Anthony Price was born in Hertfordshire in 1928. Educated at the King's School, Canterbury, and Merton College, Oxford (where he read History), he became a journalist in 1952, and was editor of *The Oxford Times* from 1972 to 1988. An interest in naval history and a weakness for spy thrillers led him into book reviewing. Now he has nineteen acclaimed spy novels of his own to his credit, and has won the Crime Writers' Association Silver Dagger and Gold Dagger awards. Anthony Price is married and has three children. This is his first non-fiction work.

By the same author

ANTHONY PRICE

The Eyes
of the Fleet

A Popular History of Frigates
and Frigate Captains 1793–1815

W. W. NORTON & COMPANY
New York   London

For information about permission to reproduce selections of this book, write to
Permissions, W. W. Norton & Company, Inc. 500 Fifth Avenue, New York, NY 10110.

ISBN 0-393-03846-7

W. W. Norton & Company, Inc., 500 Fifth Avenue, New York, NY 10110
http://web.wwnorton.com
W. W. Norton & Company Ltd., 10 Coptic Street, London WC1A 1PU

1 2 3 4 5 6 7 8 9 0

Contents

CHAPTER ONE

Six naval occasions

Early on the morning of 19 July 1793 His Britannic Majesty's ship *Nymphe* (of 36 guns) ran within hail of the French National ship *Cléopâtre* (40 guns) in the English Channel. The crew of the *Nymphe* gave King George III three cheers, and their captain, Edward Pellew, raised his hat to Captain Jean Mullon, who returned the compliment while his own men cried 'Vive la Nation!'. Then, since a state of war had existed between their two countries (and taking their cue from the replacement of Captain Pellew's hat on his head), the British opened fire.

Towards midnight on 21 September 1797 and during the following day the crew of His Britannic Majesty's ship *Hermione* (32 guns) rose in mutiny, murdering Captain Hugh Pigot and his officers and later surrendering their ship to their country's nearest enemies, the Spanish authorities in Venezuela.

On the morning of 3 April 1805 His Britannic Majesty's ship *Pallas* (36), commanded by Captain Lord Cochrane, was cheered into Plymouth after a ten-week raid on Spanish shipping off the Azores with three golden candlesticks (each five feet long) lashed to her masts.

During the long afternoon of 21 July 1808 selected members of the crew of His Britannic Majesty's ship *Lydia* (36 guns, Captain Horatio Hornblower commanding) danced in a hornpipe competition while that ship was being towed into action under the fire of the Nicaraguan rebel ship *Natividad* (50 guns), which was subsequently sunk in the Gulf of Tehuantapec on the Pacific coast of Mexico.

On the morning of 13 March 1811, while awaiting an attack by a

Franco-Venetian squadron which outnumbered his own six to four in ships and two to one in men and guns, Captain (acting Commodore) William Hoste, of His Britannic Majesty's ship *Amphion* (36), recalled his mentor and 'second father', and encouraged his men, with a final flutter of signal flags off the island of Lissa in the Adriatic Sea: *Remember Nelson*.

Early on the morning of 1 June 1813, while on blockading patrol off the New England port of Boston, Captain Philip Broke, of His Britannic Majesty's ship *Shannon* (38), despatched a letter under flag-of-truce to the captain of the United States ship *Chesapeake* (38), which then lay within sight of him in harbour: 'Sir – As the *Chesapeake* appears now ready for sea, I request that you will do me the favour to meet the *Shannon* with her, ship to ship, to try the fortunes of our respective flags.'

That these six naval incidents have something in common is obvious – at least in so far as all of them involve British captains, crews and ships during that period of naval warfare which has come to be known as 'the Age of Nelson'. But that each one is also very different from the others is no less apparent.

For example, apart from being spread over 20 years in time and half a world in space, these six British captains were each up against different enemies – Frenchmen, Spaniards, Spanish Americans, Frenchmen and Italians, and Americans, not to mention their own men in the case of the *Hermione*. But then, over those 20 years they had a wide selection of enemies to choose from at one time or another: Russians and Turks also, Swedes and Danes and Dutchmen, and other varieties of Italians and Spanish Americans. So this particular spread is in no way exceptional. It was, after all, a *world* war that was then in progress – and, more than that, a world war in which the British sought to control and command the sea against all-comers in order to survive, let alone win.

Regardless of the 'enemies' involved, however, there are essential differences in the natures of the incidents. The *Hermione* mutiny is clearly not a great and glorious episode in British naval history, but one so horrible and disgraceful that the British themselves have done their best to forget it, relegating it to mere footnotes in naval histories in favour of the bloodless and really rather good-mannered overthrow of Captain (Lieutenant, actually) Bligh of the *Bounty*. Equally, though, Captain Cochrane's homecoming was from a voyage that was profitable (and skilful), rather than heroic, as we shall see. And, while the *Nymphe*, *Lydia* and *Shannon* fights were each in their own way classic 'single-ship duels' (as opposed to the ten-ship 'battle' of Lissa), the genesis and course of each were wholly different.

Even if the area of comparison is further narrowed, to concentrate on the six British captains themselves, the differences are legion. Most obviously, of course, while the lives and careers of five of them are matters of fact and history, Captain (future Admiral Lord) Hornblower lives only in the best-selling fiction of the novelist C.S. Forester. But for him an indulgence is craved, so that through him and his career further light can be cast on his five fellow-captains, their times, their navy and their ships. He is, after all, probably the best-known (and therefore the most real?) of all of them. As of this moment and until the end of this book, anyway, Horatio Hornblower *lived*, and really was (as the late Mr Forester, his biographer, maintained) Captain Edward Pellew's favourite midshipman, just as William Hoste was Captain Horatio Nelson's: his omission from the *Dictionary of National Biography* is henceforth a matter of surprise and outrage.

Hugh Pigot is now the odd man out most obviously, as a bad man and a bad officer who came to a bad and premature end during a 22-year war in which the other five – good men and fine officers – survived. Two of those five won peerages and two were to be rewarded with baronetcies; the fifth ended the war a disgraced fugitive. Yet of the three who achieved admiral's rank, only one did so in the war, and it was to be the most unlikely of the five who long afterwards became Queen Victoria's Admiral of the Fleet.

In their origins all six were, admittedly, 'gentlemen' within the eighteenth-century meaning of the word, and at the outset of their naval careers *'young* gentlemen' in the Navy's terminology. But the spread of their parentage reflected that of their fleet's officer corps itself quite accurately: one earl (Scottish and impoverished, but none the less representing the nobility and the services); one admiral (English, rich and also professional navy); one squire (English and poor, but the English squirearchy was influential); one 'minor gentry' (poor but Cornish and 'political'); one East Anglian clergyman (poor again, and feckless with it, but Captain Nelson was also an East Anglian vicar's son); and, finally, one country doctor (only just a gentleman perhaps, and as uninfluential as poor, anyway). Poverty in this context, of course, is relative: compared with the rank-and-file of His Britannic Majesty's wartime navy, so many of whom had been taken against their will by press gangs, the debt-encumbered Scottish Earl of Dundonald and the country doctor were well-to-do. But in the Navy that was of no great consequence: it was *par excellence* the most promising career for one (or more) of the offspring of otherwise threadbare families in the social scale, from 'professional' upwards. For them, the placing of their 12- and 13-year-old sons in the Navy was both a solution and an investment. If the lads did not get their heads blown off (which Nelson's kindly naval uncle thought would solve *his* problem) they were at least provided for by His Gracious Majesty at no cost to fathers who had no money to spare. And if they lived (surviving those far greater enemies, disease and the sea) – well, as we shall discover, the investment might pay off handsomely.

And with that thought (which certainly animated Parson Hoste as he despatched his little William to the care of a captain who favoured the sons of clergy, being one himself) it is time to stop playing this 'game of differences' and consider what all these captains had in common on those six particular days between 1793 and 1813. Each of them, for better or worse, was in command of one of His Britannic Majesty's *frigates*, by virtue of which he was a fully-fledged 'post-captain' on his way to becoming an admiral.

In 1795 Mr Midshipman Horatio Hornblower was summoned by the captain of the 74-gun ship-of-the-line *Justinian* (in which he was then unhappily serving) and was offered a transfer into the 44-gun *Indefatigable*, which was then commanded by Captain Edward Pellew – now Captain Sir Edward, since his celebrated capture of the French *Cléopâtre* on 19 July 1793.

'I don't need to point out that any ambitious young officer would jump at the chance of serving in a frigate,' added Captain Keene.

Nor did he. For Mr Hornblower was well able to compare his prospects in a big ship-of-the-line with what he might hope for in the smaller *Indefatigable*. Both in theory and in practice any ship-of-the-line could blow any frigate out of the water, perhaps even with a single broadside. Ships-of-the-line – *battle*-ships of the *battle*-line – made up the great fleets which fought the great battles, most recently that of 'the Glorious First of June' only a year before. Yet all too often these monsters swung at anchor in harbour, or congealed into huge 'fleets-in-being' waiting for months (or even years) for the emergence of similar enemy fleets. Whereas *frigates* were something else: they were the busiest and most aggressive of the true *war*ships of the world's navies. Rarely in port except for refit or damage sustained in action, they were the Navy's light cavalry, scouting, patrolling, protecting, capturing – and, above all, *fighting*. In a frigate, a midshipman might aspire to gain his lieutenancy, and a lieutenant could hope for the chance of winning promotion to 'master and commander' of some smaller vessel on the way to his apotheosis as a frigate commander, which carried automatic promotion to post-captain's rank.

Not (at least, according to his biographer, Mr Forester) that Mr Hornblower actually thought all that back in 1795. He was, after all, then only a very young man, with no inkling that he would be a middle-aged one before this war ended: he saw no further than *frigate* – and the chance of *distinction, promotion, prize-money* which such a ship offered even very young men.

But, more than that, he was now about to learn the art of frigate warfare under that master-practitioner, Captain Sir Edward Pellew.

CHAPTER TWO

The French Wars, the French Navy, and Edward Pellew

Although they have not fought each other formally since 1815, the French and the English (and after the English, 'the British') have always been among the best and most traditional of enemies.

Visible evidence of this neighbourly enmity is to be found up and down the adjacent coasts of both countries. In England medieval castles (some within ancient Roman fortifications, even) plug the gaps in the coastline, augmented by Tudor 'gun-castles', the Martello towers and other military works of the 1793–1815 period, and the Palmerston 'follies' looking down on Portsmouth harbour of the mid-nineteenth century. In that last period, while he was commander-in-chief of the British Army in the Crimea, Lord Raglan was accustomed to refer to 'the enemy' (who were then the Russians) as 'the French' – much to the embarrassment of his staff, since France was then Britain's ally there. And while this unfortunate slip of the tongue has been quoted to illustrate both Lord Raglan's unfitness for command due to age and the propensity of old men to dwell in the past it is also a piece of historical truth. Not only had Lord Raglan's country been at war with France for 22 years out of his first 27 years of life (during which he himself had served most gallantly in the Army for the last eleven, losing an arm at Waterloo), but his father, grandfather and great-grandfather could equally have remembered a succession of Franco-British wars stretching back into the seventeenth century.

Wars fought back-and-forth across what the English called the *English* Channel had, of course, been a feature of endless medieval dynastic squabbles from 1066 onwards. But then the English, always short of men and money, had run out of steam during their domestic Wars of the Roses, and after that their lack of real power reduced Anglo-French confrontations to mere skirmishes for two centuries. During these years they were eventually more concerned first to fend off the Spaniards by helping the Dutch, and then to fight the Dutch themselves (who had inconveniently become the greatest naval power) by allying themselves with the French.

It was after the Dutch had been more or less cut down to size that the game began to change, and the new era of French Wars took shape. For by then the true power of France, which had been diminished by all those medieval wars and then delayed by her wars of religion, at last blazed forth in Europe just as it began to cut across the primarily commercial interests of the British in the Americas and in the Eastern seas.

Under the 'Sun King', Louis XIV, France became Top Nation. Her language was the language of culture, science and diplomacy. The discipline of her armies, which hardly lost a battle in 60 years between Rocroi and Blenheim, was the model for successful armies (General Martinet was one of King Louis' officers), while Vauban was building the best fortresses. And all this was firmly founded not so much on the grandeur of the French monarchy and its palaces, as on the size and homogeneity of the French population. By the 1680s there were 20 million Frenchmen – more than three times the population of the British Isles and many more than any of the other far less united (and more backward) major European powers. Whatever problems the French might face over the period of all the French wars to come, actual manpower was never to be one of them. In 1811, at the height of our particular French war and when the British were beginning to catch up with their 13 million, there were 28 million French-speakers in Napoleon's empire, and another 50 million in countries then taking orders from him (not to mention over seven million Americans who were then about to declare war on 'Great' Britain). Even when, two years after that, Napoleon was at last beginning to lose the war, less than half of those eligible to join his armies were actually called to the Eagles. More than a century earlier, as Louis XIV geared up his war-machine for his latest 'Dutch' war, he easily put 250,000 soldiers into the field while the British were scratching around to put 20,000 inexperienced civilians into uniform.

More to the point (since the British did then have a sizeable navy, which had cut its teeth fighting the formidable Dutch), the rising sea-power of France was no less evident. Her great disadvantage was that her main ambitions were European, directed towards a 'Great France' bounded by the Pyrenees, the Alps and the Rhine. But such was her power that Louis XIV's great minister, Colbert (1619–83), was able to expand the French Navy from 15 ships with 1,000 guns in 1660 to 200 ships with 6,500 guns, within 15 years. And what made these ships far more formidable was that they were not only supported by the new naval bases of Le Havre, Brest, Rochefort and Toulon (which had been little better than fishing ports before), but they were the product of warship design teams which had been encouraged in France when nothing of the same kind existed in England.

This whole power – armies pushing northwards to control such great ports as Antwerp, which was in slogan 'the pistol pointed towards England', and this navy to fire the pistol – came to dictate the new imperatives of British foreign policy: no one country could be allowed to dominate Europe in general and the Low Countries in particular. And no one country (except perhaps Great Britain herself) could be allowed to dominate the seas.

By 1793 these underlying principles of French and British foreign policy, springing from the conflict between the great power and ambitions of France and the rising power and commercial interests of Britain, had already caused a series of wars over more than a century. And these, unlike their brutal but small-scale medieval predecessors, had already begun to spread out from Europe as sea-power itself had become oceanic. It is even possible to call them by their American names, as well as their European ones, as Anglo-French rivalry reached the New World: the 'War of the Grand Alliance' (1688/9–1697) (when fighting France, Britain always needed allies), was 'King William's War' in American; the 'War of the Spanish Succession' (1701–13) was 'Queen Anne's War' over the water. The British did not actually join the 'War of the Austrian Succession' (1740–8) until 1744, although by then a no-war, no-peace situation was developing between them and the French in both America and India; but when they did join in officially this became 'King George's War' in America. And even that was but a prelude to the 'Seven Years' War' (1756–63) (known also in Europe as 'The Third Silesian War'), which – perhaps since one King George's name had already been used – became 'The French and Indian War' in America.

This fourth in the World Series had ended in a crushing victory for the British. Out of its predecessors and those earlier hard-fought Dutch Wars a very formidable British navy had evolved, as an integral part of a new doctrine which united British prosperity at home with naval power, as never happened (because it never needed to do so) in France. The British were indeed beginning to like their navy, their ruling classes always ready – or at least not unwilling – to vote money for warships whenever necessary, if not for the men who were forced into them in emergency. Having not much enjoyed Cromwell's rule in the mid-seventeenth century but having used soldiers (many of them Dutch) to bring them to power in the 'Glorious Revolution' of 1688, those ruling classes mistrusted large standing armies as possible instruments of royal tyranny. Armies, in any case, were expensive to maintain and, with no land frontiers to defend, the islands needed no more than a glorified military police force, augmented by an amateur militia, to deal with any civil commotions. A navy, on the other hand, was both safe from a political point of view and cheap from a fiscal one: its ships, when not required, could be left empty at anchor (though, admittedly, they had an unfortunate habit of rotting all too quickly), while the seamen who might be needed in emergency could always be conscripted (or, to use the old threat word, pressed) from the fast-growing merchant service, where they were gainfully employed and trained during peacetime at no cost to the taxpayer. 'Hostilities-only' armies, always supported by allies in Europe, were raised (or hired) as required.

This cost-effective system worked well enough for Great Britain during the first three French wars (King William's, Queen Anne's and King George's), and very well indeed in the Seven Years' War. In fact, in that fourth war, thanks to eventual good management and alliance with hard-fighting Prussian allies, it worked far too well, leaving the British supreme in India and in actual possession of French Canada. Thus glutted with victory and territory (not that Canada was considered much of a jewel in the crown), and with her amazing new industrial revolution just beginning ahead of everyone else, Britain was very much a 'satisfied power'. France, on the other hand, had been dangerously humiliated, and at once quite deliberately put in hand preparations for revenge.

These, not least, involved the further expansion and improvement of the French Navy. In spite of mounting financial problems, many new warships were built, augmented as a result of patriotic appeals to all the great provinces and to individual bodies within the state which inspired a magnificent response. Brittany, as befitted a great maritime province, presented King Louis with the huge *Bretagne*, the capital matching her with their *Ville de Paris*. Burgundy, Marseilles and other provinces and cities followed suit, while the Controllers of Postal Services contributed the *Zélé* (74), the Guilds of Paris Merchants the *Diligent* (74), the Farmers-General of Taxes two smaller ships-of-the-line and (among numerous others) 'a group of country gentlemen' the 64-gun *Union*. Nor was this all, for with these reinforcements came reorganisation. Proper classifications of warship were established and guns standardised. Ports and their facilities were enlarged. Some attempt – sadly not too successful – was made to break down the debilitating rivalry between aristocratic officers ('rouges') and the more professional commoners ('bleus'). But, significantly for the future, a regular corps of naval constructors was successfully created. France had long built good ships. Now she built even better ones – and there was still nothing like her scientific design professionalism in England at that time.

All this certainly contributed to the almighty shock which was delivered to the British in the *fifth* Anglo-French war of the series, which developed out of the rebellion of their American colonies in the mid 1770s – the American War of Independence (which, for convenience, will henceforth be referred to as the American War). Other circumstances, of course, contributed to the ensuing British debacle, not least Britain's lack of allies in her hour of need. Her recent acquisition of an overseas empire had not particularly annoyed other European powers, but she had done nothing either to keep her old friends or make new ones since her 1763 triumph. Those not against her (and Spain soon enough joined France, with an eye on Gibraltar) were quite content to see her beaten now, with 'the world turned upside down' at Yorktown in 1781 as her redcoats surrendered to a Franco-American army, signalling the beginning of the end of a lost war.

Still, to be fair to the British people and government, they in their turn harboured no such thoughts and plans for revenge after the loss of their first ephemeral 'empire' as France had done in 1763, any more than they ever contemplated trying to recover their lost American colonies. On neither side, in fact, had there been any real nationalistic rancour during all the preceding Anglo-French wars of the past century. Patriotism, increasingly, there might be, but in its eighteenth-century form, and – certainly on the British side – informed more by the desire for wealth and profitable enterprise than for any great territorial expansion. (Indeed, when accounts were being rendered back in 1763, the British very nearly traded the whole of Canada for a single West Indian island, for that very reason: sugar islands meant good business.) The armed forces of King George and King Louis, for the rest, made war as directed, on behalf of their respective monarchs, in an otherwise remarkably gentlemanly and disinterested fashion. Friendship between enemies was not only possible, but quite common: the generosity of Marshal Biron in saving George Rodney from a Parisian debtors' prison freed the English admiral in time to fight France (and eventually to win the great battle of the Saints' Passage); 'I look forward to becoming your friend,' wrote the French commander to his British opposite number during the siege of Gibraltar, 'after I shall have learned to render myself worthy of that honour, by facing you as an enemy.' Captain Edward Pellew, whom we shall meet shortly, struck up such a friendship with Captain Jacques Bergeret, whom he first took prisoner in 1799, that after they met a second time in the Indian Ocean in 1805 the two contemplated retiring to neighbouring estates in France after the war. Even during the long and hard-fought Peninsular War to come, while the French and the Spaniards were fighting a guerrilla war of unsurpassed ferocity, the rank and file of the French and British armies happily fraternised when not killing each other, exchanging tobacco and brandy when on outpost duty.

Friendships between officers-and-gentlemen and mutual esteem between front-line soldiers was not, and is not, unique to the eighteenth century, of course. But, sad to say, there were changes ahead in Anglo-French relations, due to the establishment of a new order in France which both practised and preached world revolution. From the safety of their island, many liberally-inclined Englishmen at first welcomed that revolution, but the excesses of the Parisian mob and the execution of Louis XVI shocked the country. Such barbarism, together with the behaviour of the armed ruffians who broke open his wife's coffin, turned Sir Thomas Graham from a sympathising Whig gentleman into a Tory volunteer for army service in a war which he had become convinced was 'just and necessary in defence of our Constitution' – a very different reason for serving King and Country than any which had animated the British officers of the previous five wars. It was against such a background that Nelson's advice to his midshipmen must be judged: 'First, you must always implicitly obey orders without attempting to form any opinion of your own regarding their propriety. Second, you must consider every man your enemy who speaks ill of your King. *And, thirdly, you must hate a Frenchman as you do the devil.*' Admittedly, Nelson's patriotism was of the simplest variety, and he was in reality both foremost in disobeying orders he disliked and insistent on the need for every British naval officer to learn the devil's language. But it is none the less true that there was a marked decline in the behaviour of many French officers of the new Revolutionary and Napoleonic model. British prisoners of war were later to hope that they fell into the hands of a Frenchman with 'de' in front of his name, and in praising the virtues of his captor in 1815 one British officer was to reflect that these had 'used to adorn French heroes *in a better time*'.

But all this was in the future in 1793. And, indeed, even the shock-horror events of the Terror were insufficient to bring the British into the war which had started when a coalition of European powers took it upon themselves to suppress the Revolution and restore the French monarchy in 1792. To start with it hardly seemed necessary, anyway, for the odds against the French revolutionary armies (which had lost virtually their entire officer corps by emigration, resignation or the guillotine) were huge. But the new spirit of those armies and the incompetence of their opponents soon reversed the situation: before long the French were not only fighting on all those 'natural frontiers' for which Louis XIV had squandered so much blood and treasure over so many years, but were contemplating greater conquests in the sacred names of Liberté, Egalité and Fraternité. So it was not the British, whose Prime Minister Pitt had been looking forward to his version of 'peace in our time' only shortly before, but the French themselves who declared war in 1793, to turn what had been a European conflict into a world war.

As usual – almost, indeed, by hallowed custom – the British Army was totally unprepared immediately to play any significant part in the war, let alone a successful one. Since its defeat in America it had vegetated in a cloud of wig-powder and pipe-clay, the victim of Pitt's fierce post-war economies. It would be years now before it won any sort of battle victory against the French (1801, actually, and in far-off Egypt), and even more years before it began to play any sort of substantial role successfully on European soil. Fortunately, however, the Navy was not in anything like such a parlous condition.

As has already been noted, the British – and not least the Tory gentry in the House of Commons – had a soft spot for the Navy, which had become a necessary ingredient of the new religion of 'mercantilism', with its Tory slogan of 'blue water' enterprise. It had expanded during each of the preceding French wars, with nearly 50,000 men afloat in 1714, rising to over 80,000 during the Seven Years' War and to over 100,000 by the end of the American War in 1783. Indeed, although that war had been lost, it had not in the end been lost by the Navy, which – although it had crucially lost control of the sea before the Yorktown surrender – had defeated the French fleet in the West Indies and had saved the fortress of Gibraltar.

Since then, with Pitt's economies delayed by a succession of minor overseas threats (variously from the Dutch, Russians and Spaniards) and the readiness of Parliament to give money for ships, the Navy had actually added 33 new ships-of-the-line (the battleships of the day) and some two dozen frigates to its strength. And even if its actual manpower had been cut to the bone as each threat receded (from an inter-war high of 39,000 to a miserable low of less than 14,000), its mobilisation plans had been updated by an able Comptroller, Admiral Sir Charles Middleton (the future Lord Barham).

Of course, most of its strength in 1792 was laid up in harbour and in dozens of creeks, with only six of the line (and the smallest of them) and a dozen frigates stationed in the five overseas commands of the Mediterranean, North America, the West Indies, the African coast and the East Indies, out of a total of 25 of the line and 50 frigates in commission. But so efficient was Middleton's planning that this number was doubled by February 1793, and powerful squadrons were soon on the way to the Mediterranean and the West Indies. These, together with the ships of the enlarged Channel Fleet, were certainly enough to meet any battle fleets the French could put to sea. Which was just as well, because the British Army, which was now expanding again after having been reduced only recently from 17,000 to 13,000, had to count on 14,000 Hanoverians (and 8,000 Hessians even) to make its contemptible showing against a French revolutionary army now working up to three-quarters of a million.

For the truth was that, whatever Shakespeare among others might say in misunderstanding history, the 'moat defensive' of the sea, which was supposed to serve England 'in the office of a wall', was only as good as its defending navy made it. It had failed to stop innumerable invaders in the past, most recently only a century before in 1688. Until the age of railways and better communications on land, a would-be invader could actually transport an invasion force faster by sea than any defender could move defensive forces by land to resist an attack. The sea was not a moat, but a highway.

As it was in 1793, and even apart from the speed of British naval mobilisation, the French had other and easier fish to fry in the Low Countries, the Rhineland and Savoy, in backing up their revolutionary preaching with their bayonets. But the eventual threat to Britain was none the less explicit, as delivered by Danton in the Assembly: this was no longer a good-mannered, old-fashioned limited-objective war of King Louis against King George – it was virtuous Republican Rome against decadent despotic Carthage. And as the British ruling class was as well-grounded in the classics as those well-educated Frenchmen who had made the Revolution, they knew exactly what that threat meant: Carthage, in the days of its greatness, had been a mighty sea-power. But in the end the Roman legions had ploughed salt into its ruins.

Whether Captain Edward Pellew himself grasped such allusions to the Punic Wars of the third century before Christ is doubtful. He was certainly 'a gentleman' within the eighteenth century meaning of the word, and not one of those 'old tarpaulin' captains common in the British Navy in the earlier part of that century, who had risen from the lower deck without any formal education. There were still such men commanding ships in 1793 (and he had first gone to sea over 20 years before under such a man). But, although captains of working-class origins actually outnumbered those of the business and commerical classes, nine out of ten were by then drawn from the professions, the gentry and the nobility, whose sons were more or less 'educated'. Still, as Pellew's schooldays seem to have been active rather than scholarly and had ended abruptly when he ran away at the age of 13 (to escape yet another beating), he would seem to fall into the 'less' rather than the 'more' category: his education over 18 of the 22 years since then had been mostly either at war or at sea. Born in 1757, during one French war, he had already served throughout the whole of the next one (the American War), from youth into manhood. But if he did not know what Danton meant with his talk of Rome and Carthage, he knew well what the French were about: most of the year 1792 (he had relinquished his previous command in 1791, having been fortunate in spending half the decade of peace afloat), he spent in campaigning for another ship – and, more precisely, a frigate. His problem was that there were many other captains similarly unemployed and equally experienced, and not a few senior to him. His advantage, however, was that he had 'interest'.

'Interest', in its full eighteenth-century meaning, can only be compared inadequately with our own Oxbridge 'old boys' network' in its heyday, for it was much more than that. In all human activities, in peace as in war, seniors inevitably have preferences among their subordinates: it is, after all, an important function of rank to select and advance promising juniors. And in all such activities success depends on a varying mixture of such influential 'interest' combined with actual merit and the wild factor of luck (or, as the eighteenth century might have put it, 'providence'). But 'interest' in the eighteenth century, as the successor of all the partialities and loyalties of earlier times, was still naked and unashamed as a source of power among patrons and the avenue of advancement among their clients.

Political party, geography and, almost above all, family were primary ingredients of interest. To take Pellew, the first of our special frigate captains, as an example, he was a member of an old Cornish Tory family who looked to their own Cornish Tory nobleman for 'interest' when young Edward went to sea. Later on, when already a captain, Pellew himself looked in the same direction when he wanted command. And in due course, when he had 'interest' of his own, *Admiral* Pellew advanced his young sons in the Navy as openly (and, indeed, as outrageously, by our standards) as his predecessor in the same command had done his own young relatives.

'Interest' certainly could advance the undeserving and the second-rate in all spheres of eighteenth-century activity. And, by the same token, *lack* of 'interest' could hold back better men. Yet sheer merit, given just enough luck, could triumph nevertheless, and most of all in war. Even in the British Army, where the purchase of commissions (and even whole regiments) was the custom, the long war to come in the Spanish Peninsula was to give meritorious (and lucky) officers a much better chance of promotion. In the British Navy, while 'interest' (and never mere cash) was undoubtedly still one of the keys to quick promotion, a degree of professional competence was essential because of the very nature of an officer's duties: blue blood, money and the right family and political connections were of no use at night in a howling gale off the rocky coast of France.

Actual combat, too, was another avenue by which merit and luck could advance an officer's career, especially if it was accompanied by victory. And, unlike the British Army, the British Navy was already

accustomed to winning, not only in the great set-piece battles of the
French wars, but in the hundreds of smaller engagements of sea
warfare, notably those classic 'single-ship duels' which were most
often fought by frigates. Not only could the winning captains of such
duels hope for honours, a better ship and not inconsiderable financial
gain from such successes, but their first lieutenants had a good chance
of their own commands, with the coveted promotion to post-captain
of a frigate quite likely (leaving a vacancy which would benefit all the
lieutenants beneath them). It was thus that a man like John Jervis, who
entered the Navy quite without 'interest', could rise to become
Admiral Lord St Vincent, First Lord of the Admiralty and the main
architect of the navy which Nelson used to such good effect. (Nelson
himself, by contrast, had huge 'interest' to thank for his early
promotion, meritorious and lucky though he was – and, in his turn, he
was to demonstrate the working of 'interest' at is worst and best by
accelerating the promotion of his stepson, Josiah Nisbet, as well as
that of the admirable William Hoste; but then St Vincent in his day did
no less, even while deploring undeserving promotions, as we shall see.)

Luck, inevitably, was more capricious than 'interest' or merit,
thought not always unrelated to them; those officers who had
'interest' or merit, or both, might find themselves put in the way of
luck, as Cochrane was to be in the *Pallas* when he was given a
potentially enriching cruise (as indeed also was Hornblower in the
Lydia; although his luck then, as a meritorious captain without
'interest' was to rescue a woman whose family 'interest' was to serve
him well). But, equally, luck's desertion was decisive: two of the
Navy's most outstanding frigate captains, Philemon Pownoll of the
Blonde (who had certainly been the luckiest captain in the Navy up to
that moment) and Richard Bowen of the *Terpsichore*, might well have
displaced two of this story's chosen captains but for the chance shots
which cut them off in their prime. Pigot aside (who richly deserved his
*un*luckiness anyway), it was our special captains' luck which, with
their merit and their varying degrees of 'interest', preserved them
through so many dangers as to make the stories of their frigate careers
worth the telling.

Perhaps it is not quite accurate, however, to suggest that Horatio
Hornblower was quite without 'interest', for he at least had the merest
tincture of it, sufficient for him to be accepted as a somewhat elderly
midshipman (at the ripe old age of 17), albeit in a worn-out
ship-of-the-line with a dying captain who warned him that he would
have done better to have had a lord for a father, rather than a doctor, if
he wished to make a career for himself. Actually, the medical
profession contributed a measurable number of its offspring to the
Navy's officer corps, but it would certainly have been better for
Midshipman Hornblower if he had at least had a lord *behind* him as

his patron, as Edward Pellew did during his early naval career.

Pellew's original 'interest' was geographical in origin, for his family, although it had somewhat come down in the world, were loyal clients of Viscount Falmouth, the most powerful nobleman in their part of Cornwall. As such they could rely on his political support in obtaining jobs and offices ashore. But better than Falmouth's political influence was his naval 'interest', which coincided with the 13-year- old Edward's ambition. For His Lordship's younger brother had been none other than Admiral Sir Edward Boscawen ('Old Dreadnought'), the victor of the battle of Lagos in 1759. And although the Admiral had died two years later, his 'interest' lived on in the person of his former boatswain, whose career he had advanced to such good effect that he now commanded the 32-gun frigate *Juno*. By simply calling in this debt, Lord Falmouth obtained a place on the *Juno* for the young Pellew in December 1770.

Vital though this first step on the naval ladder was (and all the more rare too, since it was peacetime, and the Navy was down to 15,000 men), it was none the less on the lowest rung, as – officially – a 'captain's servant'. But this rather odd-sounding start to the career of the future Admiral Lord Exmouth was nothing out of the ordinary. Mere children like Pellew, and the other slightly older 'gentlemen' teenagers who were also potential officers, generally first appeared in ships' books variously as 'captain's servants', or even 'able seamen', if not 'volunteers, first class'. As a 'young gentleman' Pellew might be a general dogsbody, but he certainly was not a servant. Indeed, he expected to become a midshipman or master's mate, and having served in that rate for at least two years in a total of six years' sea-service and reached the minimum age of 20, he might then present himself (with his journals and certificates signed by his captain testifying to his worthiness) for his lieutenants' viva voce examination by three senior captains.

That, at least, was the theory. But this being the eighteenth century, theory and practice diverged, often wildly. As regards sea-service, for example, this might be illegally and blatantly gained by false entries in ships' books. By the time he went to sea for the first time at the age of 18, Lord Cochrane had officially accrued over five years' sea-service in a succession of ships commanded by his uncle, Captain (future Admiral Sir) Alexander Cochrane, which was by no means unusual, 'interest' working as it did. In his case it was because Uncle Alexander had entered him without telling his father, the Earl of Dundonald, who had destined him for the Army, in which another Cochrane had 'interest' at the very top. As a risible result, the young Cochrane (who only wanted to be a sailor) was at one time simultaneously an officer in the Munster Fusiliers (the 104th Foot) and a seaman on HMS *Hind*, while actually serving in the flesh in neither capacity.

For our purposes in the young Pellew's case it is enough to understand that, in going to sea as a captain's servant, he was set fair to become a warrant officer (midshipman) as soon as possible, being already a 'young gentleman'. But this was none the less his testing time, when any romantic notions about the Navy would be dispelled. As soon as possible he would be given huge responsibilities over experienced men old enough to be his father. But immediately he was amongst not only other 'young gentlemen' like himself in appallingly dark, cramped and smelly conditions even in the biggest ships (and worse ones in the smaller ones), but among others who were very different. Some were *former* 'young gentlemen' doomed by their inadequacies never to become officers: famously, Billy Culmer was to become the Navy's senior midshipman in 1791, with 34 years' service under warrant to his discredit. Others were not 'gentlemen' at all, but warrant officers who had risen from the lower deck. Some of these might rise further (as Admiral Boscawen's favoured boatswain did) by special 'interest' or out of extra-special merit luckily catching some captain's eye. But most would rise no further.

The potential horrors of such a mixture, particularly of disappointed elderly 'gentlemen' brutalising hopeful young ones in bad ships under bad or weak captains and senior officers, are obvious: Hornblower was driven to near-suicide by an embittered senior midshipman whose mathematical illiteracy had resulted in repeated failure in his lieutenant's examination. But then, no matter how brave and strong a man might be (never mind rich), more was required of a sea-officer in the British Navy (of all navies), on whose professionalism his country's survival depended. Apart from this, while the test of this mental and physical discomfort undoubtedly exceeded anything the aspiring 'young gentlemen' had endured ashore, bullying by his peers and harsh treatment from his elders and betters at school would have been his lot there also. It was to escape the latter that Pellew had abandoned his education: by our standards the 'Age of Enlightenment' was a brutal one at all levels. This theoretically flawed system had certain practical virtues which made it superior to that which it had superseded. At the very least, it gave the fledglings experience which money and blue blood – however little the money and pale blue the blood – could not buy as they learned their trade. In former times there had been aristocratic officers who had never gone through the mill from the bottom. In the previous century generals had been made admirals, and a dangerous distinction between 'gentleman captains' and tough old 'tarpaulin' ones had developed, threatening professionalism: 'The seamen were not gentlemen,' wrote Macaulay, 'and the gentlemen were not seamen.' There were still aristocratic officers and semi-tarpaulin types in Nelson's time and St Vincent himself was to bewail the increasing presence of too many of the former in the post-Trafalgar period. But there was none of the French 'rouges' versus 'bleus' rivalry: they were all professionals who had risen through their years in the stinking darkness of the warrant officers' mess while learning the skills of seamanship on which their future survival depended more surely than on simple bravery in battle.

It also gave future captains and admirals the opportunity of understanding the men they would be called on to lead. That the less intelligent (or less psychologically robust) did not take this opportunity and learn from it will become evident in the story of Hugh Pigot in due course – just as the stories of Edward Pellew and Horatio Hornblower (standing in for Horatio Nelson in this context) illustrate very different styles of successful leadership which must have been derived, at least in part, from those formative years. In the matter of punishment, for example, Pellew was a hard man of the St Vincent school, always ready to flog and hang when it seemed necessary to him, contrasting with the Nelson school, of which Hoste was a distinguished graduate. 'The men worship him, ma'am,' Lieutenant Bush confided to Lady Barbara Wellesley during Hornblower's *Lydia* voyage. 'They would do anything for him . . . and the lash not in use once a week, ma'am. That's why he's like Nelson.' Equally, a flogging ruined Hoste's day, and his men loved him. But then, to confuse matters, the crew of Captain Edward Hamilton, who was to avenge the Pigot disgrace in the most daring fashion, would also do anything for *him* too. And Hamilton was later to be court-martialled and – albeit only temporarily – dismissed the service for brutality.

What the young Pellew learned, perhaps, was just how far he could go – at least with his men, if not with his superiors – during his early years at sea. His first voyage had been to the Falkland Islands, on a peaceful mission to re-establish a British presence there after a brief Spanish occupation. (The Spaniards, having claimed the islands by right of an antique Papal gift, then left without abandoning their alleged rights, boding ill for the British – and for certain British frigates – in the 1980s.) After this, he followed his captain to another frigate, the *Alarm* (28 guns), which served in the Mediterranean until 1776. But by then Pellew was no longer on board her: he had been dumped at Marseilles the year before for a midshipman's joke at the expense of his captain's mistress, whose presence afloat did not break the Navy rule then in force that *wives* were forbidden to sail with their husbands.

This punishment, it may be thought, hardly fitted the crime. But a captain's power over his 'young gentlemen' – even those who had been advanced, as Pellew had been in 1772, to be master's mate – was absolute; and one may further suppose that a former boatswain who had risen to the quarterdeck to be the captain of the *Alarm* frigate was both jealous of his dignity and less likely to laugh off a young

gentlemanly jape. In any case, this mischance had a marvellous result.
For, first, it served to return Pellew from the peaceful Mediterranean
station to an England in the midst of its war against the rebellious
American colonies. And, second, it then required Lord Falmouth to
exert his influence again on behalf of his protégé, which he did to good
effect by invoking the gratitude of another of the long-deceased
Admiral Boscawen's grateful officers, Captain Philemon Pownoll,
whose 36-gun frigate *Blonde* was earmarked for American service.

Philemon Pownoll (variously also Pownall or Pownal) was already
famous as one of the two luckiest men in the Navy. For, while
commanding the sloop *Favourite* and in company with the frigate
Active, he had captured the Spanish treasure ship *Hermione* in 1762.
The subject of prize-money, together with other incentives (of which
pay itself was the very least), will be discussed in more detail later, in
the story of Captain Cochrane. Suffice it to say here that the *Hermione*
and her cargo were knocked down at auction for £544,648 1s 6d. So,
when all due deductions had been made and the residue divided
according to the rules, the smallest single share of this windfall going
to every ordinary seaman and marine aboard the two frigates was
£484 2s 9d. It is not easy to render an eighteenth century pound in
modern money. But Captain Pownoll's share – £64,872 13s 9d –
effectively made him a millionaire, given that a captain's pay at that
time was some £100 a year.

It was neither Pownoll's luck nor his wealth, however which must
surely have gladdened Pellew's heart when he joined the *Blonde* in
January 1776, but the other well-known fact about his captain: that he
was one of the very best officers in the Navy, intelligent, inventive and
upright, as well as marked for distinction. To serve with him was a
great opportunity not only because of what he had to teach and where
he would lead but also because he would surely carry the best of his
followers up with him (as, indeed young Captain Nelson was to do
with Midshipman William Hoste in the next war).

But luck, unluckily, was also part of the equation. And Pellew was
not as lucky as Hoste in that his own beloved patron was killed in
action even earlier in his career. Even so, his four years under Pownoll
were none the less decisive in their influence on him, as he was to admit
to the world publicly and gratefully in naming his first son *Pownoll*
Pellew long after his captain's death. Meanwhile, however, he joined
the *Blonde* in the Medway in 1776. And there, at once, he was taught
his first Pownoll lesson (albeit one which, in later years where his own
family was concerned, he sadly abused). For, typically, Pownoll
demonstrated how 'interest' should be used for the good of the Navy,
as well as its interested parties: while it was one thing to take on board
a protégé to please his old captain's influential brother, it was quite
another to advance the young man before he had proved himself. For

this reason (and surely not because of that recent *Alarm* escapade which Pownoll would have disregarded, always supposing he even knew about it), Pellew was first disrated from master's mate back to able seaman ('gentleman').

Of course, a young gentleman volunteer able seaman was from the start much more than a modern able seaman. And in any case Pellew soon added that golden ingredient of merit which Pownoll of all captains was unlikely to miss. The years ahead would bow down Able Seaman (Gentleman Volunteer, First Class) Pellew with age, seniority and responsibility, so that he would live to grumble about his own captains' incompetence and awkwardness from the quarterdeck of his 110-gun flagship. But from the beginning to the end of his career he stood out among his peers as an exceptional leader of men. Later, as a captain on leave in Plymouth, his initiative and personal physical courage saved 500 men from a storm-wrecked troopship; later still, as an admiral, he led the axemen who cut away wreckage to save his flagship during a storm in the East Indies (when part of his crew had quickly got at the rum, preferring to drown drunk rather than sober). And as Captain Pownoll's newest 'likely lad' he must have been a high-spirited delight anyway, apart from his professional merits: the ceremonious reception of General 'Gentlemanly Johnny' Burgoyne on board the *Blonde*, en route to take up his command in Canada in the new American War, was rendered memorable by the sight of Mr Pellew standing on his head on the yardarm (but politely, with his hat still on his head), high above. However, this time at least, Mr Pellew had evidently taken the measure of his captain, who reassured General Burgoyne that his was no more than a young gentleman's frolic; and if the young gentleman fell he was a good swimmer anyway – which the young gentlemen proved soon after, when he jumped overboard to save a drowning sailor.

One may – again reasonably – suppose that Gentlemanly Johnny did not forget this episode later on, after he had surrendered to the Americans at Saratoga. By then Mr Midshipman Pellew had distinguished himself in the home-made naval flotilla which had fought its way down Lake Champlain to that disaster, and had remained with the General when winter had forced the *Blonde* to withdraw down the freezing St Lawrence, to command the little schooner *Carleton* and to be captured with the Army at the last. At least, General Burgoyne did not forget the hard-fighting midshipman who had skylarked for his benefit in happier days now that his own career was in ruins. Rather, he saved Pellew's career by choosing him as the messenger bearing his explanatory dispatches back to England, which the victorious Americans allowed to be transmitted. Thus saved from captivity and with a generous letter of recommendation from the General himself to add to those of Captain Pownoll and his officers for his earlier achievements, Pellew was able to take the next vital step up the naval ladder with promotion from warrant-rank midshipman to commissioned lieutenant.

His problem now was that he had lost his place with Pownoll, his only naval source of 'interest', who was by then at sea in a new command, the *Apollo* frigate (32). As a junior lieutenant he was forced to start at the bottom again, and very unpromisingly in the 80-gun *Princess Amelia*, a guardship anchored at Spithead, in January 1778. As a commissioned officer, admittedly, he did now possess the right to petition the Admiralty for a transfer, and as a meritorious one in a very hot war when the Navy was expanding he could hope for a more active posting. But so could many hundreds of other lieutenants who were also bombarding the Admiralty with similar pleas, so it was nearly a year before he was delivered from ship-of-the-line boredom – and then only into the elderly *Licorne* frigate (36) on convoy duty, albeit with promotion from fourth to second lieutenant. In fact it was not until another six months later that his merit, 'interest' and luck at last coincided exactly, when Captain Pownoll brought the *Apollo* into Plymouth for a refit with a vacancy for a first lieutenant, while the *Licorne* was also in port. For although, owing to the nature and course of those earlier American operations, Pellew had not latterly served directly under Pownoll, the captain had taken his measure and solicited his transfer.

Potentially, as first lieutenant of a brilliant, popular and lucky frigate captain, Pellew might now look for everything Midshipman Hornblower later hoped for on transfer to the future Captain Pellew's *Indefatigable* – only more so. For with the French at last fully involved in the American War and their big new 'revenge' navy pushing the British hard, sea-fighting was certain and single-ship frigate duels highly likely. Such duels (in which, of course, British victory was taken for granted) conferred honour on frigate captains, and not inconsiderable profit if the captured French vessel was not too battered to be subsequently bought by King George for his own navy (many of whose best frigates had been launched under the fleur-de-lys of King Louis). But a really hard-fought fight might do even more for the first lieutenant: as a compliment to his captain he might at least hope to be appointed to command a sloop-of-war as 'Master and Commander' as an interim promotion before getting his own frigate as a godlike post-captain. Even, in particularly meritorious circumstances, he might be appointed straight into a frigate as captain. And with a favoured captain like Philemon Pownoll, that was a real possibility now.

But more about the mechanics of promotion shortly. At this stage in his career, Pellew's luck and ill-fortune were inextricably mixed. Dismissal from the *Alarm* had served to bring him into contact with Captain Pownoll in the first place. Capture with the defeated General

Burgoyne had in the end ensured his lieutenancy. Now his brief service in the *Apollo* would soon mix success with tragedy, and further success. For, after an exciting patrol of the coast of Europe, the *Apollo* did indeed meet a French frigate of equal force, the *Stanislaus*. But although the Frenchman was speedily beaten into a dismasted wreck, she finally went aground in neutral (Austrian) waters off Ostend. And, far worse, before that, one of her shots had killed Captain Philemon Pownoll.

An assessment of Pellew's situation after the fight illuminates some of the factors which might influence an officer's career in this period. After Captain Pownoll's death he had taken command, and as a result of his exertions the *Stanislaus* was lost to King Louis. But she was then in the hands of the Austrian authorities (from whom the British subsequently bought her), so he was unable to bring her home as a tangible proof of victory. However, Pownoll had been a famous and much-admired officer in the Navy who, had he lived, would undoubtedly have flown his flag as an admiral at sea in the course of the *next* war – and, by seniority, probably before his junior contemporary, Captain Horatio Nelson. Now that he was dead, as a result of what had at least been a successful action, it was proper naval custom and practice – indeed, almost an act of naval piety – to honour his memory by advancing his first lieutenant. 'Sir' (wrote the First Lord of the Admiralty to Lieutenant Pellew therefore):

> After most sincerely condoling with you on the loss of your much lamented Patron (*sic!*) and Friend Captain Philemon Pownoll, whose bravery and services have done so much to honour himself and his Country, I will not delay in informing you that I mean to give you immediate promotion, as a reward for your Gallant conduct upon this occasion as well as many others which entitle you to Consideration. . . .

All that having been said, however, the First Lord was not about to devalue the reward system which paid officers without interest by results when they were lucky enough to be able to demonstrate their merits. So Pellew's promotion was to be 'master and commander' of one of the smallest, slowest, worst-armed and least desirable vessels requiring such a captain (by courtesy), the *Hazard* (10).

On the face of it, both the Navy and Lieutenant Pellew had done rather badly out of the *Apollo–Stanislaus* duel. The Navy had lost one of its finest officers, and his protégé had lost his best 'Patron and Friend' in exchange for command of a ship in which he could neither distinguish himself further nor enrich himself. Ordered on to anti-smuggling patrol on the very dangerous eastern coast of England, Pellew soon discovered not only that he could not catch anything in the *Hazard*, but that his quarries were often better-armed and better-

crewed as well. Indeed, his main achievement during his eight months
in command of her was to survive the perils of the sea as he tried to lick
her near-mutinous crew into shape, at the end of which period he
narrowly escaped final shipwreck only after jettisoning all his ten puny
guns.

This is, nevertheless, to underestimate the importance of his
promotion, and the Admiralty's recognition of his merits. The
position of 'Master and Commander' was in essence a temporary
rank, lasting only as long as a lieutenant commanded a particular
vessel of appropriate size – a sloop usually, or brig or even new-
fangled bomb-ketch. For some officers such a command marked the
height of their career: Captain Hoste was to have a very deserving and
able Master and Commander under his command in 1814 who never
achieved higher rank. But for others it was an interim appointment in
which (apart from proving themselves in sole command) they could
expect to serve until their 'interest', merit and luck combined to secure
that coveted post – (fully-fledged/permanent) captaincy of a rated
ship, which was almost invariably a frigate.

It may be thought that Pellew proved himself in the well-named
Hazard – at least to the extent that he was quickly given another and
larger sloop after the unseaworthy *Hazard*'s last homecoming. And
although the *Pelican*'s 24 guns were very small, and he was still only
her Master and Commander, he was then ordered to a much more
promising station off the coast of Brittany. There he took his first small
prize and finally distinguished himself in an action during which three
French ships were driven ashore, so that on 25 May 1782 the new First
Lord, Admiral Lord Keppel, put pen to paper at last:

> Sir, I am so well-pleased with the reports I have received of your
> Gallant and Seaman-like Conduct in the sloop you command . . .
> that I am induced to bestow on you the rank of Post-Captain . . .
> and will give you a frigate whenever I can find one . . .

It would have been better if Admiral Keppel had appointed Pellew
directly *into* a frigate, which carried automatic promotion to post-
captain's rank. From having been a temporary captain as master and
commander of the *Pelican* (which he now must relinquish, since she
was not a post-captain's command), he now faced a future which was
both certain and uncertain: as a post-captain his rank was permanent
and his seniority in it assured. But he could well be a captain without a
ship for all his merit – at least until either 'interest' or luck came to his
rescue. But, of course, they did. When he had brought his first small
prize into Plymouth a year earlier he had enviously noted the big (ex-
French) 40-gun frigate *Artois* shepherding in no less than seven prizes
of her own. Before this summer of 1782 was out he would be
commanding the *Artois* himself. But meanwhile it is time to consider

in more detail the nature of this type of ship, in which Pellew was to make his name, as were Cochrane, Hornblower, Hoste and Broke (among so many others).

CHAPTER THREE

The evolution of the frigate

In the Royal Navy's promotional calendar for 1987 the month of April was devoted to its Type 22 Frigate: 'The Broadsword Class of frigate is designed for anti-submarine role . . .' Then, after the vital statistics of the handsomely illustrated HMS *Beaver* have been listed ('designed to the metric system', the shade of Napoleon may have noted approvingly), there follows an historical footnote:

> The origins of today's missile-carrying frigates go back to the days of sail. The Royal Navy's first frigate was launched in 1757 and in Nelson's time frigates were the 'eyes of the fleet'. During the two world wars and despite heavy losses, frigates played an important role in sustaining the fight against the U-boat menace. The task of the frigate today remains the same.

For our purposes the year 1757 is certainly apposite, since it was also the year of Edward Pellew's birth. But otherwise there is quite a lot in that footnote which is at least arguable in the matter of the modern frigate's origins, even if it is conceded that its escort role now, and during the (so-called) Second World War, more or less coincides with *one* of those of the old wooden sailing frigates, although against a very different sort of commerce raider. And, for good measure, frigates like HMS *Beaver* and her sisters also perform trouble-spot patrolling tasks which Captain Pellew and his fellow frigate captains would understand. But a scrutiny of the volumes of *Jane's Fighting Ships* from 1898 through 1914 and 1939 will fail to reveal a single frigate in any of the world's fleets. And it was actually not until the middle of the Second World War that the name reappeared, when Nicholas Monsarrat's Captain Ericson received his new command, after his corvette had been sunk in 1942, in *The Cruel Sea*: 'It's a new ship, Number One: new job, new everything. They're giving me a frigate – that's the latest type of escort.'

In fact, the Navy had resurrected the name from history, just as it had done in 1939 with the corvette: '. . . a brand new type,' mused Monsarrat's Vice-Admiral Sir Vincent Murray-Forbes, 'the first of her class: a corvette – theatrical name, but an honoured one in naval history.'

The frigate had actually disappeared from the world's navies in some confusion during the second half of the nineteenth century, although not unspectacularly when applied to such ships as the Navy's first ironclad, HMS *Warrior* (now happily restored to its former glory near the *Victory* in Portsmouth). Although in reality the ancestor of the battleships of the future – the modern 'ships-of-the-line' (of battle) – the *Warrior* was classified as a steam *frigate*, having been built in 1859–60 in answer to the French *Gloire*, another ironclad warship (the French then still being, as Lord Raglan had not so long before maintained, 'the Enemy').

Be that as it may, the Navy's 1987 calendar has a point in '1757', for in that year two single-deck, three-masted warships, the *Pallas* and the *Brilliant*, were built as frigates to the design of Sir Thomas Slade, each mounting 36 guns in a single main-deck battery and displacing just over 700 tons. There had in fact been so-called 'frigates' – small auxiliary sailing ships – in the northern seas in the sixteenth century, and man-powered 'fregata' galleys in the Mediterranean even earlier; and later, in the nineteenth century, there would be much larger steam-powered warships which, because their guns were mounted on a single deck, were for a time classed as frigates before reclassification as Third Class Battleships. But the classic wooden sailing frigate of the Age of Nelson is undoubtedly a direct descendant from the *Pallas* of 1757 and the French *Aurore* of the same period (although – significantly for the future – the *Aurore* was a substantially bigger and more powerful ship than her British counterpart).

The development of this special class of warship was the result of the casting of guns of increasing weight and power. In the beginning of the great age of sail, when the abandonment of oars made broadside cannon fire possible, there had simply been bigger warships and smaller ones, all of which had mingled in combat. But as naval fighting developed during the seventeenth century (and until the development of the torpedo somewhat levelled the odds) it became increasingly obvious that smaller ships, more lightly built and with smaller guns, could not stand up in battle to bigger ones, with their more numerous and heavier broadsides. Gradually, over the century before the launch of the *Pallas*, this had served to sort warships into various 'rates'. By 1685 there were six of these, from 1700-ton 'Firsts' with up to 100 guns, down to little 199-ton 'Sixths' carrying 18 (much smaller) ones which had no place in the line-of-battle fighting which had by then evolved. Over the years this classification was further refined so that in the end the distinction of rate formally established which ships could be included in the line of battle (thus becoming ships-of-the-line) and which stood no chance there, and must be left out to perform other duties. It was from this division of labour that the frigate finally evolved, as the largest *single* gundeck warship, initially with between 24 and 28 nine- or 12-pounder guns, of the Fifth or Sixth Rate, to be commanded by a post-captain. Below her, smaller vessels – sloops, brigs and the like – dropped out of the rating altogether. Above her, ships (of the line) of from 50 to 64 guns were Fourths, 74- to 80-gunners Thirds (with the 74 becoming the most popular size), 80 to 90s Seconds, and everything bigger, with three or even four gun-decks were Firsts with anything from 98 to 132 guns and accommodation for admirals and their staffs.

As with so many weapons of war (tanks and aircraft, as well as wooden sailing ships), both the ship-of-the-line and the frigate became increasingly formidable. One result of this was that the Fourth Rate was effectively squeezed out of front-line service. But it was still true that *any* ship-of-the-line could outgun *any* frigate (at least in 1793, anyway). The convention even built up during the second half of the eighteenth century that it was beneath the dignity of the line ship to fire on any frigate which strayed into a battle *unless the frigate fired first*. The French *Sérieuse* (36) unwisely broke this convention at the battle of the Nile in 1798, bravely attempting to play David to the British *Goliath*, a 74-gun Third Rate. As much scandalised as irritated by such temerity, the *Goliath*'s Captain is reported as exclaiming, 'Sink the brute! What does he here?' – which was promptly done with a single broadside, the frigate's crew being seen to run up the rigging as their ship went down under them.

The frigate had by then found its proper place in naval warfare, which effectively covered all duties other than annoying ship-of-the-line captains by challenging them to fair fight on equal terms. Admittedly (as we shall soon see) there were occasions when well-handled frigates would harry bigger ships like dogs pursuing a bear, notably in storms, when such giants could not open their lowest gun-ports, which were closer to the sea in multi-deck ships than in single-deck frigates. But the frigate's primary battle-duty was to be the fleet's 'eyes', combining the future roles of the light-cruiser and the aircraft in spotting enemy fleets and bringing their own heavy ships to battle with them. In addition to this they were the Navy's true all-purpose cruisers, sweeping the seas clean of enemy merchant shipping and raiding cruisers (frigates themselves), while making short work of weaker enemy privateers. And with that latter protective role went actual convoy-escort, together with blockading duties and the combined operations which came to go with that work. Some of all this work devolved on smaller craft – sloops and the like – which could also take on enemy sloops and privateers. But, unable as they were to take on enemy frigates, such vessels were essentially auxiliaries: the Navy's cutting edge was always its frigates – and it was they, above all, which were consequently always in short supply.

It was thus the British Admiralty's first concern after the outbreak of war in 1793 was to get frigates to sea, to take enemy merchant shipping and to protect British merchantmen by dealing with those enemy frigates which the French were sending out as fast as they also could manage, with similar objectives. Within a matter of days, therefore, the North Sea and the Channel were reported to be 'full of frigates'. It was the moment of easy pickings: for weeks, and even months, many home-coming merchant ship captains would not know there was a war on until enthusiastic prize-crews boarded their vessels. Yet although these pickings would be there for the next 22 years, there were also and increasingly the duller duties of patrol (though some areas were much less dull and much more profitable than others) and convoy protection. For the convoy was not an invention of Lloyd George in 1917, after the lack of such a system had nearly brought Britain to her knees. The seventeenth- and eighteenth-century navies knew all about convoy systems. Major sea-battles had in the past been fought to protect convoys, and the first full-scale naval battle of the 1793–1815 period was accepted by the French to save a vital American grain convoy at all costs. The French admiral, Villaret-Joyeuse, lost the sea-fight, and the British rang their church bells to celebrate 'the Glorious First of June' (so-called because there was no nearby coast to name it after). But the convoy got through, thereby saving Villaret-Joyeuse's head from the guillotine.

Mostly, however, frigates protected British convoys. Not only did this enable the Admiralty to concentrate their battle fleets against French threats, which did not end with Trafalgar, but the use of the frigate, with a crew usually of around 200, was cost-effective in manpower, compared with the use of a ship-of-the-line, with four times as many. For the same reason, if there was *any* risky work to be done which might involve fighting, it was always better to 'send a frigate' whenever possible. And in the days of sail every voyage was potentially risky, even in peacetime, because of the perils of the sea. The greatest British naval disaster of the whole period, in which more than twice as many men died as at Trafalgar, was the wreck of the *St George*, a 98-gun First Rate flagship, and the 74-gun *Defence* in a Baltic storm. Indeed, while the French were *the* enemy, the sea, disease and accident had for long been far greater killers of sailors, in general, and of British sailors in particular. Of these great killers, it will once again be more convenient to leave disease and accident until later, and even here to consider the sea in its role of ship-destroyer, rather than man-killer.

In the former role (as also applied to disease and accident, of course), it was at least indiscriminate, destroying French ships as well as British. But here two other factors intrude to distinguish the losses sustained. First, the blockade which the British at once imposed on French ports and naval bases, although at first far less efficient than it was to become later, served to keep the majority of French ships at anchor in port. This, together with the destruction of its old naval (aristocratic, but none the less experienced) officer corps in the revolutionary purges, usefully led to a decline in French seamanship: on those occasions when it did get to sea, it could expect to sustain proportionally far greater sea-losses than the British even if it never came to battle. But these were more than offset by the fact that, because of that British blockade and British naval superiority, French ships spent far more time in harbour, safe from the sea's perils, than did the British, who were – especially in the case of frigates – exposed to those perils for months on end, even years. The statistics of losses eloquently demonstrate this. Over the whole 22-year war (disregarding, as we shall usually do, that 14-month 'phoney' 1801–2 Peace of Amiens), the British captured or destroyed some 229 frigates from all its enemies for the loss of only eight to them. But during the same period British frigate losses in the Fifth and Sixth Rates by shipwreck or foundering at sea were 66, while the French lost no more than a dozen from those causes in spite of a general (though not invariable) inferiority in seamanship.

Taken out of context and simply mathematically, these figures might have led successive French Ministers of Marine to echo Jellicoe at Jutland when another battle-cruiser blew up, in his conclusion that there had to be something wrong with his ships, especially in view of the glorious string of victories which French soldiers had notched up in their European campaigns. But in fact, whereas there undoubtedly *was* something wrong with those British battle-cruisers in 1916, the reverse was the case with these French frigates: almost without exception they were of better and more advanced design, faster, bigger and able to carry a heavier armament than their contemporaries in the British Navy. And, indeed, the same applied to their ships-of-the-line. Nothing pleased a British captain more (except promotion itself, or the sight of a French ship within range) than to be given command of a captured French ship – or, for that matter, a Spanish one – whether a frigate or a line-ship.

The sad fact in 1793 was that this was no new situation. The British *could* build good heart-of-oak ships, as the longevity of HMS *Victory*, which was built in 1764 and sailed triumphantly through Trafalgar to become a national monument, proved. But by the end of the eighteenth century oaks were in short supply. In its heyday a single ship-of-the-line swallowed some 2,000 of them, growing over 500 acres of forest. In default of any official tree-replanting programme, the great oak-woods of England vanished into her increasingly large navy. Before long oak – and often inferior oak, too – had to be obtained from abroad, in the New World and from the Baltic, together with all sorts of other naval equipment including masts, spars and cordage. As early as 1760 Britain imported nearly £1m of such supplies from Russia alone (in exchange for a mere £70,000 worth of finished goods). The importance of such imports of war material was a major reason for the country's aggressive – even sometimes brutal – northern policies, which required Scandinavian neutrality, failing actual alliance. Even so, before the end of the war ships were being built for the Navy in Bombay, of teak. This was another problem which the French never faced: with nearly all the ship-building centres in Western Europe soon at their disposal, as well as abundant forests and excellent ship-builders of their own, they could always replace their losses.

True, when St Vincent first planned to build ships in India during his fierce and controversial time as First Lord of the Admiralty in the phoney Amiens peace in 1801, it was not so much because of the material shortages, serious though these were, as because of the scandalous situation in Britain's dockyards. It is a moot point which of these was the worse, the royal or the private. That the latter were marginally better is suggested by the virtual relegation of the royal yards by then to repair and refitting (although, in an age of wooden ships required to be at sea for long periods, that was a hardly less vital service than actual ship-construction). But in both royal and private yards, in any case, negligence, incompetence and downright criminality were neither uncommon nor a secret. No one, for example, will ever know exactly why HMS *Blenheim* foundered with all hands – including Nelson's friend Thomas Troubridge – off Madagascar in 1807. There was a severe storm at the time, and the *Blenheim* was an old and worn-out ship, like the ex-Dutch frigate *Java* which went down with her. But she was also one of a number of notorious privately built ships of fraudulent construction which virtually fell to pieces as a result. And, much more famously (or infamously), the price of faulty maintenance claimed another admiral and another ship while actually in harbour:

> *Down went the Royal George,*
> *With all her crew complete . . .*
> *His sword was in the sheath,*

His fingers held the pen,
When Kempenfelt went down
With twice four hundred men

All this was bad enough. But it was also generally the case that, to bad and dishonest practices like 'the devil's bolt' (which had two visible ends, but no middle), British ship-builders added hidebound, unscientific conservatism in design. The 'old Spanish customs' of the newspaper printing industry in the later twentieth century came close to ruining it. In the late seventeenth century and through the eighteenth a few old Spanish (and French) customs would have been welcome in ship-building, when sailors' lives and the security of the realm were threatened by foreign navies as well as the sea itself. But the *Golden Hind* and the *Revenge* of Queen Elizabeth I's reign and King Charles I's *Sovereign of the Seas* (which the hard-fighting Dutch had honoured with the nickname 'the Golden Devil') had by then been forgotten by the descendants of their builders. Both the great Anson, in the 1740s, and the even greater St Vincent 60 years later, tried to clean up Britain's Augean dockyards, without success: innate rule-of-thumb conservatism, crooked politics and the endemic corruption of the age were, in alliance, too strong even for them. The best that can be said of the ship-builders (nothing good can be said of the dockyard system itself) was that they were amenable to copying captured ships, some of the best of which were literally taken apart and measured for that purpose.

There is, of course, nothing new, let alone disgraceful, in stealing foreign good ideas in wartime (or, if one can get away with it, at any other time). The great 'English' longbow evolved from uncomfortable experience at the receiving end on the Welsh marches. The unsolicited gift of a Focke-Wulf 190 to the RAF in 1942, by a German pilot who had lost his way, resulted in a radical rethink among British designers; the American Sabre jets and the Russian Mig-15s of the Korean War owed more to German design (and captured designers) than to native ones.

At sea the story goes back much further. The Romans, when getting the worst at sea in the First Punic War, took to pieces a Carthaginian quinquereme which had been stranded off Brutium (presumably marking each piece with their clumsy Roman numerals), promptly built a hundred such dreadnoughts, and won the war. The design of the ships of King Alfred's so-called 'first British Navy' surely owed most to the Viking longships they were built to repel. The French navy itself, at the beginning of France's rise to power in the seventeenth century, had started in much the same way, with the purchase and copying of a number of warships from the Dutch (then the top maritime nation) in Richelieu's time. That the French should name battleships after the Great Cardinal is altogether appropriate, for as 'Surintendant Général de la Navigation et Commerce' he was the real founder of their navy. The first notable result of his organisation of the training of naval ship-designers and craftsmen was the splendid 72-gun *Couronne*. From her was descended the even better *Superbe*, the arrival of which in Spithead in 1672 so stirred King Charles and his naval brother James that it resulted in the building of nine copies of the *Harwich* class. The French naval reform after 1763 merely continued a tradition of excellence.

From that point British designers never looked back. But, unfortunately, neither did they look forward, in spite of the succession of wars in which their country became involved. For, while the science of warship design continued in France through a succession of brilliant and highly regarded academic writers, the hidebound and unenterprising British shipwrights frequently failed even to produce good copies, let alone to improve on their models. Britannia was to rule the waves eventually in spite of her designers and dockyards, with her sailors' victories masking the inadequacies of the ships in which they won their battles. 'Slower' and 'smaller' was, among other defects, the general rule, so that more than 100 years after the death of King Charles, Admiral Rodney's flag-captain was heard by a midshipman to describe the British 98-gun flagship *Formidable* as a 'bumboat' compared with its newly-captured opposite number, the *Ville de Paris*. In Nelson's time the (notoriously cranky and slow) British-built 80-gun ships weighed in at 2240 tons, when the French were building up to 2747 tons with the 120-gun *Commerce de Marseille*, a splendidly seaworthy giant which for some reason never joined the British Navy after its capture at Toulon in 1794 (perhaps it too obviously showed up all the rest?). And, of course, the almost-legendary Spanish *Santissima Trinidad*, that four-deck, 132-gun survivor of the battle off Cape St Vincent which was to be finally cornered at Trafalgar, was the greatest of them all: humiliatingly, the Spaniards had built as well as, if not even better than, the French. And thus, all too often, the best ships in any British line-of-battle during the whole period first sailed under enemy flags if they were not more copies – ships like the ex-French *Invincible* of 1747 (which begat the *Triumph*-class copies, and inferior copies-of-copies after them) to the remarkable *Implacable* (ex-*Duguay-Trouin*, taken after Trafalgar), which not only saw Napoleon's war out but actually survived Hitler's also, to be honourably scuttled in mid-Channel under the Tricolore as well as the White Ensign in 1949.

As with our great ships-of-the-line, so with the frigates. As has already been sketched, the original 'classic' sailing ships of this type of the mid-eighteenth century were (and remained) basically single-deck warships functioning as scout–cruiser/escort vessels, designed for speed and too lightly built to withstand a line-ship broadside, but outmatching everything else from the largest privateer downwards. It was inevitable, however – or, at least, inevitable given the skill of French and Spanish ship-designers – that this class would be further improved and developed, just as the bigger ships had been. Besides the 36-gun, 700-ton *Pallas* in 1757, and other 28- and 32-gun Sixth Rates resembling her, there were soon larger 38- and 40-gun French and Spanish frigates, mounting heavier 18-pounders against the British 12s. Nor did the enemy ingenuity stop there, for by the time Edward Pellew put to sea in his 36 (18-pounder) *Nymphe* in 1793, the word was out that there was not only a new class of 40-gun French frigates of over 1000 tons (like the *Sybille*, which was to be caught at a disadvantage in the Aegean Sea next year by the old-fashioned but heavier 50-gun Fourth Rate *Romney*), but the even newer *Pomone* class, of 1240 tons and 44 guns, many of which were 24-pounders. The bad news did not end there, for the French *Forte* class would be at sea well before the end of the century which, with a displacement and weight of broadside almost exactly twice that of the 1750s frigates, constituted the most powerful custom-built ships of the type afloat until the arrival of those American super-frigates whose story must await that of Captain Broke of the *Shannon*.

By a coincidence – but, as we shall see, a by no means unique one – it was eventually the captured *Sybille* which encountered the *Forte* in the Bay of Bengal in 1799. Details of the ensuing fight must also await their turn in this narrative. But some statistics of the two ships as they then were will serve in the meantime to illustrate some of the complications in making comparisons between them. For by then the originally 40-gun, 1000-ton *Sybille* was rated a 38-gun British frigate, but actually carried between 44 and 48 guns (authorities differ here), including not only at least twenty-four long 18-pounders and ten 12-pounders, but also ten of the nearest thing to a secret weapon possessed by the British Navy – the 32-pound carronade.

The carronade, so called because of its origin in the Carron Ironworks in Falkirk, Scotland, was a large-bore, short-barrelled, close-quarters 'smasher', invented during the American War by Lieutenant-General Robert Melville (1723–1809). With its stubby barrel and small powder-charge it was useless at long range, but devastating at close quarters, and its subsequent record of success and failure is a commentary on this fact. Its lightness – the 68-pound variety weighed only about one and a half tons – enabled it to be carried higher up in a relatively small vessel, and this contributed to one of its first victories, of the antiquated British *Rainbow* over the modern French frigate *Hébé* in 1781: having received a few 32-pound carronade shots from the *Rainbow*'s forecastle, the French captain assumed that an even heavier main-deck broadside from 'long' guns would come next, and accordingly struck his flag in surrender.

The case for the carronade was thus proved, but the secret of its strength and weakness was soon well-understood, with prudent captains preferring a mixture of long guns on the main deck, one or two long 'chasers' in the bows for use in pursuit, and a few smashers above for close-quarter work. For the truth was that the *Rainbow's* captain had been lucky as well as skilful in luring the *Hébé* within range of the only guns he had. His weight of broadside then had been mathematically decisive, being no less than four times that of the Frenchman. By tradition, the British preferred a close-quarter battle, aiming low and relying on the speed and training of their gun-crews at short range, rather than too-precise accuracy (which, anyway, was problematical with smooth-bore cannon, so it seemed to them). And such tactics were to serve them well in the future, as in the past, against a succession of different enemies, even though the latter were all too often in better – bigger, faster and more powerful – ships, ships-of-the-line and frigates alike.

Mathematics *did* come into the equation, of course. And in a ship like the splendid *Forte*, which was nominally a 44, but actually carried 52 guns, they could be daunting (and all the more so when French weights and measures were different from British, with her 24-pounders firing cannon-balls weighing 27 British pounds). But, as will be shown – and most immediately in the continuing story of Captain Edward Pellew – the mathematics of sheer brute force were nevertheless only a beginning, not an end, of wooden sailing-ship warfare. And, above all, of frigate warfare.

CHAPTER FOUR

In which Edward Pellew becomes a successful frigate captain

The 40-gun frigate *Artois* was not actually Captain Pellew's first *posting* in the rank of post-captain. In Admiral Keppel's letter of 25 May 1782 Pellew was in fact named as captain of an elderly ship-of-the-line, the *Suffolk*, which was then undergoing a major overhaul-and-repair in Plymouth dockyard. But ships-of-the-line, elderly or not, were not commands for new captains on the bottom of 'the List', and the *Suffolk* was in any case already promised 'to a Captain of old Standing' (seniority on the List), as Keppel further indicated. What he – and the Admiralty – was doing was purely technical. Lieutenant (acting Master and Commander) Edward Pellew had performed competently in the *Pelican*, after having been first lieutenant of the late, gallant and much-lamented Captain Philemon Pownoll in the *Apollo–Stanislaus* duel, which also merited official recognition. If he was not now appointed to a ship of one of the six 'rates' which carried automatic promotion to post-captain's rank he would remain a mere master and commander while in the *Pelican* – and would automatic-ally revert to lieutenant when he relinquished that command. But once captain of a *rated* ship by Admiralty order he would be safe in the rank, even if the ship eventually went to someone else.

That, however, was as far as Admiral Keppel's generosity went, for he belonged to the Whig party and the new post-captain was a follower of the Tory Lord Falmouth. So, as there were always far more post-captains than there were posts (and all of them senior to Pellew, anyway), no frigate was likely to become free very quickly, if at all. For although the Navy was then bigger than it had ever been before, the

American war was drawing to its close, and when it ended the Navy would be cut to the bone again, as usual. Long years ashore on half-pay would then be the rule for thousands of naval officers, no matter how meritorious. And while none of the unemployed post-captains among them could lose their ranks (unlike all the unfortunate masters-and-commanders), ship commands would be few and far between. Indeed, while those captains would still move up 'the List' in a strict order dating from the day of their appointment as a result of deaths above them, some of them might never get a ship again. Of course, if they lived long enough they would eventually become admirals automatically once they reached the top of the list and an admiral above them died in one of the various grades. But then it was even less likely that they would ever command anything at sea if peace continued. Long years of unemployment in peacetime was the lot of almost every officer: Nelson himself was to be 'on the beach' for five of the next ten years, between the wars.

This, in fact, was a time when 'interest' and luck counted for more then merit. Pellew experienced the luck first when an old friend of his father, Captain John Macbride of the *Artois*, was temporarily detached from his frigate on special duties and was able to nominate his friend's son as his locum. However, having gained a whole year's valuable experience as a frigate captain, Pellew did finally have to face up to life ashore. But even this proved valuable in enabling him to take his place in Cornish politics in Lord Falmouth's power-base, as a burgess and alderman of Truro. And that served him well eventually, when the Tories had toppled the Whigs from government. Later in his naval career (and especially after he had become Member of Parliament for Barnstaple in 1802), his political advancement was to have the disadvantage of discouraging Lord Falmouth from securing him lucrative postings further afield, from which he could not return in time to vote. But, more immediately, it made him more than a simple supplicant, which almost certainly accounts for his two peacetime commands, of the *Winchelsea* frigate (32) and the old *Salisbury*, for five of the next seven years in a navy whose manpower fluctuated around the 20,000 mark.

That this navy was actually reduced from 24,000 to 16,000 in the years 1791–2, two years *after* the storming of the Bastille, disposes of the accusation that King George III and William Pitt either desired or planned war with revolutionary France. Indeed, while the Austrians and Prussians were on the march, looking for easy victories over a divided and disorganised nation of cut-throats, and the Tsar was breaking off diplomatic relations, a not-uninfluential part of the British intelligentsia was welcoming the Revolution's noblest aspirations, and the majority of Britons (Lord Falmouth included) still hoped at least for a continuation of peace and the prosperity which the country's own revolution – in industry and commerce – was bringing.

Whether or not Captain Pellew knew better that war was inevitable is beside the point. What he certainly knew after having paid-off the *Salisbury* in December 1791 was that if war *did* come it would immediately present a chance-of-a-lifetime (which might never be repeated in *his* lifetime) to every frigate captain at sea. For, in bombarding Lord Falmouth with the scarcely veiled demands of a useful political client over a nine-month period, it was a frigate that he wanted. And, more precisely, it was one of three which he knew to be most readily available at Portsmouth: the *Thalia* or the *Nymphe*, failing the *Andromeda*.

If he was wrong about the coming war, then at least he would have a ship again. But if he was right, then he would have the right ship in the right place at the right time: rich and fat Indiamen, both English and French, would be sailing up the Channel, blissfully unaware of the outbreak of hostilities, offering fortunes in prize-money to their respective captors as well as patriotic advantage to their captors' nations. And more (which would undoubtedly have attracted any would-be frigate captain in his prime after ten years of peace, which Edward Pellew at the age of 36 undoubtedly was, above all else), it would also offer French *frigates*, with like-minded French captains thirsting for the glory and promotion that every single-ship duel offered. In the opening phase of any war, indeed, such combats offered both in greater measure. For at the start of every war nations are at once at their most belligerent and uncertain, and therefore all the more grateful to those who can satisfy them, even in actions which may pass almost unremarked later on if the war has become victorious (or which, in the midst of defeat, their propaganda machines know how to minimise).

To attribute such thoughts to Edward Pellew is perhaps unfair, as he kept Christmas 1792 with his wife and young family – with his boys Pownoll and baby Fleetwood, whose 'interest' he was to serve so well in the long war which was to come, just as he was already attempting to push that of his brother Israel, and the younger brother of one of his old midshipman friends from his service in the *Alarm* of long before. (And both of these would owe their success to his 'interest', which made Israel a very lucky admiral in spite of all his subsequent disasters, and young Midshipman Christopher Cole the future flag-captain after the war: that, classically, was how 'interest' worked from one generation to the next in those times.)

Lord Falmouth hoped for peace right to the end, and indeed even beyond it. For, even as Pellew's repeated requests had at last borne fruit, he was still grasping at 'some faint hopes that a lucid interval in the brains of these frantic Murderers will show them that [it] is not in their interest to quarrel with us' when in fact the French Assembly had declared war on Great Britain three days before those words were written. The perception of the 'frantic Murderers' (not a few of whom would soon be going to the guillotine themselves in the Terror) was very different from his: war with the British was not only inevitable because of the French advance into the Low Countries, that ancient Anglo-French *casus belli*, but was to them desirable in itself not only for the preservation of the Revolution but also of their own heads in the course of a great national emergency requiring ruthless action against all internal and foreign enemies, real and fancied; which, variously, their friends and enemies would see respectively as liberty on the march in Europe or an echo of Macbeth's conclusion that 'things bad begun make strong themselves by ill'.

However, by then Pellew already had more pressing matters to attend – indeed, quite literally pressing as they concerned the manning of the *Nymphe*, which Lord Falmouth had at last obtained for him from Lord Chatham at the Admiralty three weeks earlier. For, although Pellew quickly expressed his gratitude in the form of a hogshead of sherry, Falmouth's misplaced hopes had lost him precious time during which 'the hottest press ever remembered' had stripped Portsmouth (and every incoming merchant vessel) clean of prime seamen. Already – and for the next whole generation – finding a crew would be the nightmare which sat grinning on the pillow of every captain newly appointed to a ship. There were, quite simply, *never* enough men – and men of any kind, let alone those trained and experienced sailors whose presence aboard in sufficient numbers could best turn those nightmares into sweet dreams.

One of the recurrent themes of eighteenth-century debate in Parliament was the need to encourage the supply of seafaring manpower. Unfortunately this enlightened concern for the country's prosperity and safety was accompanied by a foolish and short-sighted unwillingness to pay sailors in the Royal Navy a decent wage even while money was being voted for their ships. Thus, after more than a century of world-wide expansion and bigger wars during which the Navy's manpower requirements had risen progressively, actual rates of pay had not been increased since Cromwell's time, nearly a century and a half earlier. The manifest injustice of this at a time of rising inflation was to have dire results *within* the Navy very soon, as we shall discover in a later chapter. But meanwhile, as Pellew sought a crew for the *Nymphe* in 1793, it was another strong disincentive to volunteering to serve His Britannic Majesty afloat to go with the dangers, fierce discipline and notoriously harsh conditions of life at sea.

Volunteers there were, amazingly. But except in special and unusual cases (which we shall also explore later), these rarely accounted for more than one in five of any crew, and more generally one in seven or eight. The rest came from a variety of different types of compulsion:

off other ships, merchant or naval, without the volunteers' feet ever touching dry land; from the jails and 'quotas' (usually of men on the brink of jail); from foreign countries (not least the United States, whose citizens often found it difficult to convince desperate naval captains of their nationality); and, most infamously of all in popular history, the hated 'press gang' –

> *For they have taken my beau, Ben,*
> *To sail the old Benbow,*
> 　　　　　　　– wailed Faithless Sally Brown.

In fact, the Impressment Service was by then a well-established state organisation which was in this war eventually to employ no less than 24 post-captains (usually those unfit in some way for active service) full-time. Legally, its meat was anything on two legs which could be classed as 'a seafarer' (and not, of course, 'a gentleman'). But in those rough-and-ready times of extreme emergency press gangs in practice took anything they thought they could get away with, by force and not infrequently only after pitched battles both with local people and even with local constables (not to mention the crews of incoming merchant ships, which might be left almost crewless as a result). It was, indeed, the *practice* of impressment, rather than its principle (which was little more than a typically *ad hoc* eighteenth-century version of our own much more ruthlessly efficient twentieth-century Conscription Acts), which left behind a legend of cruelty and barbarity – and possibly that un-European aversion to forced military service which the British never afterwards lost.

At all events, by these means Pellew and every other naval captain expected to get their crews – or, at least, crews of a sort, an increasing proportion of whom might be going to sea for the first time, and the majority of whom were unwilling. How desperate their problem was to become will be further illustrated in the story of Hornblower's commissioning of the *Sutherland* at a time when every seaport had been picked clean a thousand times already over 17 years of war. Pellew's situation in early 1793 was itself difficult enough, after the 'hot press' of the previous month. What was most insidious and aggravating about the whole system, however, was that however successful he and his fellow-captains might be in acquiring crews by such means, they were thereby also ensuring a continuous *loss* of men – indeed, the most serious single category of manpower loss the Navy traditionally sustained during all the years of war under sail. Statistically, over the whole of this war, for every man lost – 'DD' (Discharged Dead) – by enemy action, two were lost by shipwreck, fire and to the sea. And for every man lost in those categories combined, between four and five would die by disease or accident. But far more than from *all* those causes (the exact total is impossible to arrive at) would simply disappear with 'R' marked against their names, having successfully 'Run' as deserters. The true cost of all the defects of the system – bad pay, poor conditions of service, unnecessarily harsh discipline, the press gang's brutalities – was thus paid in full.

In fact Pellew failed to get all the men he needed in 1793, but one may suspect that it was his determination to get to sea quickly as much as the endemic shortage of men which caused him to set sail in mid-February while still 30 short of his full complement of 220, with his own brother Israel – an as yet unemployed lieutenant – on board as a volunteer, only a month after 'reading himself in' as her legal captain. Otherwise, once he had bullied a set of lower masts for her from the dockyard, the *Nymphe* was everything a middle-ranking captain (of ten years' seniority on 'the List') could hope for. As the final 'e' of her name suggested, she was a French-built ship, and therefore a fair sailer although getting on in years, having been captured by the British *Flora* during the previous French war, in 1780. By British reckoning she was also fair-sized at 938 tons and, although nominally a 12-pounder 36, actually carried 40 guns – 26 'long-12s' on the main deck, twelve 24-pounder carronades on her quarterdeck and forecastle, and two 'long-sixes' in the bows. By the standards of the better French frigates of the time, even other than the new 40-gunners of the *Sybille* class, she was certainly nothing special, either in speed and size or in broadside. But, after having been worked up by a captain of Pellew's quality for four useful months, during which the unteachable had been put ashore and others had replaced them, she was as good as any frigate the Royal Navy had in the Channel in June 1793, when she finally met the French National frigate *Cléopâtre* at last, in the first of 20 years of real single-ship duels of the war.

More, actually, was riding on this fight than on any of the 'first fights' of all the previous Anglo-French wars – first, that is, if an earlier meeting between the French *Sémillante* and the British *Venus* in May is discounted. For, with the *Venus* commanded by an incompetent captain, both frigates had retired to their respective bases crippled, with the sea-war's first big question left unanswered, regarding the quality of the new republic's navy.

The French Navy, like the French Army, had by then lost the greater part of its aristocratic element through flight and purges. But in the previous war it had been a formidable force, which had battled with the British on equal terms, especially in the Indian Ocean, even though it had been decisively beaten in the last great battle of the American War. That its battle fleets were now slow in showing themselves proved very little, however. Even the relatively better-prepared British ship-of-the-line squadrons took time to bring out of mothballs, with their problems of sea-worthiness and equipment being greater than anything the armies had to contend with: unlike the good firm earth, the sea was a hostile element which showed no mercy from the moment a ship cleared harbour.

But of all the *rated* ships – the real warships – the frigate was the smallest and easiest to get to sea, as well as the most useful in its commerce-raiding (and commerce-defending) function. So it was the French frigates that the British expected to encounter first in formal ship-to-ship fight. And it was therefore the frigate that must answer the terrible question at sea which the new French revolutionary armies were posing on land, as they hammered the old-fashioned armies of the continental monarchies one after another, against all the odds: was revolutionary *élan* – 'Vive la nation!' rather than 'Vive le Roi!' on 19 June 1793 – as formidable in the Channel as on the Rhine and in Belgium?

So, even after his recent capture of the 16-gun privateer *Sans Culotte* (which really didn't count in view of the disparity between them), Pellew still had everything to prove when he at last caught sight of the *Cléopâtre* at daybreak on 19 June. And so, equally, had the French captain, Jean Mullon, as one of the few remaining officers from Louis XVI's navy, who had served under the great Admiral Pierre André de Suffren de Saint Tropez in five indecisive battles against the British Admiral Hughes in the Indian Ocean in the previous war. Indeed, Mullon may well have felt that he had more at stake than his and his country's reputation, for the successive failure of earlier French naval reformers to solve the 'rouges versus bleus' rivalry in its officer corps had made her navy a prime target for revolutionaries. He was technically a 'rouge', and many of the 'rouges' who had remained in the service had been insulted, attacked or even jailed; others had had gallows erected meaningfully outside their doors; at Toulon some had actually been hanged; one, commanding a frigate off Leghorn, had been deposed by his crew in favour of an officer of marines. This process of what the Jacobin member of the fearsome Committee of Public Safety who was in charge of the Navy was to call 'purification' was still active in the summer of 1793, so that few 'rouges' and by no means even all the humbler 'bleus' finally remained. France's best fighting admiral, Albert de Rions, was soon forced out of the Navy, and his immediate successors, over-promoted, found themselves saddled not only with equally over-promoted junior officers and in-experienced and insubordinate crews, but also with political commissars. In assessing his choices that June morning in the Channel, Captain Mullon may quite reasonably have concluded that he was already caught between a British Scylla and the Charybdis of the Committee of Public Safety in Paris. For if he fled from the former (a newer French frigate was likely to be faster than an older one), he might very well fetch up on the guillotine of the latter.

Adducing what long-dead men *may* have thought is, of course, of doubtful value at best. It is at least just as likely that Mullon was, like most French officers, quite simply brave and willing to die for his country even if he did not fancy his chances. The casualty lists of many more single-ship actions and full-blown sea battles during the years ahead bear this out: at Trafalgar more men were killed in the *Rédoubtable* before she surrendered than in the whole of the British fleet that day. But also, as an experienced officer of *Suffren* vintage, he should have been able to estimate that the *Cléopâtre* and the *Nymphe* were fairly matched. The British frigate *might* be heavier-gunned (British ships, the French always thought, tended to be over-gunned), even with a few of those new-fangled carronades. But, if it came to boarding, he would surely have more men (100 more, actually; the British, for their part, always thought French ships were over-manned). Also, although Mullon could hardly know that 80 of Pellew's crew had been Cornish tin-miners a few months earlier, he knew that his own crew was not inexperienced, his ship having been in commission for a year. And, finally, in any such encounter as this there was always the chance that a lucky shot might decide the battle – it might, in this case, kill that polite British captain who had just raised his hat in salute. Casualties on the exposed quarterdeck were statistically heavier than below, and heavier still among captains, who were prime targets. At Trafalgar, one French admiral and nine captains were killed, and three Spanish admirals and ten captains seriously wounded; in the great duel between the (by then British) frigate *Sybille* and the French super-frigate *Forte* both commanders fell, the *Forte* finally being surrendered by a junior lieutenant.

Frigate fights could be lengthy, too: that between the British *San Fiorenzo* (36) and the *Piémontaise* (40), off Cape Cormorin in the Bay of Bengal, lasted three epic days. But this one, which began when Pellew replaced his hat, only lasted 50 minutes, during which time it was poor Mullon who fell – and Pellew's brother Israel who won his spurs.

Lieutenant Israel Pellew lacked both his elder brother's luck and his pre-eminent merit, but he had risen on Edward's coat-tails to become first lieutenant of the *Salisbury* in 1791, failing anything better from Lord Falmouth, and even to the temporary rank of commander, although that had not fledged him into post-captain. Now, failing to get a ship as war broke out, he had capitalised on his brother's good fortune by shipping as a 'volunteer' on the *Nymphe* – and at this point the story becomes somewhat apocryphal, at least in so far as dreams of the future may be credited. For, as the *Nymphe* closed on its prey, Edward allegedly observed Israel taking charge of the after guns on the main deck, still only half-dressed (having presumably been off watch and asleep below). Apart from the fact that the main-deck battery was the proper concern of his first lieutenant, this is said to have given Captain Pellew's conscience a twinge, occasioning the following unlikely dialogue:

Edward: 'Israel, you have no business here, and I am very sorry I brought you from home. We are too many of us.'

Israel: 'That's the frigate I have been dreaming of all night. I dreamed we shot away her wheel; we shall have her in quarter of an hour.'

Although Israel's dream was wrong in the matter of time, if it was not anyway pure legend, there was nothing either dreamy or legendary about his deadly gunnery after that: his first shots killed the steersman, and succeeding ones killed three replacements before he finally got the wheel itself (if not also Captain Mullon himself possibly, together with the *Cléopâtre*'s mizzen-mast). Bow on to the now-unmanageable Frenchman, the *Nymphe* was then able to rake her, bringing all guns to bear with no answering broadside possible, in the sailing-ship version of the classic 'crossing the T' of the steel dreadnought tactics of the future.

After that (and in spite of an emergency when Pellew thought the French were trying to board, and ordered up his men to do the same), it was all over; only a handful of Frenchmen were alive or unwounded on deck among 60 casualties which included the captain and his three lieutenants, with the rest of the demoralised crew driven below. Not, however, that our imagined version of Mullon's estimation of the odds was too wide of the mark, for during the same time the British casualties had been almost as great, with 52 killed or wounded, including the second lieutenant, the marine lieutenant, four midshipmen and two other senior warrant officers. Later in the same year, Captain James Saumarez, of the famous Guernsey family of that name, engaged the *Réunion* (40) with his *Crescent* (36) off Barfleur. The two ships' broadsides were much the same in weight (French 310 pounds to British 315 – overgunned as usual, since the Frenchman was larger, at 950 tons to 888), while the French crew was (as usual) more numerous, at 300 to 257. But the *Réunion*, with a crew as inexperienced as it was brave, was totally out-manoeuvred from the start, suffering between 91 and 120 casualties (authorities differ) to a British loss of *nil*, which not even Saumarez's celebrated Guernseyman's skill can altogether account for, with only *one* French shot hitting his ship.

Not that casualties mattered, anyway, as the *Nymphe* struggled back to Portsmouth with her mainmast badly damaged and the battered *Cléopâtre* in her wake, to the cheers of every ship in harbour. The British positively liked a respectable butcher's bill – as Captain Cochrane was to discover to his cost after well-calculated and far more brilliant actions in the future, and as Admiral Lord Gambier's flag captain, Calendar, would approvingly demonstrate by his reaction to Captain Hornblower's report on his epic fight with (and surrender to) four French ships-of-the-line in Rosas Bay: 'Thompson in the *Leander* lost ninety-two out of three hundred, my lord.' Thompson, of course, had been knighted for his lost fight against a single more powerful French ship, so Hornblower's loss of 262 men out of 600 was positively to his credit: a gloriously bloody defeat might well reflect more credit on him than an easy victory – that was the point.

In any case, what mattered most was the presence of the *Venus* in Portsmouth, with the Union flag flying above the strange new banded red-white-and-blue of those 'frantic Murderers' in Paris, as tangible proof that Britannia's (ill-paid) 'Hearts of Oak' were still unbeatable (or, even more reassuringly, that the French republican navy was, unlike the French republican army, *beatable*). As has already been suggested, every newly belligerent country longs for that first victory, however small. Britain, as a sea power rather than a land power even then, needed a *sea* victory most urgently in 1793 (which was fortunate, since she would have to wait years for even a small success out of her element). Meanwhile, the hitherto unknown Captain Pellew was the Man of the Hour, to be feted and rewarded accordingly.

Captain Pellew doffed his hat to Captain Mullon on 19 June 1793, and then brought his battered *Nymphe* into Portsmouth two days later. Communications in those days, before the British had copied the brilliant new French invention of the semaphore signal system (which increased the speed of message transmission on line-of-sight from days to 200 mph on a few vital routes), was agonisingly slow. But in this case good news travelled at breakneck speed: within a week Captain Edward Pellew and Lieutenant Israel Pellew were kissing hands with His Britannic Majesty King George III at a royal levee in St James's Palace, on the introduction of Lord Chatham. And then, to public acclamation and politic Government satisfaction, His Majesty knighted Captain Edward and the Admiralty advanced Lieutenant Israel to the rank of post-captain.

Distinction, promotion, as Horatio Hornblower was to reflect before long, in transferring to Captain Sir Edward Pellew's *Indefatigable* frigate. *Prize-money*, however, was something else – at least in terms of real profit, which might make a frigate captain rich. Eventually, if and when a prize-court had decided on the future of the *Cléopâtre*, and some estimate of her crew had been arrived at, guineas would percolate through to Captain Sir Edward and his crew: possibly some thousands of them to the first, a hundred or two to his officers, and the equivalent of many months' pay to the rest if they were lucky (and still alive, or had not already deserted). But Captain Sir Edward, who would throughout his life have his eye firmly fixed on the just rewards a captain (and especially a frigate captain) might hope for until he qualified for the much greater (and far less well-deserved) cut of an admiral, which would be deducted from the shares of all his captains, expected more than that.

Most immediately, as he pleaded poverty in accepting his knighthood, he hoped for a colonelcy of marines, which paid ten times his captain's emolument as an honorary rank, at £1200 per annum for no work until he reached admiral's rank. That he now expected to enrich himself, even as an ordinary frigate captain, is best exemplified from the hopes of Jane Austen's Captain Wentworth, who in *Persuasion* lost his delightful Jane Elliot because he had not yet got his fortune and his frigate in 1806, but who acquired all of them eventually, albeit in reverse order, for a happy ending. Pellew in fact over-reached himself in hoping for a marine colonelcy. But he did not go away empty-handed in such favourable circumstances, even though he also first encountered some of the complications of frigate command at the same time. For, first, he received an immediate annuity of £150 (much more than his naval pay) from a grateful government, to keep the new Lady Pellew in appropriate comfort. But then he became entangled in one of those legal disputes ('legal', anyway, under naval custom-and-practice in his case, although more often – and far worse – in civilian courts) relating to his prize-money.

Prize-money, once again, will be touched on later (and frequently), and in more detail, as it raises its ugly and tantalising head; and, in any case, Pellew's real benefit from his success was fame, public esteem and the Admiralty's desire both to use his proven talents and to keep him happy, without any comeback from Lord Falmouth. So he went to sea quickly again, in the repaired *Nymphe*, as part of the British blockade which was tightening on the French coast, where he could do the most good most profitably to himself and his country. So, mercifully, it was up to the Admiralty to adjudicate on the claim of Captain Faulknor (who was later to die heroically in battle) to share in the profits of the capture of the *Cléopâtre*.

Captain Faulknor, who had failed already to take the *Sémillante* and whom Pellew was to describe as 'thick-headed', was claiming his share of the price of the *Cléopâtre* in virtue of an agreement which already existed between cruising British frigate captains – especially now that the *Cléopâtre* had become the British *L'Oiseau* (36). But although his case was soon disallowed (his *Venus* was in port at the time; and Pellew's old friend Captain Macbride was one of the arbitrators), his intervention at once illustrates the inducements of the frigate captain and the constant source of strife between captains (never mind the legal headaches) which resulted from prize-taking. All ships in view at the time of capture had an equal claim – unless the prize was adjudged illegal (neutral? semi-neutral? American?) – in which case the over-zealous captain was alone responsible.

That, however, was the least of Captain Sir Edward Pellew's concerns as he was busy taking (and re-taking) other prizes off the French coast. What he wanted was a better frigate. And what he got – failing the first-asked-for *Diamond* – was the even more powerful *Arethusa*, a heavily-armed 44 already famous for her elaborate rigging, colour-scheme and the individual heights of her crew, which was the legacy of her rich, 'very clever, but very mad', previous captain.

In the *Arethusa* Pellew began his real work in the blockade, on which his rightful place among our frigate captains is founded, when his true merit (as opposed to his 'interest' and his luck, and his somewhat flawed application of the system which had advanced him) flowered. For this was a very dangerous coast for frigate captains, whether their fleet admirals were (wrongly) keeping their fleets far off, in safe offshore British anchorages, or close in, behind the inshore screen of frigates and smaller craft which were threatened by wind and sea as well as the more powerful French ships they were blockading. No sailing navy had ever before attempted such a stranglehold. Mahan, in the most famous passage in his *Influence of Sea Power on History*, rightly spoke of those 'far distant, storm-beaten ships, upon which [Napoleon's] Grand Army never looked, [but which] stood between it and the dominion of the world.' But there were other storm-beaten ships not so far away on which the French generals and admirals frequently looked, which were the ceaselessly prying eyes of the British fleets off their coasts. And more often than not these were frigates. From the North Sea, outside the ports of the Low Countries (which, together with the Dutch fleet, would soon be under French control), past Le Havre and Brest, along the Breton coast with its little islands, uncharted rocks and deadly bays like Audierne and the rocky peninsula of Quiberon (still called 'la Côte Sauvage'), on southwards beyond the Basque Roads outside Rochefort into the Bay of Biscay, and then – when, before very long, Spain too became an enemy – all along the coasts of the Spanish peninsula and through the Straits of Gibraltar into the Mediterranean, this watch had to be kept. The losses sustained by these patrols were the price of Admiralty, and those occasions when the blockaders were temporarily driven off station by wind and storm – or, occasionally, by superior force – were not a proof of failure. Nothing like it had ever been attempted before, and it became increasingly successful. In the age of sail it was a magnificent achievement of seamanship.

This, in the area from Brest southwards, was Pellew's theatre of operations, first in early 1794 as part of a detachment of the Channel Fleet under Admiral Macbride (his benefactor from 1782, now

promoted) and then as second-in-command of Sir John Borlase
Warren's Western Squadron of frigates. It was with Warren that his
next spectacular victory came, when, in company with the *Flora* (42),
Melampus (42), *Concorde* (42) and his old *Nymphe*, the squadron
caught three French frigates and a corvette. The French were in fact
heavily over-matched, with only one 'heavy' frigate, the formidable
Pomone; and only one of their frigates escaped – even though the
slower *Nymphe* never got into action at all. But it was to Pellew that
the *Pomone* surrendered, though Warren, as squadron commander,
received the Order of the Bath together with most of the official credit
for the action. Nevertheless, Pellew's reputation as a fine seaman and a
gunnery fanatic was further established, and so was his credit with the
Admiralty in a period when there were still many French frigates and
smaller craft at sea. Thus, after his squadron had also overhauled and
captured the almost-new *Pomone*-class *Révolutionnaire* (a very fine
ship, which served in the Royal Navy until 1822 – latterly under the
command of his son Fleetwood, who was still in nappies in 1794), he
was well placed to lobby his masters for something as heavily gunned
as the *Arethusa*, but much faster. In the Western Squadron in the mid-
1790s speed (plus carronades, with 24-pounders for choice on the
main deck, and preferably in a captured French ship) was what every
British frigate captain prayed for beside his cot, after invoking God's
blessing on King and Country (and in Pellew's case, also Lord
Falmouth and the Tory Party). And it is part of his history and of
Horatio Hornblower's that his prayers were answered beyond his
wildest frigate captain's dreams – although not with an ex-French
frigate, but with a much more curious beast.

As in 1792, so in 1794 Edward Pellew would have known what was
happening – what was 'the talk of the town' – in Portsmouth
dockyard. So, late in 1794, he would have known all about the
Indefatigable, which was then being '*razéed*'. In later years, when both
Pellew's sons Pownoll and Fleetwood were already well up the naval
ladder, the navy was to *razé* three 74-gun ships-of-the-line, the
Goliath, the *Majestic* and the *Saturn*, rather desperately, in order to
combat the embarrassing United States Navy. They were even to lay
down three ultimate super-frigates of no less than 60 guns, the
Leander, *Newcastle*, and *Java*, which were almost ships-of-the-line.
But meanwhile, a *razé* was, quite simply, a ship-of-the-line cut down
by one deck to become a frigate. This suggests, more than anything
else, an unsatisfactory compromise. But it was also a recognition that
there were big French frigates at sea and a surplus of Fourth-Rate
ships-of-the-line of less than 74 guns, when 74s had become the
work-horses of main battle fleets. That other *Leander*, which
Thompson had surrendered to the French 74 *Guillaume Tell* in 1798,
was just such a Fourth Rate taken while running despatches because

Nelson lacked frigates to do the job. So in 1794 razéeing was what was happening to the *Indefatigable* (built at Buckler's Hard private yard, up the Hamble river from Portsmouth, in 1780), together with her other out-of-date sisters, the *Magnanime* and the *Anson*. But she was a fast sailer and Pellew now had his eye on her.

What the *razé* process did to these ships was to remove their old forecastle and quarterdeck, together with the middle part of their main deck, leaving a frigate-type single-decker of much greater (normal British) size, stronger, longer and broader – like, almost, any modern French national frigate of the latest type, near enough.

Although Pellew knew his ship, and then had her promised to him, his problems were not over when he got her. First, he was hit by politics, when a new First Lord of the Admiralty, George John Spencer (second Earl, 1758–1832), took over from Lord Chatham. Fortunately, although Spencer was a Whig (where Lord Falmouth was a Tory) and William Pitt's man, he was also young, energetic and quite imaginative. Very soon he would need all his qualities in the great naval and national emergency which will be dealt with in the next chapter. In due course he would go down in history as the man who singled out Nelson, and as a first-rate First Lord who got the Navy into real fighting order, and even improved its dockyards somewhat. More immediately, he evidently knew a good captain when he saw one, and honoured Chatham's promise. What he could not (or would not) do immediately was to support Pellew in his angry dispute with the Navy Board about the best way to arm, rig and ballast the razéed *Indefatigable* so as to get the best out of her in battle and on dangerous shores.

Pellew got his way in the end, though not before having to take his new ship on patrol and after surviving her encounter with an uncharted rock off Cape Finisterre. But get it he did, as he took command of a small four-frigate detached squadron which included the *Révolutionnaire* and the new midshipman who was to become his favourite for the next two years, one Horatio Hornblower, on transfer from the *Justinian*. After an episode in which he was instrumental in saving 500 soldiers from the wreck of the *Dutton* transport while his ship was in Plymouth, His Gracious Majesty King George III and Lord Spencer further expressed their satisfaction in his conduct by converting his fighting knighthood into an hereditary baronetcy. So, though his finest hour was yet to come, his pre-eminent merit, given its chance through 'interest' and the luck a good frigate captain might expect, was now pointing him straight towards wealth, his own flag and the House of Lords.

CHAPTER FIVE

The Indefatigable *versus the* Droits de l'Homme

The blockade, of which Captain Sir Edward Pellew, Bt. and his newest young gentleman Mr Midshipman Horatio Hornblower were enthusiastic parts, was still very far from being effective in 1794. Thanks to the number of ships and trained men available in 1793 the Navy had more than quadrupled in size in the first year of the war, and within three years it was to have as many men (about 110,000) and almost as many ships (nearly 600) as in 1782. But although ship-for-ship superiority was soon established in combat, its commitments were enormous, its tactical and strategic doctrines had not been perfected (particularly under the indifferent command of Lord Bridport in the Channel), and the French were far from beaten at sea.

In spite of Lord Howe's victory of the Glorious First of June, as well as several successful squadron engagements and a great many victorious single-ship encounters, the French still had plenty of ships, with many others building. In the Mediterranean the situation was critical – not least because Lord Hood had signally failed to destroy the Toulon fleet when a royalist coup had delivered it into his hands: thanks to his incompetence and the activities of the young Napoleon Bonaparte the British had carried off only four ships-of-the-line and burnt five, leaving 18 intact. And to these and the many others in their Atlantic ports the military prowess of the soldiers of France shortly added two complete fleets, that of the Dutch by conquest and that of Spain by alliance. For on land the new model Republican Army had triumphed over all difficulties finally to smash the first great continental alliance on which Britain had depended. By mid-summer 1796 the British Army – as contemptible in relative size, and far inferior in quality, to the BEF of 1914 – had as allies only the soldiers of Naples, Piedmont and Portugal for what they were worth, which was nothing.

The problem the British Government then faced (which had taxed it before, and was to tax it both for much of these wars and also in this century) was how to strike effectively against an infinitely more powerful continental enemy, whose main armies it could never take on alone, no matter how successful the navy might be. When that enemy, by design or folly, presented Britain with allies, she could encourage them with large quantities of gold, but hardly with the prospect of a major 'second front' on her own account. For three-quarters of this war, until – in a very different situation – Wellington learned how to make war in Portugal and Spain, her European adventures were brief and usually disastrous, and only the presence of the Navy offshore prevented outright catastrophe. Outside Europe, of course, she could use her naval superiority to pick off her enemies' colonial possessions one by one, and these wars certainly did complete the framework for a new British Empire, with its chain of key bases like Malta, the Cape of Good Hope, Mauritius and the rest (even also Heligoland, off the German coast), added to Gibraltar. But even these operations diffused her manpower – sometimes with humiliating failures, but most quickly with the hideous 1794 disaster in the West Indies, when yellow fever killed as many redcoats in a single year as Wellington was to lose from all causes during the whole of the Peninsular War. (And, of course, the greatest beneficiary of all was to be the neutral United States, to whom Napoleon was to sell his great untenable territory of Louisiana in 1803 – 828,000 square miles for $15,000,000 – thereby increasing American national territory by some 140 per cent.)

With all hindsight it is perhaps fortunate that the British failed for so long to open up any major European theatre of operations successfully for any length of time, since any real threat to France would have brought down the whole might of the French Army on the invaders. The fate of Sir John Moore's little army, which was evacuated from Corunna in 1809 with the enemy snapping at its heels, and of the abortive Walcheren expedition of the same year, which was defeated by disease before the French could destroy it in the field, pointed to the outcome of such temerity even much later in the war. In its opening phase the French quickly dealt with a motley Anglo-Dutch-Hessian-Hanoverian intrusion into Flanders, the diseased survivors of which were shipped home from Bremen in 1795. But by then another opportunity was opening up, which had the special attraction of risking no British lives except those in the ships which would be used to transport, supply and generally encourage Frenchmen to fight Frenchmen.

In the bizarre 1989 French Revolutionary celebration parade in

Paris all the ancient provinces of France were represented in a march-past. But while many of these sent large contingents, those from the Vendée, the maritime area of old Poitou south of Brittany, contributed but a handful (only *three*, according to one commentator): evidently the Vendéans, having memories as long as the Irish, knew that they had nothing to celebrate, and still regarded Paris much as the inhabitants of Wexford or Limerick do London.

In the aftermath of 1789 and into the 1790s the Vendée and much of Brittany had remained devoutly Catholic and royalist, to the point of open rebellion (in so far as rejection of a revolution can be so called). This flame the British now irresponsibly fanned into a fierce fire with easily delivered supplies of war material and some thousands of armed *émigrés*, with predictable results: the regular soldiers of the republic, led by the bright young General Lazare Hoche, made short work of the untrained peasants and squabbling *émigrés*, and then went on to make a terrible example of the Vendée with the full ferocity of the revolution, in which terror was an instrument of policy. It even required no great activity on the part of the French Navy, since everything delivered by the British Navy in their equipment 'drops' to the rebels soon ended up in republican hands all along that charnel-house coast, which today is a smiling Anglo-French tourist trap, with its quaint towns and villages and sandy beaches.

For Captain Sir Edward Pellew and Mr Midshipman Hornblower, however, this tragedy was just another (but more irritating) job for the inshore frigate detachment, with the rocks more dangerous than the enemy. But if the failure of the so-called 'Quiberon Expedition' and the loss of all the arms and equipment Pellew and his subordinate frigate captains delivered hardly enhanced his reputation, the seas between the two main French Atlantic naval bases of Brest and Rochefort, with their halfway house of Lorient midway, were promising hunting-grounds. First blood there actually went to the *Indefatigable*'s consort, the (ex-French) *Révolutionnaire*, which easily took the weaker *L'Unité*, but in mid-April 1796 it was Pellew's turn, when he sighted the brand new *Virginie* (40), which was commanded by an enemy who was to be his friend for life, Jacques Bergeret.

Bergeret was a man not unlike Pellew – a fine seamen and a stern disciplinarian who led from the front, albeit without noticeable charisma. But although his *Virginie* was fast and well-armed it now stood no chance against the exceptional *Indefatigable*, which not only carried 24-pounders but had been re-rigged for speed on Pellew's insistence. Indeed, during the 15-hour chase which followed the British frigate averaged 9.8 knots (11.2 mph) over 168 miles before she brought the French ship to bay. With other British frigates coming up Bergeret lost no honour in the subsequent fight, although he was careful to point out to his masters that he had been taken by a *razé*.

And, indeed, after he had been befriended and supported in captivity by Pellew, he was soon enough exchanged and restored to command, eventually to become the scourge of the British East India Company in the Indian Ocean (where, once again, he was to meet Pellew, who was by then flying an admiral's flag).

The pursuit and capture of the *Virginie* was in fact a far more brilliant action than the taking of the *Cléopâtre*. But it was soon to be eclipsed by an action during an emergency in which the British were appropriately punished for encouraging the poor Breton and Vendéan peasants to their deaths. For what was sauce for the French republican goose was also sauce for the British Protestant gander: if the Vendée offered an opportunity to make trouble for Paris, then oppressed Catholic Ireland was ready to do the same for London; and indeed, who better to fan those smouldering Irish flames than the energetic General Hoche, with his newly gained experience of his own country's rebellious Catholic peasantry? More than that even (and in the days when Irish Catholics and Ulster Protestants could still make common cause), the Irish then had a potential leader of their own in Theobald Wolfe Tone, an expatriate young Belfast lawyer, to go with France's own long experience of intervention in Ireland, which went back to the Bantry Bay landing of 1688 in support of James II.

Whether the French also cynically measured likely failure against the certainty of at least diverting British resources from further European operations can only be conjectured. But the flaw in their new Irish adventure was an old one in French strategic naval planning, which ignored weakness by glorifying the final objective – 'the mission' – at the expense of its true prerequisite, which was command of the sea. *Getting there* was taken to be all that mattered, with all the problems of resupply, reinforcement and (if the worst came to the worst) evacuation left to chance.

Consequently, military preparation went ahead and troops were collected (20,000 allocated, with arms for 30,000 rebels, but only 15,000 actually embarked), grandiose and unrealistic plans for naval superiority depending on the arrival of the newly allied Spanish fleet coming up from the south to augment the French one. This was a truly disastrous piece of optimism, since (as everyone by land and sea, on both sides, was to discover throughout the whole war) those who depended on Spanish naval and military help always came to grief. That the Spaniards were as brave as they were proud was to be proved time and again in the years to come. That their ships were incomparable when they came off the slipway was never in dispute. But that they were quite extraordinarily unreliable and incompetent as allies was a lesson which even the most otherwise intelligent commanders (not least the Duke of Wellington himself) always seem to have had to learn the hard way.

In the event, therefore, the Spanish fleet never turned up. However, the French had by then assembled a numerically formidable fleet of 17 ships-of-the-line, 13 frigates and eight corvettes (powerful sloops-of-war), many carrying soldiers in addition to those in seven transports. And (had they but known it) all that stood in their way was Captain Sir Edward Pellew and the *Indefatigable*.

Under the elderly and inactive Admiral Lord Bridport (second-in-command to the near-geriatric Lord Howe, who was treating his gout at Bath), the British blockading Channel Fleet had been more or less withdrawn to snug home anchorage at Spithead for the winter months, leaving a few line ships in the wrong places or too far out to sea on distant watch and only the *Indefatigable* in the Brest approaches, with the *Révolutionnaire*, the *Amazon* (36) and a messenger-lugger in support. Bridport's assumption was that the French would not attempt an expedition in mid-winter. The French, for their part, decided that winter offered them their best chance of slipping through a blockade which they presumed was much stronger than it looked. Indeed, they further decided that a night escape would be prudent.

Pellew, for *his* part, had realised earlier that trouble was brewing when a strong squadron of French ships-of-the-line and frigates from Rochefort brushed him aside to enter Brest. He had duly reported this to Admiral Colpoys, whom he believed to be cruising somewhere off Ushant. But then, only hours before the French sailed, he learned from a friendly (anti-republican) Breton fisherman that troops had actually been embarked. (Friendly Breton fishermen were a major source of British intelligence during the period; Pellew himself had even acquired a royalist Breton to help him navigate those treacherous waters, to whom, before long, he would owe his life). In the absence of the *Amazon* on patrol elsewhere and now desperate, he further sent the lugger and then the *Révolutionnaire* to find Colpoys, while himself heading into the Brest approaches to do what damage he could by night in increasingly stormy conditions.

What Wolfe Tone and General Hoche might have achieved in Ireland (on which they were never to set foot) is as conjectural as what might have happened if Admiral Bridport's fleet dispositions had been wiser and Admiral Colpoys had remained on station. Wolfe Tone was an able man and Hoche an enterprising and ambitious soldier whose death next year from galloping consumption removed one of young General Bonaparte's rivals from the scene. The belated appearance of the British Channel Fleet would certainly have precluded any re-inforcement of their invasion had they actually got ashore, but they might together have caused the British a lot of trouble before their eventual defeat in that bitter winter of 1796–7. And had their fleet kept together there was no reason why they should not at least have landed successfully, for there was nothing in their way – except darkness, one of the worst storms in living memory, and Edward Pellew.

The first French mistake (after their over-estimation of Admiral Bridport's ability) was to attempt that night escape, which would have sorely taxed a much better-trained fleet. Debilitated by those earlier revolutionary purges which had robbed it of its most experienced officers and further demoralised by long months of inactivity due to the British blockade, which had prevented many of its captains and crews from acquiring sea-going experience, this fleet might well have had difficulty in keeping together in stormy weather in daylight, for all that every ship had its own Breton pilot to help it out of harbour. As it was, it was soon further confused by a variety of signal rockets which attended the exodus. These – the work, of course, of Pellew – resulted not only in the destruction of the *Séduisant* (74) on the rocks, but contributed in the end as the weather worsened to the chaotic scattering of the whole fleet, the most notable absentee being the vital 'command ship', the frigate *Fraternité*, in which both its commanding admiral and General Hoche were travelling.

Pellew had done his work well, and the sea and the weather did the rest. Days later, battered French ships did actually straggle into the superb invasion anchorage of Bantry Bay in dribs and drabs, first arrivals leaving in despair, later ones running when a fresh gale threatened to drive them ashore in the snow flurries. Not one French soldier was landed, and several ships foundered on the way home.

However, if the French Navy had predictably performed badly in adverse conditions, the British Navy's performance had been almost equally abysmal – almost, that is, because the total failure of Admiral Bridport's and Admiral Colpoys' ships-of-the-line even to sight a single French ship, let alone bring it to battle, was to be somewhat offset at the end by one of the most notable frigate actions of the whole war.

It is worth pausing for a moment here to consider the enormous burden placed on commanders in the days before radio. On land the new semaphore system, with a chain of signal stations linking the decision-makers to the coast, was to revolutionise the speed of message transmission. But at sea, although British signalling methods had been vastly improved, visibility between ships was limited by the weather – as, indeed, were the ships' movements themselves. Of the pressures on any British commander, battle was the least, as we have already noted: the grand old Hymn 370, in its prayer 'for those in peril on the sea', rightly puts 'foe' last among the perils facing the sailors of those times, with rock, tempest and fire preceding. But to these hazards might very reasonably be added the stress factor, to which admirals at sea and captains on detached duties (usually frigate captains, and often very young ones) were particularly exposed for prolonged periods. With the fate of the country perhaps at stake, and certainly their own lives and professional reputations, lone commanders had to make decisions on the basis of information which might not only be sparse and imprecise, but also often days, weeks, or even months old. In the case of our six captains, the harrowing experience of Horatio Hornblower in the Pacific in 1808, when after a seven-month voyage he attacked and took the Spanish *Natividad* in ignorance of the fact that Spain was by then Britain's ally, is a case in point, and no far-fetched one: the Anglo-American land-battle of New Orleans in 1815 was fought weeks after peace had been concluded.

Extreme anxiety and fear of making wrong decisions informs Pellew's letters and reports at this time, especially after the French had sailed and the captain of the *Révolutionnaire* had reported back that he had failed to find Admiral Colpoys cruising on station: that admiral's miserable performance had included letting the weather get the better of him. 'I trust implicitly to their Lordships' Candor for believing me actuated by every motive of honor & disinterested zeal', Pellew wrote to the Admiralty; and to the First Lord, in what sounds like desperation, 'God knows, my lord, if I shall be doing right, but left in a wilderness of conjecture I can only say that the sacrifice of my life would be easy if it served my gracious King and my country.' He was one of the best and steadiest captains in the Navy, in the prime of life. But, with the French at sea (God only knew where) and a continuous month of some of the worst weather he had ever experienced, from mid-December to mid-January, the strain was beginning to tell even on him.

What befell him then, after the rest of Channel Fleet under Bridport and Colpoys had failed to prevent any of the scattered Bantry Bay expeditionary fleet returning home, gave him the opportunity to prove the truth of his words to the First Lord. For then he at last caught sight of a French ship while once more in company with another of his inshore squadron, Captain Reynolds' 36-gun *Amazon*, in hazy conditions and heavy seas some 70 miles (so he thought) south-west of Ushant, and signalled the 'General Chase' flag.

His quarry turned out to be a brand-new ship-of-the-line, the *Droits de l'Homme*, rated 74 guns but carrying 80, together with 700 of Hoche's soldiers (most of whom had been carried in warships rather than transports). Technically, the razéed *Indefatigable* and the much smaller *Amazon* were together no match for such a ship's 36-pounders, which could sink them with one broadside each – just as the German pocket-battleship *Admiral Graf Spee* could have sunk (and very nearly did sink) the British cruisers *Exeter*, *Ajax* and *Achilles* in the South Atlantic in December 1939. But technicalities are one thing and realities are another, just as much somewhere off Ushant in January 1797 as off the River Plate 142 years later.

In fact, in spite of the superficial disparity of force, Pellew actually had a number of advantages which would have been apparent to him even after he realised what he was up against. Initially he took the French ship for a large *razé*, not unlike his own beloved *Indefatigable*. She was in truth something very different: an experimental Third Rate of a new design, longer and lower (and in other conditions no doubt much faster) than her sisters. But for once French enthusiasm for exciting innovation was to betray them. The lower (or lowest) gundeck on ships-of-the-line had of necessity to be lower than the single gundeck of any frigate for centre-of-gravity reasons, because of the weight of the heaviest guns mounted on it. Consequently, however, those gunports could not be opened in heavy seas for fear of flooding – and capsizing. This, notoriously, disadvantaged many poorly-designed British line-ships; now it prevented the experimental *Droits de l'Homme* from even attempting her heavyweight punch – supposing, of course, that Pellew had given her the chance, once he had decided on fighting her. What he actually intended is open to argument. He could hardly have expected to sink her, since wooden ships were difficult to sink at the best of times in fights between equals. But, equally, he could hardly have expected her to surrender. For that civilised convention only applied to fights between out-matched enemies: for a ship-of-the-line to give in to a brace of frigates (even though one might be a *razé*) would have spelt professional ruin for a British ship-of-the-line captain, and probably the firing squad for a French one in 1797; indeed, Commodore Lacrosse of the *Droits* is reported to have said that he would rather have sunk his ship than surrender her to such adversaries.

Pellew's tactics were, in any case, those of every small carnivore in pursuit of bigger prey, as well as every frigate captain pursuing a ship-of-the-line either unable or unwilling to turn on her persecutors: he manoeuvred to hit and run, relying on the quicker reactions of his well-trained crews, helped not only by the French ship's inability to bring her main-deck guns to bear, but also by the loss of her fore and main topmasts already as a result of storm-damage sustained during her return from Bantry Bay (she was 'steering very wild', he had noted even before the action began).

What followed was, nevertheless, a remarkable fight by any standards. And what justifies the word 'epic' (apart from the subsequent official panegyric) was that the long harrying-to-the-death of the *Droits de l'Homme* was fought throughout the darkening afternoon of a foul January day and on through the night (with one 70-minute break for repairs between 2 a.m. and 3.10 a.m.) in the midst of a storm and off a lee shore famous for its shipwrecks.

That the *Indefatigable* and no less the smaller *Amazon* were well handled is easy to take for granted – or even belittled somewhat by their final tally of battle casualties, which in the case of the *Amazon* was only three killed and 15 wounded and in the *Indefatigable* only 19 wounded. Only the confusion of darkness can account for this, plus the inexperience of the French crew when assailed from both sides at close quarters – so close that on one occasion the French ship's stern flag became entangled with the *Indefatigable*'s main rigging until torn away. Nor can French bravery be faulted, with the poor devils of her 700 infantry lined up on her upper deck to give what fire-support they could 'within Pistol shot'. And all this in a storm so wild that, on the main decks of the frigates, men were fighting up to their waists in the water which gushed through the gunports and from above, and with some guns breaking their breachings 'four times over', or even drawing the ring-bolts which attached them to the ship. (An account of the horror of a gun breaking loose, and rumbling back and forth with every roll of the ship – 'a ton and a half of insensate weight, threatening at any moment to burst through the ship's side' – is enshrined in Horatio Hornblower's memory of his *Natividad* fight, as recorded by his biographer. Ships 'lost without a trace', rolling uncontrollably after dismasting, were the probable victims of such mischances.)

In the midst of all this excitement (which must have been only just preferable to that 'wilderness of conjecture' which had preceded it), another danger was then looming up in Pellew's thoughts – 'looming', though, in the almost impenetrable darkness of the night as the battle drifted north-eastwards. For, although he was by then one of the most experienced British frigate captains among the inshore blockaders, he was aware that he had a dangerously inexact knowledge of where he actually was in relation to the land after so many days of stormy and overcast weather. He evidently *thought* that he was still somewhere off the approaches to Brest, but at the westward point of the Breton peninsula, beyond the Passage du Raz and the Pointe de Saints, with open sea to the north of him. But in ordinary circumstances this would still have been the moment to attempt to claw away from the peninsula, for the safety of open sea.

But these were not ordinary circumstances: the safety of the *Indefatigable* had to be measured against the damage she was doing to the battered *Droits de l'Homme* with the help of the well-handled *Amazon*. So what Pellew did, while relying on the special knowledge he assumed the French captain ought to have ('I placed considerable reliance that her Commander would not voluntarily sacrifice his Ship and her crew by running her for a dangerous part of the Coast. . .'), was to send his second lieutenant to the bows to keep a sharp look-out, regardless of the fighting.

That, in the first place, was evidence of professional competence (merit), which left as little as possible to chance when other matters pressed hard, and 'interest' was of no use whatsoever. But then luck did the rest, and twice over. For, at twenty minutes past four o'clock, a providential appearance of the moon revealed breakers and land dead ahead where there should have still been open sea. Pellew hastily prepared to change course, believing that he knew where he now was on the western edge of the Breton peninsula, with the dangerous approaches to Brest (the proper destination of the *Droits de l'Homme*) beyond. But now the Breton royalist pilot with whom he had furnished himself to help him with his work contradicted his order: 'Non, non, Mon Capitaine! Ze odder way!'

In fact the *Indefatigable* was embayed on a lee shore, between the two arms of Audierne Bay, which any British tourist – fortified on a fine day with the Michelin No 58 Map – may descry, between the Pointe du Raz and the Pointe du Penmarch. But the sea leaves no evidence of its great dramas so that the precise point where both the *Droits de l'Homme* and the *Amazon* were wrecked is lost; and there is nothing to show for the desperate manoeuvres of the *Indefatigable*, as she raised her blue warning lights, and fired her warning rockets, while clawing first one way and then the other, to miss les Etocs de Penmark by a matter of yards to reach safety outside Audierne Bay, in the open sea.

Dawn revealed the fate Pellew had so narrowly escaped, when the *Droits de l'Homme* was observed, dismasted and lying broadside on a sandbank with the waves breaking over her, only a mile away. Later it was discovered that the *Amazon* had also gone ashore, further up the coast, though mercifully Captain Reynolds and most of his crew had been able to save themselves by good seamanship, unlike the majority of the 1000 unfortunates on the French ship.

The loss of a useful frigate, with a first-rate captain and crew, may seem a somewhat poor exchange for a French ship-of-the-line (of which there were still many) and a regiment of French soldiers (of whom there were now upwards of three-quarters of a million) at first sight. But any sort of success in those dark days was to be welcomed, and even though he did not get the reward he sought (that valuable sinecure of a colonelcy in the marines still eluded him) Pellew was properly given the credit for beating an 80-gun ship with two frigates – in the words of the First Lord of the Admiralty 'an exploit which has not I believe ever graced our naval annals'.

With that it is time to move Captain Pellew from centre-stage, although he had two more years of blockading duty ahead of him then in the *Indefatigable* (soon minus his protégé, Acting-Lieutenant Hornblower, who was to be captured while commanding a prize). In the Navy, as the destroyer of the *Droits de l'Homme* as well as the captor of the *Cléopâtre* and the *Virginie*, his reputation was well-established, and further promotion was certain. Indeed, he was now so far up the Captain's List, with his post-rank dating from 1782, that he could now expect not only a ship-of-the-line if he wanted one (or if, as it turned out, the Admiralty needed him in one), but an admiral's command to go with the automatic rank of admiral he must have when he reached the top of the list and a vacancy occurred. At least, anyway, he would certainly get that flag if the Tories were in power then; and with his luck that would be the case by a whisker, even though the next (Whig) government would quickly do its best to spoil his enjoyment of high command and its profits by then dividing that command.

But that, and his political debut as MP for Barnstaple after his transfer into the Channel Fleet's unhappy 84-gun ship-of-the-line *Impétueux* in 1799, and then into the (happier) *Tonnant* (an ex-French 80), is a story for his full biography, not for a tale of frigates and frigate captains. We shall, of course, meet him again from time to time down the years, as Hornblower's captain retrospectively, as a prize-money beneficiary (and over-promoter of his sons, in the exercise of Pellew family 'interest'), and even as an admirer (perhaps enviously) of that great young frigate captain William Hoste. But here it must be enough to note that it was frigate command and frigate warfare which made him – and, perhaps, that his frigate years were his happiest ones. Apart from all of which it is also time to catch up with the war itself – first with good news for the British Navy, and then with very bad news which will lead the story on to Captain Hugh Pigot.

The good news was that the Spanish Navy had got to sea at last, although happily (for the British) much too late to assist the French at Bantry Bay, and actually only to protect a valuable Spanish convoy from the Americas. Once again, the convoy got through. But, even more importantly for the British (for whom the *Droits de l'Homme* success was unimportant, however glorious), the Spaniards crossed the path of Admiral Sir John Jervis and Commodore Horatio Nelson near Cadiz, off Cape St Vincent. And there Sir John and his young commodore, representing the best traditions of their navy – harsh *but* efficient, enlightened *and* efficient – set the pace for the years to come in the Navy's testing time, after the failure of Bridport and Colpoys, with standards of performance which would inspire every intelligent captain for the rest of the war.

Jervis, as has been already noted, had risen solely by merit. Or, anyway, almost solely, for his longevity in active command was almost as remarkable. Born in 1735, before the War of the Austrian Succession ('King George's War'), he had been a friend of General Wolfe's in the next French war, commanding his first ship in action before all our frigate captains except Pellew were even born (as though say, a front-line admiral of the Second World War had first gone to sea as a midshipman in Queen Victoria's navy). Then, as the captain of the *Foudroyant* (an ex-French ship, of course), he had won his knighthood in a rare ship-of-the-line single-ship duel (frigates, more usually, fought such actions, of course). He would not relinquish his last sea-going command until 1807, at the age of 73 and still vigorous, irascible and dedicated to the good of the Navy as he saw it, with no time for officers whose 'interest' was greater than their merit.

In the person of Sir John Jervis, who in 1797 was already over 60 with nearly half-a-century's service behind him, old age shows at its best, to balance the record after Bridport's failure and as our younger frigate captains are winning most of the praise. 'Old Jervie' now sighted 27 Spanish ships-of-the-line (including the world's biggest, the 132-gun *five*-deck *Santissima Trinidad*), when he had only 15 (and Nelson). But the realities of his country's general situation, political as well as military and naval, the old man well understood, accompanied as was that understanding with his confidence in the fleet he commanded: 'A victory is very essential to England at this moment.'

The battle of Cape St Vincent, which he then fought and which gave his peerage its name, actually only produced four prizes, two of which were Nelson's (the second being taken across the deck of the first). The *Santissima Trinidad* (which the British thought they had taken, but which eluded them until Trafalgar) escaped: annihilating victories would have to wait until Nelson was in sole command. But the Spanish Navy was effectively eliminated from this half of the war as a result. And – perhaps even more importantly than that – the assumption of victory against any odds began to animate British captains. 'Old Jervie' – *St Vincent* ever after – was the true architect of Nelson's navy, harsh and (as we shall see) sometimes unfair, but ruthlessly set on perfection and duty. But before his stamp could be set on it for Nelson (and men like Cochrane, Hornblower and Hoste) to add charisma to the formula, the system required some further amendment. And the stimulus for this came almost immediately along with the St Vincent victory, but from the lower deck, not the quarterdeck or the Admiralty itself.

The bad news of early 1797 was that His Britannic Majesty's navy in its main base at Spithead had mutinied.

CHAPTER SIX

In which the British fleet goes on strike

Sir John Jervis's defeat of the Spanish fleet, from which Commodore Nelson emerged as a national hero, and the long run of frigate victories, which had most recently been crowned by Captain Pellew's destruction of the *Droits de l'Homme*, could not conceal the unpalatable truth that otherwise by 1797 the French were winning the war.

To make war effectively on her old enemy the British had always needed allies in Europe whose armies could make up for her own military inadequacy. At the beginning of a war into which she had been forced against her will she had had plenty of them. Now only Austria was left, and French armies were massing on the Meuse, the Rhine and, above all, in Northern Italy, where the young General Bonaparte was about to teach the Austrians lessons in blitzkrieg. Spain and Holland had actually been 'turned round', from allies into enemies. And although the Spanish Navy had now been at least temporarily eliminated, the army and navy of Holland – now transmogrified into the 'Batavian Republic' – was about to be enlisted by Wolfe Tone and General Hoche for another Irish expedition. Meanwhile, the greater part of the British Army itself had been thrown away in the West Indies, victims not of the French but of yellow fever, and a serious financial crisis was looming at home, with the Bank of England in deep trouble.

That the British government itself was all too well aware of both the bleakness of the prospect and the deep disillusion in the country even before the shock of the Bantry Bay expedition was clearly shown by its quiet despatch of a senior diplomat, the Earl of Malmesbury, to Paris in the winter of 1796 to explore the possibility of an honourable peace. The war, after all, had never been for the British the anti-republican crusade it had been for the continental monarchies of the now-defunct First Coalition. It had been forced on them by those 'frantic Murderers' of 1793, most of whom had long since gone to their own guillotine, despatched by the more reasonable men of the new 'Directory' which now governed France. Unfortunately, however, the 'Directors' were no less well aware of the strength of their position, and the Malmesbury mission foundered utterly on their refusal to give up the Austrian Netherlands (roughly modern Belgium, including the great invasion port of Antwerp). So, with a century of French wars behind them which had been fought largely to prevent that aggrandisement of French power, the British had no choice but to continue the struggle somehow, somewhere, secure only in the strength and superiority of their navy, which had purged its Bantry Bay embarrassment off Cape St Vincent so recently with that 'essential' victory. In so dark an hour it came as all the greater shock that the next great crisis of the war was that navy's mutiny.

As with the press gang, the sheer awfulness of life afloat 'in the old days' is almost a racial memory among the British. By modern standards life ashore was harsh and brutal enough for the majority in the eighteenth century, with the horrors of the industrial revolution in the nineteenth to come. But the legendary 'rum, buggery and the lash' existence of other ranks in the Navy with which Britannia ruled the seas in Nelson's time is a popular nightmare in a class of its own. Rum and the lash will be dealt with in due course below, and information about both is easy to come by. Statistics and general information on sodomy and homosexuality are much more difficult to unearth, and any attempt to differentiate between them (the former, in the absence of women over long periods, not necessarily being directly related to the latter) is impossible. Most of life afloat was lived in public, which cannot have made such associations easy, and the punishment – death for both parties – was savage. There were a good many (or, a *bad* many) courts martial for such offences, nevertheless, though in the case of officers there also seems to have been a good deal of hushing up and dismissal. Since, however, very few of those who left memoirs were disposed to include such anecdotes, one is forced to fall back on generalisations: detestation of unnatural acts was then both general and official, but where there's a will there's always a way. Much must have depended on the quality of command (which is indeed largely the theme of this whole book). Good – wise and observant – captains more often than not gradually acquired good and wise officers and warrant officers who would have worked to avoid both scandal and the loss of men by breaking up such *liaisons dangereuses*, and bad ones would either have hanged or turned a blind eye. But, in the scale of things, 'buggery' was never in the same class as a problem either in 1797 or later compared with 'rum' and 'the lash'. And, indeed, in 1797, none of that unholy trinity was the issue between the Lower Deck and the Admiralty.

The awfulness of naval service was, for all that, just as well-known afloat and ashore then as now. When Dr Johnson reflected that 'every man thinks meanly of himself for not having been a soldier, or not having been to sea', he was referring to every *gentleman*, one may suppose, not to other ranks. But, anyway, he also concluded that 'no man will be a sailor who has contrivance enough to get himself into a jail; for being in a ship is being in jail, with the chance of being drowned ... A man in a jail has more room, better food, and commonly better company.'

In fact, of course, a man in the Navy would not starve, and was certainly always better off in that respect than those 'free' men on land whose freedoms included freedom to starve to death, even though naval rations were all too frequently foul and stinking as well as fraudulently under-weight. And jail was no safe place either, in the heroic age of Nelson: it was to become an increasingly important source of 'recruitment' as impressment produced fewer victims and voluntary enlistment virtually dried up altogether (even with the £5 bounty, which every 'volunteer' could claim – even in jail).

What made warship life so unpopular, apart from the danger and discomfort of seafaring itself under sail and the extraordinarily cramped conditions in ships designed to pack the largest number of men (and guns) into the smallest possible space, was the harsh disciplinary system the Navy operated. But the many retellings of the *Bounty* mutiny, however unhistorical in outline, have rendered any detailed account of that system's most famous deterrent, the cat-o'-nine-tails, unnecessary. Harsh discipline was part of life in the services of all the European powers – except, perhaps, in some French ships where the lack of it was noted by the British as being a main reason for their own easiest victories. While hated and feared, the lash was also accepted therefore, and the question of its use did not feature in the demands of the mutineers of 1797: its connection even with the *Hermione* mutiny was, as we shall see, more complex than simple overuse.

Before further considering those factors which did finally lead to the 'Great Mutiny' of that year (in which the *Hermione* mutiny also took place), it is not inappropriate to look at some of the things which sustained the men in their misery, of which their chewing tobacco and – most important of all – their rum ration figured largely. The devotion of British fighting men to alcohol was proverbial: their determination to lay their hands on as much of it as possible almost equalled their determination to desert at the first opportunity, and when desertion was impossible the rum ration was always their solace. In battle, especially when well-led, they could be relied on to do their duty bravely, and to the full: Nelson's celebrated signal expecting them to do as much irritated some of his senior captains for being quite unnecessary. What they could never be relied on to do, however, was to stay sober – it was a problem which taxed their commanders much more than it did French officers, whose men both wanted it less and seemed to be able to hold it better. On land, after having performed one of the war's great feats of arms in storming the fortress city of Badajoz in 1810, Wellington's incomparable army went on a three-day drunken spree of plundering, rape and murder before it was flogged and hanged back to duty. At sea, when Admiral Pellew's flagship in the eastern seas was once in danger of shipwreck during a storm, members of the crew wasted no time in breaking into the liquor store. And at all times the rum ration, while considered essential to keep a crew amenable, was the biggest single cause of offences which led to flogging or worse – especially among those strong-minded men who contrived to save it up so that they could go on a real bender, into alcoholic oblivion if possible.

When added to brutality and boredom, alcohol was a dangerous fuse, the best antidote to which was ceaseless activity, and fighting the enemy the best cure. Winning such fights, the British sailor by then (and his officers with him) more-or-less took for granted. No matter how badly treated, the sailors considered themselves better men than any of their enemies:

Monsieurs, Mynheers and Dons, your Country's empty boast,
Our Tars can beat all three, each on his native coast.

Success in battle, and a rough patriotism which went with it even among men who still seized every chance to desert, not only conferred a certain self-respect, but otherwise offered at least the illusion of freedom through an eventually victorious peace to crews otherwise sentenced to serve 'for the duration', if not released by death first. But also (and what of course makes this war-at-sea so different for its participants) it dangled the chance of some great 'pools win' of prize-money cash, together with a share of the head money paid according to the size of the defeated enemy crews.

This cash incentive (as distinct from actual pay) will be considered in more detail later. What is important meanwhile is to realise that in the two fleets involved in the 1797 mutinies there was as little chance of such windfalls as there had been of battle. While the Mediterranean Fleet, under the hard-driving Sir John Jervis (now Earl St Vincent) and with the inspiration of Nelson and other successful captains, had seen plenty of action and had just won a glorious victory, the Channel and North Sea Fleets, spending much of their time at anchor at Spithead and the Nore, had festered and decayed, and had then failed ignominiously to catch the Bantry Bay expeditionary force. Lord Bridport had once been a brave captain, but he was a bad admiral and his fleet, in particular, had become a bad fleet. Even when it had eventually attempted to get to sea – from the wrong place and far too late – it had done so in an incompetent fashion more reminiscent of the French Directors' navy than King George's: the 98-gun *Prince* rammed the 84-gun *Sans Pareil*, the equally large *Formidable* (98) did the same to the huge *Ville de Paris* (110 guns – and the French names betray their origins, so they must have been good ships), and the *Atlas* (also 98) ran aground. All in all, with Bridport himself taking two days to reach his fleet from his comfortable home ashore in Somerset, the Channel Fleet covered itself with shame, which Sir John Colpoys' performance only made worse – and which, significantly, was not lost on his men, when as mutineers soon after they were to sing:

> He, like a base coward, let them get away,
> When the French and their transports sailed to Bantry Bay.

However, this loss of self-respect was the backcloth to the ensuing mutiny, rather than its occasion. For it was, in appearance if not in ultimate reality, a long-fermented industrial dispute, rather than the result of demoralisation after failure.

What is probably most surprising to us, in our age, is that (apart from this loss of self-respect) all the horrors of life afloat and the injustices attendant on the manning of the fleet did not result in a political act in the climate of those times, after the French Revolution had very loudly and successfully proclaimed those very 'Rights of Man' which had occasioned the naming of Captain Pellew's recent victim on the sandbanks of Audierne Bay. Indeed, the roll of ship-names in the Republican Navy as a whole rings down the years like an early form of propaganda.

By this period tradition and custom, patriotism and a devotion to classical and mythological history (which dominated every gentle-man's education) actually provided the main sources of warship names. Of the first, sentimental attachment to honoured old ships in which men's ancestors had fought and sometimes died, was strong enough to ensure that the most tongue-twisting name lived on. Among many others which appear in these pages, there was an *Indefatigable* at Jutland in 1916 (sunk by a single German salvo), and another of the same name at the Japanese surrender ceremony in Tokyo Bay in 1945. It was, very much by custom again, a 'big ship' name (our *Inde-fatigable* was a razéed ship-of-the-line, remember), so her twentieth-century successors were, respectively, a battle-cruiser and a fleet aircraft-carrier – which would surely have pleased Pellew. And he would also have spotted *Ajax, Orion, Superb, Temeraire,* and *Conqueror* in the lines of Jellicoe's battleships, and with them the proper monarchist-historical patriotism which put *King George V* and *St Vincent* with them: the fleet of his times had its *Royal George,* its *Prince of Wales,* and its *Queen Charlotte.*

Where sonorous nouns and adjectives, royalty and heroes, were favourites for the big ships, something more dashing was more generally favoured for frigates. Captain Marryat, who went to sea in Cochrane's *Impérieuse* in 1806 and lived to become a best-selling naval novelist, sums up the views not only of their Lordships of the Admiralty but also (allegedly) those of the Jack Tars themselves in his *Peter Simple*:

> No name can be too fine for a pretty girl, or a good frigate, Mr Simple ... all our gun-brigs ... have nothing but low common names, such as *Pincher, Thrasher, Boxer, Badger* ... which are quite good enough for them; whereas our dashing saucy frigates have names as long as the main-top bowline, and hard enough to break your jaw – such as *Melpomeny, Terpsichore, Arethusy, Bacchanty* – fine flourishers, as long as their pennants ...

These, signalling a triumph of the classics which the educationists of the time had surely never envisaged, continued on into the twentieth century, fortified now by proud tradition, with *Argonauts, Penelopes, Cleopatras,* and even ill-fated *Hermiones* in both its world wars, and a *Eurylaus* in attendance when Admiral Cunningham used the language of the old navy in 1943: 'Be pleased to inform Their Lordships that the Italian battle fleet now lies under the guns of the fortress of Malta.' Shades of Nelson!

As with the British Navy, so with the old French Royal Navy, exactly. While the Spaniards had a somewhat inappropriate tendency to mix religion and war, with their *San Salvador, San Francisco de Asis* and – the greatest of them all – *Santissima Trinidad* (although they also had a classical *Argonauta* and a *Netuno* too, admittedly), King Louis XVI's fleet was easily translated into English. The royal names were, of course, slightly different (*Royal Louis* and *Dauphin-Royal* for *Royal George* and *Prince George*). But the classics were just as strongly represented – *Argonaute, Pluton, Trojan* – together with recent French naval heroes like *Suffren, Duguay-Trouin* and *Tourville* which were also afloat. The Revolution changed much of this, if not all of it. *Royal Louis* and *Dauphin-Royal* became, respectively, *Sans-culottes* and *Republicain* as a whole litany of new revolutionary names went to sea: *Trente-et-Un Mai, Révolutionnaire* (the ex-*Bretagne,* 100-guns, as well as that frigate which the British took, and never renamed),

Vengeur du Peuple, Tyrannicide, and so on. To these, also, even foreign revolutionaries were added, like (Benjamin) *Franklin* and *Guillaume Tell* – rather as those other revolutionaries, the Bolsheviks, were to rename one of the Tsar's battleships after the scrofulous Jacobin Marat, as well as her sisters in the French revolutionary style. Even the old classical custom was adapted, to take account of the devotion of France's new masters to the heroes of the Roman republic, with *Mucius, Brutus* and *Scipion*.

The renaming process was indeed an example (if a somewhat esoteric one) of the revolutionary propaganda which the French eagerly sought to export to all nations – and did successfully first to the Dutch, whose navy soon had a *Vrijheid* ('Liberty'), a *Gelijkheid* ('Equality') and a *Brutus* of its own when it was to meet the British in battle before the year was out. That some of this propaganda penetrated to the lower decks of the British Navy, arriving *via* the press gang, the jails and the quota system (which scooped up more educated, or half-educated, victims) can be taken for granted. Yet, in spite of the French Revolution and its naval propaganda, the 1797 mutinies were astonishingly apolitical – as those agents sent down from London to find the Jacobins-in-the-woodpile discovered when they looked for such a conspiracy. Would-be revolutionaries there must have been, and disaffected Irishmen there certainly were, since before Bantry Bay Wolfe Tone had actually promised Hoche an Irish mutiny in the British fleet. But although there were eventually to be some political nuances in the later Nore mutiny, which blew up after that at Spithead had been settled amidst scenes of friendly reconciliation, extremism was kept in check by the leaders of the mutineers. Even in those moments when matters took a dangerous turn at Spithead, the mutineers there unfailingly supported the war effort: if the French put to sea, the fleet would fight them, come what may, they promised. One lieutenant, well-placed to observe what was happening, reported privately that his crew was 'most excessively enraged at the idea of any republican agents stirring them up to sedition', and one of those agents sent to Portsmouth to investigate the motivation of the mutineers found that 'nothing like want of loyalty to the King or (lack of) attachment to the government can be traced in this business'.

This was all a great mercy. But, nevertheless, Britain was at risk for two whole months, from mid-April to mid-May at Spithead, and mid-May to mid-June at the Nore with the greatest danger being that the government might reject the basically reasonable demands of the moderates at Spithead, attempting somehow (and without any chance of success) to suppress that mutiny by force before it could spread.

Fortunately, Lord Bridport won time initially by not doing anything stupid, and after some havering and several close calls Pitt sent down the popular old Admiral 'Black Dick' Howe to give the sailors most of what they wanted, together with a Royal pardon for all concerned. By doing this job brilliantly, as the last act in a long lifetime of service to his country, Howe cut the ground away from beneath the extremists among the Nore mutineers just in time. After first being led and then bullied by more intransigent and potentially revolutionary leaders, the Nore asked for more and seemed prepared to go further to get it. But the government was now able to stand firm with public opinion as well as the greater part of the fleet on its side. So this second mutiny petered out, this time to be followed by courts martial and executions (albeit only 29 of them), although not without another close call when Admiral Duncan, left with only two loyal ships in the North Sea, deceived the enemy with the old trick of signalling to a non-existent fleet.

A detailed record of these events is no more within the design of this narrative than are blow-by-blow descriptions of the two great sea battles of that action-packed naval year, the first having been at its beginning, off Cape St Vincent, and the second at its end, when Duncan's restored fleet captured eleven Dutch ships-of-the-line out of 18 at Camperdown. Our concern, rather, is with the underlying causes of the 'Great Mutiny' as they bear on what befell Captain Pigot and the *Hermione* in the far-off Caribbean in September of that same year.

Superficially, the former does *not* resemble the latter: the 'Great Mutiny', with its better-wages-and-conditions demands, resembles nothing so much as one of our own industrial disputes of the twentieth century: the sailors' hardships then become intolerable working conditions and the delegates from the individual ships who together managed the mutinies turn into shop stewards empowered to negotiate with the management and government further 'to improve pay in line with inflation'.

Of course, such historical analogies have many pitfalls: that these eighteenth-century naval strikers did not include the abolition of flogging in their list of demands warns us to beware taking this one too far. But, equally, they were well aware of the effect of inflation on naval wage rates which had actually not been improved since the middle of the seventeenth century. One of the anonymous petitions sent to Admiral Howe at Bath *before* the mutiny (which he most unwisely ignored) referred specifically to 'the rise in the necessaries of life, which has almost doubled'. The ill-judged parsimony of successive governments and parliaments, who so often voted money for new ships, but never for the men who sailed them, is shown by the actual cost of the settlement of 1797 – a mere £372,000 in a war budget of some £12.5 million. What undoubtedly made this parsimony unendurable then was the knowledge that the Army had had *its* wage increase two years before. For, however different were the attitudes of these eighteenth-century men from ours (in, for example, that matter of flogging), the effect of manifest unfairness is always corrosive, and in this case must have been all the more so because of the Army's abysmal record not only to date in this war, but in the previous one, with its capitulations at Lexington and Saratoga.

In a lecture delivered at the 1989 conference of the British Association for the Advancement of Science, Professor Keith Oatley of Glasgow University enlarged on the importance of the five basic emotions – happiness, sadness, anger, fear and disgust – as keys to action in a world that can be understood only imperfectly. Reporting on a study he had carried out, Professor Oatley said that happiness was predominantly triggered by achievements, sadness by losses, anger by frustration, and fear by threats ('disgust' having not yet produced enough data). 'Emotions are not just vestiges of an infantile and bestial history', he told the conference (gently suggesting that Darwin might not have got everything right). 'They are important now in our lives, in the everyday management of action.'

We would not wish to involve Professor Oatley too deeply here, in an inquiry into events at Spithead, and Spithead in 1797, let alone those in the *Hermione*. But Lord Bridport's sailors' only happiness can have come from their rum rations, not from any real achievements. And they would have been angry and disgusted by the failure of Lord Howe and the Admiralty to attend to their just and moderate demands, already delivered in anonymous petitions and relating to pay and poor rations. But, as important as anger and disgust, it will be argued that *fear* also informed and triggered their actions – and that fear was the mainspring of the more terrible actions of the crew of the *Hermione*. Which, in turn, brings us back to that industrial dispute analogy.

It has long been an axiom of business and industry (though tardily in Britain) that industries get the unions they deserve, and that there is no such thing as a bad workforce, only bad management. But, even before the penny dropped among capitalists (and has yet to drop among politicians?), the much-maligned military had concluded that defeat was the product of bad officers, bad generals (and admirals) and bad staff work, rather than the fault of front line fighting men.

This was certainly true of all the British fleets and squadrons, and of individual storm-tossed ships large and small far from the help and the advice of elders and seniors. For there was no mutiny in St Vincent's fleet, for all that that old admiral was a hard man, quicker to flog or hang than Bridport. Nor, for that matter, did Sir Edward Pellew ever aspire to winning any popularity contests: in his younger days he had been a notable flogger, the records show. And even in St Vincent's fleet all was not sweetness and light. The *Goliath*, under Captain Sir Charles Knowles, was a useless ship, until Knowles was forced to exchange with Captain Foley of the *Britannia*. Very soon the *Goliath* was a crack ship (and Foley, of course, became one of Nelson's favourite captains). And the *Britannia*, in turn, soon became drunk, disorderly and useless.

If the captain was good, then the scope for poor officers to become bad was severely restricted even before those officers were eliminated. If the captain was bad (or merely weak) even good officers had a problem – and bad officers got worse, breeding bad warrant officers, to bring sadism to perfection in a system well-designed for the practice of that art. That the men themselves were more often than not the victims, rather than the villains, of the tragedies which ensued is neatly illustrated in the traumatic experiences of Lieutenant Peter Bover, first lieutenant of the *London*, Sir John Colpoys' flagship at the Nore in 1797. Peter Bover was the officer who obeyed orders during one of the crisis moments of the mutiny, when a confrontation between officers and men finally exploded. Some of the latter began to unlash a gun, to point it at the quarterdeck, and Lieutenant Bover threatened to shoot the next man who moved, having his admiral beside him. One of the men continued to turn the gun, and Bover shot him: after which all was pandemonium, with casualties on both sides until the marines deserted their officers and Colpoys (in what was probably his finest hour, and his greatest service for his country) conceded defeat, enabling the steadier mutineers to calm their men. Nevertheless, Bover had shot straight, mortally wounding his man, and some of the insurgent sailors had seized him and were about to string him up when one of their delegates (shop stewards?) intervened, shouting, 'If you hang this man you shall also hang me, for I shall never quit.' And this gave Colpoys time to come forward very bravely to take the responsibility for what had happened. This began to turn the men's fury against him – but the moderates recoiled from insulting a man who, in spite of Bantry Bay, was still one of their admirals. So Bover was hustled below, still captive, but alive.

Now this can, quite properly, be an illustration as much of both the moderation and the authority of the senior mutineers, and their common sense, as of Colpoys' courage in action (as opposed to his ability as a squadron commander). But its importance in this examination of the springs of mutiny and murder is that it now illustrates very clearly how the system of merit and promotion worked at its best. For, among the ships of the unhappy Channel Fleet, the *London* was one of the better ones – and, in it, Lieutenant Peter Bover was known to be one of the very best officers. At the height of this fracas he was also defended by a rank-and-file mutineer, who protested that he was 'a brave boy'; and, later, a delegate from another ship who had served with him spoke up for him. He was in fact one of the *London*'s favourite officers, and after he had been finally sent ashore to stand trial for murder and had been freed on a verdict of justifiable homicide he insisted on keeping his promise to the crew that he would return to his ship. His friends advised him against this, thinking that his life was at risk, but he knew his men better: he was welcomed back on board with three cheers and a plea not to leave them again.

That there were many such officers as Peter Bover may reasonably be taken for granted, for the Navy could not have functioned so well without large numbers of such men. But, as the mutineers' unshakeable demand for the permanent removal of other officers shows, there were also many bad ones, some of whom were sadistic bullies. Where such men were in the ascendant, in ships like the *Winchelsea*, the *Nassau* and the *Amphitrite*, the agonised pleas of the men – necessarily anonymous pleas which, until 1797, were invariably ignored – testify to the hellish conditions which resulted.

Once 'read in' under the Articles of War, the breach of most of which rendered every man liable to 'death, or such less penalty', sailors were in the hands of the captain and his officers, not God or the Common Law. And although that 'less penalty' generally meant flogging, which without a formal court martial was theoretically limited to only twelve strokes, that could be stretched in practice to worse-than-death not merely by ignoring the rules (which was common) but by those thousand-and-one imaginative variations to cruelty which have characterised bullies down the ages. 'Bullies like bullyin', as Kipling's M'Turk observed in *Stalky & Co*. 'They mean it. They think it up in lesson and practise it in quarters.' But these bullies were the real thing, not inky schoolboys: if not sadists by nature, then elderly midshipmen who were never going to make lieutenant, or frustrated lieutenants who saw post-rank receding, or captains bowed down by responsibility and aware of their own inadequacies, consciously or unconsciously – all flawed men, but flawed men with near-absolute power over their victims.

Unfairly inadequate pay, often in arrears; rotten food, corruptly supplied by fat shore-based profiteers; inhumane treatment of the sick and wounded – all this (plus the demoralisation of the fleet through inaction and failure) served to bring Spithead to the boil in 1797. And the government's virtual capitulation to these just demands, made in conjunction with a Royal pardon delivered by a man the mutineers trusted, ended the crisis. But it may also be argued (and in the next chapter *will* be argued) that it was a failure in command – simply, bad *officers* – which made pay and conditions finally unendurable to those moderate men in whom the majority put their trust: 'Our first Lieutenant, he is a most Cruel and Barberous man. Beating some at times until they cannot stand, and not allowing them the satisfaction to cry out,' wrote the desperate crew of the *Amphitrite* to Howe at the height of the mutiny. 'If your honr. be pleased to look Round you may find many ships that Want men and as wee want another ship by granting one Wee will Remain In duty Bound to Remain, Your Ever lasting Servants and petitioners. . . .'

The *Winchelsea* men had asked the same, back in 1793: any ship but the one in which they were. But, in spite of pressure on him not to give in to this particular demand, old Black Dick knew at last by then what all the best captains (like Nelson's Collingwood) already knew: 'However ineligible the concession, it was become necessary.' So, quite crucially, the Spithead settlement included the removal of some 60 officers and warrant officers, including an admiral (Colpoys) and four captains. And, significantly, although Colpoys was appointed to another ship, he was never allowed to take up his command, or any other command at sea again.

The mutinies at the Nore and Spithead, although successful in obtaining so many of the mutineers' demands, did not radically change the British Navy. There were still brutal officers who commanded ships – not least, as we shall now see, the *Hermione*, among others. And other brutal officers would obtain commands, the system being what it was, and sometimes with tragic and disastrous results (which we shall also encounter). There would even be other mutinies – and, even mutinies for reasons other than brutality. Poor (or, anyway, *inexperienced*) leadership would cause trouble for Captain Edward Pellew's accident-prone brother, Captain Israel Pellew; dissatisfaction about the payment of prize-money would cause near-mutiny for Pellew himself (who in the spring of 1797 was struggling to blockade Brest with only one frigate – his own – as a result of a mutiny). Even the small frigate *Danae* would be taken from a quite decent captain by a group of Franco-American pressed men in an under-strength crew, and handed back to the French, from whom she had originally been taken. And, of course, British sailors would continue to be flogged by the dozen, and would continue to desert in ones and twos adding up to hundreds and thousands over the years.

But although too late for the *Hermione*, some sort of line was drawn in 1797, which the halfway intelligent captains must have noted, even if the brave beasts and the stupid brutes did not. Good and enlightened captains continued to get the best from the most unwilling crews. But so did harsh ones, sometimes quite amazingly. The difference, as the next chapter in this story will illustrate, was that with hard men like Pellew – and, judging by his performance too, Lieutenant Bover of the *London* – their men knew where they were, so that discipline and performance were not corroded by constant fear of arbitrary and irrational punishment.

It was that fear – as one of Professor Oatley's 'keys to action' – which was to be the death of Captain Hugh Pigot in the frigate *Hermione*.

CHAPTER SEVEN

The Hermione *mutiny*

Of our six chosen frigate captains, only two had reached coveted post-rank by 1797, and – having disposed of Pellew, who was now well up in the List on his way to a ship-of-the-line and his admiral's flag – it is time to consider the second of these, Hugh Pigot.

Before embarking on his tale, however, it is worth taking stock of the progress of the other four officers, even though the careers will be considered in turn at greater length in due course. For, although they were still in the fledgling stages of midshipman, acting-lieutenant (qualified and put forward for promotion) or commissioned lieutenant, those factors of 'interest', merit and luck were already distinguishing them from the others.

Cochrane, born in 1775, had not gone to sea until he was 18, but with 'interest' strong enough to bend the rules, he had already become a lieutenant when barely 20 (and with only two years' genuine sea-service) and was now serving in St Vincent's Mediterranean Fleet.

Broke, although only a year younger than Cochrane, was still a midshipman in 1797. But, although virtually without 'interest', his steady merit and years of experience at sea since 1792 would soon bring him to his lieutenancy.

Hornblower, another late starter with no 'interest' at all, had been lucky in catching the eye of Captain Pellew in the *Indefatigable*, to become an acting-lieutenant before his luck ran out early in 1797, when he was taken prisoner by the Spaniards. Although his acting-rank was confirmed shortly afterwards, his naval career – and his chances of 'distinction, promotion, prize-money' – had come to a halt: the grand old eighteenth-century custom of exchanging prisoners was still in force, but the Spaniards were taking few British prisoners. And, of course, he was in that maximum security prison of his officer's word-of-honour, which precluded escape absolutely. Things were to change there before long, and notably for the future Captain Hornblower. But in 1797 no British officer would break the rules.

Finally Hoste – 'Little Hoste', who was then still a teenager and the youngest of the four. But in him, thanks to merit and luck, 'interest' was now working overtime, for he was the special protégé of the Navy's greatest admiral who was now Britain's favourite wounded hero: the confirmation of his accelerated acting-lieutenancy would be only a matter of time after it had been endorsed by one of Nelson's first shaky signatures after the loss of his arm at Tenerife. So Acting-Lieutenant Hoste's future, in 1797, looked as bright as Hornblower's looked dim. But then, so too did Hugh Pigot's future seem promising, with the three years' seniority as a post-captain of a frigate which he already had in 1797.

In Pigot and his father (another Hugh), the worst working of the 'interest' system is exemplified, exacerbated by politics. 'Interest' and politics attended his birth in 1769, into a Whig Party family which had served the country vigorously during the century's French wars (and enriched themselves in the process) in the Honourable East India Company as well as in both the Army and the Navy. By mid-century, one Pigot had already been Governor and Commander-in-Chief in Madras, while another served in Europe and America, to become a general. Hugh Pigot senior, the third brother, had risen to command Admiral Saunders' flagship, the 84-gun *Royal William*, during the Seven Years' War, and having secured post-rank while still young his seniority on the List even by that war's end augured well for him: all he needed to reach admiral's rank was longevity, and all he needed to fly his flag at sea then was the conjunction of the next (no doubt) French war with the coming to power of the party of which he was a member.

Unfortunately for him, while time made him an admiral and advanced him up through the red, blue and white rungs of admirals' promotion within that rank, it did not quite coincide with war and politics to get him to sea again for many years, until the tail-end of the disastrous American war. Or perhaps in the end that delay was fortunate, for his lack of experience might well have proved disastrous both for him and for his country when the new Whig Government which came to power in 1782 gave him Admiral Sir George Rodney's command in the West Indies, where there was a large French fleet of equal force commanded by the Comte de Grasse. But, fortunately or unfortunately, Rodney solved that problem for him: almost exactly on the day of Pigot's appointment he caught de Grasse near the Saints Islands off Dominica and defeated him.

The news of this victory reached London just too late to prevent an embarrassed Government from cancelling Pigot's appointment, hard though they tried to catch him up. So Commander-in-Chief, West Indies, he remained, albeit mercifully not for long since peace was concluded within a year. But that was long enough to launch Midshipman Hugh Pigot on his career in his thirteenth year in the most favourable circumstances, with strong enough 'interest' to ensure his employment at sea during almost the whole of the decade of peace between the wars. The first seven of those ten years he spent across the Atlantic, two on the American station and the rest in the death trap of the West Indies, home of the hurricane and – far worse – the adopted home of the greatest killer of all, yellow fever.

Disease was not so much a problem in those days as a fact of life (or, rather death) in a struggle in which medical science had so far made slow progress. In war it was very often – even usually – by far the greatest killer, given its chance. It had won battles from Biblical times, when it had wiped out Sennacherib's Assyrian army, onwards; as late as the turn of this century the British were to lose four times as many men in hospital beds as from the bullets of the notoriously sharp-shooting Boers of South Africa. At sea in Nelson's (and Hugh Pigot's) time, sickness deserved to rank with the rock and tempest of Hymn 370, well ahead of fire and foe in the litany of perils, even though it was in this period that the naval authorities had at last got the measure of that greatest of all sea-going killers, scurvy.

Scurvy – simply, vitamin C deficiency, as simply cured by lemon juice – was still killing men in 1797. The year before, on the very day that the first French ships were straggling into Bantry Bay in a howling blizzard, HMS *Monarch* (74) was taking shelter in the next inlet after a dreadful three-month voyage from the Cape of Good Hope, with only eight days' provisions left and so many men sick with scurvy that there were too few to man the rigging. That, admittedly, was a bad luck situation, rather than due to the ignorance which had killed 1,300 of Admiral Sir George Anson's men on his famous raid into the Pacific 50 years before, when he had brought the *Centurion* back loaded with treasure, having lost only four men by enemy action during the whole expedition.

By 1797, barring such accidents, scurvy was not a major killer. But there were still several other killers abroad in the late eighteenth century, stalking civilians as well as soldiers and sailors, but particularly favouring the fighting men. In the more northern and colder latitudes the louse-borne disease of typhus (which was still prevalent on the Russian front and in the death camps of the Second World War, before DDT) loved dirt and overcrowding. Consequently, this was prevalent in both prisons and ships, and not least because the former fed the latter, so that its common English names were, variously, 'jail fever' or 'ship fever'. What made it worse was that the receiving ships which generally took men straight from prison were themselves often grossly overcrowded. Of 200 such recruits taken from such a ship into one frigate at the Nore in the 1770s, over one-third were diagnosed as having the fever by the time she reached the Channel, and the whole crew had to be hospitalised at Spithead. Things were not much better 20 years later at the Nore. Just before the mutiny there, the decrepit receiving ship *Sandwich*, which would have been well packed in her sea-going days with a full complement of 750, had almost twice as many poor devils sandwiched into her, including hundreds of sick. 'It is my professional opinion,' wrote the ship's doctor in a desperate appeal to the Admiralty, 'that there is no effective remedy, but by considerably reducing the number that have been usually kept for months in the *Sandwich*.' Such conditions were, of course, ideal for the breeding of disaffection, as well as lice and typhus.

Ships' doctors were rarely among the cream of their profession, Hornblower's in the *Lydia* succumbing to the complications of syphilis and drink early in his South American mission. But there were famous exceptions, like Dr (eventually Sir) Gilbert Blane, Admiral Rodney's personal physician, who became a Commissioner for the Sick and Wounded and was a strong supporter of Dr James Lind, the advocate of lemon juice. Blane was also an advocate of clean clothes and soap, as were Doctors Harness and Weir, who helped to make St Vincent's fleet as healthy as it was battle-worthy.

Hygiene helped to keep typhus (and dysentery, 'the bloody flux') at bay, vitamin C in various forms reduced scurvy, and Dr Jenner's vaccination was the answer to smallpox (though it was not yet compulsory). That however, left another pox, venereal disease, which was usually reported too late for mercury, the only known treatment. Men never allowed on shore enthusiastically contracted the disease from the hordes of women allowed on board in harbour, if they did not have it already, and the 15s for treatment further discouraged them from reporting it until this was wisely abolished in 1795. But far worse were those two endemic 'maladies of intemperate climates', malaria and yellow fever, the causes of which were to baffle medical science for nearly another century.

Malaria was at least partially treatable with 'Peruvian bark' (quinine itself was then still 50 years in the future). All the same, it plagued almost everyone who served in the lands ruled by the Anopheles mosquito, not least both Nelson and Hoste. But 'Yellow Jack', the mosquito's deadlier gift, totally baffled medical science.

As the price of discovery and wealth, if syphilis was the New World's revenge on the Old, yellow fever was West Africa's on those who enslaved her people. First recorded off the African coast in Drake's time, where it was a mild local disease, it swiftly established itself in the mosquitos of the West Indies, wrecking an otherwise successful English attack on Puerto Rico as early as 1598. By the mid-seventeenth century it was killing Europeans and native Americans alike throughout Central America, northward to the Carolinas and south to Guiana in South America, particularly favouring those in the prime of life, rather than the very young or very old. With the fate of so many military expeditions to the coveted sugar islands of the West Indies depending more on health than the battle tactics there was no shortage of theories about it, once the doctors had stopped confusing it with malaria and typhoid (two of these doctors even killed each other in a duel over their conflicting ideas, both of which were wrong). The only real progress made by the end of the eighteenth century was the strong suspicion that it was neither contagious nor infectious: one brave doctor inoculated himself with blood from a victim and drank black vomit to prove his point (an act of courage to be repeated by a Royal Navy doctor on an anti-slave-trade patrol vessel off West Africa a generation later.) But while what the disease was *not* gradually became apparent, it was not until long afterwards, in 1881, that Dr Carlos Finlay suggested the mosquito as the villain of the piece – and not until 1900 that the United States Army's Yellow Fever Commission finally pinpointed *Aedes aegypti* as the certain carrier.

All this, then, was far in the future when Mr Midshipman Pigot completed his first period of American service and returned to Britain in 1789 on passing his lieutenant's examination at the minimum age of 20. For in this case the Devil looked after his own. Many other (and, for sure, better) young men must have perished on the West Indian Station during those years. We must be grateful that both Nelson and Collingwood also survived such service, while consecutively holding their first post-captain commands of the frigate *Hinchingbroke* during the American war: 'with a complement of two hundred men,' wrote Nelson, 'eighty-seven took to their beds in one night; and of the two hundred, one hundred and forty-five were buried in mine and Captain Collingwood's time; and I believe very few, not more than ten, survived of that Ship's crew'. Nelson's experience was by no means unusual, as the records of all service of military garrisons and naval 'combined operations' repeatedly testify. West Indian, tropical, and even Mediterranean (malarial) postings were never popular: Adam Duncan, the victor of Camperdown, refused the Mediterranean command on health grounds. The 40,000-plus casualty list of the 1794 British West Indian expedition, to which reference has already been made, discouraged those able to refuse such service, in the knowledge that yellow jack was no respecter of rank, and much more dangerous. Indeed, although men at sea were obviously safer than those on shore (where the wastage of soldiers was appalling), ships' officers were probably at greater risk, since they were free to come and go when in port. Poor young Captain Lord Proby, the innocent victim of the *Danae* mutiny in 1800, was appointed to the 44-gun (ex-French) frigate *Amelia* in 1803, and posted to the West Indies. Before that year was out he was dead, together with his first lieutenant and the ship's doctor, among his frigate's first dozen fever victims. Earlier in the war, the *Topaze* (36) had struggled into Port Royal commanded by a warrant officer, every other officer being dead, together with nearly 200 of her complement of 250.

Altogether, life was more or less permanently in the midst of death for those in His Majesty's forces sentenced to serve among those 'pestilential islands' so beloved of parliamentary and mercantile interests, and extremes of behaviour among them, including frequent duels, heavy drinking and debauchery, were an understandable consequence. The only plus among all these minuses was that there were plenty of 'dead men's shoes' to step into: disease was a greater accelerator of promotion and chance-giver than battle, among the survivors. So, while Lieutenant Hugh Pigot's various moves within rank after his 1789 elevation may well have been due to paternal and family influence (for a start he was soon appointed to a ship, even though total navy personnel stood at less than 20,000 then), his eventual wartime posting to the West Indies made further promotion virtually certain.

How well he performed during the last years of peace, it is impossible to say. Having risen from fifth lieutenant to third in the *Colossus* (74) he reverted to fourth in the *London*. But then, she was a 98, and her commander was the excellent Richard Keats, who was to become one of Nelson's favourite captains among his 'band of brothers'. In any case, with the huge expansion of the Navy after war broke out augmenting the 'interest', he moved briefly to the 38-gun frigate *Latona* before his career really took off with his first command appointment. This itself – to that lowest form of naval life, the fireship *Incendiary* – was only a device to make him a master and commander before his posting to the *Swan*, an 18-gun sloop in the West Indies. Family influence, it may be conjectured, may then have coincided with Admiralty commonsense: as a West Indian veteran survivor of yellow jack for ten years in the Americas, young Pigot's promotion both served naval needs and did him and his family a good turn.

In the event, his command of the *Swan* (as captain, but not yet post-captain, since 18-gun sloops were lieutenants' ships) revealed a first hint of his cloven hoof, through an acrimonious dispute over a collision with the merchant ship *Canada* while in convoy. But that did not prevent his final apotheosis in the Navy, when command of the frigate *Success* (32) became vacant in one of those typical West Indian redistributions, which also moved Captain Philip Wilkinson to the frigate *Hermione* (32) in September 1794.

That the *Success* was a small (680-ton, 12-pounder, 13-year-old, British-built) ship mattered not at all: it was only off the French coast that fast super-frigates were at a premium. All that mattered was the fact of that frigate appointment: from that moment Hugh Pigot had made post on the Captains' List in a rated ship, as from 4 September inevitably to become an admiral if he lived long enough, before any other (slightly less lucky) officers who became post-captains on 5 September or thereafter.

To chronicle in detail Pigot's post-captain career, in the *Surprise* for the next 30 months and then in the *Hermione* for the last eight months of his life, is once again beyond the scope of this narrative, which is not intended to be fully biographical. Rather, as with Pellew in some of the preceding chapters and our other four frigate captains in chapters to come, the briefest summary of that career serves to illustrate certain of the themes already touched on, most notably those relating to mutiny, discipline and punishment, but in the first place the mechanics of promotion.

As a result of service in earlier wars Pigot's family had acquired 'interest', to which he now added the good luck of being in the right place at the right time. The outbreak of war in 1793 was providential for him, as a young (early-to-middle-twenties) naval officer sprung from an influential naval and military family. If he had not had the opportunity to demonstrate any special merit he had evidently not shown himself to be incompetent in any of the subordinate positions he had occupied up to then. It was now his fate (in the circumstances one cannot continue to refer to his good luck) to become one of the favoured protégés of his new Commander-in-Chief, Admiral Sir Hyde Parker.

There was, as has already been indicated, nothing in the least unusual, let alone outrageous, in the senior officers of Nelson's time having such favourites – 'followers' – whom they carried up with them. Ideally these younger men were not only loyal and reliable subordinates: their future success would also honour their mentors (and might even enrich them). Nelson himself owed his success to the help of his uncle, Captain Maurice Suckling, whose 'interest' equalled that of the First Lord of the Admiralty when he became Comptroller of the Navy; and it was as a 'follower' of Captain William Locker, in whose frigate *Lowestoffe* he served on promotion to lieutenant, that he was introduced to his captain's good friend, Sir John Jervis. 'My *élève*', was how Locker described him, thus inaugurating the Jervis–Nelson partnership which was to lift their navy out of the dark days of 1797. But where the 'interest' of Suckling and Locker advanced

Nelson (who in turn advanced Hoste, among others) that of Hyde Parker was to lead directly through Pigot to the *Hermione* mutiny.

Himself the son of an admiral (who had fought the Dutch off the Dogger Bank in 1781 and been lost at sea somewhere in the South Atlantic the next year), Parker was very much a senior officer of the Pigot family type, whose 'hot war' service was long in the past and whose rise had been largely due to the 'interest' system and his place on the Captain's List, after many years spent ashore. Apart from a spectacular ability to amass prize-money, such talent as he had would seem to have been administrative. Possibly it was the latter which led the Admiralty to move him from the Mediterranean, where he had failed to distinguish himself in the first years of the war: the West Indies was an area of rich pickings but little danger (except from fever and shipwreck), only the constant nagging difficulties of convoy duty, the depredations of French and Spanish privateers and the endless complaints of American neutrals. As with young Pigot he must have seemed a round peg in a round hole.

So Pigot went to the *Success* as one of his favourites, since frigates were the main agents of British control among the islands. And, indeed, his various cruises in that ship were not unproductive of prizes. But then, the profitable suppression of enemy trade was the main duty of West Indian frigate captains, whose presence in good hunting areas was very often far from accidental. Parker's favourite frigate ace Captain (later Admiral Sir) Robert Otway earned his chief £25,000 in six years from his 200 captures, returning home himself £50,000 richer, with his captain's bigger share of the prize-money (after which, as a further reward, he became Parker's Captain of the Fleet at Copenhagen, in the 98-gun *London*). But not even the sweet prospect of a small share in such good fortune was to be enough to inhibit the crew of the *Hermione* in due course, after eight months of Pigot's brutality.

In our age, when the ruling elites of all western nations (if not the public at large) have turned against all forms of corporal punishment, it is difficult to imagine the days when few escaped a 'good thrashing' in their youth, and then themselves meted it out to others in turn, by custom and practice if not inclination. It was certainly the common fate of all midshipman in the navy of His Britannic Majesty King George III, both as an officially sanctioned punishment and as part of the endemic bullying they had to endure, both of which were equally the norm in the public schools of the time (young Pellew, remember, had run away to sea to escape another beating back in 1770). As the son of Admiral Hugh Pigot – at least while his father was on board with him – Midshipman Hugh Pigot may have escaped the grosser extremes of punishment but it is unlikely that he avoided it altogether. It may be that he then got a taste for it, having been on the receiving end, and in that climate of normalised violence – midshipmen repeatedly beaten and sailors even more often 'started' with the rope's ends which warrant officers almost habitually carried on deck, never mind in those ceremonial floggings at the gratings. Whether all that appealed to something deep in his nature, we shall never know. All that is certain is that, in an age when flogging was the established sanction in all the armies and navies of all countries, he was an exceptionally enthusiastic flogger.

Yet even that does not by itself account for the *Hermione* mutiny. On the one hand, as has already been noted (with some slight surprise), no direct mention was made to the use of the dreaded cat-o'-nine-tails in the demands of the Spithead and Nore mutineers of 1797 in spite of the presence of all those bad officers. And half a century later, during the public scandal which followed the death of a soldier in the 7th Hussars after a peacetime flogging (150 lashes) at Hounslow Barracks, one newspaper editorial suggested that, although the naval cat was a heavier instrument than the army one, 'we do not believe that flogging is unpopular in the Navy'.

Yet, on the other hand (and as another editor – an ex-midshipman – was quick to point out during the Hounslow scandal), flogging was a fearful punishment. There is plenty of evidence that it frequently had the most appalling mental effect on the sufferers, apart from the purely physical result which (as the Hounslow case had shown) could be fatal. That men usually survived the punishment is curiously illustrated in the old *Shorter Oxford Dictionary* in its 'jocular' definition of 'Shellback' as meaning '(a hardened or experienced) sailor' as well as 'a tortoise'. The sailors of those times were hard men, and some of them were flogged many times, often receiving more than the regulation twelve strokes (a regulation so generally ignored that its abolition in 1806 was no more than acceptance of a well-known fact). But some men *did* die, especially after too-quickly-repeated floggings, even though such deaths were always logged as being due to other causes. 'Fever', for example, was so common as to be unremarkable: in the *Flame* mutiny of 1813, which sorely taxed Captain (by then Sir Horatio) Hornblower, the mutineers accused Lieutenant Augustine Chadwick of killing 'the boy James Jones – but we think he said in his report that he died of fever'. 'Accident' was another euphemism which could conveniently cover constructive murder. At the best of times sailing ships could be dangerous places, as testified by the steady loss of men due to injuries and mishaps recorded even in the best ships. Setting and taking in sail in bad weather or at night was particularly hazardous. Men enfeebled by sickness or as a result of flogging were inevitably at greater risk; in the *Hermione*, as we shall discover, there would be fatalities caused not by carelessness or misadventure, but by the fear of the flogging in store for 'the last man down'.

Fearful and feared punishment though it was, flogging was nevertheless taken for granted as part of life in the Navy to an extent which requires a conscious suspension of incredulity on the part of the modern reader. The quality of that life depended in the end on the quality of the captain. For it was in the shadow of Number 36 of the Articles of War that every captain commanded and every sailor lived, which covered the use by the former on the backs of the latter of the cat-o'-nine-tails for 'all other crimes not capital' – for all offences, that is, which did not call for a court martial. And in practice (since courts martial were time-consuming, troublesome and involved outsiders) this meant that discipline was routinely maintained in all ships by the lash. Some captains – Nelson, Hornblower, Cochrane and Hoste among them – were famous and beloved for their sparing use of it. But they were in the minority. Great admirals like St Vincent were great floggers; Pellew, especially in his uncertain younger days, frequently resorted to flogging. On the deck of the *Victory* which is today thronged by tourists Nelson's admirable Captain Hardy flogged one in eight of his crew in the half-year before Trafalgar (statistically a flogging every other day). Yet, further to confuse matters, that notable flogging captain, Edward Hamilton, commanded the *Surprise* frigate successfully (as we shall in due course discover), while Captain Lord Probyn's much lighter hand did not save him from the *Danae* mutiny.

Still, it was the captain who mattered, for Hamilton was much more typical, and Probyn was particularly unlucky. Admirals themselves had a part to play in demoralising whole fleets, as Black Dick Howe (good, but worn-out), Bridport (brave, but too old) and Colpoys (brave, but incompetent) did with theirs. But even in St Vincent's Mediterranean Fleet, in which Nelson was setting new standards of enlightened leadership for others to imitate, the quality of ships' captains was crucial, as the battle-worthiness of the *Goliath* and the *Britannia* demonstrated, according to whether they were commanded by Foley or Knowles. And the smaller the ships, the more important its captain: where a badly captained ship-of-the-line was likely to become a public scandal, a badly captained frigate on detached duty was a private hell.

By 1797 Pigot's lack of judgement had in fact already created problems for Admiral Parker, after his newest 'follower' had unwisely – but very typically – given the bumbling and arrogant captain of a convoyed merchant ship one of those good thrashings to which allusion had already been made. True, the captain in question well merited a reprimand, having compounded earlier bad navigation by finally ramming the *Success* amidships. But the man was an American, in an American ship, and that turned his just deserts into the very sort of diplomatic incident which a more judicious captain might have avoided. To be fair to Pigot, the Americans were notoriously touchy over their newly-won independence – and particularly in its exercise where their divorced mother country was concerned. Long after these events and the last of the French wars, when the chief role of the Royal Navy (apart from the defence of America's Monroe Doctrine) was the suppression of the slave trade, the American ambassador in London was asked if there was anything worse than that vile business; to which he (the great and good John Quincy Adams) replied that to allow any British cruiser to stop any ship flying the Stars and Stripes was a much worse evil, since that made slaves of the whole American people. But then, in Mr Adams' defence, the memory of the most recent Anglo-American war, in which the British insistence on the right-of-search had been a major issue, was fresh in his mind. It is an historical irony that when the United States nearly came to blows with the British in mid-nineteenth-century, national positions would be neatly reversed over these same issues, during an American Civil War in which the anti-slavery Union sought to stop and search British vessels. But meanwhile, in Pigot's defence, there was nothing new in young frigate captains falling foul of Yankees in the Tom Tiddler's ground of the West Indies. Some years before, the young captain of the *Boreas* (28), Horatio Nelson, had so rigorously applied his interpretation of his country's Navigation Laws that he was pursued all the way back to London by American captains claiming £20,000 damages. Not the least of the nightmares besetting such ardent (but often inexperienced, if not unwise) officers was the possibility that their prize-winning profits might be swallowed up in endless litigation with angry 'neutrals', leaving them facing huge costs.

Back in the 1780s, Captain Nelson reached the point where he dared not go ashore in the West Indies for fear of arrest (originally the damages were £40,000). But he returned home to be vindicated in very different circumstances from those in which Pigot now found himself in the dark days of a French war which was being lost. It may be that Sir Hyde Parker liked Pigot personally, but he was in any case a Parker 'follower' and the 'interest' system imposed an almost feudal responsibility downwards as well as upwards, and a protégé's fate reflected personally on a patron. Already the Admiralty had forced a court of inquiry into Pigot's behaviour, and although Parker was able to turn that into something of a whitewash, he could not prevent the *Success* being ordered to escort a homeward-bound convoy. All his life the Admiral was bowed down by his responsibilities, most famously when he tried to cut his losses during the battle of Copenhagen a few years later, and Nelson ignored his order to disengage by allegedly turning his blind eye to it. Now, possibly because he feared that Pigot might yet be court-martialled once back in England to placate the Americans (which would reflect badly on his patron, of course) he sought to avert trouble simply by exchanging the young captain into another ship within his command. It was thus that Pigot took over the ill-fated *Hermione* from Captain Philip Wilkinson.

Wilkinson was another flogging captain of that not uncommon type which seems to have been particularly common in Parker's West Indian command, so it may reasonably be surmised that the *Hermione* was already an unhappy ship (and perhaps all the more so as she had not been a successful prize-taker either; though that may equally have been because Wilkinson was not one of the Admiral's favourites, so may not have been allotted one of the more profitable cruising areas). But Pigot soon made her unhappier, beginning by taking some of his own favourites with him – inevitably bad choices and unreliable men – and continuing with an increasingly brutal regime. While in command of the smaller *Success* for less than a year before exchanging into the *Hermione* he had ordered a total of about 1,400 lashes, and there had been deaths among her crew which can surely be related to this tally, with its sad record of 'crimes' dominated by 'drunkenness', 'disorderly behaviour' (related to drunkenness, no doubt), 'drunkenness *and* contempt', 'disobedience', 'disobedience *and* contempt', 'insolence *and* contempt' and 'neglect of duty' (plus of course, attempted desertion). Having learned nothing from that experience, Pigot found much the same pattern in his new ship.

For all this, however, it would be unwise to attribute the ensuing mutiny merely to accumulated brutality – even when another essential ingredient, that of detached duty in the absence of other naval ships, is added to it. Pigot's devotion to the lash *was* probably extreme, but other captains then and later were only relatively less brutal (and we shall meet several of them). And, of course, most frigates and nearly all smaller craft were engaged on detached duties and patrols. If brutality and opportunity had together been sufficient to turn cruelly disciplined men into desperate murderers, then there would surely have been more *Hermiones*.

Two additional factors, it may be thought, were the death of Pigot, only the first of which was purely due to his defects of character. As we have seen, even a strong and self-confident man like Pellew (who was also a fine seaman and a highly successful captain) could be bowed down by the cares, problems and pressures of command. It would seem more than likely that Pigot, a weak and worried young man whose cruelties may have been as much attempts at self-assertion as sadistic inclination, was by then unbalanced, if not clinically insane, with the result that his behaviour had become both irrational and unpredictable.

The actual incidence of insanity among officers is another subject which will be further examined in a later chapter: it must be enough here to note that it was a recognised occupational disorder in the Navy – and all the more dangerous since its victims even today are frequently *not* recognised by those around them until some tragedy occurs. But it requires little imagination to guess what a sadistic madman might achieve under the 'Captain's Cloak' of Number 36 of the Articles of War, and this in turn brings us back to those emotional 'keys to action' of Professor Oatley's. Pigot's floggings, and the actual deaths which his crew observed as their 'accidental' results, must have gone far beyond the normal bounds of naval cruelty to arouse a full measure of anger, disgust and above all fear. Men were being flogged not only for all the usual major and minor offences (including that tell-tale subjective 'contempt'), but for simply being the last man down from aloft. In such a jungle, neither the old 'shellbacks' nor his ill-chosen ex-*Success* toadies were safe. Otherwise ordinary decent men and habitual malcontents, those who had been flogged already (justly or unjustly) and those who had not, pressed men (ever the majority) and volunteers' English and (possibly already disaffected) Irish as well as foreigners – literally *no one* on the lower deck was safe any longer under such a regime. All, rather, were united at once by their uncertainty as to who would be next and the certainty of the floggings and deaths they had witnessed. Such a powder-keg only needed the small spark of a few men to explode the whole crew.

To this, however, the year 1797 added a final special ingredient which rendered every ship in King George's navy much more volatile. For by that September every sailor afloat had heard of the 'Great Mutiny' at Spithead and the Nore. Indeed, this was no less a problem with which discerning captains were grappling: St Vincent himself was then receiving 'infected' Channel Fleet ships with the gravest doubts, and Pellew disliked his deliberately ordered promotion from his crack *Indefatigable* to the much bigger *Impétueux*, a fine ex-French 74 which was also notoriously mutinous. That such thoughts did less than justice to the majorities of such ships' crews may be gauged from the grubby piece of paper picked up on the quarterdeck of Nelson's new flagship –

> Success attended Admiral Nelson! God bless Captain Miller! We thank them for the Officers they have placed over us. We are happy and comfortable, and will shed every drop of blood in our veins, and the name of the '*Theseus*' shall be immortalized on high as the *Captain's*' – (signed)
> SHIP'S COMPANY

Yet even such loyal and grateful sentiments betrayed that whiff of lower-deck common purpose which had immobilised the fleet at Spithead. St Vincent, for one, refused to tolerate such tendencies. On receipt of a garbled account of the *Hermione* mutiny while cruising in his flagship off Portugal, the irascible old man wrote at once to the Admiralty, lumping it with Spithead and the Nore as 'these disgraceful events'. Years later, when briefing Captain Sir Horatio Hornblower on the *Flame* mutiny, he had clearly not forgotten the bad days of the 1790s: not only were there to be 'no negotiations with mutineers!', but he had done his best already to isolate the outbreak, with the loyal hands who had brought the news under lock-and-key until they could be shipped out in the next vessel bound for India. And the enlightened Hornblower, who privately sympathised with the mutineers, approved this precaution: *Mutiny was like an infection*, he was forced to reflect. *The plague spot must be isolated until it could be cauterised.*

No such isolation was possible in the West Indies in 1797 after those 'disgraceful events' in England's two greatest naval bases. But, far worse, the word was also out in the islands of a murderous little home-grown West Indian mutiny, in which the crew of the naval schooner *Marie Antoinette* had killed their two officers and gone over to the French. Crudely, the 'copy-cat' urge is always to be feared. More intellectually, Alexis de Tocqueville was to conclude in his study of the overthrow of Louis XVI that harsh and repressive regimes are most unbearable and most at risk when their weakness is exposed and they no longer seem to be inescapable. In retrospect it says much for the competence of the majority of British naval officers – and perhaps even more for the moderation and patriotism of their men – that Spithead and the Nore not only turned out as they did, but that in the long years of war afterwards there were never any *Hermione* repeats, red in tooth and claw.

For red in tooth and claw the night of 21 September 1797 and the next day were in the *Hermione*. Already driven to the edge of desperation by excessive irrational punishments, prodded by the knowledge of those other recent mutinies, that ship's crew was finally pushed over the edge by the 'accidental' murder of three terrified men who fell to their deaths from the rigging while trying to avoid a 'last-man-down' flogging. The very disorganisation and spontaneity of the mutiny which followed both explains its beastliness and demonstrates Pigot's command failure. For if there eventually emerged ringleaders there was no one Fletcher Christian to control an uprising which quickly degenerated into an orgy (soon a drunken orgy, too) of violence and score-settling once Pigot had been hacked, slashed, bayoneted and finally thrown overboard. And while less than 20 men out of some 160 were directly involved in the killing, many more were active or acquiesced, and only eight – plus one or two surviving warrant officers – were finally exchanged by the Spaniards as loyal. The very lack of any real resistance (except by Pigot himself and his first lieutenant) is, when taken with these statistics, another telling indictment of bad leadership.

In effect, the *Hermione* mutiny was an act of 'general will', even among those who took no direct part in it, but simply leaped at the chance of getting mindlessly drunk as quickly as possible. For even before the rest of the hated officers followed Pigot – and even before rum brought oblivion – every man must have known the score: they could 'run' with the ship itself to the enemy (in this case to the Spaniards), and might be welcomed. But thereafter they would be running for ever because they well knew that their country would hunt them anywhere and everywhere throughout the world for the rest of their lives. And if that, in those far-off days (and in the middle of a war), sounds like a needle-in-a-haystack search, the risk of capture was real enough. For, after all, most of them were simple men and the sea was the only calling they knew. So in the nine years following the mutiny nearly a quarter of those who scattered were spotted, caught and identified and brought to trial. And although it says something for navy justice that the proceedings were then not mere vengeful formalities, for nine of those luckless or rash ex-*Hermiones* were judged innocent, 24 of them ended up swinging from the yardarm.

It is, in fact, hard to avoid the conclusion that, while the 'Great Mutiny' at Spithead did result in a number of long overdue improvements which were at least sufficient to avoid any repetition of such 'industrial action' during the war, the *Hermione* mutiny has been properly relegated to historical footnotes as a uniquely awful one-off event, which had very little effect on either captains or crews.

The more intelligent (or, anyway, the more imaginative) among the captains *may* have had more *Hermione*-nightmares to go with their *Bounty* ones. Yet they, and all their less-imaginative colleagues on the List who were at least intelligent enough to take notice of the methods of men like Nelson and his pupils, really had no need of such fears: a varying proportion of their crews might still 'run' if they could, though there would also be examples of enlightened (and prize-money-successful) captains who gave their men shore leave and were not disappointed. But if such leaders were rare, significant disaffection in well-run ships was non-existent.

Much more interesting are the records of those captains who quite obviously learned *nothing* from Pigot's fate – or even less than nothing: captains (of frigates, and usually on detached duty) who *were* brutal – even who caused themselves professional problems and set-backs *because* of their intemperance ... but who nevertheless triumphed (or, at least, survived for a time) in spite of it.

Of these, Captain Edward Hamilton of the *Surprise* (28 – and well named), is the most immediately interesting, as will become apparent in the next chapter. But we shall here note for the future two other names of brave, promising and brutal officers who would in the future become frigate captains and whom we shall also meet again in due course (and who, indeed, are both *proxime accessit* main characters in this narrative, together with frigate Captain Stephen Decatur, USN):

Robert Corbet (who had been commissioned lieutenant in 1796) and Midshipman Nisbet Josiah Willoughby, 'The Immortal', who had entered the Navy in 1790 at the age of 13 and had already made good money in the *Orpheus* frigate (32) with the capture of the *Duguay-Trouin* in 1794 and the Dutch bases at Amboina and Banda in the East Indies. He would soon be promoted lieutenant just before being court-martialled and dismissed for the first (but not the last) time.

All of these, among many others, would help to make naval history so absolutely absorbing in the years to come. But, more immediately, after its darkest hours the British Navy was entering its most glorious period, lashed by Admiral Earl St Vincent and inspired by Admiral Sir Horatio Nelson.

CHAPTER EIGHT

In which lack of frigates blinds Admiral Nelson, but Captain Hamilton avenges the Hermione and Lieutenant Lord Cochrane 'makes post'

For the British Navy, 1797 was a year of extremes: victory over the Spanish Navy in the winter, the mutinies at Spithead and Nore in the spring, the *Hermione* disgrace in later summer, and finally victory over the Dutch Navy at Camperdown in the autumn, in which the Nore mutineers redeemed themselves.

In fact, although the French Navy itself was growing stronger and had not been decisively beaten in battle since 1794, a new age of British naval supremacy surpassing anything previously achieved was now dawning: the age not only of St Vincent and Nelson and Nelson's 'band of brothers' – men like Troubridge and Miller, Foley, Hallowell and Ball – but also a galaxy of senior talent – Keats and Saumarez, Pellew and Sydney Smith – and a host of rising stars among the younger frigates captains who were to shine over the next decade: Bowen and Blackwood, Cochrane and Hornblower, Hoste and Broke. Where Napoleon Bonaparte was to have his dashing generals and near-legendary marshals, King George would now have his daring frigate captains and invincible admirals whose exploits would fill the columns of the *Naval Gazette*.

In 1798, however, all this naval glory still lay in the future, very near though its first triumphs might be. Indeed, as things stood, Britain was still in a fair way to losing the whole war, with its fully stretched navy reacting to each new French threat rather than initiating operations of its own in conjunction with the puny British Army. In fact, it had already been been humiliatingly saved from possible disaster the year before by a signal failure of French intelligence to learn of the 'Great Mutiny' in time to gain any advantage from it – a failure as gross as that of German intelligence during the French army mutinies of 1917 – when Wolfe Tone and General Hoche had planned their second attempt on Ireland. And early in 1798, as a new crisis loomed in the Mediterranean, the weather in the North Sea and the Channel then crucially delayed the sailing of the invasion force which the Directory had at last cobbled together after the defeat of the Dutch.

That the British are obsessed by their weather is perhaps at least in part due to racial memories of the part it has played in their history. In 1588, after the defeat of the Spanish Armada, Queen Elizabeth I had a medal struck thanking God for dispersing the enemy with His tempest, with no mention of her fleet. A century later exactly, an allegedly 'Protestant wind' (blowing in the opposite direction) had made the Glorious Revolution of 1688 possible. It had certainly been God's midwinter tempest of 1796–97 which had been largely responsible for the failure of the Bantry Bay expedition. Short of blaming God in 1798, poor tragic Wolfe Tone reckoned anyway that 'there seems to be a fate in this business . . . The sea was open (in 1797) . . . and now at last we are ready here, the wind is against us, the mutiny is quelled and we are sure to be attacked by superior force'.

That was exactly how the second Irish expedition turned out, only worse. Because of the delay, the rising of the native Irish (Presbyterian Ulstermen as well as Catholic southerners) was premature, and ruthlessly suppressed. The French then arrived, far too late (and also now without the able young Hoche, who had long since coughed himself to death). Of the French naval squadron of one ship-of-the-line and eight frigates, (which had this time carried a mere 3,000 men) only two ships survived capture or shipwreck, having failed to land one single soldier; while the next (and even smaller) reinforcement wisely turned back before it had ever got close to Ireland.

But if this was not a British disaster, thanks to the weather, Franco-Irish incompetence and the overwhelming strength and fighting superiority of the British Navy when it actually found something to fight, it was no decisive deliverance. For the French were then busy building a much more dangerous invasion fleet in every port from Antwerp (which now effectively belonged to them) to Cherbourg, as Hitler was to do in 1940. But just as the Germans did not like the odds after the Battle of Britain, and turned to the east, so the French Directory's brightest new general (and commander-in-chief of his latest 'Army of England'), Napoleon Bonaparte also did not like what he saw – and liked much better another eastern enterprise, which was not to be his last mistaken turn away from his country's true enemy.

Still, to defend his marvellously imaginative ambition, this lateral solution to his (and his country's) own problem of *what to do next* to strike at the British fitted some of the facts, as well as meriting admiration. For, while that part of the contemptible British Army which wasn't dying of yellow fever in the West Indies or harrying Irish peasants was tied up in home defence, the rather formidable British Navy was very busy defending its country and commerce in home waters, and was weak in the Mediterranean. An 'Army of Egypt' not only stood a better chance of getting to its destination than an 'Army of England', but it beckoned the greatest military genius since Alexander the Great to follow Alexander's path towards India overland, to threaten the British there with an invasion which their fleets could not be expected to hinder. (Apart from all of which, anyway, the pragmatic Directors who still ruled France rather incompetently were only too glad to encourage their most charismatic and ambitious young general to try his luck as far away from them as possible.)

In the event, this extraordinary adventure turned out very differently for all concerned. For General Bonaparte and his army it was not so much a great chance as a huge risk, with the Mediterranean almost as dangerous with Nelson loose in it as the English Channel might have been. But the risk paid off at first in dazzling success, against the odds, as General Bonaparte reached Egypt and then conquered it. But then the British fleet turned the tables on him in the first and most brilliant of all Nelson's victories, which changed the expectations of future admirals at sea with the annihilation of the enemy, much as Bonaparte was rewriting the rules of land warfare. And then, with the British suddenly successful (albeit still only at sea) and a French army trapped far away, a new coalition of vengeful or greedy European powers was encouraged by British gold to restart the war – which, in yet another unexpected turn of the wheel, was to bring the Directors down and raise General Bonaparte to supreme power in France.

All this, of course, lay in the future in the spring of 1798, as the Irish emergency and news of the build-up of the French Army (and Navy) of Egypt combined to present the British with a major problem in simultaneously dealing with the former while attempting to frustrate the latter – while all the time both attempting to contain the French and (remaining) Spanish navies in their main bases by blockade and protecting British maritime trade world-wide. Her own navy had been effectively driven out of the Mediterranean in 1796 and must now operate from one end of that sea to the other without a single naval base east of Gibraltar. Fortunately, in St Vincent (as overall commander-in-chief) and Nelson (in command of a Mediterranean Striking Force) the Navy possessed not only the two greatest admirals of the age, but two men who had confidence in each other and in their captains. Unfortunately, however, not even St Vincent and Nelson together could make up for the British fleet's shortage of frigates, which was largely to dictate the course of events in the coming naval campaign.

Conveniently, Nelson himself supplies the most quotable proof of the truth of this most memorably *after* he had won the Battle of the Nile, in a note to the First Lord of the Admiralty: 'Were I to die this moment, "Want of frigates" would be found engraved on my heart.' Indeed, at that actual moment he was so short of frigates that he sent his despatch off in his weakest ship-of-the-line, the obsolete *Leander* (which was captured on the way home, anyway). But his desperation then was nothing compared with what it had been before as he attempted unsuccessfully to intercept the French expeditionary force: 'My distress for frigates is extreme . . . frigates, the Eyes of the Fleet . . .'; and, writing helplessly to the British consul in Alexandria for news of the French, of whom he had last had word from an obliging Tunisian corsair, 'Pray do not detain the *Mutine*, for I am in a fever at not finding the French.' (The *Mutine* wasn't even a frigate, but a mere brig, doing a frigate's work.)

Nothing more completely sums up the frigate's classic fleet operational role (as opposed to all its other functions) as the great might-have-been of the Egyptian adventure, besides which that adventure's actual outcome was in the longer view disastrous for the British for all that they dealt with both the French fleet and the French Army there in the end. For the great potential prize was the interception of both while still at sea, complete with General Bonaparte himself. And nothing, equally, better demonstrates the difficulties of naval intelligence gathering and reconnaissance in those days of sail and slow communications than the complete failure of the greatest admiral of the age to intercept a convoy of 400 troop transports during its leisurely passage across the whole length of the Mediterranean Sea from Toulon to Alexandria, with a stop en route to take Malta.

That the French expedition was escorted by 15 ships-of-the-line was quite beside the point: Nelson would make short work of most of them once he did at last find them at anchor in Aboukir Bay. That they were also escorted by 16 frigates (never mind eight sloops) would have cut deep, however: with that many 'eyes' his chance of ending General Bonaparte's career by catching him out of his element would have been vastly increased.

Why (it may be asked) was Nelson not provided with more frigates at this crucial juncture in the war – and provided with them by St Vincent, his admiring commander-in-chief, who was well aware of their importance? The answer is, of course, quite simple. By then the British had upwards of 200 of such 'eyes' of the Fifth and Sixth Rates, from big 44s (many of them ex-French) and the odd hybrid *razé* like the *Indefatigable*, through the most numerous 36/32 classes, down to smaller 28s and diminutive 22s which were little more than overgrown sloops (except that, by the requirement of their rate, they were post-captains' commands). But although this was the greatest 'cruiser' force the world had yet seen, more than half of it was always under repair, fitting out or otherwise non-operational. Not until the last years of the next round of this war, when there were some 250 of such ships in commission and France's frigates and privateers had been almost driven from the oceans and seas would there be British frigates to spare. Meanwhile, at the tail-end of the eighteenth century, the blockade of France had to be maintained, the approaches to the British Isles patrolled, and dozens of convoys escorted somehow while the main ship-of-the-line fleets were kept 'in being'. Across the Atlantic, for example, an attack on one West Indian convoy by a Spanish 64-gun ship-of-the-line, supported by a 44-gun frigate and a 16-gun sloop, was being driven off by two smaller British frigates. And the defenders were fortunate that those odds were not longer, a second Spanish frigate, the 44-gun *Santa Cecilia*, having failed to reach Havana. Now, in fact, she was HMS *Retribution*. But her original British name had been *Hermione*.

That the lost *Hermione* had stuck in Admiral Parker's throat is hardly surprising. Up-gunned and renamed (after another Spanish frigate lost off Trinidad the year before), she was a useful addition to Spanish strength as well as a living reminder of an unavenged disgrace to his flag and the Navy. Certainly, his spies seem to have kept their eyes on her as the Spaniards strengthened her armament and assembled a crew of nearly 400, almost double that of Pigot's time. By the autumn of 1799 she was ready to sail from the fortified harbour of Puerto Caballo in Venezuela to rendezvous with the more strategically placed Spanish squadron in Havana. To prevent this (as well as to avenge Pigot), Parker detached one of his best captains, Edward Hamilton, of the *Surprise* frigate (28), to cruise off the South American coast. Specifically, Hamilton was ordered to use his 'best endeavours' to intercept his quarry at sea, rather than attempt anything more risky. That a 28-gun British frigate (which had in fact started life as a French corvette, but had been up-rated like the *Danae*) could handle a Spanish one which now had 44 guns and almost twice as many men, the Admiral took for granted. Attacking the ex-*Hermione* at anchor under the protection of the 200 guns of the Puerto Caballo fortresses he considered to be out of the question. But that, in defiance of his orders, was what Captain Hamilton proceeded to do.

Edward Hamilton (1772–1851) fits interestingly but awkwardly into the story of frigate warfare and frigate captains, combining the best with the worst. Like Pigot, he came from a distinguished service family. He is believed to have gone to sea while still a child in a ship commanded by his father, who had won his baronetcy for bravery during the siege of Quebec in 1759. Having entered the Navy in 1787, he was promoted lieutenant six years later, serving in the frigate *Dido*, in which his elder brother Charles (future Admiral Sir Charles) was a senior lieutenant. After active service in the Mediterranean, under Hood and Jervis in the *Victory*, he was given command of the fireship *Comet*, under orders for the West Indies. 'Interest', one may presume, was now working for him, as the son of a distinguished captain, the younger brother of (now) Captain Charles Hamilton, of the *Melpomene* (44), and nephew of the Earl of Abercorn. Certainly, he became one of Admiral Parker's favourites, making post-rank in the *Surprise* (ex-*Unite*) in June 1797. But to 'interest' he added both considerable merit, as a 'dashing' frigate captain and highly successful prize-taker, but also an *un*meritorious harshness which, if it was not of the irrational Pigot (and, as we shall see, Robert Corbet) variety, was more than mere Pellew-type taut discipline – and a world away from the enlightened practices of Nelson and his imitators and pupils.

Still, to be fair to Hamilton, he may nevertheless be taken as representing an extreme of the St Vincent school of command, which combined harsh discipline with inspirational leadership. And also (and, again, as we shall see), its worst behaviour occurred after he had sustained a serious head injury. But more immediately, having decided to disobey his orders – possibly because he did not fancy his chances of intercepting the *Santa Cecilia* once she had put to sea – he had two options in dealing with her while she was at anchor under Puerto Caballo's guns: either he could use some 'infernal device' to destroy her, or he could cut her out.

Infernal devices (most usually fireships) had a long history of use against anchored and protected ships, having been employed most famously against the Armada fleet in 1588. If such attackers rarely destroyed anything themselves, they often enough caused a destructive panic among the enemy; indeed, so horrible were they in imagination that some British admirals of this period (most notably Lord Gambier later) regarded them as 'not quite cricket', and disliked their use. But, in any case, ex-fireship commander Hamilton did not have any such devices, so consequently chose the equally dangerous (and equally time-honoured, but much more gentlemanly) method of direct assault by the small boats of his frigate, aiming not to destroy the enemy ship, but to take it in hand-to-hand combat in a night attack, in the best Hollywood tradition.

Hollywood aside, the vast majority of all naval victories of this period – either in full-scale battles or in single-ship engagements – were actually achieved by gunfire, with the winners being those who fired faster and more accurately (which is to say, until 1812, always the better-trained and disciplined British). But when it came to inshore operations, in which British frigate captains would become increasingly expert as the nature of the war changed, the cutting out of enemy ships in either defended or difficult anchorages was an essential skill, as well as being more productive of prize-money. But it also caught the imagination of the journalists of the *Naval Gazette*: it was not so much Nelson's decisive disobedience in leaving the line at the battle of St Vincent to win the battle almost single-handed which caught the imagination of his countrymen as the way in which he then boarded the 80-gun *San Nicholas* from the deck of his smaller *Captain*, and then boarded and took the 112-gun *San-Josef* across the *San Nicholas*'s deck ('Nelson's Patent Bridge for Boarding First Rates', as the headline-writers of the time put it): this was the very stuff of that naval superiority-over-odds which the British public and navy alike now came to believe in, and to rely on.

Decisive and enterprising leadership was the key even before Nelson added his 'Nelson touch' to it, to make men follow his best pupils out of something more than fighting madness in alliance with confidence, discipline and patriotism. This was what Pellew and Hamilton had: if their crews never loved them (and in Hamilton's case may have actively feared and disliked him), they followed them enthusiastically. So there was no shortage of volunteers when Hamilton led a mere 100 men (but half his crew) to overwhelm the *Santa Cecilia*, which had nearly four times as many defenders, and 200 fortress guns as well as her own. Nor can this extraordinary feat of arms be simply attributed to Spanish cowardice, even though the British lost only a dozen men, because more than half the *Santa Cecilia*'s crew was either killed or wounded before her surrender.

For this great feat of arms *and* as the captor of the lost *Hermione*, Edward Hamilton was instantly acclaimed. The merchants of Jamaica (always keen to encourage their protectors) voted him a 300-guinea sword. Captured on a homeward-bound West Indian by a French privateer, he was quickly exchanged for a French officer (after, according to one report, having been interviewed by General Bonaparte himself). In England a knighthood, a gold medal-of-honour, a celebration dinner given by the Lord Mayor of London and the offer of a £300-a-year pension awaited him. That last he refused, accepting command of a bigger frigate, the *Trent* (36), instead, fearing that it would be used as an excuse to invalid him out of the Navy because of the serious head injury he had received in leading the first dozen of his men aboard the *Santa Cecilia*. If that was the Admiralty's intention it may have been well-advised, if his wound can be blamed for his subsequent behaviour, for in 1802 he was court-martialled and dismissed the service for gross cruelty. Although he was reinstated in the following year the only ships he ever commanded again were royal yachts (1806–18) in which he could do no harm, and he never flew his flag after reaching admiral's rank (by seniority on the Captains' List, of course) in 1821.

Captain Sir Edward Hamilton's brief years of frigate command illustrate a number of our recurrent themes. In a frigate a man could get rich quickly (he made some £50,000 in two years from prize-money). But, much more importantly for Britain and her navy, these were the high days of the Age of Nelson: British captains and crews believed that they were invincible, and acted accordingly, within or in spite of orders (Edward Hamilton and Horatio Nelson equally), on their own initiative, relying on leadership and training for success and on success for justification. But while leadership (plus, of course, the common currency of bravery) could – and very often *did* – make up for many other different defects of a captain's character, those defects in the end might distort or impede such an officer's career, if they did not (as we shall see) end it. Which brings us to the quite extraordinary story of Thomas, Lord Cochrane.

It is hardly to be denied that *our* Cochrane (there were other distinguished naval Cochranes of the same family) was the greatest frigate captain of them all, and the greatest and most daring fighting *captain* (with Nelson the greatest fighting *admiral*). But, in the amazing ups and downs of his active life he was something even more than that: he was the greatest captain in fact *or* fiction, whose successive triumphs and disasters on the way to becoming Queen Victoria's Admiral of the Fleet (also by way of Chilean, Brazilian and Greeks wars of independence and a fictional appearance as 'Captain Savage' in Marryat's *Peter Simple*) out-fiction anything a novelist would dare to include, for fear of reader disbelief.

In addition to all this, he provides a continual wealth of examples of the bizarre working of the navy's system, even from his first appearance in ill-fitting uniform. We left him in an earlier chapter, mentioned in passing as a newly-promoted lieutenant at the minimum age of 20, for which the qualifications included six years' sea service, in his case purely on paper. Notionally, as a young man of outstanding bravery, ability and ambition, the young Cochrane might have prospered as a soldier. For, although his father lacked the cash to buy higher ranks, good officers *could* rise in the Army in defiance of its purchase system. Certainly, if he had reached the British Peninsular army in the later stages of the war, when merit and the drain of casualties were securing promotions for poor but deserving officers under Wellington's discerning eye, he might have ended up on the staff (or among Colonel Colquhoun Grant's intelligence officers), even if he never rose to command a regiment – except possibly in the Portuguese service, anyway. But where in the *next* world war, with its huge citizen armies, there would be 'boy brigadiers' leading their conscripts to break the Hindenburg Line in 1918, there was no scope for his particular brand of leadership in semi-independent command in which planning and cool calculation cancelled risk in land warfare. In that *next* world war (short of a brigade in the trenches), his qualities required the opportunities of a T.E. Lawrence. In the world war after that one, he might have been another Orde Wingate in Burma, or a Long Range Desert Group commander in Libya, or – perhaps most likely of all – another Guy Gibson or Leonard Cheshire of the RAF. Winston Churchill would have recognised Cochrane's qualities – and his publicity value (even if Wing Commander Lord Cochrane would undoubtedly have voted Labour in 1945). But in the last French war, given the right conjunction of 'interest' and luck to go with his merit, only the Navy could give him the chance of independent command and spectacular action.

For only the Navy (given at least two of those ingredients) provided such scope for such men when they were still young. Nelson himself never had the chance of becoming a dashing frigate captain in combat with the French, but his post-captaincy came to him at the tender age of 21, so he was ideally placed to become a dashing admiral while still young by the geriatric standards of the time. Hoste, his pupil, reached the Captain's List only a year older; Pellew, Pigot and Broke made post-rank in frigates in their mid-twenties (and even Hornblower, totally without interest, when he was 29). Maximum 'interest' ensured maximum promotion: Peter Rainier, nephew of the C-in-C East Indies, jumped from midshipman to post-captain in 13 months, at the age of 22 (and soon a very rich post-captain, too); Pellew's sons, when he commanded the same lucrative station, were even more disgracefully promoted.

Post-captaincy *and* a frigate to go with it were, as has already been observed, the keys to success, so much so that the mere expectation of such a command formed the basis of Jane Austen's Captain Wentworth's first proposal of marriage to Anne Elliot. What makes Cochrane remarkable (or, anyway, *one* of the things which does so) is that he achieved fame initially without either, in one of the most amazing single-ship actions of all time. What makes him more immediately interesting in the context of our six frigate captains, however, is the way in which his qualities, and the strengths and weakness of his character, influenced his career and cast light on the Navy of his time.

That most captains had their eyes fixed as firmly on their own interests as on their country's may be taken for granted without devaluing them. A nice calculation of the benefits of success and victory to both was common to their time, and quite frankly (not to say proudly) revealed by Nelson himself on the eve of the Battle of the Nile, when he confided over dinner that 'before this time tomorrow I shall have gained a Peerage or Westminster Abbey'. Just as there was a marshal's baton in every French soldier's knapsack, so every aspiring young British naval officer – and most particularly every young frigate captain – believed that there was not only an admiral's flag and a knighthood, but also the promise of a fortune in prize-money in his sea-chest. Thus, to establish that Thomas Cochrane was very definitely a young-man-in-a-hurry – a 'pushy' young man and, for good measure, a pushy young *Scotsman*, with an ambition as fiery as his red hair – is hardly a slur on him in itself. He had entered the Navy relatively late, at the age of 18 in 1793, so he had to move fast. And (like so many young Scotsmen heading south) he was poor, in spite of being the heir to the earldom of Dundonald, his father having squandered what family fortune there had been on a series of ingenious scientific-industrial projects.

At the same time, if anyone knew the risks attendant on leadership, young Cochrane surely did, for the corners of many foreign fields were already forever Scotland, with Cochranes planted in them. Three of his ancestors had fallen in the War of the Spanish Succession at the beginning of the century. The 7th Earl had been killed at the siege of Louisburg in the Seven Years' War, and most recently the 8th Earl had been picked off before the Yorktown surrender in the disastrous American war. So he can hardly have believed that he bore a charmed life.

Nevertheless, it was action that he wanted. And, after having proved an apt midshipman in his uncle's *Hind* frigate, passing his lieutenant's examination at the first attempt, he was unhappy with the comfortable promotions which established him in the flagship on the unexciting American station in the mid-1790s, under an admiral who was accustomed to rent a house ashore in pro-British Virginia during the inclement months of winter, where the company of Southern belles could be enjoyed. His unconcealed dissatisfaction, together with the first evidence of certain radical political sentiments (which in America inclined him towards sympathy with the successfully revolted ex-colonists), probably helped his posting to duties in European waters, first in the *Thetis* frigate and then in Admiral Keith's flagship *Barfleur* in St Vincent's former fleet, which was now blockading the battered but still substantial remains of the Spanish fleet off Cadiz.

This was another disastrous posting for him, although many young (and courtesy-titled) lieutenants would have jumped at the chance of service in a flagship – and, not least, *Scottish* lieutenants, since Admiral Keith was a fellow-Scot. Nelson's navy (or, at least that part of it which was not actually foreign) was a predominantly English one, with three-quarters of its officers and men coming from coastal shires and the majority of them from the West country, the south and south-east, East Anglia and London. In proportion to her population, Scotland's contribution was much the same as England's, but her population was very small. More significantly, however, English prejudice against Scotsmen (whom they more usually and derisively referred to as 'Scotchmen') was extreme. Once again, Dr Johnson has left the most quotable evidence of this English contempt with such gems as 'the noblest prospect a Scotchman ever sees, is the high road that leads to England' and 'Seeing Scotland, madam, is only seeing a worse England.' 'I do indeed come from Scotland, but I cannot help it', said Boswell defensively. 'That, Sir, I find, is what a great many of your countrymen cannot help', came the reply. Significantly, Lord Keith's *Barfleur* was known throughout the fleet as 'a stinking *Scotch* ship'. Much more important in the long term for the young Lieutenant Lord Cochrane, nevertheless, was Admiral Earl St Vincent's own extreme, irrational and shameful hatred of everything Scottish. Upright in so many respects (at least by eighteenth-century standards), dedicated to the good of the service, unflinchingly firm even to the point of unwisdom against corruption, and critical of the grosser forms of 'interest' though he was, St Vincent could not bring himself to return the admiration of that fine sailor, Adam Duncan, even after the Scotsman had first maintained the blockade of the Dutch coast during the Nore mutiny and had then crowned this achievement by defeating the Dutch fleet at Camperdown.

As fellow-victims of such prejudice, Admiral Keith and Lieutenant Cochrane might have been expected to get on together, with beneficial results for the younger man. That the Admiral was at best a fair-weather friend, and very critical of Cochrane behind his back, nevertheless most probably owes more to Cochrane's behaviour than to Keith's. Dull service in a blockading flagship was, at all events, exactly the sort of duty which brought out the worst in Cochrane, with the winged chariot of his ambition at his back. His failure to get on with his equally bored (and much duller) fellow-officers soon enough blew up into a formal court martial after a ridiculous contretemps with his first lieutenant after he had omitted to report back officially on returning from a duck-shooting expedition in Morocco. And although he escaped from this with a 'Not guilty' verdict one may presume that 'his card was marked' as an awkward subordinate again. Troubles enough his seniors already had, and the need to get rid of him, as much as his undoubted abilities, may well account for his subsequent temporary posting as prize-master to bring in the dreadfully-battered French ship-of-the-line *Généreux*, the last survivor from the Battle of Nile which had finally been captured off Sicily. Perhaps, even, his brother-officers may have hoped he would go down with that prize, which he only saved by brilliant seamanship. That this proof of ability in command was followed (to the joy of the *Barfleur*'s wardroom no doubt) by a much more important genuine promotion is not proof of Admiral Keith's favour; if Keith *had* liked him he would have been appointed to command the beautiful little (ex-French, of course) *Bonne Citoyenne* corvette, which had then become available but which was given to the Admiral's secretary's brother as a mark of favour to the former, while Cochrane had to make do with what was probably the least desirable vessel in the whole Mediterranean fleet, His Britannic Majesty's coastal brig *Speedy*.

Except that she carried with her the temporary rank of master and commander (and the courtesy title of captain), the *Speedy* was not so much a reward as a joke. Ill-named (because she was pitiably slow), she boasted no less than 14 guns, seven a side, but these were all four-pounder popguns, of little use except at point-blank range. And, indeed, when Cochrane begged a couple of more powerful 12-pounders to mount as chasers he was quickly forced to abandon them when the *Speedy* protested at the force of their discharge by springing a leak. In such a cockle-shell, it would be an achievement to catch an enemy (although at this stage in the war there were still many enemies to be caught), never mind to capture one, it must have seemed. And to escape an enemy (for at this stage of the war the Mediterranean was still far from the British lake it was to become, in spite of Nelson's recent victory in Aboukir Bay) – that would be more like a miracle. But she was none the less the first real command of Master and Commander Lord Cochrane, one of whose future biographers was to describe without hyperbole as 'after the death of Nelson, the greatest naval commander of that age of glory'. Miracles – as both the enemy and the British Navy were soon to discover – were what Cochrane dealt in during a career which surpassed all the fictions it actually inspired, from those of Captain Marryat (one of his future midshipmen) to those of the Hornblower–Ramage vintage. And, most immediately meanwhile, it was the *Speedy* under his command which also must rate a special place in the story of frigate warfare.

In the ensuing 13 months Cochrane scooped up more than 50 prizes, which although all relatively small must have both improved his own cashflow and somewhat endeared him even to his commanding officer, who automatically took his percentage of the profits. However, if he was a natural pirate, combining skills and daring with successful pirate's luck, his fame and reputation were to come not from encounters with defenceless merchant vessels but from his meetings with enemy warships.

His first close call came when he chased a promisingly large ship, only to discover that she was a Spanish frigate which could easily have blown him out of the water. However, he was then disguised pirate-fashion as a neutral Danish brig known to be in those waters, and discouraged the Spaniards with information that he had plague from Algiers aboard (delivered in Danish, by a man dressed in Danish uniform and looking like a Dane), which precluded closer inspection.

(Plague, as Midshipman Hornblower was to discover, was the more-or-less endemic danger in rat-infested North Africa, hanging like a nightmare over captains who had beaten scurvy and were thankful that they weren't cruising off yellow fever coasts.)

After a year at sea, nevertheless, either that subterfuge was threadbare or Cochrane himself (and, according to some versions, his crew no less also) by now had other ideas when his luck finally ran out early on the morning of 6 May 1801 off Barcelona, in the form of the 32-gun Spanish frigate *El Gamo*.

His proper course of action – or, anyway, the only sane course – would have been to strike his flag, which would also have been a perfectly honourable one. Ships of more-or-less equal class (that is, for example, frigates of the Fifth and Sixth Rates, and ships-of-the-line from Fourth to First) were expected to engage in single combat when they met, and to fight until one was sufficiently damaged to render further combat suicidal. Surrender then was not regarded as disgraceful; even, as has already been mentioned, one of Nelson's captains, Thompson of the *Leander*, was knighted after such a surrender, because of his gallant defence. (Only in our own supposedly enlightened days are ship-captains – and aircraft pilots, though not soldiers – expected to fight to the death against hopeless odds.) But out-classed ships hardly needed to fire a single gun by way of a gesture before giving in, and the *Speedy* was hopelessly, even ludicrously, inferior to the *El Gamo*.

Perhaps that incredibility initially gave Cochrane a breathing space in which to manoeuvre – a moment which he now lengthened by running up the American Stars and Stripes as he closed with the Spanish ship. Flying false colours was, in those days, a quite legitimate *ruse de guerre*. Although it was also consequently a cobwebby old ploy by itself, it served its purpose in further delaying the Spanish captain, neutral Yankee shipowners being notoriously litigious when their property was illegally detained or damaged. Even so, Cochrane was lucky to survive the two broadsides the Spaniards managed to get off before he finally ran the *Speedy* alongside her under true British colours: she could quite easily have been dismasted, if not actually blown out of the water, but in fact only suffered six casualties. And then – at least for the moment – she had her first advantage: simply because of the disparity in the two vessels' sizes, the *El Gamo* could not depress her larger and more numerous guns sufficiently, while Cochrane's puny four-pounders, elevated and double-shotted, could fire upwards at point blank range through the frigate's side and deck.

This they did with terrible effect, to inflict 50 casualties not only among her gun crews, but much more decisively on her quarterdeck. Indeed, the God of Battles who does sometimes reward gamblers like Cochrane now served him generously, for his shots killed the Spanish captain and his ship's master. Nevertheless, Cochrane had still only exchanged the fire for the frying-pan itself. For, as he could not have failed to presume, Spanish frigates were no less over-manned than French ones, so that what he did next was hardly less mad than what he had already done. 'The great disparity in our force rendering it necessary to adopt some measure that might prove decisive,' he reported subsequently, 'I resolved to board . . .'

A few moments before, the *El Gamo* had a crew of over 300 sailors and marines. That had now been reduced to around 250, but Cochrane's own nominal complement of 90 had been reduced by six casualties, with another 26 men absent sailing his most recent prizes to the nearest British-occupied port. So now it was 48 (including the ship's doctor and the little powder-monkeys) against five times as many – even longer odds than Captain Hamilton had accepted in cutting out the *Hermione* with 100 against 400, especially as his attack had also been a surprise night operation.

The rest, however, is history, not fiction: by a mixture of mad brute force and bluff, the *Speedy* took the *El Gamo*. The brute force consisted of twenty men swarming up amidships and another twenty over the bows, all fighting mad and with blackened faces, leaving only the boys behind and the doctor at the wheel. And the bluff strengthening that force came when Cochrane shouted down to his almost empty ship for 'reinforcements' as one of his men took advantage of the confusion to sneak aft and lower the Spanish flag. Leaderless and bewildered (and having suffered another 50 casualties), the Spaniards on the main deck surrendered, and were given no chance for any immediate change of mind. After which, when deck-guns had been swung round to overawe the prisoners, Cochrane's only remaining problem was how to get the *Speedy* home herself (which was achieved with a crew of a dozen).

The aftermath of this amazing episode was, in the first place, predictable, and then sad (though, given the characters of the protagonists, perhaps equally predictable).

First, although still only a lieutenant, Cochrane became famous outside the Navy as well as in it. His fellow-professionals were of course well-placed to judge his achievement (though the rank and file may have been even more impressed by his short casualty list, which was to become a hallmark of Cochrane operations). But the public at large, even though as accustomed to victory at sea as to defeat on land, was tickled by the encounter's David-and-Goliath quality, flocking to admire a Nicholas Pocock painting of the action. (Pocock was a fashionable artist of the time whose own son had been one of young Hoste's fellow-midshipmen under Nelson, and instant paintings of naval successes were the nearest thing eighteenth-century England had to television.)

Cochrane himself, while generously attributing his victory to the bravery of his crew, wanted promotion more than fame, and fully expected it too, as his due and with public opinion behind him. Indeed, one of St Vincent's colleagues – undoubtedly a bad psychologist – is said to have advised the old man that they must make Cochrane 'post'. Whereupon St Vincent, never one to be pushed into doing anything and contemptuous of public opinion, replied that, for the First Lord of the Admiralty, there was no such thing as 'must' – least of all (one suspects) where a damned insubordinate young *Scotchman* was concerned.

Nevertheless, with naval custom-and-practice as well as public sympathy on his side, and the exercise of some self-control on his own part, Cochrane should not have had to wait too long for post-rank, and certainly for an appointment to something better than the *Speedy*. But self-control in the face of injustice was a virtue he lacked: when not safe fighting his country's foes he could invariably be relied on to become his own worst enemy. So now, failing to receive promotion himself, he entered into a protracted and acrimonious correspondence with St Vincent – lieutenant to First Lord of the Admiralty – over the lack of advancement of the gallant First Lieutenant of the *Speedy* (which was, of course one of the usual sequels of successful frigate actions). And when St Vincent once again demurred – this time with the ignoble excuse that the *Speedy*'s casualty list was too small to justify such a compliment – he reminded the old man that the Earldom of St Vincent had been conferred after an action in which the new earl's flagship had lost only one man killed. This unforgivable – almost suicidal – act of lese-majesty being added to an equally bitter letter on the same subject to the influential Secretary to the Board of Admiralty, both the Master and Commander of the *Speedy* and his first lieutenant speedily found themselves back in their cockleshell, which was in turn ordered back to the Mediterranean, but now relegated to the role of messenger-boat to the fleet.

Thus, quite typically and not for the last time, did the second 'greatest naval commander in that age of glory' retard his progress towards the rank of Admiral of the Fleet as much by his own imprudence as because of the system. Worse still, he learned nothing from the experience; rather each new unfairness and injustice seemed to make him more himself, as red-reforming-radical as he was red-headed (and often wrong-headed with it). It was fortunate now that the French – foremost among his enemies, but much more admiring once they stopped trying to kill him – now took a hand in the game.

More precisely, his luck and that of the *Speedy* finally ran out on one summer morning off Alicante in 1801, after he had been busily harrying coastwise Franco-Spanish traffic as best he could (with no great profit to himself) while acting as postman to the fleet. For there he was caught by three powerful French ships-of-the-line packed with men and en route from Toulon to Cadiz, where the Spaniards had agreed to transfer six of their own battleships to French crews, as part of a plan to reinforce her beleaguered army in Egypt.

Playing games with the *El Gamo* was one thing. But taking on two 80-gun ships and a 74, a shot from any one of whose main-deck 32-pounders outweighed the entire broadside of the *Speedy*, was out of the question even for Cochrane. Short of immediate surrender, his only chance lay in escape. Yet even there his chances were virtually nil, since the French ships were between him and the open sea. And, of course, French ships were notoriously fast sailers anyway. So any such attempt would be near-suicidal.

Being Cochrane, however, he took that only chance. During the hours of manoeuvring which followed, first the useless four-pounders were jettisoned and then all the ship's stores, in an attempt to increase her speed. Sweeps (oars) were got out (the *Speedy* was small enough to be rowed), and at one point she tried to sail between two of the big Frenchmen, on the theory that they would not endanger each other by opening fire. But in the end, although none of the enemy broadsides actually blew her apart with direct hits, their smaller shot so damaged her sails and rigging that she was brought to bay.

It was ironic that from this small British disaster, which left him a prisoner in Franco-Spanish hands, and also from a greater British failure which followed it, Cochrane's promotion finally emerged. For, having dealt with the little *Speedy*, the French pressed on the Algeciras Bay, with Cochrane on board the *Desaix* (74) still wearing his sword, which the chivalrous French captain positively refused to accept from an enemy who had so bravely resisted the inevitable. Indeed, he was breakfasting with his captor when a cannon-ball crashed through the ship's stern-windows as British ships-of-the-line under Sir James Saumarez attacked the French squadron where it lay close in-shore, under the protection of 14 Spanish gunboats.

What followed was one of the British Navy's rare defeats in an attack which was as daring as it was ill-judged. With little room to manoeuvre on a dangerous shore, all Saumarez's ships were hard-hit, with the 74-gun *Hannibal* actually having to surrender – an almost unheard-of event – after she had gone hard aground. And although the three French ships were also grounded after cutting their cables, a strong Spanish squadron was able to break out of Cadiz to sail to their rescue.

This, however, was now the 'age of Nelson' – of Nelson and his band of brothers, and of St Vincent, Pellew, Hamilton and Saumarez himself. Undeterred by their recent bloody nose, the Admiral and his captains and crews worked round the clock to repair most of their damaged ships sufficiently to sail against the Spaniards. Captain

Richard Keats, another of the Navy's Pellew-type heroes, took one ship-of-the-line in what became a pursuit, and two other huge Spanish 100-gun three-deckers were destroyed by fire following a collision as their squadron was driven off into the Atlantic.

All these exciting events were compressed into a very few days. Cochrane was taken prisoner on 3 July (1801 now), to breakfast with the admirable Captain Pallière in the *Desaix* (named after one of Napoleon's equally gallant generals) during the British defeat in Algeciras Bay on 5 July. Two days later he was free in Gibraltar, having been no less chivalrously paroled by his captor, and a week later he became unconditionally free to fight again, his parole having been turned into 'exchange' in return for the Spanish second-captain of the *Sainte Antoine* (74), which Captain Keats had captured with his *Superb* in the recent battle.

The technicalities of parole, exchange, and indeed, escape will be further considered in due course, in tracing both Hornblower's problems and the adventures of Captain Hoste's first lieutenant, Dermot Henchy O'Brien. Meanwhile, Lieutenant Lord Cochrane's return to duties was automatically delayed by the court martial he had to face after the loss of his ship. But, this, too, was held quickly in the *Pompée* (the worst-damaged of the Algeciras survivors) and it was very different from his previous Gibraltar court martial. Rather, it was a formality which established for the record how devotedly and skilfully he had done his duty in the *Speedy* when even an immediate surrender to such superior forces would not have been regarded as dishonourable.

In effect, he was a hero again. And this time even St Vincent could not ignore his merit, so that in less than another month Lieutenant Lord Cochrane was on the post-captains' list at last.

Nevertheless, the old admiral's surrender in this matter also allowed him the last laugh. For such a promotion did not automatically carry with it a ship – a frigate, properly – as it always did as part of an appointment *to* command such a ship. And, indeed, there was not the slightest chance that there would be any such command for the young Scotsman, because peace with France was now a fast-approaching reality. Within a month of Captain Lord Cochrane's elevation British civilians were actually crossing the Channel to savour the long-denied pleasures of Paris – even before peace preliminaries, to be ratified six months later, were officially concluded on 1 October 1801. And by then, as custom and financial prudence demanded, the Royal Navy was already being run down.

Of our original six sailors, one was now dead, and two – the 21-year-old Hoste and 25-year-old Hornblower – still not captains (although, with Nelson behind him, Hoste would not have to wait too long). But even of the three *on* that magic list, only Pellew was far enough up it and famous enough to hope for employment at sea in a peacetime navy. Cochrane and Philip Broke, at the bottom of the List as 1801 promotions, were instantly high and dry on the beach on half-pay, together with large numbers of more senior captains, numerous masters and commanders (who now became lieutenants again) and innumerable junior officers. It might be years before they went to sea again. And if peace lasted they might never go to sea again at all.

Peace, of course, did not last. Indeed, it was hardly a peace at all, but more like a mere breathing space in a war which had already lasted eight years, but was not yet half-finished.

CHAPTER NINE

Captain Cochrane and the flying Pallas

If there were some in Great Britain who continued to view the new French Republic with grave suspicion, a war-weary majority among the ruling classes welcomed the Peace of Amiens and hoped – indeed, expected – that it would last, with no such thoughts of a *revanche* as had animated the French back in 1763.

Indeed, that angry old man St Vincent was among those who presumed on at least several years of peace, not a mere 14 months, as he embarked on a long-overdue attempt to flush corruption out of the Augean stables of the British naval dockyards – a project which, in the event, proved as unwise for the disorganisation it caused as for the unpopularity it earned the First Lord among the powerful vested interests he offended. And, anyway, this long-term undertaking was also accompanied by those slashing cuts in naval manpower with which the British traditionally greeted every war's end. A navy upon which, as the preamble to the Articles of War put it, 'under the good providence of God . . . the safety, honour and welfare of this kingdom do chiefly depend' was speedily reduced from the 130,000 men voted in 1800 to 50,000. Britain's answer to French military might and naval expansion (and the despatch of an expedition to the West Indies and plans for the development of Louisiana) was a massive tourist invasion of Paris, with the great and good admiring the latest fashions and jostling to catch a glimpse of the newly-created 'First Consul', the famous General Bonaparte.

The extent to which the war had been lost, nevertheless, was all too apparent in the provisions of the peace, by which Britain agreed to hand back all her overseas conquests except Trinidad (taken from Spain, not France) and Ceylon (taken from the Dutch). Captured naval bases right across the globe were thus to be surrendered, not only Minorca in the Mediterranean (returned to Spain) but also incomparable Malta, which was to be returned to the moribund Order of the Knights of St John under Russian protection, with various footling international 'guarantees'. With the loss of those bases went all the hard-won ascendancy of the British Army's first victory over a French one for many years, won in Egypt in 1801 after its most brilliant sea-borne invasion between Quebec (1759) and Normandy (1944).

But more eloquent of defeat even than this was that France (now fast becoming incarnate in Napoleon Bonaparte) gave nothing in return which had not already been agreed earlier in her separate treaty with defeated Austria at Luneville. Thereby the independence of the Low Countries, Switzerland and Northern Italy was 'mutually respected' – weasel words which recall nothing so much as the Munich agreement of 1938. That those three countries had been transmogrified into the Batavian, Helvetian and Ligurian republics respectively was evidence of that same devotion to classical history which had just turned Napoleon into a Consul (the *First* Consul, then Consul *for life*), as well as naming half of all the rated warships afloat. But under whatever names, these countries were little better than French quisling states, and in conceding their status Britain was giving up the cause for which she had fought for so many years already.

Given Napoleon's character and ambition such a peace could never have lasted long. Yet given also Britain's war-weariness and the popularity of Prime Minister Addington's 'peace and retrenchment' policies it might have lasted longer if Napoleon had not embarked on such nakedly expansionist policies in Europe and overseas, compared with which the dilatoriness of the British in evacuating Malta and certain Indian forts was a quibble. After all, they were at the same time planning to reduce their navy further, down to 30,000 by 1803– 4, and their regular army, though larger at 95,000 than it had been pre-war, was none the less derisory by continental standards.

As it was, Napoleon's actions during the brief Amiens peace months – and not least his expansion of his ship-of-the-line strength from 43 to 66 – turned British hopes and complacency into fear and anger between March 1802 and May 1803, uniting the country as it had not been in 1793. A 'hot press' in every major British port this time preceded the withdrawal of their ambassador from Paris on 12 May, five days before a declaration of war which was this time delivered from London. And on 19 May the British Navy seized its first prizes in Pellew's old stamping ground, Audierne Bay.

That this was going to be a different kind of fight even from that with the 'frantic Murderers' of '93 became immediately apparent when Napoleon seized hundreds of British tourists on the pretext that they were of military age (16 to 60) and *could* be militia officers (many of them were rich peers, too) – which was against all the customs and usages of the past, even as practised by the revolutionaries. And if Luneville–Amiens smelt of Munich, the cloud of propaganda which accompanied this action also has a sulphurous twentieth-century smell about it. The British (*perfide Albion* now) replied in kind with jingo patriotism as the largest and finest army in Europe gathered across the Channel under the greatest captain of the age and his galaxy of new marshals and generals: Boney, 'the Corsican Ogre', and his band of frog-eaters would soon be seen off by Britannia's 'Hearts of Oak', the pamphleteers and cartoonists confidently predicted.

Not least among those Hearts was the Member of Parliament for Barnstaple, Sir Edward Pellew, who was already at sea in the *Tonnant* (80), cruising not far behind his screen of frigates and in-shore sloops – one of which was now commanded by Lieutenant (Master and Commander) Horatio Hornblower, formerly his favourite midshipman. Elsewhere, although the worthy Captain Philip Broke would have to wait several long years for *his* frigate (having no 'interest'), the very young Captain William Hoste, whom Nelson's 'interest' had promoted into his first frigate during the peace, would not have to wait so long, way down the List though he was, for his next command. (Everyone liked young Hoste, whom Lady Hamilton had spotted as another Nelson in-the-making and who had actually been made post while assisting a British diplomat, a certain Lord Elgin, pick up some marble fragments lying around in Athens the year before.)

Everyone did not, however, approve of Thomas, Captain Lord Cochrane, who had also not yet got his frigate. While thousands of men were being conscripted into every available ship as each was brought back into commission – and while every homecoming merchantman was being stripped of its crew before it could dock, with Americans and other foreigners (and even Thames watermen) all illegal grist for the mill – Cochrane's vociferous demands for a command in which he could serve his country in its hour of need came to the attention of the First Lord himself, Earl St Vincent. 'I have not forgot Lord Cochrane,' replied St Vincent to those soliciting on the fellow's behalf. But, in the matter, of his request for an 18-pounder frigate (which would have been most likely a big 40), there were of course 'so many senior captains of great merit without ships of that class', which were much in demand.

However, St Vincent had to give in eventually, but apart from being a very great admiral he was nothing if not a good hater, and ingenious with it. For the ship which Captain Lord Cochrane finally received from the Admiralty was the *Arab*, a (nominal) Sixth Rate frigate appropriate to an officer of post-rank and therefore satisfying those who believed that the heroic victor of the *El Gamo* fight deserved a command. But also, one must suppose, this appointment satisfied St Vincent no less.

Even compared with the *Speedy*, the *Arab* was hardly a warship. She was indeed hardly a ship at all, but a converted North Sea collier, old and broken down, in which no captain would have gone to sea happily in peacetime, never mind in a hot war as a unit of Admiral Lord Keith's squadron off Boulogne, where the *Grande Armée* of the Corsican Ogre was massing for the invasion of England.

The perfection of St Vincent's revenge (if that was what it was) lay in the fact that Cochrane, with his natural aptitude for in-shore commando-type operations, was exactly the right man for such a posting – but now in exactly the wrong sort of no-hope ship, never mind under an admiral who was no friend of his. Even surviving in the *Arab* in those notoriously treacherous Narrow Seas was something of an achievement, regardless of the enemy. But, having done so, Cochrane once again proceeded to ruin his chances quite typically, in a manner which it would be churlish to imagine even St Vincent had foreseen: in the best Pigot/Nelson manner he high-handedly detained a neutral American ship, threatening another international incident of the sort Britain could not afford, hard-pressed as she was. And that fully justified his exile (still in the *Arab*) to fishery protection duties in the far north, off the Orkney islands.

For 14 months Cochrane remained banished among fishing boats, fretting through the whole emergency of 1804 while Napoleon schemed to get his unbeatable army across the Channel, at first so certain that this ditch would be crossed that he had his victory medal struck in advance commemorating the *Descente en Angleterre . . . Frappé à Londres en 1804.*

On the other side of the ditch preparations were being made the like of which had not been seen since the days of the Armada, and would not be seen again until Hitler took his telescopic view of the White Cliffs in 1940. Thousands of troops, some regular but most more-or-less irregular, massed in the southern counties, behind a string of look-out beacons, strong points and a line of Martello Towers on the foreshore (constructed to the design of a tower on Cape Mortella in Corsica, which had given the British a deal of trouble ten years before). The evacuation of women and children, the driving off of livestock and the disposal of corn and haystacks by scorched earth action were planned, in an atmosphere in which amateurishness, incredulity and grim determination (also reminiscent of 1940) were curiously mixed.

What short work the veterans of Marengo, Rivoli, Hochstadt, Hohenlinden and all those other French victories would have made of one-third of a million ill-armed volunteers, stiffened by a mere 28,000

regulars (with almost as many of their comrades busy holding down
Ireland), does not make pleasant thinking. But, of course, it never
came remotely near to reality, though every port along the adjacent
European coast was packed with landing craft designed and built to
get the *Grande Armée* across. The Royal Navy stood in between,
unshakeable even in the worst weather (and the months of Cochrane's
absence, from November 1803 onwards, were again among the
stormiest in living memory). From Keith in the Narrow Seas, with only
six-of-the-line, but now no less than 32 frigates (how *that* must have
galled Cochrane's soul!) to Cornwallis's fleet off Brest (with Pellew in
the *Tonnant* and Hornblower in the little *Hotspur*), and other
squadrons off the French bases of Rochefort and Toulon, France's
navy could not hope to clear the way for her army, even for a few
hours. Addington, though a much-underrated politician, was hardly
the man to inspire the nation in Churchillian style. But old St Vincent
managed a truly memorable – and memorably true – summing-up of
the situation: 'I do not say, my Lords, that the French will not come. I
only say that they will not come by sea.'

All this, which led Mahan to his conclusion that it was 'those
distant, storm-beaten ships' which stood between Bonaparte and
world dominion, was what Cochrane, in his equally storm-beaten and
even-further-distant *Arab*, missed, thanks to his own and St Vincent's
failings, and the system itself. But eventually it was the system, as it
interlocked with British politics, which came to his rescue.

The emergency of war had at first actually strengthened Addington's
government, for purely patriotic reasons. But when his appeal for
volunteers to defend the country produced a huge Kitchener-like flood
of them, and they then experienced the ensuing chaos of his ineptitude
as a war minister, this patriotism rebounded on him, and broke his
resolution to continue. Out of this, in a tangle of personalities, William
Pitt rose again, for the last time. And with him rose his old friend and
ally, Henry Dundas, to become First Lord of the Admiralty as Lord
Melville, while out from that post went John Jervis, Earl St Vincent.

Melville's career in parliament went back over a quarter of a century
already, to before the American War (in which he had opposed any
concessions to the Colonies), and his close interest in the Navy dated –
fatally, as it turned out – from 1782, when he was its Treasurer. But
for our purposes now (that is, for Cochrane's) the important thing
about him was that he was a Scotsman. Educated at Edinburgh
University, he had become Solicitor-General for Scotland at the age of
24, in 1766. Later he organised the notoriously venal Scottish
parliamentary vote for Pitt in government (Scottish votes were usually
available for the government of the day, on the basis that those who
were poor needed the jobs each succeeding government had in its gift).
Not backward in accepting lucrative posts himself, Dundas was a

convivial fellow who equally did not forget his Scottish friends, who of course did not forget theirs either. So now, when the Duke of Hamilton (another Scot) advised him of the sad fate of that brave young (Scottish) captain, the Earl of Dundonald's boy, Thomas Cochrane, he reacted quickly, and in the most obliging fashion: in less than two months the former captain of the *Arab* was sailing out of Plymouth in the brand-new frigate *Pallas*.

Compared with many of the most modern frigates (particularly with so many French prizes among them), the *Pallas* was small – a mere 667 tons – with only 32 (or, as later advertised by Cochrane himself, 36) guns, and certainly not to be compared with Pellew's splendid *Indefatigable*. Also, in the rush to get her to sea after having been out of the limelight for several years, Cochrane experienced considerable difficulty in acquiring a crew in Plymouth, which, like all western and southern England, had been picked over by many desperate captains before him since the outbreak of war in 1803. As a result he had to make use of the press gang, leaving behind (also like many of those captains) a summons for assault taken out against him by the Mayor of Plymouth, whose constables had been roughed up by his men in carrying off the sweepings from the bottom of the barrel.

That, however, was the last as well as the first time that recruitment was ever to be one of his problems. For, in addition to the *Pallas* herself, the new Scottish First Lord had given Cochrane an almost unrivalled opportunity to enrich himself, to become one of the most popular captains afloat.

Three months earlier, when it had become apparent to the government that Spain was a *de facto* ally of France, a pre-emptive strike worthy of Drake himself had been mounted against her: a frigate squadron under Captain Graham Moore (brother of General Sir John Moore, the future hero-victim of the battle of Corunna) was ordered to intercept the main Spanish treasure convoy from America. Ostensibly, the bullion on board was then to be held in trust, as it were, to be returned if and when British suspicions of neutral Spain turned out to be wrong. In fact, of course, the Spanish escort fought to protect its country's honour and property and was dealt with accordingly, and the treasure carried off. After which, inevitably, Spain was soon officially at war again with Britain. It was because of this, in due course, that it was a Franco-Spanish fleet that Nelson faced at Trafalgar. But, more immediately, it enabled Dundas to reward Captain Lord Cochrane for all his past sufferings with a roving three-month cruise in the Azores region, right on the main Spanish–American–West Indian trade route, before he reported for convoy duty.

At this early stage in the new Anglo-Spanish war there were still many Spanish merchant ships at sea, not a few of which – given the poor communications of the time – did not know of the outbreak of hostilities. As a result, within a few weeks of the *Pallas*'s hurried departure Spanish prizes not only valuable in themselves (for the Spaniards built good ships) but also carrying quantities of cash, jewels, gold and silver ingots and highly saleable Spanish-American exports like mahogany and sugar began to arrive in Plymouth, to the enrichment of Captain Cochrane's commanding admiral and his crew, but most of all to Captain Cochrane himself.

Years later, on the eve of Waterloo, the Duke of Wellington observed that the rank-and-file of his volunteer army had 'enlisted for drink'. A large part of the British Navy had not enlisted at all, of course, but had been forcibly conscripted. It is, nevertheless, appropriate to consider here some of the rewards and incentives which then existed, and which – even if they were altogether insufficient to crew the Navy with volunteers – did at least encourage about one-third of other ranks and all 'young gentlemen' potential officers to serve their king afloat. Among these, as in all wars, the quest for excitement, genuine patriotism and – not least – the simple requirement to earn a living played their parts. Not all our special frigate captains were captivated from childhood by the idea of going to sea, but the lure of the sea was a genuine force among many 'young gentlemen'. And in spite of all those hardships, dangers and even horrors which have already been detailed, the majority of *them*, at least, came to love the life, and desire no other. If life could be (indeed, *was*) hell under a bad captain, under a good one it could be happy: William Hoste's good war certainly began so under Captain Nelson, and Nelson's example made Captain Hoste's ships happy ones.

One thing that did not attract anyone to the King's service, either ashore or afloat, would-be officer or other rank, was pay, even with the immediate prospect of some sort of bounty on enlistment. Successive governments in both peace and war had been dedicated, with full support in Parliament, to maintaining the Navy on rates of pay far inferior to those in the merchant service. These, as has been mentioned in the context of the Great Mutiny, had remained unchanged since the seventeenth century, and were among the mutineers' (or strikers', rather) main grievances. Even after they had been adjusted then, an able seaman received only £20 2s a year (before stoppages, £1. 13. 6d every month), usually in arrears, and often disgracefully so. Ordinary seamen and some others got even less, including boy volunteers, who had actually received nothing at all at the start of the war. The emolument of the middle non-commissioned ranks varied somewhat, according to the rate of their vessel, quite substantially in relation to each other, but in niggardly fashion overall, few being paid more than £30 a year, and many much less. Perhaps the only advantage they had over their opposite numbers in the Army was that they had fewer opportunities to spend what little they got.

Those fledgling half-officers-and-gentlemen, the aspiring midshipmen, fared just as badly – or, indeed, worse if they had to keep up appearances on the quarterdeck without any pocket money from home for the captain to dole out to them. Even fully fledged officers, the lieutenants, had to make do with little over £100 a year at the lowest grade, and not much more at the highest – at least after the Government's wicked new income tax had been deducted (which at that rate of pay was only just under the outrageous maximum of 10 per cent).

If junior officers who depended on their pay were always poor, however, the rewards of command obeyed logarithmic rules. Sloop 'acting-captains' and post-captains of the smallest (Sixth Rate) frigates just about doubled their lieutenants' pay, with the scale then rising rate-by-rate, through £283 for the captain of a standard 74-gun Third to £386 for a First Rate. And to this, various expenses and allowances were added, which in practice could add between £25 and £50 at the bottom and could virtually double the income of the captain of a First Rate if an admiral was aboard her. And, of course, every captain knew that if he lived long enough he must become an admiral, and that if he was then fortunate enough to fly his flag at sea his starting rate (without expenses and allowances) would be over £600, rising to a maximum of £1,820 (with even more generous extras).

In modern money, allowing an inflation multiplier of perhaps 100, this sounds a substantial reward until it is set against the £5,000 which the captain of a fat East Indiaman might clear on a single round trip with all his opportunities for making money on the side. But it is far from the whole story, because any of the captains in the preceding paragraph *could* become a millionaire (in modern money) on a single voyage if he was lucky – and most particularly if he was a frigate captain on detached duty; and every admiral in command of a station *expected* to come home even richer than his luckiest captains, in whose successes he automatically shared.

The source of this enrichment, which provided by far the greatest single financial inducement for any man to serve King George (however illusory it might prove for so many in practice) was prize-money, the formalised and legitimised descendant of the legendary semi-piracies of Francis Drake and Henry Morgan: in law, every enemy ship and its contents taken by the King's navy in war belonged to the King, but the King had graciously (and wisely) surrendered all of this loot to his loyal navy, to be divided up according to Admiralty custom and regulation.

Just as everyone knew about the press gang, so everyone knew about prize-money. But to help them remember in Nelson's 'age of glory' and in the hope of luring simpletons to volunteer in order to make their fortunes, dozens of posters advertised it in every town and city, issued by newly appointed captains at their own cost. Cochrane in January 1805 was no exception to this rule, and his poster provides an eloquent example of all captains' first headache, the acquisition of a crew. Hornblower, in the same boat a few years later, reflected that unlike 'dashing frigate captains' he could not advertise actual figures of prize-money won on previous voyages. Cochrane's problem (though it was thereafter never to be a problem for him again) was that his *Speedy* exploits had been forgotten, and he first had to inform his public that he had not been 'drowned in the *Arab* as reported', and was now commanding 'the flying *PALLAS*. . . of 36 guns. . . a new and uncommonly fine Frigate. Built on purpose. And ready for an EXPEDITION, as soon as some more good Hands are on board' (which, being translated, meant that the flying *Pallas* was as short of men as every other newly commissioned ship).

But all that was a mere postscript to the important message at the top of the poster, after 'GOD save the KING: Doubloons. . . Spanish Dollar Bag (consigned to Boney)':

My LADS,
The rest of the GALLEONS with the TREASURE from LA PLATA, are awaiting half loaded at CARTAGENA, for the arrival of those from PERU at PANAMA, as soon as that takes place, they are to sail from PORTOVELLO, to take on the rest of their Cargo, with Provisions and Water for the voyage to EUROPE. They stay at PORTOVELLO a few day only. Such a Chance will never occur again.

The burden of the poster is plain enough, even before Cochrane added, with a real touch of class, that he only wanted 'SEAMEN, or Stout Hands' able while carrying 'an hundred weight of PEWTER' (gold and/or silver) 'to run without stopping, at least three Miles'; and then, in a final challenge to the patriotism and impudence of 'British Seamen', 'BONEY'S CORONATION' (General Bonaparte was about to crown himself Emperor of the French) 'Is postponed for want of COBBS' (Spanish pieces of eight).

This moving appeal, which failed abysmally because Cochrane then had no better track-record than Hornblower when he appealed to all 'Hearts of Oak' to join him in the *Sutherland*, offering them 'a Hatful of Golden Louis d'or for PRIZE MONEY', exemplified the beginning and the end of the attraction of prize-money, which – at least for those who succumbed to such advertising – began with promises and fed on hope derived from the tales of the great jackpot windfalls, some of which were true but none of which lost anything in the telling.

Still, this story is part of that telling. And if few ordinary Hearts of

Oak made their fortunes from prize money, or kept what they had made, or even lived to spend it, not a few frigate captains retired more enriched by their accumulated profits over many years of war than from their pay, who had gone to sea as poor midshipmen or 'captain's servants'. Cochrane was one of those who got rich quickly. Pellew, more slowly rewarded, probably made a much greater fortune than he ever admitted from his years as a flag-admiral. Even Hornblower did not do so badly from his *Sutherland* cruise (from which few of his men survived to take their paltry shares), netting some £3,000. But for rather special bad luck, Hoste would have retired rich, rather than merely well-to-do. Broke (as we shall eventually see) was a special case, retiring richer in honour and fame than cash money. But few captains relinquished their frigate commands empty-handed, even apart from Jane Austen's Captain Wentworth, who won Anne Elliot's hand in the end as an additional prize of his frigate-captaincy.

Captains (and, of course, admirals) were better placed to make their fortunes because of the division of the spoils. Before the rules were slightly adjusted in 1808, the captain's share of their ship's share (which was proportionate to the number of ships in view at the time of the capture) was three-eighths of the total. But even when one from those three-eighths had been subtracted as their commanding admiral's share, that still left him with a full quarter. So taking the average knock-down value of a foreign frigate which was not too badly damaged to be bought by the Navy at £16,000 – and during the war some 132 of them were purchased – a single-ship victory might net a British frigate captain £4,000 (maybe £400,000 today?), while leaving his country with a similar profit, since the cost of a new British frigate was around £20,000.

Of all the remaining eighths, one was divided among the more senior officers (lieutenants, captains of marines, masters and, surprisingly, physicians), another going to marine lieutenants and other 'principal persons' (senior warrant officers, masters' mates and the like, including the apparently less important chaplain). After another eighth share had gone to these principal persons' immediate inferiors –midshipmen, marine sergeants and inferior warrant-officers – the final quarter was split between the rest of the crew equally.

Such a sub-division did not go unremarked on the lower deck. A famous cartoon of the Trafalgar period pictures a sailor on his knees, hands clasped in prayer. 'Why, Starboard!' cries an officer. 'How is this, at prayers, when the enemy is bearing down on us? Are you afraid of them?' 'Afraid?' replies Starboard. 'No! I was only praying that the enemy's shot may be distributed in the same proportion as the prize money, the greatest part among the Officers.'

There is, nevertheless, a certain injustice in that. For, in the first place, the enemy's shot *was* more concentrated on the open and unprotected quarterdeck, which was particularly the target of French sharpshooters (as Nelson ought to have known). And anyway, much was given to those from whom much was expected, and who worried most and had most to lose. It was the captain, not the crew, who faced automatic court martial for the loss of his ship for any cause, and dismissal and disgrace if his sword on the court martial table pointed towards him at the last. And, anyway, it was the captain who paid the bills if his prize-taking turned out to be unwise, involving him in endless litigation with angry neutrals (or litigious half-neutrals). 'Stout hands' who could run three miles carrying a hundredweight of pewter were always in short supply, and would never be without employment in this war, whether or not they wanted to serve. But young captains wanting ships were ten-a-penny, posted or unposted, with the threat of fishery patrol off the Orkneys, if not unemployment, always hanging over them if they got it wrong, never mind shipwreck or defeat. Hugh Pigot cracked under this strain and Cochrane became increasingly awkward because of the different pressures the system imposed on him. Who shall say that a captain's share of prize-money was greater than his responsibilities, compared with those of the ship's physician and her chaplain, or her powder-monkeys?

One downside of this, of course, was that the temptation to amass prize-money could distort duty. The presence of frigates in lucrative waters (especially when commanded by very successful or favoured captains) was on occasion the result of avaricious admirals, if not because they just happened to be off-course (or, as in the case of Captain Cochrane and the *Pallas* now, added an extra week or two to their patrols). But there were other captains – like Broke and Hornblower – who were poor *and* despised profit. And, anyway, there were enough true stories of unsullied good fortune to dignify prize-money: the capture of the (different) Spanish *Hermione* not only rewarded Pellew's Captain Pownoll with £65,000 *after* his admiral had had his share, but had made his officers and warrant officers rich men while paying every one of his 'Starboards' a record £485. But before any more of such tales, other naval perks merit consideration, not least that one designed to encourage captains and their crews to do their first and foremost duty, which was to eliminate enemy fighting fleets, rather than line their pockets most easily with the proceeds of merchant ship captures. By the late eighteenth century this had been compounded into head-money, paid at the rate of £5 per caput for every man in any warship they destroyed. However, as simple multiplication soon reveals, this was still no great incentive, compared with their *taking* the enemy vessel or some enemy merchant ship bulging with valuable cargo. Thus, the profits of battle, whether Nelson's Trafalgar (shared by the whole of his fleet, with few prizes actually surviving) or Hornblower's final bloody fight with the *Natividad* (sunk; although he would probably have had to return it to the Spaniards anyway), tended to be small indeed, compared with a single-ship prize-taking cruise, either of the Pellew or – most of all – the Cochrane variety.

Much more profitable (but much less publicised, for obvious reasons which will emerge) was 'freight-money'. Simply, this developed because when it came to moving small, but very valuable, cargo the safest way of doing it, and the fastest, was inside one of His Britannic Majesty's armed ships. Of course, this was how governments usually moved their own money, from the United States' delivery of tribute to the Barbary States of North Africa in the 1790s to the transfer of Russian gold in HMS *Edinburgh* (an equivalent of a heavy frigate of the latest type, relatively) on the Murmansk run, with such disastrous and contentious results when she was sunk during the 1939–45 war. In the great French wars of the eighteenth and early nineteenth centuries, private individuals and companies also hired the Navy for such work, to the great profit of the captains and admirals involved, on a strictly private custom-and-practice basis of percentages. This, as with so many of our diversions, is actually a subject in itself, which both naval and legal historians may enjoy exploring further, as it developed both before and after our particular French wars. Suffice it to say here, however, that our good old 'control', Pellew, complained, as C-in-C in East Indian waters long after his happier and less complicated frigate-captain days, that a small adjustment in his admiral's percentage-cut had reduced his annual share by some £2,000. Still, like Cochrane's old flag-officer enemy, Admiral Lord Keith, he split tens of thousands of pounds of it with his captains during every year of his command without lifting a finger. Even, at the very lowest level, one of the reasons why the court martial of Lieutenant (Commander) Lord Cochrane, after his heroic loss of the *Speedy*, was so quickly and happily concluded was because he was at the time illegally carrying valuable commercial mail with his flag-officers' unofficial agreement.

For better or worse, prize-money, head-money and freight-money were important parts of the incentives of Nelson's navy. Sometimes the resultant stories are cautionary, if not actually disgraceful. Cochrane, for example, must have expected a substantial windfall after he took the *El Gamo* frigate, while his handful of men would have also been looking to receive big dividends from their madness, with a frigate pay-out dividend among so few. Perhaps because Cochrane was unpopular, however, the *El Gamo* was sold cheaply as a merchant ship, to be encountered next by him and his men in a Barbary Coast port, under the Algerian flag; and, once in the egregious hands of prize agents (as opposed to admiralty ones appointed by local flag-officers if the Navy was interested in the prize) such profits might be so swallowed up by high charges that some unfortunate officers came away *owing* money to the middle-men.

It was a snakes-and-ladders game, in which other men's ladders to fortune were always better-remembered by everyone, as they drowned their sorrows, than the snakes, which were inevitably dismissed as the *mis*fortunes of war, which all fighting men expect as their lot. Fortunes were famously won and lost through recaptures: one junior lieutenant (with his £100 a year, no more) heard his captain mourn the loss of £40,000, when a prize was lost. But then he had just taken another ship, worth almost £10,000, from which the same young officer himself was looking to receive at least one hundred guineas, if not his originally hoped-for £800. After that famous other *Hermione* capture, each lieutenant's share had been £13,000; and after the capture of the *Santa Brigida* and the *Thetis*, over £5,000. And perhaps the lower deck also talked of Hornblower's coxswain, who qualified for his deck's whole share of £400 (£40,000?) after the recapture of the *Witch of Endor*, far outdoing the warrant officers' £242 shares at the capture of the ports of Banda and Amboyna, which netted Pellew's predecessor, Admiral Rainier, £28,000. All of which was good for recruiting.

But Cochrane was now to do even better, during his short *Pallas* cruise. With the vagaries of wind and weather, orders could rarely be precisely obeyed to the week, never mind the day, and captains often took any opportunities for independent action chance gave them, both to prolong their activities and to stray into more promising areas. For one of the attractions of single-ship operations was that prize-money did not have to be shared (except with the flag-officer, of course), as it did if any other naval ship was in sight. Even Hornblower, arriving early at a rendezvous in the *Sutherland*, seized the chance of a few days' private enterprise (albeit in his case for the good of the country, naturally). Exceptionally, as we shall see once again in the story of Philip Broke, a good captain might be prepared to forego what he had not earned. But that was the exception which Pellew's experiences have already shown. And his *Indefatigable* profits would usually have been considerably reduced by the presence of the other ships of the Inshore Squadron cruising with him.

No such constraints worried Cochrane in the *Pallas* during his ten-week cruise which he lengthened to three months in 1805. 'Such a Chance will never occur again', he had guessed in his recruiting poster, and for him, in spite of all the glory he was to win in the next four years, it never did. But those months were enough effectively to solve all his financial problems, netting him an estimated £75,000, the equivalent of (say) hardly less than several million pounds in modern money, or (more precisely) rather more than two hundred times the annual pay of a captain of a Fifth Rate frigate.

Not that this golden voyage was to end without high drama. For, just as the *Pallas* was about to set sail for home, loaded down with plunder and with her crew reduced by the detachment of the men who were taking her prizes back to Plymouth, she was bounced out of the morning mist off the Azores by three French ships-of-the-line. Once again, as in the *Speedy*, Cochrane had been ambushed by greater unrelated naval operations, for these French ships were one of those many small squadrons which had been ordered to break out from wherever they were, to rendezvous on the other side of the Atlantic, off Martinique, as part of the plan to invade Britain. Admiral Villeneuve himself, at that very moment, was escaping from Toulon in what became the indecisive-decisive first phase of the 1805 campaign at sea, which was to end so decisively seven months later at Trafalgar. Meanwhile, Cochrane was again facing death or capture, only this time with his ship loaded with loot. For the *Pallas*, although far more powerful than the *Speedy*, was still immeasurably inferior in broadside to any ship-of-the-line. And although she was also a frigate, with a frigate's turn of speed, she was up against French-built ships-of-the-line which were actually faster than she was, so that during the ensuing day-long chase they were able to overhaul him, one on each side, within easy range.

Providentially, however, a storm had risen during the chase, so that (as with Pellew and the *Droits de l'Homme*) the big ships were unable to open their main-deck gunports to blow the *Pallas* apart; and by suddenly reducing speed (an old trick which a well-drilled crew could manage far more quickly than a lubberly one and which had also saved Hornblower, in the little *Hotspur*, from the *Loire* frigate in the approaches to Brest), Cochrane caused them to overrun him, thereby escaping them until darkness fell; after which they followed his stern-light in the night, only to discover at dawn that they had been sailing in pursuit of a barrel bobbing in the sea, carefully weighted to give them glimpses of the lantern fastened on top of it. As with music-hall jokes, so with naval subterfuges: the old ones, recycled, were still often the best ones.

So Cochrane returned in triumph to Plymouth with his three big golden candlesticks lashed to his masts. And if that typically Cochrane flashiness offended the more respectable and fastidious (most notably, one may confide, St Vincent himself) it was no less the sort of showmanship which established him as one of those dashing frigate captains under whom sailors might actually want to serve – and all the more so when he was to gain a reputation also for not getting them killed when he led them. He was on the way now to that ultimate accolade of being a hero to the generations of British boys who would be the readers of the novels of Captain Marryat and G.A. Henty, who had no need to gild the facts to make him 'Cochrane the Dauntless'.

Unfortunately, however, his brilliance and luck as a ship-captain in the face of his country's enemies was equalled by his bad luck and lack of judgement when ashore among his own countrymen. First came the bad luck, when his patron, the First Lord of the Admiralty (now Lord Melville), was overtaken by the priorities and hatreds of British politics, which had earlier toppled St Vincent to the young captain's advantage. As the great friend of Pitt, Melville was a target for all Pitt's many foes, and a committee of naval inquiry which had been nosing into certain inevitably smelly aspects of past naval administration came up with improprieties which dated back to his tenure (as Henry Dundas) of the post of Treasurer of the Navy back in the 1780s. In fact, careless and convivial as he was, he had been no more than negligent in the eighteenth-century style in administering a system wide-open to abuse. But the anti-Pitt committee had no more mercy on him than Pitt's followers had had on St Vincent for unwisely trying to reform the dockyards. With tears running down his face (which his friends shielded from his enemies' views by crowding round him) Pitt was now forced to ruin his friend's political career to save him from actual impeachment.

This political drama, which began in April 1805, not only removed the only good friend Cochrane had in both the Admiralty and the Establishment, but also must finally have driven him into disaffected opposition to both just when he might have either been brought safely 'inside', or at least so usefully and busily employed afloat that his energies would have been fully expended against his country's enemies. Indeed, without Melville to protect him he was at once ensnared by the pettifogging clauses in the small print of the prize laws, which so often sowed dissension between naval officers. As a result his final share (*c.* £75,000 nevertheless) was arrived at only after a slice of it had been handed over to his nominal flag-officer in Plymouth, Admiral Sir William Young, on the purely technical ground that he had *copied out* Melville's direct Admiralty orders for the *Pallas* cruise.

In just what proportion all these events encouraged Cochrane to combine politics with his naval career must remain conjectural. No doubt his disreputable uncle and evil genius, Colonel Andrew Cochrane-Johnstone, played some part in the decision. For Cochrane-Johnstone, with an utterly deplorable West Indian career already behind him, was by then a Member of Parliament – appropriately representing the non-existent electors of Grampound, that most rotten of all rotten boroughs, which he had purchased in the open market because parliamentary seats brought with them immunity from prosecution for debt. (Grampound was, indeed, so obviously indefensible that it was abolished even before the Reform Bill of 1832.) Yet, ironically, even while he was associated with his blackguardly uncle, young Captain Cochrane was no less inspired by that great enemy of the corruption and dishonesty of the age, William Cobbett (1763–1835). For Cobbett, the one-time farmer's boy, solicitor's clerk and sergeant-major of the 54th Regiment whose new career as a reforming political journalist had just taken off, had appealed for an honest man to contest the (fairly rotten) borough of Honiton, in Devon, where the standard tariff for votes was five guineas each.

Therefore, after having obtained leave-of-absence from the grateful Admiral Young (whom he had enriched), Cochrane spent the late spring of 1805 contesting Honiton, before taking up the dull convoy duties to which he and the *Pallas* had now been sentenced for the rest of that year, when he would have been more safely employed hunting the French.

That year, indeed: 1805.

In that year the French fleet had been chased back and forwards across the Atlantic, had been slightly blooded, and would be at sea again, in company with the Spanish fleet in that autumn. Pellew, now an admiral, had sailed away to take up his East Indies command. The at-last-promoted Captain Horatio Hornblower, still virtually without 'interest' never mind a ship, was engaged in cloak-and-dagger work. Captain Philip Broke, also uninfluential, had finally been appointed to the elderly *Druid* frigate after four unemployed years, and was patrolling from the Channel to the Irish coast, unspectacularly. More happily, Captain William Hoste, two years Broke's junior on the List but Nelson's protégé, was to graduate from the elderly *Eurydice* frigate to his patron's own favourite, the crack 36-gun *Amphion*, on 13 October.

Hugh Pigot, of course, was long-dead, and better forgotten. But the battle of Trafalgar was then about to be fought, and the Emperor Napoleon was busy conquering all Western Europe.

CHAPTER TEN

The rise and fall of the captain of the Impérieuse

Cochrane lost the First Battle of Honiton, not because he was a naval officer up against politicians, or even because he stood as an independent reformer against the Government candidate, but because he refused to pay five guineas in advance to any of the handful of electors who would otherwise have been perfectly happy voting for a dashing hero in the war, against both Boney and the British Government.

Certainly, no one thought any the worse of him for temporarily abandoning his duties at a time of national crisis in order to play politics: politics was – and had long been – a perfectly respectable game for serving naval officers. Control of the Navy had passed from the Crown to Paliament at the beginning of the eighteenth century. If politicians in those corrupt days were to play at being admirals, it was perhaps not a wholly bad thing that admirals and captains should become politicians in both the Lords and the Commons. Even if they failed to act as a sailors' pressure group in the matter of pay until almost too late, they knew more about the sea than the dominant rural squirearchy, although as a malignant result political interest in the Navy then all too often worked more strongly against pure professional merit.

Still, there it was, the naval-political connection, as exemplified not least by the career of that meritorious officer, Edward Pellew, who was by the turn of the century a loyal follower of old St Vincent, and who was therefore more-or-less put up in that role in the hotly-contested Barnstaple election of 1802. The then unpopular First Lord needed all

Frigate versus frigate: Captain Pellew, in the *Nymphe*, makes short work of the French *Cleopatre* in the first decisive single-ship action of the war, on 19 July 1793, thereby reassuring the British Admiralty and public that the French revolutionary navy is not as fearsome as the French revolutionary armies which are stunning Europe. This engraving of a Nicholas Pocock painting nicely mixes accuracy with artist's licence: the crippled French ship did finally collide with the *Nymphe*, but there was no boarding-attack (hardly any Frenchmen were alive on the upper deck by then), and the fight took place out of sight of land.

Brig versus frigate: the bows of "Captain" (by courtesy, not in rank) Lord Cochrane's ridiculous little *Speedy* are barely visible beneath the *El Gamo*'s stern as his handful of men storm the Spanish ship. This is hardly one of Nicholas Pocock's best naval pictures, with its poorly-placed *Speedy* and inaccurate millpond sea. But at least the shot-holes in *El Gamo*'s lower sails are right: Cochrane's 4-pounders were by then firing at maximum elevation, upwards through the deck of the enemy, who could not depress his far heavier guns in response.

Frigates versus ship-of-the-line: the *Indefatigable* and the *Amazon* begin their harrying-to-the-death of the 80-gun *Droits de l'Homme*. Much of the battle took place in almost total darkness, on occasion with near-collisions. But the stormy conditions which prevented the French ship from using her main battery tell the story well enough; although Pellew's gun-crews were little better off, "up to their middles in Water" and with their guns breaking loose time and again.

Frigates versus battle-fleet: the morning after the night before during the Basque Roads action. After Captain Lord Cochrane's destruction of the defensive boom with an explosive vessel during the night and the break-in of his fireships, the majority of the French fleet are either helplessly grounded or actually ashore. But now triumph is turning into tragedy for Cochrane as Admiral Gambier fails to rise to the occasion, fearing to lose his fleet in the same way.

LEFT: The evolution of French frigate-design and the superiority of British crews were illustrated in the capture of the French *Forte* by the ex-French *Sybille* in the Bay of Bengal in 1799. Displacing nearly 1400 tons and mounting 30 24-pounders in a total of 52 guns, the *Forte* was actually a second-generation improvement on the 1000-ton *Sybille*, an 18-pounder frigate rated 38 by her new owners, although actually carrying 44 guns. But British ship-handling, training and gunnery were such that she battered the French ship into submission in an hour and forty minutes, for the loss of her captain and 21 men. The French lost their captain and 172 men, nearly half their effective strength. (From an engraving by C. Tiebut after a painting by T. Birch.)

Captain Lord Cochrane strikes a characteristically Napoleonic pose, which may have pleased h
Westminster parliamentary constituents in 1807 (from the engraving after P. H. Stroehling, b
probably further irritated all his many enemies in the Admiralty and in politics. But the background is right: Cochrane's ships had a permanent smell of victorious battle. It was only on lan
and then only on his own soil – that he came to grief . . . at least, until the days of Queen Victo
and Prince Albert, anyway.

John Jervis, first Earl of St Vincent (1735–1823): not only the victor of the battle off Cape St Vincent and Nelson's commander and friend, but also the main architect of the navy which Nelson led to victory. However, in our story, although he was the navy's greatest adversary of corruption, indiscipline and unmeritorious promotion, he hated Scotsmen in general irrationally, and Lord Cochrane among them (but perhaps not so irrationally) in particular: tragically for the navy, Admiral Lord St Vincent and Captain Lord Cochrane were chalk and cheese.

Bravery is not enough: that British captains were brave could be taken for granted. But, then, so were French captains brave too, and frequently to the death – and those of all the other navies at the receiving-end, from Spanish and Dutch to American ("Don't give up the ship!" Lawrence of the *Chesapeake* died shouting). So Captain Nesbit Josiah Willoughby was brave as a lion – and, as "The Immortal", survived not only innumerable wounds but also Napoleon's retreat from Moscow. Only, that was not enough to make him a great frigate captain.

How not to fight a frigate battle: of the four British frigates attacking a more powerful French frigate squadron in the difficult Grand Port anchorage in Mauritius, only the over-confident Captain Nesbit Josiah Willoughby's *Néréide* is in position (left), where she will be battered to pieces. The *Iphigenia* (centre) is too far away to help, but she will not escape either. The *Sirius* and the *Magicienne*, also incompetently navigated, never even get into the picture: they are already helplessly aground and will be burnt. And worse is to come outside before the main British invasion fleet arrives. (Drawing by N. Ozane.)

the help in the Commons he could organise, and at considerable financial cost Pellew secured one of the two seats on offer, with 166 votes out of a total of 585 cast for the four candidates. At the same time, Nelson's beloved Thomas Troubridge and St Vincent's cousin, Thomas Jervis, together with another of St Vincent's followers, Captain John Markham, came in from other constituencies. And how 'interest' worked was then once again illustrated by Pellew's expectation of a reward for his loyalty: he was near the top of the List and had already set his sights on his flag, and the lucrative East Indies command, both of which he eventually received. Meanwhile, of course, all the greater events of 1805 were taking place, which were to dictate much of the wider course of the war for years to come.

Popular British histories of the years 1793–1815 are dominated by the war at sea up to Trafalgar in 1805, and then by the war on land afterwards, as the Duke of Wellington replaces Nelson as the nation's hero. This, however, leaves something of a gap between Nelson's death and the future Duke's arrival in the Spanish Peninsula (just as, in the Second World War, there seems to be a gap between the Fall of France and the Battle of Britain in 1940 and the eventual arrival of Russia, the United States and Japan in the war during 1941).

If great naval battles are allowed to dominate naval history, this is fair enough. For there were no great naval battles during the last ten years of the last French war. Indeed, for the British Navy there were no great battles at all for the next century, if one excludes shore bombardments like the Algiers 'battle' of Admiral Lord Exmouth (formerly Edward Pellew) in 1816 and the Allied massacre of the Turkish Fleet at Navarino in 1826. Up until the outbreak of the next world war in 1914 the world's most powerful navy was to be an interested onlooker at other countries' battles, in which the Austrians, the Americans and the Japanese were to demonstrate the changes which steam power, iron and steel and rifled breech-loading guns were imposing on naval tactics, at the expense of the Italians, Spaniards, Chinese and Russians. And as for that long saga of Anglo-French naval confrontations, the next time a British fleet was to open fire on a French one was to be even further in the future and very tragically, in the pre-emptive strike at Oran in 1940.

Nevertheless, it was during the ten years *after* Trafalgar that Britain's maximum naval effort in the age of sail occurred. To enlist statistics once more, the number of men voted for the Navy (which had risen from 16,000 to 130,000 between 1792 and 1802) had quickly fallen to 50,000 in 1803–4, thereby filling every port with unemployed sailors and desperate half-pay officers (Broke and Cochrane were both unemployed, and Hornblower was forced to live by his wits, near starvation). But by 1805 the total was back to 120,000, rising through the 130,000 mark by 1807 to a peak of some 145,000 – with a 20 per cent increase in ships, to over 1,000 – for the years 1810–14.

The strains which this 'maximum effort' placed on the Navy even during a period of almost unbroken victory were enormous, with the constant drain of manpower due to accident, disease, shipwreck, enemy action (least of all) and desertion (most of all). Yet this was merely the price of exercising and capitalising on the supremacy at sea which had been finally won in the Trafalgar period, as the Navy countered every attempt by Napoleon to turn the tables. For he continued to build dozens of fine warships, with all the shipyards and resources of Europe at his disposal. And even more dangerously, he was to resort to the weapon of economic warfare.

More immediately, however, while the British Navy was sweeping up the last remnants of the Franco-Spanish Trafalgar fleet and mourning Nelson, Napoleon himself was busy smashing the latest of the Continental coalitions which his ambition and British gold had lined up against him. At the very height of his amazing powers, he had been unable to cross the Straits of Dover, but no power on land could long withstand him. Even before the sound of British church-bells celebrating Trafalgar and tolling for Nelson had died away, he had disposed of Austria at Austerlitz. At Jena and Auerstadt he humbled the once-mighty Prussian war machine so that it never rose again in its old form. And finally, in 1807, he brought Imperial Russia to a standstill at Friedland, then going on to divide Europe (at least temporarily) into spheres of French and Russian influence at the Peace of Tilsit.

Great Britain was once more at bay. For although (just as in 1940) one of her fighting services had saved her for the time being, she was not only far too weak militarily then to take on her great enemy on land, but there was also not the slightest prospect that she could ever field an army big enough to do so, unaided. Implacable she remained, with every bit of the rest of the world that had a coastline at her mercy. But without powerful land allies she was powerless against Napoleon and his great armies in Europe, and was condemned to wait for Something to Turn Up, fighting to survive until her enemy came to her aid by making some mistake.

In the end, of course, something did turn up, in the rather unlikely form of Spain, where Napoleon contrived to rouse a nation whose hatred of foreign domination and consequent resistance to him was greater than its habitual military incompetence. And in Spain the British were to be doubly lucky. For, after one overwhelming Personal Appearance (which resulted in the speedy evacuation of Sir John Moore's battered little army from Corunna, by courtesy of the all-powerful Royal Navy), the Emperor always found more important things to do than to settle accounts personally with Moore's successor and the next British Expeditionary Force the Navy delivered to the Peninsula.

But that, in the aftermath of Trafalgar, Austerlitz and Jena, still lay in the future. Meanwhile, Napoleon still had other battles to win, and France and Europe to reorganise, while the British Navy went about its accustomed business of gripping the coasts of the whole world in its blockade, with the enthusiastic aid of all our young frigate captains.

In the case of Captain Lord Cochrane, this at last brought him to duties for which he was ideally suited, in the course of which he was not only to prove himself an incomparable frigate captain but also the finest exponent of post-Trafalgar naval operations.

As regards the acquisition of prize-money, while the first voyage of the *Pallas* deserves its place in the record books, Cochrane was still only one of a number of captains who combined luck with ability and judgement. Even in the matter of ship-duels, while the *Speedy–El Gamo* fight must have a special place, there were innumerable other great fights and daring actions which merit special mention, in which the true odds were equally daunting, from the wrecking of the *Droits de l'Homme*, through the recovery of the *Hermione* and the sinking of the *Natividad*, to the as-yet-untold final duels in this book, among a host of others. As a gallant captain and a fine seaman, Cochrane was only one among many, not a few of whom died poor and unsung.

As a fighting admiral, Nelson obviously reigns supreme. And although Cochrane (and, indeed, all our frigate captains) never had a chance to demonstrate how he might have led a great fleet 'on campaign' and into a fleet battle, it seems unlikely that he would have inspired that peculiar affection bordering on love which Nelson did among his captains, even when they disapproved of some of his actions and (more often) his personal behaviour. That over-worked word charisma exactly describes what Nelson had in full measure, which exerted its force throughout every ship and every fleet he commanded, equally on their quarterdecks and below deck. That Cochrane had a touch of this magic too can hardly be doubted: the performance of his crews suggests it, anyway – as does the testimony of Midshipman (future Captain) Marryat, who served under him. But *under* Cochrane was perhaps the best place to serve, one may equally suspect.

When it comes to land operations, particularly combined operations of the commando type, Nelson's record is not so laurel-wreathed. As a very young captain – 'a light-haired boy' – he had performed competently in the appalling conditions of Central America during the American War, and certainly did not disgrace himself in the Corsican operations of 1794 (during which he lost his eye). But his inshore operations at Cadiz and Santa Cruz in 1797 proved to be messy affairs, and the assault on Tenerife ended in disaster, in which one of the Navy's great heroes, Captain Richard Bowen, was killed, and Nelson himself lost his arm and nearly his life. And, finally, nothing very spectacular emerged from his operations against the French invasion flotillas at Boulogne later on.

It is unfair to conjecture that things would have gone better *if* a certain arrogant young Scottish captain had been in charge of any of these operations (or, for that matter, that equally meticulous planner of land–sea operation, Edward Pellew; or even – by adjusting their ages and ranks – if either of those other two talented combined operations officers, Hornblower and Hoste, had been present. All that is certain is that Captain Cochrane, having survived near-shipwreck off the Canadian coast (due to corrupt dockyard work in England which rendered the *Pallas*'s compass unreliable) was at least transferred from dull convoy duty at the end of 1805, to be let loose on the French Biscayan coast as part of Admiral Edward Thornborough's inshore blockading squadron.

Forethought was a hallmark of Cochrane's operations, and he actually arrived on his new station complete with a fast little galley which he had designed himself and had had built at his own cost. With this and the *Pallas* he now proceeded to cause trouble and loss to the enemy all the way from the splendid beaches of Les Sables d'Orlonne (which are the favourites of today's French holiday-makers) to the Gironde estuary. Merchant shipping was carried off, or driven ashore and then burnt by landing parties; a corvette guarding the approaches to Bordeaux was cut out by boarding, and several of her sister-ships which threatened the *Pallas* (undermanned as usual, in the absence of boarding parties and prize crews) were first outsmarted and then themselves driven ashore; a French frigate was rammed and left disabled and aground; a French signal station on the Isle of Re, near the naval base of Rochefort, was destroyed after marines (led, naturally, by Cochrane himself) had frightened off the local militia. And British casualties in all these operations were negligible – another Cochrane hallmark.

This whirlwind mini-campaign brought Cochrane's name to the attention of Napoleon for the first time, but also to the attention of an unforgiving Admiralty. Unfortunately, in spite of Admiral Thornborough's approving reports (he got his flag-officer's share of the prize-money, of course), this additional fame in no way melted old St Vincent's heart. So, while some lip-service had to be paid to these daring exploits, their architect remained for those in power what he had always been – variously 'proud', 'wrong-headed', 'violent', 'mad', 'not truth-telling', 'money-getting' and generally 'not to be trusted out of sight' ('Scotch' was presumably to be taken for granted).

To be fair to St Vincent he was just as great a hater of corruption in the navy, of young nobility and incompetence unjustifiably promoted, and of anything else which in his opinion harmed his beloved service. Nevertheless, his and the naval establishment's continued failure to recognise and use Cochrane's talents to the full was not only a crime but a blunder. It was a crime because, given greater force and a reasonably free hand, Cochrane would have done even more damage to the enemy, and would have tied down thousands of troops. But it was a blunder because, as soon as his energies were not fully extended in that direction, he once more turned his attention to politics, not only to the establishment's eventual embarrassment, but also in the end to his ruin and his country's loss.

As it was, cold-shouldered by the Admiralty (who once again failed to buy one of his most useful captures, the corvette *Tapageuse*), he now returned to contest Honiton once more in the general election which eventually followed the death of William Pitt.

The outcome of the second battle of Honiton was very different from the first not so much because he came back with fresh battle honours and an enthusiastic contingent of officers and men from the *Pallas* to help him campaign as because of a modest but ingenious investment he had made there after his defeat, when he had rewarded all those (few) honest electors who had spurned his opponent's five-guinea bribe with a gift of £10. The memory of his generosity now proved sufficiently vivid to swing the result his way in 1806 – only for the venal majority to discover that their new MP's already-stated principles prevented him from repeating such a gift, which had been a reward for honesty, not a bribe for the future.

It would be a mistake, nevertheless, to dismiss the second battle of Honiton as merely another example of Cochrane's cheek and ingenuity – or even a typical bitter Cochrane victory, when the outraged electors revenged themselves by running up huge bills for 'celebrations' which were to dog him for years afterwards. Unwise though he often was in his friendships, intemperate though he was in his reactions to injustice (real or supposed), and ill-judged and wrong-headed though he was to be in so much of his political behaviour, he was undoubtedly a man of principle, and a reformer by nature as well as from experience. For better or worse, also, he was the very antithesis of another of Dr Johnson's libellous characterisations of all Scotsmen – that they were as abject to those above them as insolent to those below. Rather, those who served under Cochrane could rely on his unfailing concern for their lives and their careers, as those in authority above him could rely on his arrogance and criticism. As the newly-elected Member for Honiton he very quickly made more powerful enemies by threatening the Admiralty on behalf of those gallant subordinates of his who had been denied promotion, not only the officer who had boarded and taken the *Tapageuse* but also his old first lieutenant in the *Speedy*, who was still not a master and commander as he deserved to have been after the capture of an enemy frigate five years before.

Still, all this did have one good result for Cochrane (in addition to the belated promotion of both of those meritorious junior officers): it finally convinced the Admiralty that he would be better employed at sea – and in a ship and on a station worthy of him and which he would accept, rather than be left to cause further trouble at home in Parliament.

On the face of it, the *Impérieuse* was a plum command: a big 38-gun, 1,046-ton ex-Spanish frigate, taken two years before and now with a 300-man crew ideal for his purposes (and, with his flying *Pallas* reputation, there would never be any need for posters and press gangs when he needed men). Also, for posterity, he now had young Frederick Marryat as one of his admiring midshipmen, to immortalise him in print.

However, although the *Impérieuse* was a fine ship, she was totally unready for service. But the Admiralty was so desperate to get Captain Cochrane safely away that to sea she none the less unsafely went, with her supply lighters still loading her and her guns not properly attached; and within less than a week she was scraping over the rocks off Ushant, a victim of the same dockyard corruption which had nearly destroyed the *Pallas* on her first voyage, because of the substitution of cheap iron for expensive copper round the compass binnacle.

For a man dedicated to the extirpation of naval corruption and incompetence, it was perhaps a fitting start to a mission (although the irony of St Vincent's dedication to the same cause a few years before, equally to his professional and political disadvantage, may have escaped him: sadly, neither of these two heroes appears to have been endowed with a sense of humour). And the *Impérieuse* nevertheless survived, albeit by an even narrower margin than had the *Pallas*; although this time also irritatingly for the Admiralty, who later had to reject Cochrane's demand for an inquiry into the mishap, which would have washed far too much dirty linen in public. So then she once again went to work – Cochrane's real work, which he had already perfected in the *Speedy* and the *Pallas*, and now demonstrated again along a coast which he knew like the back of his hand, from the future holiday-beaches of Les Sables d'Orlonne to the Gironde estuary and beyond, in the Bay of Biscay.

The result was even more spectacular: any French ships which dared to go to sea, both protective warships and the merchantmen which were still by far the cheapest way of shifting goods and supplies, were now at Cochrane-risk: if not taken, they were once again forced ashore; and even if beached and protected by shore-batteries and soldiers they were still not safe from the man whom Napoleon himself had described as a 'sea-wolf'. When ships were not available for the taking, there were still the forts which had been built to guard them to be attacked and destroyed. The Impérieuse, according to Midshipman Marryat, smelt permanently of battle.

It might have been better if Cochrane had now remained at sea. But hard-worked wooden ships were in constant need of repair – especially one which had scraped over the rocks off Ushant. So he returned just in time to take part in the next general election, with the latest turn of Great Britain's ramshackle wartime politics, which had now brought the so-called 'Ministry of All the Talents' down. But in this election, although as a previously-elected member he could not be denied leave of absence to take part in the campaign, a third battle in the corrupt borough of Honiton, which he had so recently held up to ridicule, was ruled out. Yet after what he himself had seen and experienced during his last cruise he was even more determined than before to pursue his campaign against naval corruption and incompetence. So he had to find another seat.

The system of representation by which members were elected to the House of Commons in the 'Mother of Parliaments' during this first world war was such that, viewed across two centuries, it is difficult to know whether to laugh or cry. There had been a time when, relatively observed, it had been the most advanced assembly of its kind – far superior, by the happy accidents of its historical development, than (say) its pathetic French equivalent, which had been reconstituted too late in 1789, and had then spawned bloody revolution in spite of its high principles. Now, with the scandal of the pocket boroughs (not only pocket-sized, but also in someone's pocket), never mind those famously rotten ones like Grampound and old Sarum (which were mere grassy mounds), the British parliamentary system had quite obviously been overtaken by the country's own revolution in which the population had been redistributed by the development of industry and commerce but was unrepresented. But, although demands for reform were increasing, another action-packed quarter of a century was to pass before those in power were at last compelled to accept change.

With his prize-money, Cochrane might conceivably have bought a seat somewhere (cash in advance by custom – and particularly with his past record). But his principles were against that, and he was now quite without any powerful patron who might have had influence, or even an actual seat in his gift. A popular hero he certainly was: with no soldier-heroes to catch the public imagination as Napoleon's marshals were doing on a dozen victorious European battlefields, the British adored their admirals and captains of that time, while dabbing away the odd tear in memory of the immortal Nelson, whose glamour rubbed off on all Hearts of Oak. But cheers were not votes, and it was

'the public' which was disenfranchised in the old unreformed House of
Commons. Except, that is, in the City of Westminster, in which
constituency that otherwise egregiously unrepresentative assembly
actually met.

Just as Grampound and Old Sarum were indefensible anomalies at
one extreme of the *1066 and All That* democratic joke which was
Parliament, so the City of Westminster was an anomaly at the other
extreme: *all* its ratepayers were entitled to vote, returning two
members to Parliament, and although those ratepayers were no better
individually than in any other constituency (Honiton included), there
happened to be far too many of them to bribe effectively for a certain
majority. Indeed, as it turned out, no less than 13,893 of them were to
vote in the coming general election (though, to be fair to psephologists
studying this phenomenon, that remarkable figure may be somewhat
inflated by those who were allowed to vote more than once at the end
of this election, when the result was no longer in doubt and Cochrane
had generously withdrawn his scrutineers so that the defeated
candidates might make a slightly better showing).

For the dashing captain – 'FRIEND OF REFORM' and 'The pride
of our coast' in the election songs of his partisans – did win one of the
two seats on offer with 3,708 votes, over 1,000 more than the
unsuccessful Government candidate, the playwright Richard Brinsley
Sheridan, who had previously been Treasurer of the Navy in the so-
called 'Ministry of All the Talents'.

It was a famous victory, considering that Cochrane had stood as an
Independent in a five-horse race, for Naval Reform and with even the
Radicals against him. Nevertheless, it was also another typical
Cochrane Pyrrhic victory, since he had not only humiliated the
government's (and the Admiralty's) candidate, Mr Sheridan, but
during his campaign had implicitly denounced both the Admiralty and
St Vincent himself for causing the loss of two blockading ships which
had become unseaworthy but had been kept at sea. That, it was widely
considered, was going too far: it was disloyal to the service and not the
action of a gentleman. In the naval corridors of power, from being a
nuisance Cochrane had become a menace.

Once back in Parliament, moreover, from the opposition benches
he returned to his themes of naval corruption and incompetence. But
the new Government, now led by the colourless but shrewd and brave
Mr Spencer Percival, had much more pressing matters to deal with.
Apart from its perennial domestic problems (Catholic emancipation,
the Irish Question, et cetera), it had to find some way in which to
continue the war when Napoleon was dictating terms to a prostrate
Europe. Compared with all that, Captain Lord Cochrane was a mere
irritant, no matter how the Admiralty felt about him. And, in any case,
the Admiralty could solve its Cochrane problem quite simply by

tempting him with another commission which would take him so far away that he would have to choose between fruitless political opposition or glory and prize money.

This solution came adrift somewhat when the still-admiring electors of Westminster gave their hero leave-of-absence, so that he would be able to return to the political fray in future. But it worked well enough in the main by removing Cochrane into the marvellous Tom Tiddler's ground of the Mediterranean (the Channel being out of the question, since St Vincent was still in command there). No frigate captain worthy of his salt could have resisted such an opportunity, and the *Impérieuse* was now ready for action again with her enthusiastic crew. So Cochrane went where he could do the most good and was much safer.

In fact he could with advantage have been sent even further afield. On land almost everywhere on the continent the French might be going from victory to victory, and from peace treaty to peace treaty in the wake of Napoleon's victories. But at sea the British were flexing their muscles from the Baltic (where they were to fight their old allies the Russians in 1808), via Portugal (whose Royal Family and navy they carried off under the noses of the invading French), to the Dardanelles (where they were rebuffed – and not for the last time – by their former allies, the Turks). Even further away, having earlier destroyed one of the French squadrons which inevitably broke out from time to time in the West Indies, and scattered two others, the Navy had also been busy recovering such earlier conquests as the Cape of Good Hope, and had much to do in the Indian Ocean. Additionally, between 1805 and 1808 the war with Spain dangled the chimera of rich and profitable South and Central American trade, if not actual conquest, when the French were making business very difficult in Europe. At this very moment (as will be explained in more detail later), Horatio Hornblower was being despatched in the *Lydia* to encourage one of the early liberation movements in an empire which was starting to slip from Spanish grasp at last; it would have been a smart move to have sent Cochrane instead of Hornblower in that direction.

Still, to the Mediterranean Cochrane was now sent, under the command of Nelson's 'dear Coll' of Trafalgar fame – Cuthbert, Admiral Lord Collingwood. And, with all the European coasts of that sea hostile but the Navy at last secure in its great new base at Malta as well as in unconquerable Gibraltar, Cochrane and the *Impérieuse* were well-posted indeed.

Initially, however, after having escorted troop reinforcements to both these bases, he had his problems as senior officer of the Adriatic blockading squadron (where, in due course, young Captain Hoste was to shine). In one operation, against a privateer operating equivocally under a British flag, his men suffered heavy casualties to which he was unaccustomed; and in this and other actions he sailed into the sort of prize-money complexities which, in those great areas of neutral, semi-neutral and falsely-neutral trade, so bedevilled enterprising young frigate captains. The upshot of this (apart from the stack of legal problems and the complaints made against him) was that he was demoted from his squadron command. But, although informed against, he was this time not disgraced. For among Nelson's 'band of brothers', Cuthbert Collingwood was among the most discerning and admirable. Perhaps most gracefully immortalised as one of the heroes of Alfred de Vigny's *Servitude et Grandeur Militaires*, the prematurely aged admiral (who was to die afloat at his post within two years, worn out in the service of his country) recognised qualities in the unpopular young Scottish captain which were too good to waste. Accordingly, he returned him to those coasts of France and Spain which he knew so well from his *Speedy* days.

It was at this moment that the crisis in Franco-Spanish relations was developing. Ostensibly to deal with awkward little Portugal, which had refused to fall into line with his plans for Europe, Napoleon had already marched an army through Spain while she was his ally. But even then it seems likely that he had plans to replace the ramshackle Spanish monarchy and government with French rulers who would organise the country more efficiently to further his plans for the war and for Europe. So, while Cochrane's first operations were against both the French and the Spanish, another 100,000 Frenchmen were crossing the Pyrenees. And in the late spring of 1808 the captive Spanish monarchy was bullied into handing over the crown to Napoleon's brother, Joseph.

The intervention of other countries in Spain's internal affairs had a long history. As far back as the fourteenth century the French and the English had backed rival royal claimants, with the veteran longbowmen of Crècy and Poitiers famously demonstrating their skill at Najera in 1367, under the Black Prince. But although Spain was now a third-rate power whose army was quite unable to defend the country, her people were none the less proud and brave. As a consequence, a six-year 'War of Liberation' now commenced, with spontaneous and bloody risings across the country. At Baylen in the far south, the Spaniards even won a rare (or, rather, unique) victory in mid-summer over the temporarily disorganised French; and, for the British, that something which they had been hoping would turn up had done so at last, with the beginning of what was for them to become the Peninsular War.

Meanwhile, this succession of major events, coupled with his removal from the Adriatic, combined to place Cochrane exactly where his perfected talents as a combined-operations commander had most scope: along a coast where the people, both civilian and military, were now on his side – against a hated foreign army of occupation which could never be everywhere at once in sufficient strength. And this time, at last, he operated with the blessing of his discerning commander-in-chief, being ordered to assist Britain's new ally 'with every means in his power'.

'Every means' for Cochrane were now enlarged. Where before he could only briefly raid, while taking anything afloat along the coast of a country whose roads were proverbially bad, henceforth he could attack much more ambitiously. In his grasp of what could be done at full stretch of naval power, he provided the perfect model for Hornblower's operations on the same coast in the *Sutherland* a year or so later, and probably an inspiration to Hoste in the Adriatic in due course.

During this period, also, that slur of St Vincent's, that he was 'money-getting' was given the lie: his record over the rest of that year as a fighting captain, in dangerous operations which offered no chance of profit, is second to none in the annals of the war. Only in his somewhat foolish contention that the war could actually be won by such means can his judgement be faulted. For the rest, otherwise, what he achieved with the *Impérieuse* (later with the aid of another frigate, the *Spartan*, commanded by the excellent Captain Jahleel Brenton) remains a classic text-book example of inshore frigate warfare.

Moving faster at sea, as though on an interior line, he tempted French garrisons out by destroying coastal roads – and then hit their depleted garrisons when they sent men to repair his work (an extension of his old Isle of Ré operation). With Spanish guerrilla help he assaulted more powerful forts, and took them. Famously, by a brilliant bit of seamanship witnessed by the admiring Brenton and later emulated by Hornblower, he caught and destroyed a French cavalry regiment with the unexpected close-quarters broadside of the *Impérieuse*. Blowing things up was one of his specialities, not least signal stations (where he would leave the secret code-books carefully burnt after having copied them). Deception was indeed another speciality: on one occasion he dressed up the boys of the *Impérieuse* and the *Spartan* as red-coated marines, landing them on one side of his objective while his real marines attacked on the other. And the Mediterranean coast of France was no safer from his depredations than the friendly coasts of Spain: when his ship ran short of water he sent boats up the Rhone to replenish his supplies with fresh river water. In fact, during the 1808 cruise of the *Impérieuse*, fiction continually has to withdraw gracefully before fact, as chronicled both in official reports and by Midshipman Marryat.

Even as the French poured more men into Spain, both from their own armies and their allies, to counter the first British military interventions by Sir Arthur Wellesley in Portugal and then by Sir John

Moore in Spain itself, Cochrane embarked on what was perhaps his bravest and most ambitious land-battle, by occupying the old Fort Trinidad in aid of the Spanish defenders of Rosas, a small seaport now much favoured by British holiday visitors to the Costa Brava, near the French frontier. His ingenuity in re-fortifying the fort, which over-looked the town but had no escape-route except down a cliff above the sea (which, of course, belonged to him), was rewarded by a regular siege which he resisted by both conventional and unconventional means (mines and a generous application of cooking grease to the approaches) as his handful of seamen and marines were attacked time and again. It was during this action that he was painfully wounded by a fragment of stone which broke his nose and pierced the roof of his mouth, but he continued to command his defenders from the front for another whole week, until the fall of Rosas town and the surrender of the Spaniards made the end inevitable. Even then, after having set another of his celebrated demolition charges, he was one of the last two men to escape by rope-ladder down the cliff, to ship's boats waiting on the beach below.

There were then no medals of the modern variety for such singular acts of gallantry, so Cochrane could receive no Victoria Cross for Fort Trinidad, to add to the DSOs and DSCs he would by now have acquired if his exploits had been performed in the world wars of this century. But word of his latest achievements had reached England through Collingwood's frankly admiring despatches, to be made public in the *Naval Gazette* and trumpeted in the *Naval Chronicle* and the British Press. Whatever the Admiralty might still think of him (and, with supreme meanness, they complained about his 'excessive use of powder and shot'), they now had to swallow his 'zeal and activity', 'skill and ability', 'consummate prudence' and 'astonishing exertions'. Even that other old slur that he had sustained few casualties was weakened by Collingwood's testimony that all this had been effected with but a handful of men. And (what was also important) Britain's newest allies, the Spaniards, were no less taken by 'this gallant Englishman' who had deserved their 'admiration and gratitude'. Politically, in the House of Commons, Cochrane might still be unimportant. But politically, also with the British Army just driven out of Spain (from Corunna, leaving its heroic general dead behind it), the government was in no position to ignore the demands of the opposition press that their hero must be properly employed.

As it happened, however, the government was quite undeservedly lucky at that very moment. For what might seem the perfect mission for 'that gallant Englishman' Captain Lord Cochrane now lay waiting for him off that French Biscayan coast which he also knew so well.

Modern British holiday-makers, drawn either to Pellew's (and Hornblower's) old hunting grounds along the south Breton coasts, or directly down the French motorways to the Dordogne (or, even further, to Cochrane's and Hornblower's other hunting-grounds on the Costa Brava), less often divert to the flat Biscayan shore of France north of Bordeaux. But some, more discerning, do take in the lovely old ex-Huguenot seaport of La Rochelle before hurrying southwards again, past Rochefort, the little fishing village which Colbert in the seventeenth century had transformed into one of France's main naval bases.

In fact, Rochefort itself was a poor choice for a base, being situated too far up the shallow Charente. But seawards of the river estuary there were certain anchorages – *rades* or 'roads' – in which fully laden ships could ride safely (at least in peacetime), even at low tide. Beyond the Ile d'Aix, within the pointing fingers of the bigger islands of Ré and Oléron, there were the Basque Roads, while closer in, between Oléron and Aix islands and the mainland, there were the much safer Aix Roads. It was in the latter, protected by shore batteries on the islands and an enormous boom made of cables totalling two and a half feet in diameter secured by five-and-a-half ton anchors, that a French fleet now lay, inviting urgent attention lest it escape.

This fleet, consisting of ten ships-of-the-line (including the 120-gun *Ocean*) and four frigates, had been assembled for the relief of Martinique in the West Indies, one of the last unpicked plums of the French overseas empire remaining. Originally it had been in two parts, at Brest and Lorient, and somewhat larger. But during its break-out and concentration it had been sufficiently harried by units of the British blockading Channel Fleet to lose three frigates (on the sands of Les Sables d'Orlonne) and a ship-of-the-line before it was driven into the Basque Roads, and finally into the Aix Roads inside the great boom.

One may fantasise that, if the young Hornblower had been in the Brest approaches in the *Hotspur* with Pellew in the *Tonnant* nearby and Cornwallis' fleet not far out to sea beyond them, this fleet might never have united, let alone reached the Basque Roads. Or, if it had got so far, it would not have remained unattacked long. But Hornblower was by then on the way to the Pacific in the *Lydia* and Pellew was in the Indian Ocean, and the Channel Fleet was commanded by Admiral Lord Gambier.

James Gambier provides another cautionary example of the defects of the system which at its best produced admirals like Nelson and Collingwood, Keats and Saumarez, or even the Channel Fleet's present second-in-command, Admiral Eliab Harvey, who would all have been far better suited for the Channel command. Influential connections, notably with the Pitt family and with that of Charles Middleton (the able First Lord during the Trafalgar campaign, albeit also another of St Vincent's *bête noires*) had helped Gambier to his present command, together with his seniority, even though the greater part of his long service had been spent ashore. It was not that he had been a bad captain in his time, and least of all a coward. No ship was handled better or more bravely than his *Defence* (74) at the battle of 'the Glorious First of June' in 1794; munching a biscuit in the thick of it, he had inspired his men by his coolness and leadership, drawing praise from Howe himself: 'Look at the *Defence*! See how nobly she goes into action!'

The First of June made Gambier's name. And his seniority and 'interest' eventually gave him his flag and command at Copenhagen in 1807, when he bombarded the city into submission and finished what Nelson had begun six years before, by carrying off the entire Danish fleet and (much more valuable) the contents of the Danish naval dockyard and arsenal. But that had been an easy victory (unlike Nelson's earlier one) and Gambier was far better known throughout the Navy for his religious fervour than for his naval ability.

This fervour was no new thing. Back in '94, in the aftermath of the First of June, as the friendly captain of the *Invincible* sailed past the partially dismasted *Defence* he had shouted 'Never mind, Jemmy! Whom the Lord loveth he chasteneth!' By 1808 Gambier's convictions had, if anything, strengthened. In that dawning age of elegance, gambling and regency rakes (and foul-mouthed, hard-drinking sailors), he was the shape of a later Victorian England to come. A friend of the great reformer, William Wilberforce, and of the 'Saints' of the Revd Joseph Venn's Clapham Sect, he took his piety with him to sea as commander-in-chief, deploring the rum and bad language as he showered his officers and men with religious tracts. This did not endear him to his fleet. As we have seen, although the abuse of alcohol was a real problem which frequently brought them to the cat-o'-nine-tails, rum was even more the men's solace than it became to their suffering descendants in the 1914–18 trenches. And for the officers, Gambier's uninspiring and unenterprising command was rendered further unpopular by the suspicion that an ostentatious devotion to God offered them a speedier path to promotion under him than the efficient discharge of their naval duties in the service of King George.

What made the present situation worse was that Gambier was not without an inkling of what ought to be done. The Basque and the Aix Roads were far from unknown territory to the British Navy, treacherous though these waters were known to be. As far back as the days of Charles I, in the time of the Duke of Buckingham and Richelieu (and d'Artagnan and Milady de Winter), one of their fleets had descended (unsuccessfully) on the island of Ré; during the Seven Years' War Admiral Hawke had destroyed a fleet in the Basque Roads, thereby helping Wolfe to take Quebec, far away in Canada; and, of course, that whippersnapper Cochrane had most recently raided the whole area in the *Pallas*. While it might be too dangerous to attempt to take the whole fleet into such an enclosed space, it was essential that the French should not be left in peace where they were. For sooner or later the weather must turn to their advantage, driving off the blockaders and opening the way for an escape to the West Indies. Indeed, it was not only essential to do something from a naval point of view, but also from a political one: a French relief of Martinique was less important than the havoc such a raid might cause among British shipping in the West Indies, which would outrage the powerful commercial interests so well-represented in Parliament, Lords and Commons alike.

Difficult for a fleet as such an attack might be, it was none the less an ideal location for a fireship operation to lead the way. Fireships (as already noted) were a time-honoured weapon – not only historically, with those Armada memories when the English had used them against the Spanish in a war designed to help the Dutch, but by the Dutch against the English in the Medway three-quarters of a century (and most humiliatingly) later – and most recently (although unsuccessfully) by the Spaniards against the British at Gibraltar. Fireships rarely burnt anything but themselves, but only the best-trained fleets could resist them. And the French were not best-trained, however brave.

In this case, however, Admiral Gambier was not the man for the job. He did not like the look of that great boom which protected the Aix Roads (confusingly, since the eventual battle was named after the outer 'Basque' *rade*). And he also feared all the shore batteries, most of which existed only in his imagination. Although there was no shortage of fireship volunteers from Admiral Eliab Harvey downwards, he not only believed that the operation would fail, but disapproved of such 'a horrid form of warfare'. For him, carronades were acceptable, but fireships and other 'infernal devices' represented the unacceptable face of warfare.

Cochrane, of course, had no such scruples, let alone any fears or doubts about the feasibility of such a risky operation. Indeed, while there must have been some in the Admiralty and others in politics who would have wept no tears at his death in a heroic (and preferably successful) action, he undoubtedly *was* the man for this job. Like his father, the inventor-earl, he was a man of flexible mind – very much, in fact, a nineteenth-century man, rather than of the eighteenth century. Later, after having spent most of his life at sea under clouds of billowing and beautiful canvas, he would be quick to see the advantages of dirty and noisy steam-power. War, to him, was about killing the enemy while preserving his own men, and any means to hand – including any infernal device, fiery or explosive – was welcome. Before long even (and also many years later), he would be among the earliest advocates of chemical warfare.

Now, nevertheless, when summoned post-haste from the

Impérieuse at Plymouth into the suspiciously friendly presence of the First Lord (now Colonel Lord Musgrave) in London, he did his best to refuse the assignment. Being the man he was and with his expert knowledge of both special operations and the Basque Roads, the planning of such an attack was no great problem for him. The problem lay in Admiral Gambier himself and in the officers of his blockading fleet. As for the former, 'Preaching Jemmy' would be unlikely to welcome any junior officer (a captain of eight years' seniority only) sent in to do what he had failed to do – particularly an officer like Captain Lord Cochrane. As for the latter, whatever they might think of Captain Lord Cochrane personally, they would detest any man sent to do what they had already volunteered to attempt, with its implication that they were not up to the job.

Cochrane was absolutely right in all these assumptions. Not even his own well-publicised reactionary Protestant views on Catholic emancipation made him acceptable to Preaching Jemmy, and Admiral Harvey exploded in a series of public rages on his arrival off the Basque Roads. Harvey already disliked Gambier as an incompetent quite as much as Cochrane did (while Gambier himself disliked both men as unregenerate sinners). Now Harvey became the first victim of the Admiralty's stratagem, destroyed by his own incandescent anger at Cochrane's appointment, which he somewhat unfairly blamed on Gambier. Unfortunately, to his public declaration that he would haul down his flag and resign from the service Harvey added all his pent-up opinions of his commander-in-chief both as man and an admiral. As a result, while Cochrane was grappling with the problem of getting at the French, one of the Navy's bravest admirals, who as a captain had nearly overtaken Nelson in breaking the enemy line at Trafalgar in his famous three-decker, Turner's 'fighting *Téméraire*', was being court-martialled and dismissed from the service before he could quit it. And, although he was subsequently to be reinstated and honoured, he never served afloat again.

For Cochrane, this introduction to Gambier's fleet worsened an already unhappy situation. He had, of course, finally given in to Lord Musgrave's pleas after the First Lord had told him frankly (though disingenuously) that no one else wanted the job, and had promised (equally disingenuously) that he would soothe the ruffled feelings of Gambier and his officers – a promise which was unfulfillable even before the Harvey scandal. In reality, Cochrane was trapped from the start, not only by his status as a national hero and his sense of duty, but by the overriding fear that the longer he temporised, the more likely it was that the French might break out. (And, indeed, the enterprising Captain Jacques Bergeret, Pellew's old friend who had been freed from his second captivity by exchange now, must certainly have been advocating just that, whether or not he and other captains knew that the famous 'Sea-wolf' had arrived to direct operations, for he can have had no illusions about the dangers of the anchorage.)

Whether time was or was not of the essence, events moved fast thereafter under the stimulus of Cochrane. Arriving in his *Impérieuse* in the Basque Roads on 3 April, he immediately carried out a night reconnaissance of the French positions in a small boat, which Gambier had signally failed to do. To his experienced eye, the shore batteries did not yet amount to much. Given men and official backing he believed that the island of Oléron could easily be seized, which would have made the destruction of the whole French fleet certain and would have permanently neutralised the Rochefort base itself. Short of this solution, however, the boom had to be blown up to open the way for fireships to enter the Aix Roads, where the French fleet was moored in three lines, two of ships-of-the-line behind one of frigates. The picket-boats guarding the boom would have to be brushed aside.

Cochrane's final plan was actually neither very complicated nor even new, for the admirable Captain Richard Keats had advocated just such an assault on a squadron in this anchorage some years earlier. It was, however, hideously dangerous for the boom-breakers, who must sail small ships crammed with gunpowder alongside the boom under fire from the enemy. To give them a better chance, diversionary attacks must be made by small craft on the islands to draw the enemy's fire, while other small craft marked the approaches to the boom with lights (all this must be done at night, of course), also giving the explosives ships covering fire and generally causing as much chaos as possible. The boom having been blown apart, the fireships would then enter the gap, followed by a flotilla of the fleet's boats and (eventually, presumably) the fleet itself.

In the event, Cochrane was both lucky and unlucky on the actual night of 11/12 April, when the attack took place. He was lucky first in that he survived it, of course. But rough weather confused the assault, so that only one of the explosive ships reached the boom, and none of the fleet's boats was operable. However, the bad weather also hindered the French guard-boats, and the single explosives ship to reach the target – commanded of course by Cochrane himself – shattered the great boom in one single monstrous explosion. The frigate *Mediator* then led the way through the wreckage for the fireships – which, as usual, then burnt nothing but themselves. But fear of fire and the wildness of the night had the desired effect, nevertheless: the French fleet cut its cables in panic, to be driven ashore on the shoals of the Charente estuary as the tide turned to leave it high and dry – and helpless.

Having saved himself and his little explosives ship crew and the fireship crews in all this confusion, Cochrane returned to the *Impérieuse* and also took her into the Aix Roads as dawn broke, signalling to Gambier in the Basque Roads outside that the French fleet was at his mercy. But Gambier now failed to rise to this invitation: first, he acknowledged Cochrane's increasingly angry signals belatedly, and then he answered them ineffectually, with piecemeal reinforcements. Eventually, over the long and heart-breaking hours which followed, Captain Bligh (John, not the celebrated William, formerly of the *Bounty*) came in with the two 74s of the line, the 80-gun *Caesar*, and two frigates, Pellew's old *Indefatigable* and Cochrane's own old *Pallas*, together with some smaller craft. But the work of destruction was cautiously undertaken (especially after the *Caesar* grounded for a time) and ill-completed. In all – even though the little *Beagle* sloop gloriously assaulted the stranded 120-gun *Ocean* flagship with her nine-pounders – only four of the French ships-of-the-line were destroyed before the British attack finally petered out in a further series of half-hearted gestures.

Back in England, the 'Basque Roads' was hailed as another triumph for the British Navy in which, under Admiral Lord Gambier, the dashing Captain Cochrane had once again performed gloriously. For, after all, apart from the destruction of four enemy ships-of-the-line, the rest of the French fleet had either been badly knocked about, or had been forced to damage itself by jettisoning guns and stores and cutting off masts in order to refloat itself off the shoals. It would never sail as a fleet again and – most important of all – the West Indies were safe from it. And, anyway, both the Admiralty and the public were satisfied with Admiral Gambier's generous despatch, which after noting that 'the Almighty's favour to His Majesty and the nation' had been 'strongly marked', had conceded that on this occasion the Almighty had been assisted by Lord Cochrane's 'accustomed gallantry and spirit'. Accordingly, and on Admiral Gambier's recommendation, Captain Cochrane was very properly admitted to the company of the Knights Commander of the Order of the Bath.

If ever a hero had everything going for him, Captain (Lord by courtesy, but now Sir by merit) Cochrane had it then. All he had to do, for his own good and that of his country, was to keep his mouth shut. For then, for reasons of expediency if not for nobler ones, even the Admiralty and the political establishment might be relied on to forget his past excesses and make their peace with him, perhaps even giving him some appropriate (if distant?) new command worthy of his talents and fame while he was still by seniority too far down on the Captain's List for them to make an admiral of him. But that, predictably, was what he was altogether incapable of doing.

One must be fair to Cochrane, nevertheless, by adding the Basque Roads to all the wounds he had received over the years, in which his own defects of character and his virtues and great qualities had been so inextricably mixed with the defects, injustices and virtues of the system. He had accepted command of the attack while still exhausted from his Mediterranean activities, and hardly recovered from his physical wounds. Taking 1,500 barrels of gunpowder into a defended passage on a foul pitch-black night, and then his frigate among a dozen or more enemy ships-of-the-line in notoriously dangerous water, had itself been hideously dangerous (although all that was nothing more than Admiral Harvey and others had been only too willing to attempt). But during that day inside the Aix Roads, he believed that he had had something in his grasp that *no* British officer had possessed since Nelson had led his fleet into Aboukir Bay in '98: the chance to destroy a French fleet in its entirety, equalling Nelson's annihilating victory – even, since he was still no more than a frigate captain, surpassing it. Nothing he had done before, and probably nothing he would ever have the chance of doing again, came close to that. So, perhaps understandably, his rage was colder and even more self-destructive than Admiral Eliab Harvey's hot rage had been when the possibility of such a triumph had been denied him.

At all events, and in spite of all pleas to desist, he now warned the First Lord that, in his capacity of MP for Westminster, he intended to oppose the traditional Vote of Thanks to Admiral Gambier which was to be proposed in gratitude for his victory. Such a scandal left Gambier no choice but to demand a court martial to inquire into his conduct. And that, in turn, with all its echoes of the judicial murder of poor Admiral Byng years before, united both the Navy and the establishment in implacable opposition to Cochrane.

Also, in the cold and unromantic light of the burdens of admiralty, there was not such an open-and-shut case against Gambier as the Cochrane's-eye-view which has deliberately been given so far. The approaches to Rochefort *were* a death-trap for unhandy 74s, as not only the earlier loss of the French *Jean-Bart* on a shoal there a month before the battle proved, but also the dangerous grounding of the British *Caesar* during the action. Captain after captain (hardly poltroons, any of them, and few of them admirers of Gambier) testified to the dangers, not least those who had performed best there, Bligh of the *Valiant* and Kerr of the *Revenge* as well as the captains of the smaller ships, like the *Pallas* and the belligerent little *Beagle*. In fact no one – not even the one captain who first supported Cochrane, but then wilted under cross-examination – supported Cochrane in his indictment of Gambier.

The truth is that, by the very highest standards – the standards of Nelson at the Nile and Copenhagen – Gambier had failed to take the fullest advantage of a very risky situation. But (and perhaps not least with the near-disaster of Algeciras Bay in mind, as well as Admiral Byng) that was the beginning and end of it: if everyone was to be publicly disgraced who failed to equal Nelson, no one would be safe.

As it was, with the burden of the actual evidence given at the court martial never mind Cochrane's unpopularity in both naval and political circles, the outcome was foreordained. Gambier was honourably acquitted, with his 'zeal, judgement and ability' commended into the bargain. However, the reality behind this finding – and the proof that this reality was widely discerned – was also that he then only remained in command of the Channel Fleet for the minimum decent period, never to be employed either at sea or on land again. Indeed, a proposal to make him First Lord was scuppered by none other than old King George himself, who was on occasion a shrewd judge of men during his periods of lucidity. Not even the King, though, could tamper with the seniority list, which only death amended. So, as a reward for longevity, Gambier was to become Admiral of the Fleet in 1830, holding that ultimate naval honour until his death in 1833 and thereby pipping his almost-exact contemporary, Edward Pellew, who died in that same year.

As for Cochrane, it is properly time for him to leave this narrative, for the outcome of the court martial and his consequent humiliation in the Vote of Thanks debate in Parliament effectively ended his wartime career in the Navy as the greatest frigate captain of all time, in all wars. However, since the rest of his long life was hardly less action-packed, almost like a gloss on Kipling's *If* and with outrageous incident to provide material for a dozen novels, he demands a few final paragraphs.

The Basque Roads episode was not the end of his disasters, but the beginning, as the *Impérieuse* and her adoring crew sailed away under a new captain. Henceforth, while his radical politics continued to make him unacceptable to those in power in Parliament, his imaginative projects for combined operations against Napoleon's 'Fortress Europe' were equally ignored as the government and their military advisers embarked on the disastrous Walcheren expedition of 1809. Worse was to come, just when Cochrane was eventually offered another command in 1814, of Pellew's old *Tonnant* (80). For then he was falsely charged with complicity in an ingenious fraud perpetrated by his villainous uncle, Andrew Cochrane Johnson. Expulsion from the Navy and Parliament, imprisonment, escape, re-election to Westminster, recapture and further imprisonment all followed. During this period of increasing disgrace and financial disaster, while his honours were being stripped from him, he contracted a wonderfully happy and successful runaway marriage, nevertheless. And, after finally fleeing the country, accompanied now by his beautiful and formidable wife, he went on to glory (and, as always, new disagreements) in command of the fledgling navies of Chile, Brazil and Greece in their wars of independence, leaving behind him streets in their cities (and, in the case of Chile, warships too) named in his honour.

But not even that ended his stranger-than-fiction career: with no cannon ball or musket shot bearing his name on it, in the end he even beat the system which had broken him, by outlasting it. For the years killed off his enemies, one by one, as his fame grew into legend. New friends, made at a distance through an appreciation of his achievements, espoused his cause. He was reinstated in the Royal Navy, as an admiral, in 1832 (while Gambier was Admiral of the Fleet: it is only as the instrument of Cochrane's disgrace that Preaching Jemmy is remembered, in one of history's neatest revenges). Gradually all his honours were restored to him, with the admiring approval of Queen Victoria and Prince Albert. He even served afloat again, as commander-in-chief in the North American and West Indian Station in the late 1840s, and actually offered himself for active command during the Crimean War, before his death in 1860. And the government was still involved in doing right by his family in the 1860s and 1870s, to remedy the injustices of more than half a century earlier.

But this long-delayed justice hardly makes up for the great might-have-been if his courage and skill in battle had been accompanied by a little of the modesty, tact and diplomatic skill of Horatio Hornblower.

CHAPTER ELEVEN

Adventures in Spanish America

The narratives of the late Mr C.S. Forester, on which any biographical sketch of the life of Admiral Lord Hornblower must be based, did not originally present their subject's naval career chronologically: they began like every good epic, *in medias res*, when Horatio Hornblower was already a post-captain of five years' seniority and in command of a frigate, the *Lydia* (36), off the Pacific coast of Central America in 1808. Yet this departure from the strict sequence of Hornblower's adventures (whatever the original reason for it) cannot be regarded as inappropriate. For, while we shall of course trace the process of his rise to frigate command very shortly (and later meet him again from time to time) his achievement in the *Lydia* as a great frigate captain was central to that career. Everything which occurred before the *Lydia's* South American mission may be seen to lead up to it, and everything which followed was in some sense its consequence. For our purposes, however, it also quite dramatically illustrates the mixture of the problems and opportunities of frigate captains on detached operations.

On the face of it, Hornblower's opportunity at that moment was dazzling. He had sailed secretly, under sealed orders, all the way from Plymouth to catch the enemy (in this case the Spaniards) by surprise on a coast unvisited by the British Navy since Anson's voyage 60 years before and potentially rich in prizes. And, for good measure, he was under direct Admiralty orders, with no intermediate flag-officers either to badger him or to share his prize-money. Against that, on the other hand, his mission to supply and encourage a colonial rebellion also included a warning not to offend any of the local inhabitants with whom British commercial interests hoped to trade after they had expelled the Spaniards. And even before he could begin the thereby much more complicated process of enriching himself he had to deal with the Spanish navy ship guarding these waters, the two-decker *Natividad*, of 50 guns.

Actually, there was nothing too unusual by then in an Admiralty clerk blithely assuming that a medium-sized frigate, with 12-pounders as her main armament plus a few 'long nines' and carronades elsewhere, could take on an old-fashioned 'intermediate' ship-of-the-line of the sort that was obsolete in European waters – and a Spanish one, too. The clerk probably could not remember when the British had last lost a single-ship action; and he undoubtedly recalled how Pellew had harrièd the *Droits de l'Homme* to destruction, even if he hadn't been among the London crowds which had admired Nicholas Pocock's picture of the *Speedy* taking the *El Gamo*. That Captain Hornblower could deal with the despised Dons somehow, he may have confided; or if things went badly, so long as the gold, guns and ammunition had been first delivered to the Nicaraguan insurgents then the main objective of the mission would have been accomplished. And frigates were not in such short supply now as they had been in 1798.

As for Hornblower himself, he was less worried about the *Natividad* than the accuracy of his navigation after seven months at sea, but most worried of all by the state of his unreplenished supplies when so far from any friendly harbour. His lime juice was already exhausted, which meant that there would be scurvy in the crew soon. Worse than that, however, he was almost out of water, tobacco and rum – and lack of that last was as dangerous as a shortage of the slimy-green water ration. A crew without the solace of rum could not be trusted, inspiring memories of Bligh and the *Bounty* with the paradisical islands of Tahiti somewhere to the west, if not darker recollections of Pigot and the *Hermione*.

Finally, to spoil that bright June morning in 1808 as he put on the threadbare second-best uniform coat of a frigate captain who had not yet been lucky in winning prize money (which he had to do to attend a flogging – which he also hated), he was irritated by the sight of a bulge below his ribs, which he identified as a sign of future corpulence. In fact (as we know from his biographer), it was no such thing, for he was an uncommonly abstemious and weight-conscious man for his times. Rather, it was merely a sign of age, which was already afflicting his former patron, Admiral Sir Edward Pellew more than him. Their war – at least, their war discounting the brief Peace of Amiens, which Hornblower preferred to forget – had been in progress for 15 years now. While Pellew (who had fought a previous war, anyway) was by

now in his fifties, most of our special intake of 'young gentlemen' of
1793 were now in their thirties, excepting only that intake's luckiest
teenager, 'little Hoste' (now Captain Hoste of the *Amphion*).

However, Hornblower would still not be anywhere else. For he was
now a frigate captain, and although still poor he would rather be a
captain and poor than anything else and rich. If he lived and the war
continued he might yet become an admiral – say, in the 1820s.
Meanwhile he thought himself lucky to be a frigate captain.

In fact (though he would be the last to admit it), merit had been the
main ingredient of his rise, with the element of luck decidedly mixed
(to be despatched on this expendable mission he regarded as luck,
undoubtedly), with the element of 'interest' coming a poor third.

For, like so many young hopefuls, Hornblower went to sea in 1793
with the bearest minimum of 'interest', which was just sufficient to
find him a berth on what was probably an elderly 74, with its worn-out
lieutenants, elderly midshipmen and dying captain. Possibly it was the
captain's state of health which gave him this vestigial opportunity, in
return for a free consultation from his father, a country doctor who
evidently could do nothing more for his son thereafter. Not, statistically, that the medical profession did not play its full part during the
war in contributing its offspring to naval service. The year before
Hornblower reached the Nicaraguan coast, crusty old St Vincent was
bemoaning the intrusion of the sons of Members of Parliament, both
Lords and Commons, into his beloved navy, now that its victories had
made it popular (as distinct from the unvictorious army, into which
they could always easily be inserted by the simple purchase of a
commission). But then, even though he was to use his politics, St
Vincent always hated their too-close connection with the Navy (which
was surely another nail in Cochrane's coffin), preferring the deserving
and meritorious sons of (English) naval officers to anyone else.
Nevertheless, although the 'ruling classes' of the peerage, baronetage
and gentry which dominated Parliament contributed nearly four out
of every ten officers then, out of all proportion to those classes' actual
numbers, the sons of men in the professions still contributed more
officers numerically, with the 'other classes' (business, commercial
and working) the final 10 per cent (and usually in the lower ranks).

Among the professions from whose children officers were drawn
during the war (things were to change quite significantly during the
long peace after it), the Navy itself easily came top, with the Church
(Nelson and Hoste, for example) and the Army respectively second
and third. But after them, each with over 5 per cent of the professional
intake, and nearly 3 per cent of the total, came the law, the civil service
and medicine. So, as a doctor's son, Hornblower was far from unique.

Nor was his misery in the midshipman's berth unique, which in a
badly commanded ship surpassed even the worst public schools of the

time in that its bullying took place in far more cramped and uncomfortable conditions under the guise of the Articles of War, as sadistically imposed by the victim's seniors. It was only his cold-blooded coolness in a famous duel (perhaps added to his mathematical excellence, enjoyment of whist and his captain's wish to die in peace), that eventually delivered him from this purgatorial existence, though still as an example of luck rather than merit. For (at least, so Mr Forester avers, though there is no other evidence for it), Captain Pellew of the *Indefatigable* not only had a midshipman's vacancy in 1795 but was partial to a game of whist, and was therefore prepared to do Captain Keene, of the *Justinian*, a small favour.

Pellew and Hornblower were well-met, for the captain's frigate operations were such that they both required and provided scope for intelligent young warrant officers able to take command of boats in his off-shore operations and to take his prizes back to where they could be bought by the Navy or auctioned to the highest bidder. It was under his able tuition that Hornblower learned his trade, as Pellew before him had learned his under Captain Pownoll and Hoste was to learn his under Nelson. Indeed, it was a Nelson–Hoste marriage exactly, for years later, when Hornblower was Master and Commander of the *Hotspur* sloop and Pellew had returned to inshore duties in the 80-gun *Tonnant*, the famous captain welcomed back the unknown lieutenant (temporary commander) with a letter to gladden Hornblower's heart:

> My dear Hornblower,
> It is with greatest of pleasure that I hear that you are serving under me, and what I have been told of your actions already in this war confirms the opinion I formed when you were my best midshipman in the old *Indefatigable*. Please consider yourself at liberty to make any suggestions that may occur to you for the confounding of the French and the confusion of Bonaparte.
> Your sincere friend,
> Edward Pellew

That was how merit (and potentially, 'interest' too, Hornblower might now hope) really worked, to the benefit of both parties. Also, Hornblower had some claim on Pellew's sympathy, even apart from his merit, since he had been taken prisoner by the Spaniards some six years before while in command of one of Pellew's prizes as an acting lieutenant. That hiccough in his service, which had stopped his career in its tracks when he was a warrant officer (and might have left him an 'other rank' in captivity until the Peace of Amiens four years later), was somewhat remedied by the confirmation of his lieutenancy in August 1797 while he was still a prisoner (in circumstances which those interested may discover in that episode of his midshipman career entitled *The Duchess and the Devil*). But, even then, it was only because of his courage and enterprise (more merit) that he was to be unconditionally freed by the Spaniards for saving the lives of some local fishermen and then honouring his word-of-honour parole when he could have escaped. Arguably, he could have done no less than return to the PoW status on that occasion, since the British government was very strict in such matters, refusing to employ – and even dishonouring – those who broke their paroles (obeying rules throughout the war which Napoleon most dishonourably encouraged his own officers to break). But, by the same token, this Spanish gesture was in the best traditions of eighteenth-century military courtesy: however incompetent and often brutal the Spaniards might be, they were – and prided themselves on being – gentlemen.

Ideally, Pellew ought then to have taken back Lieutenant Hornblower into the *Impétueux* (84), into which he had been promoted from the *Indefatigable* in March 1799. But one may assume that his best former midshipman's unexpected return found him busy at sea, so that the Admiralty's speedy appointment of the otherwise uninfluential (but meritorious) lieutenant to a ship-of-the-line was reward enough, on the face of it.

In fact, Hornblower's experience on the *Renown* (74, Captain Sawyer) was to be an education far surpassing that on Captain Keene's *Justinian*. For, where Captain Keene was merely dying, Captain Sawyer had become unbalanced under the weight of his responsibilities, not so much in the sadistic manner of Captain Pigot of the *Hermione*, who brutalised his men, as in that of Captain Queeg of the USS *Caine*, who more subtly victimised his officers.

In the Hornblower canon, his time in the *Renown* is particularly interesting because it seems to have been uniquely compiled not through Hornblower's own recollections, but through those of Lieutenant (future Captain) William Bush, who was his superior in that ship (since his lieutenant's commission, as inexorably fixed as those on the Captain's List, pre-dated Hornblower's). Bush, in both this narrative and in the history of the whole navy of this period, must represent the greater part of the junior officers of the British Navy, as in that of any of the better armies and navies (and now air forces) throughout history. He had been brought up and shaped by the traditions of the service. And, more than that, his education was in a war at sea, which eliminated many of the weaker and the incompetent, if not the nastier. However, although he learned to do his job competently, and understood how to bring the best out of the men he commanded, Bush was quite without imagination and flair. In command he would do his duty bravely and unhesitatingly to the best of his ability, no matter what the difficulties or cost. But if those difficulties were great then that cost might be great also, and the outcome doubtful. The first battle at Algeciras and its victorious sequel back in 1801 were typical 'Bush' battles, bravely but rather unwisely started and then heroically finished, final success being due to superior seamanship and training allied to invincible morale and determination. The British Navy had by then become accustomed to almost invariable victory over nearly half a century. Rodney had thrown away the old Rules of Engagement book at the battle of the Saints' Passage in 1782 and St Vincent and Nelson had set new performance standards for what was expected of the Navy whatever the odds or risks. British commanders and captains henceforth did their best to live up to these standards in the confident assumption of victory, almost as a matter of course. But less able men were thus both inspired and imprisoned by Nelson's example, even though they lacked the Nelson touch. And because of this, as we shall see, there were some nasty shocks in store for them in the future.

Meanwhile, Lieutenant William Bush's misfortune in being posted into the *Renown* as third lieutenant was to be offset by his burgeoning friendship with Hornblower, the fifth and most junior lieutenant. Before very long it was on Hornblower's back that he was to move up the naval ladder, and higher than he might otherwise have expected to do although eventually to his death: this was luck, merit and 'interest' working at the lower levels, indeed. More immediately, however, we are indebted to him not only for his portrait of the future frigate captain and admiral as a young man, but for what that portrait also represents as an example of *any* exceptional young officer at the time who stood out from his fellows by reason of his intelligence and initiative (with physical courage and professional skill being taken for granted as basic requirements). What Bush at first discerned rather hazily as a not-over-intelligent equal and then did his best to describe was not only what Pellew had already and more professionally observed: it was what Captain Pownoll and others had noted in Midshipman Pellew himself many years earlier, what Nelson saw in little Midshipman Hoste (in contrast to what he saw in his own stepson at the same time, in the same ship), and in due course what Captain Hornblower himself was to see in other promising young men (like the young *Lydia* seaman he promoted to midshipman in the *Sutherland* and, most notably and equally tragically, Lieutenant Mound of the bomb-ketch *Harvey*). The possession of such promising subordinates, from whose pockets the tip of a future admiral's flag peeped, not only lightened every captain's burdens and potentially increased his reputation (and his prize-money too). It was also both his duty and his pleasure to fan such bright sparks with promotion. Even, as in the case of Admiral Cornwallis and Commander Hornblower of the *Hotspur* later on, it was his final job-satisfaction, more valuable than rubies, as anyone who has himself been fortunate enough to reward merit will testify.

It was typical of Bush (as of others saddled with Lieutenant Lord Cochrane in his wardroom, no doubt) that he at first found Hornblower's restless intelligence irritating: good solid Englishmen, averagely thick, tend to be prejudiced against brains, where a Frenchman might find it difficult to render 'too clever by half' accurately in his own language. Nevertheless, in Bush's case that unimaginative, conformist and philistine Englishness was relieved by golden veins of common sense, lack of self-regard and honesty of the sort epitomised in higher command by men like Cuthbert Collingwood when he had Cochrane as a subordinate. And these now made Bush's friendship with Hornblower possible, and then mutually beneficial, and finally good for their service and their country as his younger friend outstripped him and friendship became loyalty. But most immediately in the *Renown* it was to be put to the test in the mysterious case of Captain Sawyer's 'accident', which providentially incapacitated him before he had driven his officers to an action which, even if it had not been judged mutinous, would surely have ruined all of their careers.

Accidents, as has already been noted, were commonplace in the old sailing navy, but that proportion of them which occurred *un*-accidentally among hated officers and warrant officers is no more to be guessed at accurately in this war than in the 1914–18 trenches ('Sir, we've shot our corporal!' – 'Good God! By accident?' – 'Yes, sir, we meant to shoot the sergeant.'): memoir writers then were no more likely to tell the truth about such events as to detail homosexual scandals. So whether Captain Sawyer *fell* down the hatchway as the ship rolled or whether he was *pushed* by the victimised Acting Midshipman Wellard will never be known. Conveniently, Sawyer never recovered from his head injuries before he was murdered in an uprising of Spanish prisoners which won Hornblower his promotion to acting Master and Commander in the West Indies, where such vacancies were most likely to occur. And, equally convenient, Wellard himself was to die in another accident a few months later.

In the context of Captain Sawyer and Midshipman Wellard, it is worth considering accident here in more detail as a source of naval casualties. As has already been indicated desertion was always the Navy's single biggest headache when it came to loss of manpower, and enemy gunfire the smallest. But, of course, deserters *could* be recovered and reused, whereas a far greater cause of permanent loss (also as we have seen) was always disease, particularly because of the need to station fleets permanently on unhealthy stations like the West Indies. This accounted for half the losses there in any average year. Major naval disasters like shipwreck, fire and explosion distorted the overall statistics in particular years, as when the 100-gun *Blenheim* and the *Java* (32) were lost with all hands off Madagascar in 1807 –

or, above all, in the dreadful loss of the *St George* (98) and other ships at the mouth of the Baltic in the great storm of December 1811, when more British sailors were killed than in all the major battles of the war added together. But famous (or infamous) though such disasters were, they still probably accounted for no more than from 10 to 12 per cent of deaths on average, while the steady drain of individual accidents in each of the thousand ships at sea killed three times as many, and disabled many more inexorably year after year.

Among these, Wellard's death was remarkable only in that he drowned, at a time when officers were at least more likely to be better swimmers than other ranks. Indeed, many of the latter, positively refused to learn to swim, in the widely held belief that a quick (and supposedly merciful) drowning was better than a hopeless fight for life. The extent to which this was already true lay in those frequent situations when it was either impossible or too dangerous to recover men who fell overboard in the days of sail. Even Cochrane, who was famous for doing his utmost to preserve the lives of his men in the most desperate situations, rejected a plea from Midshipman Marryat to lower a boat to save a man during a gale, muttering 'Poor Fellow!' but rightly refusing to hazard other lives.

Falling *in*board, from the high masts and rigging, was no less a source of fatalities. Some men, like Pigot's three victims in the *Hermione*, fell because of fear of flogging if 'last down'. More simply fell because of frozen or slimy ropes in heavy seas, whether or not they were trying to do their work smartly under the uncompromising eyes of their superiors. Even those who did *not* fall could very easily injure themselves, both while attending to the sails and in all the other heavy jobs round the ship, by overstraining their stomach muscles and rupturing themselves, as the issue of so many thousand of trusses by the Navy during the war years testifies.

Finally, there were all the run-of-the-mill accidents of the rough (and often drunken) life of sailors at sea in cramped conditions in ships never designed for comfort, where only pigmies could stand upright below decks (tall men like Admiral Duncan and Captains Cochrane and Hornblower, if not little Nelson, must have learned to walk with a more-or-less permanent stoop). Head-injuries were among the commonest ones. It could have been that it was the stress of command which finally cracked Pigot and Sawyer, not an accumulation of minor concussions; it was certainly a head injury, whether incurred as a result of pure accident or a judicious shove from behind, which transformed the latter from an uncertifiable madman to a raving lunatic. But, whatever the circumstances of this particular accident, the Navy was certainly not unacquainted with that risk, for its foremost physician, the great Sir Gilbert Blane, actually identified accidental head injuries as one of the Navy's problems. That he did so at all – and that he was in his time highly regarded and knighted for his service to the nation – is evidence of the importance which the Admiralty and all intelligent admirals and captains attached to health, with the result that the British Navy became healthier during the war – and notably more so than the much less hard-pressed French Navy. Still, while general hygiene improved steadily, treatment was at best primitive even where there was some sort of cure. With the real killers (apart from scurvy), the medical profession was helpless, as has been noted. With those venereal 'maladies of indiscretion', which the system encouraged by allowing prostitutes on board in harbour, much harm was done up until 1795 by the 15s charge made for what was already an unpleasant (and only partially effective) cure. However, syphilis (like hernia) was more common among other ranks, whereas head injuries (and lunacy) appear to have been more significant among those in command, although Blane also related it to carelessness due to the drunkenness which was also so common on the lower deck.

Captain Sawyer, at all events, became an accident statistic first, and was 'Discharged dead' by fortunate enemy accident soon enough before he could become a lunacy statistic. And his bad luck served to concentrate Hornblower's good luck, as a meritorious young officer without 'interest' arriving on an unhealthy West Indian Station, where there were more often vacancies but no unlimited supply of un-employed officers, as at home. Indeed, the heavy officer losses on the *Renown* offered the flag-officer in Jamaica gratifying openings for his own protégés first: favourite frigate captain to ship-of-the-line (in Captain Sawyer's place), favourite commander to post-captain's rank in a now-vacant frigate, and no less than three lieutenancies for the as yet unpromoted but qualified midshipmen sons of his friends (adding 'interest' to luck and merit, as usual). That Hornblower did not feature in this distribution of promotions in being appointed to the vacancy created by that commander-to-post-captain move indicates his lack of solid 'interest'. However, his very evident merit displayed in the recapture of the *Renown* from her Spanish prisoners, the loss of which would have been both embarrassing and awkward for the flag officer, was none the less rewarded with his appointment as commander into the best of the Spanish prizes taken earlier by that ship as a result of his efforts, an 18-gun sloop.

Now, however, his luck turned horribly against him, as a result of greater events in far-off Europe. For, although the rank of commander was an important one, often presaging advancement to post-rank, it was also a strictly temporary captaincy, held only by virtue of the command of a particular ship below frigate-rating. So, on his return to England, he was caught by the Peace of Amiens and the instant reduction of the Navy, to be thrown ashore like many hundreds of other officers, with his commission as acting-commander lost and unconfirmed. And, by a typical act of clerical meanness of the sort for which the Navy was famous, he was not even left with the half-pay of an unemployed lieutenant until he repaid the difference between that and the (acting) commander's pay he had drawn for the months of his ship-command. For those without influence, peace was always a disaster, and even promotion a considerable hazard when it involved removal from an existing command. Cochrane's adventures during this period have already been chronicled. But poor Philip Broke, another meritorious officer who had actually graduated through command of smaller ships to the glorious status of post-captain at last during the Amiens negotiations was to remain without another ship for the next four years.

It was Napoleon who saved them all in the end, of course. And it was Hornblower's luck – mediated once again through his skill as a whist-player (if Mr Forester and Lieutenant Bush are to be believed) – that he was exactly in the right place and among the right senior officers when the British Navy remobilised in 1803.

His appointment to the sloop *Hotspur* (16) was nevertheless both just in time and a beginning with no guaranteed future ahead of him. Some appointments to master and commander were almost in the nature of promises for the next available frigate made to lieutenants qualified one way or another for post-rank by seniority, merit or 'interest'. But other such commands were hard-earned rewards for older men (or men without 'interest', however competent) who might never make post thereafter. Hoste, in his final brilliant Adriatic operations, would have just such an able and deserving sloop-commander as his subordinate, John Harper of the *Saracen* (18). Harper was in his forties by then (1813), eight years older than Hoste, who had his eleven years' seniority as a post-captain. Hornblower, ten years earlier, was already in his thirtieth year, and – although lucky even then to get a ship of any kind – a beneficiary of the British Navy's top priority requirement, which was to get as many small craft as well as frigates as close as possible to the French coast, and particularly to the dangerous approaches to their main naval base at Brest, before war was declared. Indeed, if the captains of such little ships had rather better life-expectancy than RAF flight-lieutenants in 1940, Hornblower's successor in the *Hotspur* was to lose her on the Black Rock reef within days of taking command in 1805. Back in 1803, having lost his chance to hang on to the coat-tails of Captain Pellew back in '97, Hornblower still had everything to win – or lose – with the odds actuarially against him without 'interest' on so dangerous a shore. Given luck *and* a long war, plus merit, he still might make post. But, unlike all our other surviving special heroes, he needed all three ingredients now to reach the List with any hope of becoming an admiral. On the other hand, if this turned out to be a *short* war he might never reach the List at all, doomed to languish forever in the limbo of commander (by courtesy), if not lieutenant, on peacetime half-pay.

As all his admirers know, things were to turn out very differently for him, thanks primarily to his professional merit, which more than deserved that necessary infusion of luck which helped to generate 'interest' where there had been virtually none.

He was lucky, in the first place, to catch the eye of Admiral Sir William Cornwallis (1744–1819), whose eyes he was in the approaches to Brest. 'Billy Blue', the younger brother of that other Cornwallis who was forced to surrender at Yorktown (yet went on to become an able Governor-General of India), had entered the Navy nearly half a century earlier, seeing active service at the seige of Louisburg and the battle of Quiberon Bay in 1759. Having distinguished himself as a young officer in the Seven Years' War he saw more action as a captain in the American War, and reached admiral's rank when the next war broke out in 1793. His most famous action had been a fighting retreat in 1795, when he had brilliantly extricated his squadron of five ships-of-the-line and three frigates from a pursuit by a faster (as always!) French fleet of twelve ships-of-the-line and 15 frigates without losing a single ship. He had commanded the Channel Fleet in 1801, and now reassumed command. This, in a true sense, was his finest hour, to which Trafalgar was, in another true sense, the postscript: he was one of that band of admirals – St Vincent and Barham on land, Nelson and Collingwood (among others) at sea – who brought Napoleon's invasion plans to nothing.

It may be that Pellew, who became part of the ever-tightening blockade to the south in his 80-gun *Tonnant*, had some part in Hornblower's advancement, for he himself had served under Cornwallis in the *Impétueux* in 1801, having been strongly recommended by St Vincent not only as a 'meritorious and judicious' officer, but also as one who filled 'the eye of the public'. But the then unknown captain of the *Hotspur* won his spurs with Cornwallis by his own efforts on a coast the dangers of which the admiral well knew from his own youthful service in Quiberon Bay, as well as from his 1801 admiralcy. To his skill in surviving the hazards of this hostile no-man's-land, Hornblower here added a reputation for intelligence-gathering, after having also survived an encounter with the French frigate *Loire* which exemplified the communication problems of the age: with no wireless to give him either information or orders, he did not know – as the captain of the *Loire* did – that the second half of the last Anglo-French war had actually been declared when they met.

To this merit, more significantly in the *Naval Chronicle* for all fellow-officers to see, was added the credit for his part in the capture of the French frigate *Clorinde*, in company with the *Naiad* (36) when his conduct was deemed by Cornwallis to be 'highly commendable'. But more important to him was the arrival of Captain Pellew himself in the *Tonnant*, whose letter has been quoted earlier. For Pellew then ensured that his favourite ex-midshipman now had opportunities to distinguish himself, before himself leaving the squadron to hoist his own flag elsewhere on his appointment to admiral's rank. Pellew's no doubt enthusiastic despatches to Cornwallis, reporting his protégé's actions, must further have confirmed the admiral's own views, which in turn inclined him to reward such a 'meritorious and judicious' (and poor) young officer by attaching him to that frigate task-force which was detached under Captain Graham Moore to intercept the Spanish treasure fleet in 1804, before war between Britain and Spain had actually broken out (and to which reference has been made earlier).

This act of state piracy in fact further illustrates not only the use of frigates (rather than ships-of-the-line) for special operations, but also the working of 'interest' and the snakes-and-ladders nature of the prize-money game. The Spaniards had chosen frigates to transport their bullion, despatching Captain Moore to intercept the Spaniards in 1804 the Admiralty also chose frigates for the job. But it was Cornwallis who exercised his 'interest' in selecting the captains concerned, and then by adding Hornblower and the *Hotspur* for good measure, believing that he would make them all rich thereby: Hornblower, with his mathematical bent, would have had no difficulty in computing his captain's share, which would undoubtedly have made him a millionaire in modern money. In the event, of course, he forfeited his share by nobly heading-off a French frigate which would have given the game away, so that he was out of sight (and therefore out of prize-money) when the Spaniards were caught. But in the end he lost nothing by this nobility, because of the small print of the prize laws: prizes of war – 'Droits of the Crown' – belonged to King George, who had waived his claim in favour of his navy. But prizes of *peace* – 'Droits of Admiralty' – belonged to the Admiralty (and the government), and as neither the British nor the Spaniards had yet declared war on each other, the captors got nothing.

Still, Cornwallis eventually gave Hornblower something he valued more, by exercising his admiral's right to make a post-captain promotion on relinquishing his flag. Years before, when he accepted a midshipman's berth in the *Indefatigable*, Hornblower had looked for 'distinction, promotion, prize-money'. If he had signally failed to get much of the third of those so far, he now obtained the second through the first. And although, like every other ambitious young officer, he had hoped to become rich, he nevertheless summed up what the best of them felt no less in thanking his patron: 'I'd rather be a captain and poor than anyone else and rich, sir.'

For all that, his post-captaincy promotion was of the least desirable variety: like so many other newly made post-captains who lacked 'interest' (Cornwallis having then retired), he had thus exchanged the command of an unrated ship for post-rank but no ship at all, and like them he now had to wait for a frigate vacancy. Philip Broke, in a similar situation in 1801, remained on the beach for four years; Hornblower, indeed, was further required to prove himself in one of the most nebulous chapters of his career, which his biographer only hinted at – a cloak-and-dagger mission which is alleged to have contributed to the sailing of the Franco-Spanish fleet into Nelson's grasp at Trafalgar through the planting of false orders. Somewhat romantic though this tale may seem, it was not without precedent. On at least one occasion the French themselves had earlier deliberately allowed a ship of theirs containing disinformation about their Irish intentions to be captured.

Even after Trafalgar – which victory was, of course, followed by the promotion of many first lieutenants to post-rank – the command he eventually received was on the face of it a reflection of his lowly position on the Captains' List. Indeed, the *Atropos* (22, nine-pounders) was not really a rated ship at all and therefore hardly a post-command, but more like a French 'corvette' which, like the *Danae* and the admittedly somewhat bigger *Surprise*, the Admiralty none the less sometimes declared to be post-ships rather like the Catholic priest who found himself eating beef on a Friday, gave it his blessing, and declared it to be fish. However, whether the *Atropos* was merely an overgrown sloop or a stunted frigate, there was more in this posting than met the eye, if not in the ship herself.

Even as a ship, actually, the *Atropos* was preferable to the *Arab*, in which St Vincent had just sent Captain Lord Cochrane to sea – and in which Captain Lord Cochrane was then guarding the Orkneys fishing fleet. The only worse commands post-captains were to receive somewhat later were those worn-out frigates or obsolete ships-of-the-line of the Fourth Rate which the Admiralty was to convert into troopships for Wellington's Peninsular Army reinforcements. In these a captain had no chance at all of winning distinction or prize money, for all that his cargo was the most valuable of all, since it was both desperately needed and in short supply; and, indeed, troopship commands were in fact *not* given to junior or dead-beat captains as dead-end appointments, but to more senior ones who could expect to be delivered from their purgatory in due course, into ships-of-the-line. But newer and younger captains (and although the oldest of our special ones, and with 13 years' service on his record, Hornblower was still only 31 in 1806) expected frigates as their first post-command, and it is only from a deeper analysis that the *Atropos* posting can be assessed – and, indeed, compared with the fate of the more senior and much better-known Captain Cochrane while St Vincent was First

Lord. For, while the Sixth Rate *Arab* was a deliberate punishment for a man St Vincent disliked and did not trust (but who had to be given *something*), the smaller *Atropos* was a ship with a mission, entrusted to a young captain in whom the First Lord had confidence. Indeed, Hornblower's task was an extremely tricky one (and a very typical *frigate* job, from which his next mission in the *Lydia* – a *real* 36-gun frigate – must have been partially derived, with his knowledge of the Spanish language as an additional qualification): he was required to recover a British military chest (£250,000 = £25m in modern money?) illegally from Turkish waters, which had been lost in an 1801 shipwreck en route to Egypt, while the Turks were still Great Britain's allies. (Wrecks, of course, belonged not to their original owner, but to whomsoever's territorial waters in which they had been lost – 'Droits of Admiralty'?)

But, more than that – at least if the evidence of Lieutenant (future Admiral Sir) Anthony Bracegirdle can be relied on – Captain Hornblower was now St Vincent's protégé, having now been not only presented to His Gracious Majesty as such, but also having been entrusted with an obscure German relative of His Majesty's as a midshipman (Midshipman Mr Prince). For St Vincent, blue-blooded recruits to the now-fashionable Navy were anathema, and the claims of deserving officers came ahead of the upstart sons of Scotch earls, but – as with Nelson – his duty to his King always came first. In this case, however, he could do his whole duty with a clear conscience. Captain Hornblower was not only a Cornwallis recommendation, but also the pupil of Admiral Sir Edward Pellew, who – although now far away in his East Indies command, sadly – had been a reliable Member of Parliament among the First Lord's 'Friends' there. In fact, Captain Hornblower was not only a meritorious officer, but also a *judicious* one, on whose professional competence the Admiralty could rely; which, translated into eighteenth-century realities, meant that Hornblower was at last beginning to acquire 'interest'.

'Judiciousness' (which Cochrane above all lacked) was what the Navy now needed. Meritorious officers were two-a-penny, insanely-brave ones the norm and competent seamanship the result of years of experience at sea. These had been enough, under the direction of admirals like St Vincent and Barham and the inspiration of Nelson, to win all the great battles. But after Trafalgar there were no more of such battles. More, of course, had always been required of many of the very young men who found themselves in command of single detached ships, even small ones like Hornblower's *Hotspur*: 'There's folly and there's foolhardiness on one side, and there's daring and calculation on the other. Make the right choice,' Cornwallis had warned him in 1803. 'One can make mistakes,' added St Vincent in 1806. 'Let them be honest mistakes.' More and more there would be a premium on judgement in complex situations, tact in handling foreigners (allied or neutral) and superiors, and even real diplomatic skills requiring an understanding of higher policy. Before the war's end a captain like Hoste would be taking the reactions of the Emperor of Austria and the Tsar of Russia into account as he made war on the French; Cochrane, in making war on Admiral Gambier, failed even to take into account the likely effect of his actions on his own Admiralty and fellow Members of Parliament.

In a passage to be found (appropriately, as will soon be shown) in a chapter on early nineteenth-century independence movements in his *The Age of Revolution*, Professor Eric Hobsbawm actually identifies Cochrane as 'the original' for Hornblower. But while some of Cochrane's inshore operations in the Mediterranean do mirror some of Hornblower's and the latter's private politics inclined towards radicalism, there was no similarity in character. Unlike the Scotsman, the Englishman learned to hold his tongue, win the confidence of his superiors and – almost above all – steer clear of politics, which were the bane of so many otherwise successful officers. It was politics, indeed, which were nearly the ruin of his first patron, Pellew, at the height of his naval career after he had been given the East Indian command by *his* patron, St Vincent, and the Addington Government, only to have it unworkably divided by his (and St Vincent's) political enemies, Melville and Pitt. (The bitter quarrels caused by this petty piece of revenge which he had with Nelson's friend – now Admiral – Troubridge were to drive Pellew to reflect rather irritably that he would 'rather command a Frigate with her Bowsprit over the rocks of Ushant' all his life than be where he was, flag or no flag.) As it was, even later on, when he had quite incidentally acquired real political 'interest' of his own through his marriage into the Duke of Wellington's Wellesley family and had become a popular naval hero in place of the now-ruined Cochrane, Hornblower kept out of politics. It is in this, perhaps (certainly rather than in his disdain of prize-money, which he shared with Captain Philip Broke), that he is most nearly too good to be true among his contemporaries. For them – for Pellew equally with the reforming Cochrane – politics and 'interest' were simply facts of life, and of the system, to be used (and abused) accordingly. Even St Vincent, who always deplored the malign influence of both, never scrupled to use either.

Facts of life and the system notwithstanding, however, the evidence suggests that meritorious *and* judicious officers without much 'interest' (but with, of course, a little luck) could get on in the Navy. Even Broke by now, after his years of unemployment, commanded the powerful *Shannon* (38). And in 1807, after successfully recovering his country's lost war-chest and assisting the *Nightingale* (28, and another 'corvette'-sized frigate) in the capture of the Spanish *Castella*

(40), Hornblower was rewarded not only with a *real* frigate, the *Lydia* (36), but with a special frigate-type mission-of-mischief which British naval supremacy had now made so tempting and which was particularly suitable to a judicious and Spanish-speaking captain.

During the war the foundations of the British Empire of the future – the Second British Empire, if the loss of the American colonies marks the end of the First – were being laid, but not deliberately. Colonies, as the American experience had demonstrated, could be expensive and troublesome. It was trade and commerce that made for wealth and comfort at home, where such things could be best enjoyed. So, although money-making also involved overseas *possessions* in profitable but otherwise unstable parts of the world (especially where there was tough foreign competition, as in the West Indies and India), there was no great drive for the acquisition of the vast new territories which then lay open for the taking. A few more plums might be picked, certainly. But larger fruit – even like the rich (Dutch) island of Java, which Pellew was to conquer in 1811 – were not retained at the end of the war. Even the immensity of Australia was useful only as a refuse dump for convicts. Much more valuable were well-situated harbours, strategic in war and convenient in peace, from which British naval and merchant ships could safely operate – and which, when taken from enemies, denied others such advantages. Gibraltar, captured a century before and held against all odds ever after, was one of the first and greatest of these jewels in the British imperial–commercial crown. Malta, a jewel of increasing brightness, had quickly proved so useful that its retention during the months of the Amiens peace provided Napoleon with his best reply to British accusations of bad faith as that peace broke down. (In the fullness of time he would end up imprisoned on another of Britain's days-of-sail stepping stones, St Helena, which the East India company had held since 1659; and his exile there led the British directly to the annexation of Ascension Island also, whose role as a staging post to the South Atlantic was to be reanimated over a century and a half later, during the Falklands War.)

To Malta were now added other enemy bases one by one, in the Cape of Good Hope, Ceylon and eventually Java – all possessions of Holland ('the Batavian Republic'), and finally the last main French naval base in the Indian Ocean, Ile-de-France, the future Mauritius. Of these, Java alone was to be restored to its original owner in 1815, commercially very valuable though it was. But it is the Cape of Good Hope which concerns us here and now because of its indirect influence on the *Lydia* mission. This strategic 'Batavian' colony had been seized once before, in the first half of the war, but had been restored to its owners under the terms of the Amiens treaty, in 1802. When the war started again, its reconquest was a British priority, for fear of some new Napoleonic move against India and in the knowledge that a

French occupation would be easy with the Batavian Republic itself no more than a French colony. Accordingly, a quite substantial expeditionary force of 5,000 men, commanded by one of Britain's better generals, Sir David Baird, was despatched at some considerable risk before Trafalgar had been fought, escorted by a naval squadron under the command of Captain Sir Home Riggs Popham, as 'commodore' (a temporary appointment indicating the importance of a small detached command – and also conferring temporary flag-officer status in such matters as prize-money).

Even though – or even, perhaps, *because* – he was never a successful frigate captain, Home Riggs Popham (1762–1820) ranks among the most interesting of the up-and-coming senior naval officers of the post-Trafalgar period, not least in that both he and his career were far from typical. A one-year Cambridge undergraduate and accomplished linguist, he had entered the Navy during the American War and been commissioned lieutenant in 1783. In 1789, however, he had obtained long leave-of-absence, and during the next five years had involved himself in the China and East Indian trades, commanding an *Austrian* East Indiaman, and nearly ruining himself when his ship was seized for alleged unlicensed trading. A Fellow of the Royal Society, his present knighthood (of Malta) had in fact been conferred on him not by His Britannic Majesty, but by the Tsar of Russia for services in the Baltic during a period of Anglo-Russian alliance. And since his return to the Royal Navy he had distinguished himself during the Duke of York's disastrous campaign in Flanders in 1794, when he was promoted to post-captain. Ever since he had been involved in the Copenhagen campaign of 1800, when as captain of the *Romney* (50) he had transmitted messages between the fleet and negotiators on shore, he had interested himself in the Navy's signalling system. This had been infinitely improved over the previous 25 years by the innovations of Admirals Howe and Kempenfelt, from its primitive and restrictive state, which had been largely to blame for the many unproductive battles of previous eighteenth-century wars. Over the next decade, Popham was to continue this work of improvement, greatly to the Navy's operational advantage: he was, all in all, an unusually intellectual and thoughtful officer.

However, though already marked as somewhat different from the majority of those on the Captains' List, Popham was not simply an intellectual eccentric – he was also very much a man of action and initiative, which were combined with imagination and daring almost of Cochrane proportions. And before he had sailed for southern Africa in the autumn of 1805 he had been in contact with certain Creole (Spanish-American) exiles who had assured him that their homeland was disaffected with Spanish rule and ripe for British intervention.

This, as it turned out, was both true and false. The British (and before them the English, in the persons of such men as Hawkins, Drake and Raleigh) had long been interested in the commercial possibilities of the Spanish Central and Southern American empire – or, failing commercial openings, in the profits of freebooting and semi-piracy. In early days, however, the power of Spain had been too great, and even after that power had declined the increasing rivalry between France and Britain had served to protect Spanish America by ensuring that one of the rivals would always be concerned to stop the other from dismembering it. Also, in spite of Anglo-French perceptions to the contrary, Spanish colonial rule had been neither excessively incompetent nor particularly oppressive in many respects, and the eighteenth century had witnessed a period of relative stability and increasing prosperity in her American colonies. But as the century advanced some of those same processes which had worked eventually to transform *British* Americans into *United States* Americans worked to turn *Spanish* Americans into *Americanos* or *Creoles* who came to resent incoming European Spanish officials and the rules and regulations which they imposed. This evolutionary process prepared the ground for the ideas of the successful American and French revolutions, which fell on fertile patches of soil among the more prosperous Creoles who had inherited that same fierce Spanish pride which was soon to confound Napoleon himself.

All this, by the turn of the century, had resulted in the arrival of Creole revolutionary exiles and émigrés in both France and Britain, including such men as Francisco de Miranda and the great Simon Bolivar himself. In Britain, particularly, their dreams of revenge and independence found a ready welcome. For not only did the British need new markets for their goods as trade with Europe became more difficult, but the ascendancy of the British Navy had at last provided the ideal conditions for colonial revolt. Even before the Amiens peace the Spanish American colonies had been effectively cut off from their motherland, further weakening the ties between them. And once a motherland's navy is seen to be no longer able to defend its colonies and dominions from outsiders an imperial relationship is changed forever – as Britain in her turn was to discover after the 1939–45 war. Spanish Trinidad, a West Indian sugar island, had indeed been one of Britain's few acquisitions under the Amiens settlement. Faced, after Trafalgar and Austerlitz, with the problem of making war somehow, somewhere, with a great navy, but with a contemptible army and virtually without allies, the British were not unnaturally tempted to embark on overseas sideshows against their main enemy's weaker allies – the more so as such operations could now be viewed as commercially essential.

Against this background, Commodore Sir Home Riggs Popham's South American adventure becomes much more explicable. And, indeed, in spite of its outcome and his subsequent court martial the City of London later presented him with a Sword of Honour in appreciation of what was viewed as a gallant attempt to open up new markets. What makes the adventure extraordinary, nevertheless, is that it was a pure bit of private enterprise. For (emboldened, one must assume, by the Nelson tradition of initiative, without or against orders), he went on from the conquest of the Cape of Good Hope to an unscripted dash across the South Atlantic to invade South America in 1806.

Arriving quite literally out of the blue in the River Plate, he was at first successful, capturing Buenos Aires and despatching a million Spanish dollars home with the news of his exploit. Surprised but not averse to a victory, the British government hastily scratched some reinforcements together. But these were only swept up in what turned out to be a disastrous miscalculation: there were indeed disaffected Creole elements in Buenos Aires and Montevideo, but they were no more willing to exchange British for Spanish domination than were the official Spanish authorities. Popham's troops were too few in number (even before they started joyfully to desert into an attractive country, just as so many Redcoats had done during the American colonial war), and the incompetent General Whitelock's reinforcements were insufficient. Also, both the Spanish Viceroy, Sobremonte, and the local Creole leader, Liniers, proved to be energetic commanders. So the invasions failed dismally, ending in capitulation, the cashiering of Whitelock and a severe court-martial reprimand for Popham. Rather surprisingly, the latter lived to fight again (as we shall discover later), to become an admiral and to be knighted by King George. But Popham's only lasting South American achievement, one may suppose, is that he laid firm foundations for the eventual liberation movements on the River Plate – and perhaps the idea among the future Argentinians of General Galtieri's time that the South Atlantic was too far away for British military operations.

Meanwhile, the British had learned the hard way that any conquest of the mainland Spanish American territories was fraught with danger, and that an earlier policy, formulated in instructions to their governor of newly-conquered Trinidad to explore the possibility of supporting local independence movements, was better-advised. To this end and at the urging of men like Miranda, they began to assemble a real expeditionary force of some 9,000 men at Cork in Ireland to support a Mexican revolution. Interestingly, this was in the time of the first Foreign Secretaryship of young George Canning, who after the war was to be the real enforcer of the Monroe Doctrine ('no European intervention in the Americas'), which the might of the British fleet ensured. Perhaps more immediately interesting, however, the command of this American invasion was given to Sir Arthur Wellesley, the up-and-coming and politically influential young general who had distinguished himself in India and, most recently, during Admiral Lord Gambier's Copenhagen operations.

In fact, whatever the outcome of the Mexican expedition *might* have been, it would have constituted a foolish dispersal of Britain's limited forces far from the real war against the real enemy, under the command of the man who was to emerge as her greatest soldier (who himself only accepted the – to him – uncongenial role of encouraging revolutionaries in order to escape from a political post in Ireland). Arguably, also, almost as much might have been achieved anyway, and at far less cost and risk, by the judicious use of frigates in the way that Captain Hornblower was soon to demonstrate. To give the British government the benefit of the doubt, however, it is altogether possible that the *Lydia* mission was in reality a diversionary operation designed to help Sir Arthur by drawing off Spanish forces from Mexico to Nicaragua, as well as away from Panama.

Be all that as it may, Hornblower's unexpected arrival off the Nicaraguan coast illustrates classically that frigate role which Pellew had demonstrated less successfully in the *Indefatigable* in aiding Breton and Vendéan rebels and which Cochrane was soon to do so brilliantly in the *Impérieuse* off the Costa Brava. For he not only supplied and transported the Nicaraguan insurgents, but also ambushed the unsuspecting 50-gun *Natividad* and captured her virtually undamaged. But then, after having turned his prize over to his allies for perfectly justifiable diplomatic reasons (and he had no crew for her, anyway), he was overtaken by history just as he was setting off to make his fortune in prize-money in those very waters which had enriched Drake over two centuries earlier, and Anson in the 1740s.

It was his *mis*fortune, but his country's crowning mercy, that some three months before, just as he was rounding the Horn in the *Lydia*, Napoleon had ruthlessly ejected the Spanish monarchy and roused a great Spanish national rising. Indeed, while the *Lydia* had been sailing up the coast of South America, delegations from Spain and Portugal had been hurrying to London, eager to solicit alliance and help against the common enemy. And help, of course, was for once providentially ready to hand, in the form of Lieutenant-General Sir Arthur Wellesley and his army, which was instantly diverted from Spanish Mexico (to fight the Spaniards) to the Spanish Peninsula itself (to fight the French), much to General Wellesley's relief and 'General' Miranda's bitter rage. But all this, thanks both to the huge time-lag in communications of those days and the secrecy which Hornblower's own Admiralty orders had enjoined (which did not allow him to call at any port en route), now forced the British captain to seek out and retake the *Natividad* while further burdened by the presence on board of General

Wellesley's sister, Lady Barbara, who had insisted on joining his ship to escape the horrors of a yellow-fever epidemic in Panama.

The resultant single-ship action, which made Hornblower's reputation as a frigate captain, was at once typical and atypical of such actions during the war. It was typical in the first place in the disparity of the contestants' broadsides, the *Lydia*'s fewer and lighter 12-pounders against the *Natividad*'s 24-pounders. Fortunately, however, it was also typical in the superiority of British ship-handling, training and gunnery and – almost above all in this instance – damage-control, which usually more than evened that disparity in guns. At the same time, unfortunately – and highly atypically – the *Natividad*, under officers as fanatical as brave, was not only fought much harder than any other ships of the time, French *and* British, but literally to the death. As a result, even though Hornblower manoeuvred his ship brilliantly to deliver several raking broadsides, the rebel captain refused to strike, and the first round of the fight continued until both ships were partially dismasted, heavily damaged and unmanoeuvrable. Only those advantages of training and damage-control (and temporary repair), which the British Navy had earlier demonstrated after their defeat in the first round of the battle of Algeciras in 1801, enabled Hornblower to get the *Lydia* back into action again next day. And even so this process involved heavy casualties (and the famous episode of the hornpipe competition) while she was being towed into range by her own boats in windless conditions under enemy fire. But then the wind freshened and the helpless *Natividad* – still refusing to strike – was beaten into a burning wreck and finally sunk, not in eighteenth-century style at all but rather in the cruel twentieth-century 'no-surrender' manner.

One may imagine that the hornpipe story did the rounds of the coffee-shops in Portsmouth, Plymouth and every navy anchorage, as well as those of London, even with popular ballads sung in 'Horny's' honour, as they had been for Pellew and the *Indefatigable* and Cochrane and the *Impérieuse* – and Nelson's capture of the *San Josef* and the *San Nicolas* (perhaps there was a *Lydia* v *Natividad* Nicholas Pocock painting too . . . but that, alas, has eluded all researchers). But Hornblower's peers and seniors would have been more impressed by the duration, dreadful casualty list and outcome of the fight. Single-ship actions (as we have already seen and will see again most spectacularly in the *Shannon*'s last fight) were more often brief affairs, minutes rather than hours in duration. A quick succession of well-aimed broadsides, delivered at close quarters on the 'downward roll' to hit the hull – and ideally from the raking position, at right-angles to the enemy's stern or her bows to do maximum execution and damage – had a cumulative effect, slowing down the enemy's own broadsides (if they even managed an organised reply). Indeed, such fights

Indeed, such fights resemble nothing so much as those medieval archery duels, when the Black Prince's longbowmen maintained that 'after the third or fourth, or at most the sixth, draw men knew which side would win'. But longer fights did sometimes occur, particularly when both sides had sustained damage aloft, as in the *Lydia–Natividad* fight. Famously, the duel between the British (ex-French) *San Fiorenzo* (36) and the French *Piémontaise* (40) off Cape Cormorin in the same year lasted for no less than three days. What made the outcome of the *Lydia–Natividad* encounter more unusual still was that the beaten captain refused to strike, his ship being in the end sunk by gunfire in battle. Sinkings *after* battle and surrender were far from rare, due either to accumulated damage or to damage plus weather, most of the Trafalgar prizes being lost that way. But wooden ships were notoriously hard to destroy *in* battle by gunfire, being then more often destroyed because of fire or explosion, more or less accidentally and especially after poorly trained and inexperienced crews had been further demoralised by casualties and ship-damage. In both the French and Spanish navies ships were regularly lost in battle in this way, including the huge *Orient* flagship at the Nile and two giant Spanish 112-gun ships during the pursuit at the second battle of Algeciras. That the British lost not one ship from such causes *in battle* says much for their higher standards of training and discipline in combat; that they lost a number *in harbour* – including Sir John Jervis's 98-gun flagship *Boyne* in 1795 and the *Amphion* frigate (32), commanded by Edward Pellew's brother Israel, a year later – probably says more for rum-induced carelessness than anything else.

The performance of the *Lydia*'s crew was, therefore, routinely excellent rather than unique, and, so far as Captain Hornblower himself was concerned, a victory of a British frigate over an elderly and obsolete 50-gun Spanish two-decker was praiseworthy rather than headline-grabbing after so many other victories over so many years of war. It was, after all, what the Admiralty clerk who had drawn up his orders expected, and their Lordships of the Admiralty were probably more gratified by the length of the British casualty list (more than one-third killed or maimed), which proclaimed British heroism, than by that expected success. Captain Hornblower had once again shown that he was a meritorious and judicious officer. But then, equally, he had once again been an unlucky one: the autumn of 1808 was hardly the moment to trumpet the double humiliation he had inflicted on the navy of his country's newest and most valued ally when the struggle against the Corsican Ogre was going rather badly. His unfortunate handing-over of the *Natividad* to the insurgents was best forgotten, and himself with it (and, of course, there would not even be any head-money for the crew he had thus disposed of, let alone prize-money for a ship now at the bottom of the Gulf of Tehuantepec). Without 'interest', the best Captain Hornblower might now expect was blockade duty off Brest, for which his previous experience fitted him, always supposing that the *Lydia* was still seaworthy; or, if she was worn out (and Admiral Pellew, his old patron, was far away in the East Indies), he would have to wait his turn for another command, like every other post-captain of a mere four years' seniority.

But, of course, it was not like that at all. For Captain Hornblower now acquired 'interest', and at the very highest level, in the formidable person of Lady Barbara Wellesley, who was not only the daughter of the Earl of Mornington and the sister of General Sir Arthur Wellesley (now in command in the Peninsula), but also the sister of Lord Richard Wellesley, shortly to become Foreign Secretary, and who was herself shortly to become the wife of Admiral Sir Percy Leighton, whose friends controlled 20 seats in the House of Commons. And in virtue of his political 'interest' rather than any noticeable naval talent, Admiral Leighton was then earmarked for command of a small detached squadron of ships-of-the-line in the Mediterranean, charged with supporting his country's valued new Spanish ally.

'Interest', as has either already been shown or will further be shown, operated through many different channels, from the service-familial (Nelson and Pigot), through the service-nationalist (Cochrane) to the geographical-political (Pellew), and even – as we shall see – the geographical-ecclesiastical (Hoste). It is hardly to be doubted that it also worked through that most traditional of routes, the bedchamber, in Hornblower's case. He was a meritorious but unfortunate officer, whose recent successes had been embarrassing and whose only patrons, Cornwallis and St Vincent, were respectively too old and out of office. But he was not connected *politically* with the latter, and it may reasonably be presumed that Admiral Leighton would not have refused a solicitation from his bride, who was as formidable in character as she was influential by birth, and it was thus that Captain Hornblower was appointed to the command of the (ex-Dutch) *Sutherland* (74) in the spring of 1810. That he would otherwise have been unemployed may be inferred from the complete (and compulsory) transfer of the *Lydia*'s crew to become the nucleus of the *Sutherland*'s, which meant that the frigate was being de-commissioned. But although in retrospect the transfer for him (if not for all but two of his crew) opened a new chapter in his career leading through defeat and captivity to fame and fortune it also put an end to his frigate career, in which he might have won as much by more conventional (frigate) means: as a Pellow-pupil and Cochrane-imitator he was born a frigate captain – indeed, the *Sutherland* was to behave more like a frigate than a ship-of-the-line on many occasions during the months that followed before he finally sacrificed her to prevent the escape of a squadron of French ships-of-the-line. And, without Lady Barbara's intervention yet as a meritorious *and* judicious captain of at least six years' seniority on the list, he should sooner or later have got another frigate.

Still, all that is in the realm of might-have-been. As it is, Hornblower must now sail out of this story as a notable frigate captain like Pellew before him, as a ship-of-the-line captain, better-paid and with more men and more and bigger guns, but less chance of the individual fame and fortune which a frigate might bring. And how he made his own chances (although, of course, nothing but years of seniority could make him an admiral) is another story. Meanwhile, however, it is necessary to take stock of the progress of the whole war before taking up the tale of the youngest of our special captains – youngest and arguably luckiest, since it was his good fortune in the Age of Nelson to win by merit the devoted 'interest' of Nelson himself.

CHAPTER TWELVE

Convoys and clergymen's sons

When Admiral Sir Percy Leighton's squadron sailed for the Mediterranean the war – except for the Amiens breathing space between
rounds – had been in progress for 17 years, having started before many
of his 'young gentlemen' and powder-monkeys had been born. But
although in some respects it must have seemed as unchanging as it was
endless a new phase was beginning for the British: the squadron's first
duty might be to escort a convoy southwards, as so many departing
warships had long been required to do, but while Captain Hornblower
continued further south protecting four fat Indiamen as far as
Gibraltar, Leighton himself split off to take a troop convoy into
Lisbon. The British Army had returned to Europe, and this time it
would not be evacuated with the French breathing down its neck – it
would leave the Spanish Peninsula *via* France.

But that would be four long years ahead. And there were meanwhile
some things which Captain (now Admiral Sir Edward) Pellew would
have recognised from 1793, even apart from that convoy duty (of
which more very soon): before she had sailed the *Sutherland* had been
desperately short of men, which Captain Hornblower had partially
solved by raiding Cornwall by surprise with his press gang in his ship's
boats after the Bodmin and Truro assizes had supplied him with only
60 jailbirds. And then, in bidding farewell to his Indiamen, he had
stripped each of them of 20 prime seamen – which, unlike the Cornish
raid, *was* strictly illegal; but which, given the many months before the
East India Company protests filtered back to London from India, was
a well-calculated risk. Under-strength crews made up partly of

untrained riff-raff and largely of unwilling men who would desert at the first opportunity were the lot of most British captains. And *all* British captains (at least, except the Cochranes among them) filled the gaps ruthlessly and high-handedly as the opportunity presented itself, for choice with British sailors, but with anything two-legged and likely (particularly Americans) when they had the upper hand. And the upper hand, of course, they usually had now at sea. Hornblower, as captains went, was an enlightened and inspirational captain. But even Nicholas Monsarrat's equally enlightened and inspirational Captain Ericson of the *Saltash* in the 1939–45 world war was brutalised by experience and necessity by 1943, after only four years of combat. Hornblower and his peers, after 17 years of war and half-a-dozen or more years of command under a much more brutal system in a harder age were no longer soft-hearted.

Plus, no less, the last of the great French Wars in 1810 in no way resembled the last of the German Wars in 1943. At sea even though Britannia ruled the waves, French warships – and quite substantial squadrons of them, as Hornblower and Hoste were both to discover, as well as Captains Willoughby and Corbet in the Indian Ocean – might still have to be fought by numerically inferior British ones. And on land, although Sir Arthur Wellesley might now be in command of a British army in Portugal and Napoleon's 'Spanish ulcer' had opened up there, the French dominion of Europe from the Atlantic to the Russo-Polish frontier, and from the Baltic to the Adriatic down to the heel of Italy, still seemed as absolute as it had been after the battles of Austerlitz and Jena and the Treaty of Tilsit. Even with her Portuguese and Spanish allies, Britain had still not solved the problem of tackling the full might of the French Army, augmented as it now was by the soldiers of France's own subject-allies. If Napoleon had given his undivided attention to that Spanish ulcer, it would surely have been cauterised, however painfully.

Also, the war had, and had always had from its very beginnings in 1793, another dimension, which presented both great problems and great opportunities for both sides in the area of economic warfare. Most obviously, this dimension affected Britain, both because she was becoming the workshop of the world by virtue of her lead in the industrial revolution and because, as an off-shore entrepreneurial island, she lived by her maritime trade. It had been this development, after all, which had provided the stimulus for her to launch the world's greatest navy while other European nations – even far poorer and smaller ones like Prussia – had raised far bigger armies to protect their land frontiers.

Establishing naval superiority either by sinking enemy battle-fleets or by penning them up in their harbours is one thing, but making the seas safe for essential merchant shipping is another – as both twentieth-century world wars have demonstrated frighteningly. In each of those later wars British (and allied) command of the sea-lanes was not only challenged, but also twice almost wrested away by enemies whose main target was merchant shipping: on both occasions the still-great British Navy fought its most important sea-war against the great *new* German submarine navy, to the death. Indeed, the 1917–18 and 1940–43 Atlantic Sea campaigns, which all too easily seem an endless blur of continuous action, deserve in reality to be regarded as a sequence of individual sea-battles, for all that they have gone into the record simply under the code numbers of hundreds of inward and outward-bound convoys. And the final Homeric convoy encounters of 1943, from late winter into early summer, in which new high technology was blended with old-fashioned professional excellence and courage on both sides, fully deserve to rank not only with any other sea-battles of that war, but with any of Nelson's victories.

Our 1793–1815 world war bears some comparison with those modern wars, very different though the ships and their technology and organisation were in the age of sail. For, disastrous though the French Navy's performance was, the professional skill and ingenuity of their commerce raiders was very damaging, added to the effects of the Napoleonic economic warfare, which sought to counter the British blockade by closing all ports of Europe to British goods. In fact it was the latter, rather than the former, which almost brought the British to their knees during the depression of 1807–8, combined with a United States embargo on trade, which was the American 'plague-on-all-your-warring-houses' reaction to their own situation, caught as they were between the Royal Navy at sea and Napoleon on land. Goods piled up in every warehouse from London to Liverpool, with unemployment, hardship in the new manufacturing centres and finally riots following. Fortunately for the islanders, however, their industrial revolution had changed the world commercially quite as much as the American and French revolutions had changed it politically: neither America nor Europe could do without cheap British machine-made products – they needed them, they wanted them, and one way or another they were going to have them – together with all the re-exports which also passed through her ports in both directions. Not all the bayonets and customs officers in Europe could stop smuggling from becoming a major European service industry; ports from Archangel in the most distant north, through all the North German and Baltic ports (where the authorities were surprised how many hearses were to be seen along the quaysides – until they looked behind the curtains), to Trieste and the Italian ports in the south, soon emptied those British warehouses, and demanded more. Most famously, many of Napoleon's future invaders of Holy Mother Russia marched in British boots, wearing British greatcoats (if they were lucky), to be repelled by similarly equipped Russians. By 1810–11 the British depression of 1807–8 was forgotten in an economic boom.

But all that, in greater detail, lies outside the scope of this story. For, notwithstanding all its other duties, the British Navy was not concerned to *prevent* the export of whatever Britain could sell or re-export to anywhere other than France (directly, anyway). Rather, the Navy's job was to see such goods reached their proper destinations, transhipped from such halfway houses as Heligoland Island (another British base now) and Malta, which waxed fat on trade as never before. And, more importantly still, the thousands of ships bringing goods into Britain as their final destination, or trading with the rest of the world, had to be protected from enemy raiders at sea.

How dangerous the French Navy could be, before it was tamed, had been amply demonstrated in the earliest years of the war, when a French squadron of three ships-of-the-line and six frigates took 30 merchant ships and one convoy escort (a 74-gun ship-of-the-line) off Cape St Vincent in 1795, leaving only two escorts and one merchant man uncaptured. Fishing boats were no less fair game, and had to be protected (as Cochrane had learned the hard way): a French squadron decimated the valuable Newfoundland fishery fleet in 1796. As late as 1810 another French squadron escaped to capture a quarter of a 200-ship convoy off Norway. Regular French navy ships, with big crews available to be spread among prizes, could make short work of merchant shipping, not least the big (and most prized) Indiamen which might carry 18 or 20 guns and were barely distinguishable from warships. (Indeed, on one celebrated occasion, in the Straits of Bali in 1797, the senior captain of an unescorted group of Indiamen bamboozled a powerful French squadron by raising a British admiral's flag and forming line-of-battle, convincing the French admiral that he was up against two ships-of-the-line and four frigates.)

Much more dangerous than the French Navy, nevertheless, were the countless smaller French 'private enterprise' raiders, the privateers, which lurked in every port and creek, varying in size from formidable 20-gun sloops and corvettes, which could – and on occasion did – master their British opposite numbers, down to mere rowing boats packed with armed men. Often faster and usually more manoeuvrable than the British Navy vessels hunting them, these were crewed by skilled sailors who knew the British coastline as well as their own, many of them ex-fishermen whose business had been ruined by their enemies. Some of their captains became legends on both sides of the Channel, and also much further afield. If there were no great French admirals of the age to rank with the best among Nelson's colleagues, and few French frigate captains of the quality of Pellew's friend Bergeret, there was no shortage of brilliant privateer captains: men like the famous Blanckmann and Leveille, from Dunkirk, Lemême and

Surcouf from Ile-de-France, and Leroi in the West Indies – not to mention foreigners like Bavastro in the Mediterranean. In their own sphere, and pitted against the most powerful navy in the world, these were the Pellews, Cochranes and Hostes among the enemy for their daring, enterprise and seamanship, and the injury they inflicted was substantial even if it never approached that achieved by the German U-boat aces of the twentieth century.

As with the U-boat, the only effective answer to these predators was the convoy system, some consideration of which is necessary now not simply because of its importance in the story of the whole 1793–1815 sea-war, but also because all six of our frigate captains – and, indeed, *all* British ship-commanders and their crews, and the admirals above them – spent a good part of their service either as convoy escorts or on associated defensive patrol duties.

Mention has already been made of the significance of the great Atlantic convoy-battles of 1917–18 and 1940–43. But the history of the convoy and the convoy system begins much earlier, even though it was so unaccountably misinterpreted by the British Admiralty during the years 1916–17 that the Navy came much closer to losing the war then than the Allied armies in Flanders and France were to do during the last great German offensive of 1918. By contrast, the British Admiralty and Parliament of 1793 made no mistake from the start firming up previous custom, practice and experience immediately with a convoy act which was given more teeth with the *Compulsory* Convoy Act of 1798, in which taxes on awkward ship-owners were added to the fines imposed on disobedient captains. What is not least interesting in the history of the convoy is, indeed, that the convoy's importance was better understood by the Admiralty in 1793 than by the merchant captains themselves. In both the last French and the first German war merchant captains chafed at delays in convoy assembly, the orders which then tied faster ships to slower ones under naval discipline, and to the delays caused by their simultaneous arrival in port. The 1793–1815 merchant captains did, admittedly, have a greater incentive to break the rules (with their owners' approval): the huge profits which first arrivals could expect outweighed the danger of meeting Captain Blanckmann and his friends in that final dash for port (which, under sail, might be argued away more easily as unintentional, but which was a constant source of apoplexy among harassed escort captains, who were held responsible).

Still, at the higher levels the value of the convoy was never questioned on both sides. Indeed, the whole war started with a great convoy battle which the French won, even though the British celebrated it afterwards as the victorious 'Glorious First of June'. Honours were then showered on the British admirals and captains who had defeated the French Navy in the first sea-battle of the war, confirming what Captain Pellew had proved in his frigate victory. But the French admiral, though beaten in battle, congratulated himself on thereby bringing in a vital grain convoy from the United States to the starving French Republic, saving his head from the guillotine as well as his country. And, equally, on the British side, no less than 34 ships-of-the-line, together with frigates and smaller ships, escorted a military convoy to the West Indies (where yellow jack soon massacred the soldiers thus safely delivered) in 1794.

Many of the ships of that escort fleet were, of course, also heading for foreign service. But then almost every outward-bound British squadron or warship was automatically conscripted for escort duty, like Hornblower's in 1810. For in this war, as in its predecessors and successors, there were never enough escorts available, with all the other calls on the Navy. And it was always an unpopular duty, not only because of the recalcitrance of merchant captains, but also because in the days of sail the escorts often faced tremendous difficulties in keeping convoys together, especially during storms, fog and at night. In dead calms or very light winds, convoys were prey to attack by oared raiders off the French coast, and to galleys in the Mediterranean and off Cadiz. As a midshipman, Hornblower experienced an attack by Spanish galleys, and, as the captain of a 74 he was to discover how difficult it was to protect even a small convoy against simultaneous attacks from different directions by small French luggers which he could sink with half a broadside if only he could catch them. In bigger convoys there were often small 'whipper-in' escort vessels whose job it was to keep convoys together, even towing persistent laggards to keep them in formation. Even the convoy formations were strictly laid down, but (as in the 1939–45 war) there always seemed to be merchant captains who could not or would not keep station: such ships were in this war on occasion actually fired on to bring them to heel. But at least Nelson's Admiralty had grasped a great truth, later forgotten until the findings of trained twentieth-century statisticians prodded his descendants into rediscovering it: that few and bigger convoys were better than many smaller ones. This was revealed in the 1940s by comparative loss statistics, which showed that the number of ships lost was not in proportion to the size of the convoy. And the logic of it was simple: not only was the ocean so great that any one convoy stood a chance of getting through undetected by the enemy (so the fewer, the better), but also, by simple geometry. The perimeter of a large convoy was not directly proportional to that of a smaller one, so that its escort requirement was more economical – or it could be better-escorted. Without benefit of such statistical expertise, but only by experience, the hard-headed admirals of 1793–1815 needed no advice. And if they had needed allies in support of the convoy system itself, the immensely influential Committee of Lloyd's and its underwriters were also powerfully on their side. All of them knew what was to emerge conclusively from historians' subsequent analyses: that during even the first five years of the war, before the French and Spanish fleets themselves had been defeated, thousands of ships were convoyed with an overall loss of only 0.6 per cent – and that, even in its last months, when there were some highly skilful Yankee privateers loose, this rate had been reduced to 0.53 per cent.

Of course, by then many of the greatest privateer 'aces' (like their U-boat-captain descendants) had been eliminated – the Bergerets of the regular navy and men like Blanckmann (who was finally cornered after a nine-hour pursuit by one of the Navy's fastest sloops-of-war) even if St Malo's favourite son, Surcouf, 'the King of the Corsairs', was never caught. Given the right circumstances, convoys always could be – and were – penetrated; and, of course, there were always rich pickings among the legal 'independents', who sailed out of convoy, and that substantial number of coastwise shipping which for various reasons also ran the gauntlet outside the regular convoys. Thus, actual British ship losses rose annually from 1803 (222) to a peak in 1810 (619), with only one decrease (to 469) in 1809. Thereafter they fell steadily until 1813 (371) and sharply in the last proper year of the war, to a mere 145 in 1814, disregarding those same enterprising Yankees. Convoy duty was always tedious and arduous for naval captains and their crews – not to say unprofitable. But these statistics were as much the measure and reward of naval supremacy as any of its more spectacular benefits. So, just as men like Captain F.J. Walker, the greatest escort commander of the 1939–45 war (who worked himself to premature death in 1944), deserve to be ranked among the great naval officers of the twentieth century, so do forgotten admirals like Alan Gardner, who regarded the conscientious shepherding of convoys to their destinations as 'of the greatest importance to the common interest of the Country', deserve to be ranked with the better-known Troubridges and Pellews of Nelson's time.

The importance of the other routine naval activity which took up so much of our frigate captains' time, the *hunting-patrolling* duty, is both much more controversial and – not least in Nelson's war – much harder to quantify. Mahan, with his customary acuteness, recognised that, compared with the convoy system, patrolling, 'even when most thoroughly planned, still resembles looking for a needle in a haystack'. And generations of naval officers have instinctively chafed at the superficially defensive nature of convoy work, brought up as they have been in the offensive Nelson tradition and blinded by it to the beautiful twin truth of the convoy system: that, if a raider finds a convoy, *then it has to do battle* – but also, if it *fails* to find that needle in the haystack, it is just as surely losing its own war as if it had been defeated, because its time is wasted.

Mahan's conclusion was neither 100 per cent correct in its age-of-sail application nor absolutely applicable to the modern technologies of the 1939–45 war. During the latter, the development of the long-range aircraft revolutionised patrol of the sea-lanes (statistically, an aircraft actually escorting a convoy by patrolling directly above and around it was still far more cost-effective than scouring the ocean-haystack, looking for U-boat-needles, even then). During the 1793–1815 period, the greater sea-patrolling capacity of wind-powered escorts, compared with those which soon ran out of fuel, was perhaps a minor factor, since it applied equally to the larger raiders. But the real difference between the wars against merchant shipping in the age of Nelson and in the twentieth century did nevertheless lie in the transformation of the old *guerre de course* which technology, in the form of the submarine, brought about. In the sailing ship war attacks on merchant ships were not only restricted by civilised conventions which distinguished such actions from piracy, but also by the profit motive. Privateering – legalised private warfare under official letters of marque – flourished during the eighteenth century, and was not internationally banned until 1856, by the Declaration of Paris. But the object of the privateer captain (and also, in practice, every frigate captain too) was to capture enemy ships as expeditiously as possible *and get them home intact*, thereby enriching himself and his crew as well as helping the war effort. In the early part of the 1914–18 War, captains of German surface raiders often tried to do this, and invariably behaved chivalrously to merchant crews who surrendered. But it was out of the question that prize-crews could be supplied from the tiny complements of submarines, even if there had been a chance of getting the prize back to Germany: their captures *had* to be sunk. And soon enough the logic and dangers of submarine warfare resulted in the unrestricted sinking of merchant shipping without warning or mercy: the submarine was not simply the old *guerre de course* warship – privateer or frigate – in a different form, it was a new kind of weapon in a new kind of war.

The convention of the last French war, as has already been noted, allowed naval captains to surrender against hopeless odds without loss of honour. Indeed, soldiers could do the same: the famous General Cambronne is popularly supposed to have replied that his Guards would die, but would not surrender (or, even more famously, shouted '*Merde!*') when all was lost at Waterloo. In fact, according to Wellington himself, Cambronne surrendered 'without a wound'. This is not to say that there were not innumerable examples of heroic defences and disgraceful massacres during this war. But few of these were Anglo-French occasions, and none (other than those mutinies already mentioned) occurred at sea. It is to the credit of the fighting men on both sides that neither the inordinate length of the conflict nor

Napoleon's tendency to break the old PoW rules (which will be considered in due course) put an end to all the old practices of the previous French wars: in spite of the harshness and brutality of day-to-day existence at sea and the rumours of cruel captivity, gentlemanly treatment of prisoners prevailed. The wife of a French officer, a passenger on a ship captured by William Hoste, hid below, fearing not a fate worse than death, but English cannibalism. Six years later she was still singing her captor's praises. On the other side, many of France's privateering aces were almost as celebrated among their victims for their humanity and engaging good manners as for their daring and seamanship.

To be realistic, however, such (French) reputations were also good for business, in that the prospect of decent treatment discouraged merchant crews from fighting too hard for their lives – and not least the crews of those well-armed Indiamen. And decency thus not only saved losses among privateering crews (who were needed as prize-crews), but also ensured that the prize itself was taken in a relatively undamaged condition, and so could be sailed safely and quickly by its captors. Many such prizes were indeed *re*captured intact: the recapture of captured British ships was an important source of frigate prize-money, especially among blockading ships, long after genuine French merchant prizes had become scarce.

All this – thankless convoy duty, endless patrols and dangerous blockading – made up most of everyday life for the majority of British frigate captains. But for the luckier ones there was still that 'eyes of the fleet' role in the years after Trafalgar, when enemy warships succeeded in outwitting the blockaders. Most often these escapers were frigates, the best long-range raiders of all, not a few of which headed immediately for the rich hunting-grounds of the Indian Ocean, in which they could operate out of the strategically placed French bases on the isles of France and Bourbon, modern Mauritius, sometimes called the Gibraltar of the East. It was in the Indian Ocean that the (ex-French) *San Fiorenzo* fought her terrific battle with the *Piémontaise* in 1808, and in due course we shall be returning to that Gibraltar of the East to consider the frigate-fighting there and the lessons which the British failed to learn from it. Meanwhile, in that same year, a small French squadron also escaped *via* the Basque Roads from Rochefort under Admiral Allemand to rendezvous with other escapers from Toulon, under Admiral Ganteaume, for a daring Mediterranean operation. Yet, no matter how well-handled, the French Navy could not long escape the British Navy's 'eyes', and among those frigates soon snapping at Ganteaume's heels – apart from the crack *Spartan* (38), commanded by that established frigate ace Jahleel Brenton – was Nelson's own *Amphion* (36) now commanded by none other than his own former favourite midshipman, Captain William

Hoste, still only 28 years of age, but already a post-captain with six years' seniority on the List.

Anno Domini 1808: in a war, which effectively, had already been going on for 15 years (and which, to its very end, had another *seven* years to run), most of those who had been in high military, naval and political office at the start were now too old to play active parts, if they were not already history in graveyards. Lieutenant Bonaparte was now Emperor of the French and master of most of Europe (even though the Spanish Peninsula was about to give the lie to that). Great men like Pitt and Fox in England were dead and as forgotten as the Jacobins of '73 and the Directors of the French Directory, never mind all the bit players like General Hoche and Wolfe Tone, and the thousands of poor Vendéan and Irish rebel-patriots they had taken with them in their hopeless revolts. But there was a hecatomb of new victims still to come, under the management of a new generation of leaders now rising, from the lines of Torres Vedras in Portugal to America in the west and Moscow in the east, and even to the further east, in the fantastical islands of the Indian Ocean and the East Indies. The First World War was getting into gear now.

Among our original 1793 intake of naval officers, at one extreme Captain Pigot was as dead as Pitt and Hoche, while Captain Pellew had become the rich Admiral Sir Edward Pellew, Baronet, commanding in the Eastern seas. Captain Lord Cochrane was at the height of his fame, with everything still to win (but actually to lose, in the Basque Roads), like *and* unlike the unknown Captain Hornblower, off Nicaragua, but unlike Captain Philip Broke, meritorious but without either 'interest' or opportunity to distinguish himself on his routine convoy-patrol duties in his frigate. All, of course, were veterans now: Pellew was in his fifties and Cochrane, Hornblower and Broke were in their thirties, having spent all of their teenage and adult lives in uniform, at war and afloat.

As for the youngest of the intake, 'little' Hoste had not even been a teenager when he had joined his first ship off the Downs of East Kent in the Narrow Seas in '93, for convoy duty, so that half his whole life now had been spent at sea. And, according to the fraudulent record of his service, more than five-sixths of it had been entered on ships' books: when he had *actually* gone to sea at the age of 12 he already had five years' sea service, having made his official debut at the age of *five* in 1786, as a 'captain's servant' in HMS *Europa*, thanks to the 'interest' exercised by his father, the Reverend Dixon Hoste, Rector of the Parish of Tittlesham in Norfolk, a living advantageously in the gift of the Coke family, an ancient and influential house representing the Whig political party in that county.

In fact, the introduction into the Navy of our William Hoste, the Reverend Dixon Hoste's second son, illustrates the way 'interest'

worked *in general* in the England of the late eighteenth century quite as
much as it does the system of recruitment of future naval officers *in
particular*. That the little boy was a clergyman's son was, as has
already been statistically noted, far from unusual: the Church of
England, with the medical, legal and civil service professions, was a
significant contributor of its offspring to Nelson's navy. Indeed,
Nelson himself was one such a contribution, being the son of the
Reverend Edmund Nelson, Rector of Burnham Thorpe, another
Norfolk parish not far from Tittlesham, as well as the nephew of the
Comptroller of the Navy.

For all that they were both Cambridge graduates as well as
neighbouring rectors in the same part of the country, the Reverend
Edmund Nelson and the Reverend Dixon Hoste were actually chalk
and cheese: Mr Nelson a quiet scholar, while Mr Hoste was the
archetypal sporting parson, whose interests were secular and political,
and whose inclinations profligate. And, for good measure, where the
Hostes were the clients of a great East Anglian Whig family, the
Nelsons' connection was with the Tories. But dissimilar personalities
and contrary politics did not rule out civilised back-scratching among
gentlemen of the clergy, whose stipends often did not match the size of
the families with which they were blessed and whose sons required
employment. That Mr Hoste and Mr Nelson would at least have
agreed on the need to resist the godless French revolutionaries of 1793
is likely, but irrelevant, since the Most Christian King Louis XVI still
ruled France when the five-year-old William's name was put down for
the Navy; and, indeed, little William was then neither consulted nor
seven years later showed any particular inclination to go to sea, as had
both Pellew and Cochrane. Rather, his entry on the *Europa*'s books
must be taken as a rare example of his father's prudence in financial
matters, not to say his presumption that sooner or later there would be
yet another French war. For, in the first case, if a 'young gentleman'
ought at least to have pocket money (as well as a useful accumulation
of fraudulent sea-service) on joining the Navy, his penurious father
was not required to buy a commission as in the Army. And, taking the
longer view, if the boy survived and prospered he could become rich –
as he never could in a red coat.

As it turned out, Mr Hoste (who was always to be in arrears with
that pocket money, actually) was able to take advantage of this
investment of his flesh and blood in 1793, when Mr Nelson's boy
Horatio was at last given a ship on the outbreak of war in 1793 after
five years' unemployment. Indeed, with his useful 14 years' seniority
on the Captains' List (having been made post at the early age of 21, in
1779), Captain Nelson was given a ship-of-the-line which, albeit a
rather small one, brought with it patronage in the appointment of
quite a number of 'captain's servants', 'volunteers' and (for older lads)

midshipmen. Accordingly, with the Coke family as go-betweens, a meeting between the young Captain Nelson and both the Hostes was arranged, at which – with that not invariably good first-sight judgement of his – Nelson took to both father and son, expressing himself willing to take the latter into his *Agamemnon* (64) as soon as she was ready for sea. Yet there was, of course, nothing particularly special in this: across Britain many other hopeful youths, from the very young (like Hoste) to the not-so-young (like Hornblower and Cochrane) were converging on those captains with whom their families had influence – just as those captains themselves who did not yet have ships (like Pellew) were bombarding their patrons and the Admiralty itself with their own pleas for employment as the Navy expanded to a war footing. Nelson, like all the rest of his lucky brother-captains, had no trouble finding quarterdeck material among the young. He already had on his books Josiah Nisbet, his stepson, and William Bolton, the son of his sister's brother-in-law (another clergyman), together with two more Norfolk clergy offspring, the Weatherhead brothers. In the case of Nisbet and Bolton, of course, he was doing no more than family duty expected of him, in providing employment for younger relatives; 22 years earlier his own father had presented him in the same way to his uncle, Captain Maurice Suckling, when the latter had been appointed to command the (ex-French) *Raisonnable* during a Spanish war-scare before the American Revolution.

In the years to come, although Nisbet and Bolton were to reach the Captains' List thanks to their Nelson connection, neither did their patron much honour during their naval careers. By contrast the careers of both Hoste and the elder Weatherhead (John) were to unfold very differently, both glorious, although Lieutenant John Weatherhead's was to be cut tragically short. What united all these boys in 1793, however, was their good fortune. For although they had missed out in being taken into a ship-of-the-line (and a technically obsolescent one of 64 guns, too) rather than a frigate, they were now in the charge and under the eye of the greatest sea-commander of the age, whose influence and example was to dominate their lives, and before long the Navy itself in which they served.

Of books on Nelson – Captain Suckling's 'poor Horace. . .who is so weak' of 1770 – there is no end, such is the fascination of the man, but this is not one of them. Yet he has in some sense overshadowed the whole story already, and in considering the career of William Hoste – Nelson's own 'poor Little Hoste' of the early 1790s – he has a centre-stage part to play briefly now, as of right.

In fact, Nelson's early career coincides and contrasts with that of Edward Pellew quite neatly. Pellew was almost a year and a half older (born April 1757) and went to sea a year earlier, in peacetime; and, indeed, both were lucky, in the first place, in their possession of sufficient 'interest' to secure them employment in the smaller navy of the early 1770s (there were only 14,700 men on the books of naval ships in the year of Pellew's entry, and some 27,000 in the war-scare year of Nelson's acceptance into the *Raisonnable*, which total soon fell below 20,000 again). They were thus able to acquire all the purely technical skills of their profession before the next (American) war broke out in 1775, and then old enough to demonstrate their merit in the hunt for promotion in wartime, when opportunities to distinguish themselves multiplied, and casualties created vacancies.

However, if Pellew and Nelson shared those vital ingredients of luck and merit, where the older midshipman's 'interest' was somewhat indirect, albeit not insignificant, the younger one's was of an altogether superior order before very long. For Captain Suckling, who soon identified his nephew's promise and superintended his career accordingly, was appointed Comptroller of the Navy in 1776 – a post which, involving as it did the mustering of all naval manpower and the building and repair of naval ships, was hardly second to that of the First Lord of the Admiralty himself in power and influence. Nelson was by then already acting fourth lieutenant in the *Worcester* (64), even though still more than a year short of the minimum age for commissioned rank. But this was the eighteenth century, and notwithstanding his youthful looks the prudent captains who conducted his viva voce examination for lieutenant readily accepted his *appearance* as being that 'of a young man of more than 20 years of age' without pressing the matter before passing him, then to discover (to their surprise, it is alleged) that he was the Comptroller's nephew.

Thus was Nelson appointed second lieutenant in the frigate *Lowestoffe* (32), which was then earmarked for the Jamaica station under the command of the excellent Captain William Locker, luck, merit and 'interest' having all played their parts. So now the new (under-age) lieutenant was heading for those sickly waters in which the chances of action and promotion as well as death were maximised, not to mention prize-money – and in a frigate under a good captain who was himself not without naval influence as Admiral William Parry's son-in-law.

As second in the *Lowestoffe* Nelson did well, and was taken into Admiral Sir Peter Parker's own flagship, the *Bristol*, as third lieutenant after little more than a year, becoming the first lieutenant the next month (September 1778) in a typically quick West Indian turnover. The familiar pattern of the advancement of the admiral's favourite then continued smoothly: by December he had cleared the last fence before the big one, with his appointment as Master and Commander of the brig *Badger* (16), a sure sign in his case of the shape of the things soon to come. And things came in June 1779, when he was still nearly four months short of his twenty-first birthday, in the form of the frigate *Hinchingbroke* (28): 'I got my rank by a shot killing a Post-Captain,' Nelson recorded. 'And I most sincerely hope I shall, when I go, go out of the World the same way.'

Arguably, that particular shot came not a moment too soon, for by then Comptroller Suckling himself was dead. He left Commander Nelson £500 in his will (a not inconsiderable sum, allowing for the inflation of the next two centuries), to which William Suckling, another uncle and chief beneficiary, added the dress sword which his brother had carried with honour as captain of the *Dreadnought* in battle with the French in 1759 (and which Nelson himself was to carry at St Vincent, and at Tenerife, first in his right hand, and then in his left after his right arm had been shattered). But what he left his country, by the accelerated advance in the Navy of his nephew, young Horatio, was far more important and valuable. For, to be fair to Nelson, his merit had by then so commended him to Admiral Parker in addition to Captain Locker's high regard that the *Hinchingbroke* (and, more importantly, the post-captaincy which went with her) may be regarded as almost all his own work.

In fact, neither that frigate (a converted ex-French merchantman) nor Nelson's next command, the *Albemarle* (28, and another conversion of a French prize) were the sort of ships which later frigate-aces would have preferred, up against a French 44-gunner. But there were no big French frigates in the West Indies then, and Nelson himself never had the opportunity to prove himself a great ship-fighting frigate captain, even though one of his hardest fights was a frigate action. It was not as a captain, but as a commodore already flying his broad pendant in the run-up to the battle of St Vincent that Nelson fought that action, when, while being carried in the *Minerve* (42, ex-French) and in company with the *Blanche* (36), he fell in with the Spanish frigates *Santa Sabina* and *Ceres*. Both Spanish ships were captured, the *Santa Sabina* after a hard-fought fight in which more than half her crew was killed or wounded, her only surviving officer being her captain, Don Jacobo Stuart, the grandson of King James II of Great Britain, after 50 of his crew of the *Minerve* had also been killed or wounded. And then, shortly afterwards, other units of the Spanish fleet arrived, including eventually two ships-of-the-line, to retake both prizes together with their prize-crews. Even Nelson himself was almost captured – which would certainly have changed history; but he escaped, and in due course Lieutenant Hardy, who commanded one of the prizes, was exchanged with his fellow prize-master for the brave Don Jacobo: such were the good-and-bad fortunes of the more civilised days of *taking*, not *fighting-to-the-death-and-sinking* of our own less civilised times.

But all that was nearly 14 years after Nelson's appointment into the

Hinchingbroke, of which eight had been years of peace and a small navy for the British, and those five unemployed years on the beach for Captain Nelson. However, thanks to Captain Suckling, Captain Locker and Admiral Parker, he had also moved inexorably up the Captains' List, with others less deserving, to have those 14 years' seniority. Which, in turn, brought him the *Agamemnon* as the last French war broke out – and provided employment for William Hoste, among those other sons of Norfolk clergymen.

CHAPTER THIRTEEN

From the Agamemnon to the Amphion: *the making of a frigate captain*

'Interest', as has been shown in the case-histories of five of our special captains so far, could be exercised both externally and from inside the Navy, and at different stages of a young officer's career. Two of the five – Pellew and Hoste – entered the Navy with the help of powerful civilian patrons (Lord Falmouth and the Cokes of Norfolk respectively), while Pigot and Cochrane owed their initial advantages to their naval families. Later on Pellew was in fact further advanced both by Lord Falmouth when already in post-rank and additionally by St Vincent for his political value as well as on account of his merit. Hornblower, starting from nowhere, obtained post-rank purely meritoriously by winning the 'interest' of Cornwallis first, but thereafter owed much (if not everything) to Wellesley influence.

All five, however, benefited from the patronage of senior officers *under whom they served* to a greater or lesser degree. Pigot – probably because of his influential service family provenance rather than his proven merit – became one of the protégés of Admiral Parker, who actually gave him post-rank. Pellew was talent-spotted by the famous Captain Pownoll, whose untimely death was then a set-back. Cochrane, in spite of his awkwardness, undeniably received his first command from Lord Keith, a fellow Scotsman. Hornblower, until captured by the Spaniards, was Pellew's favourite midshipman. But Hoste was undoubtedly the luckiest of all in becoming Nelson's special protégé for the first twelve years of his naval career: Nelson was, indeed, not only his patron, teacher and friend, but – in his own words – his 'second father'.

If it was the 13-year-old Hoste's supreme good fortune to fall into the hands of such a man immediately he went to sea it was none the less out of his own merit this special relationship grew. That Nelson was, from his earliest days of command, an enlightened and inspirational teacher of the mere children whom the system gave him to lick into shape is attested to by the wife of his commanding officer in the Leeward Islands back in the 1780s, who noted his 'infinite kindness and goodness of heart' in the management of his 'Younkers'. Before long he – and the Navy – would expect these babes-in-arms not to duck on the quarterdeck when under fire, and to command men old enough to be their fathers – or even their grandfathers, perhaps. Meanwhile, this young captain (whom Lady Hughes rather fancied as a suitable husband for her daughter Rosie) led by example, always doing first himself what he then ordered them to do. But, for all that, he was no 'soft touch' in those days with those who would not (or could not) follow his lead: he rejected not only the son of his patron, Captain Maurice Suckling, as never likely to make a 'good sea officer', but also Lady Hughes' own boy (as well as poor Rosie for the role of Mrs Nelson).

In the *Agamemnon* in 1793, admittedly, he was not quite so ruthless when he had on board his own stepson, Josiah Nisbet, as one of his older midshipmen among all that clergy-offspring intake from East Anglia: Josiah would never make a 'good sea officer', but Nelson (like Pellew) was a man of his time, so Josiah would get on in the service faster than even the excellent John Weatherhead, never mind the much younger (and dreadfully sea-sick and accident-prone) 'little Hoste'. But although (unlike Pellew and Cochrane) Hoste had had no vocation for the sea, and was at first no more than an eager-to-please and likeable boy who endeared himself to his captain, he speedily also showed himself to be a natural-born sea-officer of the sort – the Pellew–Weatherhead–Hornblower–Broke sort – that any discerning captain (of the Pownoll/Pellew/Hornblower/Hoste/*Nelson* variety) derived pleasure in nurturing, to his own future honour as well as the good of the Navy and the country.

The happy conjunction of Nelson and Hoste (and, although it was tragically brief, Nelson and Weatherhead) exemplifies the 'interest' system at its best, just as Nelson's concern for Josiah Nisbet and Pellew's promotion of his sons, among so many other 'interest' promotions, shows it at its worst – and as do the early experiences of Midshipman Hornblower (*without* 'interest') show it at its very worst. Sea-sick and brutalised almost to the point of suicide, Hornblower escaped through a duel which he cold-bloodedly sought with his persecutor. In the happy and well-run *Agamemnon*, whose officers and crew quickly came to idolise their captain (just as those of the *Albemarle* frigate had done years before, when they volunteered to a man to serve in his next ship), 'little (sea-sick) Hoste' was immediately looked after, even before he found his sea-legs and began to show his quality as a sea-officer. In the *Agamemnon*, whose captain not only made sure his 'young gentlemen' wrote home regularly, but made up the deficiencies of their pocket-money out of his own (when the Reverend Dixon Hoste fell into arrears), there was no scope for bullying; and (almost as good, short of the opportunities of a frigate like Pownoll's and Pellew's), the *Agamemnon* under Nelson was a ship in which every man and boy could show his mettle in action. So, before very long, Hoste was writing home about her running fight with five French frigates, and then of her great duel with the big *Ça Ira* (80) and the *Censeur* (74), in which his beloved Captain Nelson made his name as a rising star in the Navy.

Hoste was only in his fifteenth year, but a battle veteran by then of the seige of Calvi, and a survivor of disease (probably dysentery; although he was soon enough to catch malaria, which was endemic in the Mediterranean), and accident (he broke his leg while in command of one of Nelson's smaller prizes). And by now he had graduated from (unpaid) 'captain's servant' to the rate of midshipman (pay: £14 8s per annum) within a year of going to sea, having been recognised by Nelson as 'without exception one of the finest boys I have ever met with'.

As such, in the classic role of a young protégé who could be relied on in due course to do his patron honour, he followed Nelson's rising star as Sir John Jervis breathed new discipline, life and purpose into the British Mediterranean Fleet in the run-up to the battle of St Vincent. For, just as Nelson had marked 'my dear William', so old Sir John now marked Nelson by appointing him Commodore (First Class). Writing home, 'dear William' exulted in 'this additional mark of distinction conferred on him' – 'our good Captain' – 'which . . . his merit richly deserved. His Broad Pendant is now flying; therefore I must beg my dear father to draw an additional cork'; which, the Reverend Hoste being the man he was, would certainly no sooner have been read than done.

And there was soon much more, and better, news to be sent to the Norfolk rectories and vicarages, and to the Reverend Hoste both by his son and the new Commodore himself, after Nelson had broken the Spanish line at St Vincent, to take those two bigger Spanish ships, from the *Captain* (74), into which Hoste had followed him. To his chagrin, the 16-year-old boy had not been allowed to join the boarding party with other (and older) 'old *Agamemnons*'. But his gallantry had been such, wrote Nelson to Hoste's father, 'that each day rivets him stronger to my heart'.

From the battered *Captain*, Hoste once again followed Nelson, first briefly into the *Irresistible* (74) and then – with certain other

enthusiastic officers and men from both the *Agamemnon* and the
Captain – into another 74, the *Theseus*. The First Lord of the
Admiralty confided to the new Lord St Vincent in his new flagship, the
100-gun (ex-French) *Ville de Paris*, that the new Admiral Sir Horatio
Nelson preferred handy 74s to three-deckers. But one may equally
'confide' that both the Admiralty and St Vincent also believed that
Admiral Nelson and his friend Captain Miller would transform their
new ship from one of the worst in the Navy, with her bad reputation
from the Spithead mutiny, into another *Agamemnon*, or another
Captain.

How that transformation was achieved – much of it very quickly by
Nelson's charisma and Miller's common sense and humanity, together
with proper rations (including fresh vegetables) – undoubtedly taught
Hoste further lessons, since he had never served in a bad ship before.
But he was soon to learn other lessons too, some of them relating to the
small print of the system and very irritating to a young man fired by his
admiral's example and career, but others much harder and more
brutal, relating to wounds and death and defeat in operations of the
very type in which he would eventually become a specialist.

As a good patron Nelson was concerned now to do his best by that
1793 intake, with his own star in the ascendant. However, in spite of
all his true preferences, he gave the undeserving Josiah Nisbet first
prize, with a lieutenancy solicited from St Vincent, followed before
very long by another for Midshipman Bolton, who was promoted into
a 74 with the promise of a frigate lieutenancy (and who would
thereafter sail on serenely to a post-captaincy and a knighthood even
though Nelson was later to refer to him as 'that goose'). The problem
with the otherwise far more promising Weatherhead and Hoste was
their lack of qualifying sea-time overall for lieutenancies, though both
now had their necessary midshipman years. But even this could of
course be circumnavigated sooner or later with the backing of such a
patron in such times, just as it had been in Nelson's own case back in
'77: with Weatherhead, who was older, it was soon enough accomplished, but Hoste had to wait until November 1797 before the
various elements of his service could be added up Navy-fashion
(counting eleven years 'on the books', rather than four years' real
service), enabling him to take his examination the following February
(by which time Josiah Nisbet was already captain of a small ship as
master and commander).

By then however, Hoste was already an *acting*-lieutenant, advanced
by the tragic death of his great friend Weatherhead in the Tenerife
defeat, which had also robbed the Navy of one of its finest young
frigate captains, Captain Richard Bowen, of the *Terpsichore* (36), and
from which Nelson himself emerged minus his right arm as a lucky
survivor of naval surgery. Hoste had tried to join his admiral in that

disastrous combined operation, but had been out-ranked by Nisbet and Weatherhead. In its aftermath he was to watch his friend's painful death from a stomach wound, recording in a letter home the sorrow he felt that his acting-lieutenancy was its result. Yet although such windfall promotions were the natural order of things in this and every bloody war, leaving promotion and the future to the lucky survivors, his substantive lieutenancy was already certain: as a Nelson protégé when Nelson himself was a St Vincent protégé he was soon on the quarterdeck of Nelson's friend and flag-captain, Captain Miller of the *Theseus*.

Miller's is one of that drum-roll of names which constitutes Nelson's 'band of brothers' during the period from the battle of the Nile in 1798 to Trafalgar. After the dark times of the mutiny, the Navy suddenly had an elite of inspirational captains in its main fleet, as well as headline-grabbing frigate commanders: Troubridge of the *Culloden*, Hallowell of the *Swiftsure*, Foley of the *Goliath* and Hood of the *Zealous*, never mind all the other choice 74-gun captains St Vincent had deliberately given to his admired subordinate for the reconquest of the Mediterranean. There were still duffers in the pipeline, among the admirals and on the Captains' List, coming up. But there was now a wealth of talent equal to anything Napoleon had in the meritocracy of his Generals' List, who would command the seas more effectively than he would finally aspire to hold down Europe. Among this elite, Captain Miller was actually not an Englishman at all: he was born a New Yorker, in a loyalist family driven from the new 'United States', who – if he had lived – might have fought his family's old enemies all the more ruthlessly later on, in Captain Philip Broke's days. But meanwhile, with Lieutenant Hoste as one of his likeliest young officers in the *Theseus*, he now followed the most daring of his fellow 'brothers' *inside* the anchored French battle-fleet in Aboukir Bay in 1798, in succession raking and dismasting the *Guerrier*, then blasting the *Spartiate*, *Aquilon* and *Conquerant*, before presiding over the capture of the *Heureux* and the *Mercure* (while someone else captured Pellew's future *Tonnant*). In the course of these fire-fights Lieutenant Hoste was seconded from his gun-deck duties to take possession of one of those French frigates, the big 40-gun *Artemise*, which had also unwisely opened fire during the battle, and had quickly been battered into surrender accordingly.

Much to Captain Miller's outrage, the *Artemise* was set on fire by her crew before she could be seized. But even if she had not been, she could hardly have been left in the hands of a junior lieutenant, however meritorious, who was still only in his nineteenth year. So, after the battle, Hoste was appointed first lieutenant of the dismasted French *Tonnant*, the 80-gun ship which Pellew later commanded in the Channel. This further vote of confidence in his abilities was also, nevertheless, only a temporary posting for a young man on whose promotion his captain and admiral were equally set, one must suppose. For very shortly afterwards Lieutenant Hoste became master and commander (and, by courtesy, captain therefore) of the fast-sailing (ex-French) brig *Mutine*, which the Navy had bought after Captain Hardy had captured her off Tenerife the previous year.

In a fleet tragically short of frigate 'eyes', handy ships like the little *Mutine* (14 guns) were the next-best all-purpose messenger/cruisers. But command of the *Mutine* was a greater test of any young officer's quality than that, since she was a notoriously indisciplined and unhappy ship, which required a mixture of St Vincent firm hand and Nelson–Miller humanity to discharge her duties efficiently in the very hot war of 1798–9, and after. Not only were Spithead and the Nore recent memories, but General Bonaparte was still loose in Egypt and up the coast to Acre, with French frigates and surviving ships-of-the-line from the Egyptian expedition still at sea, while the war in Europe had also rekindled meanwhile, after Admiral Nelson's victory and in General Bonaparte's absence. Malta was under seige (by the British, and for the first and last time successfully), and a British counter-invasion of Egypt was being planned by right of sea-power: not for the last time, King George's ramshackle war-machine was now *re*acting to the actions of the enemy.

The *Mutine* was therefore an exciting command in a fluid situation, as well as a testing one. Even, perhaps, it was another example of Hoste's luck (compared with Lieutenant Weatherhead's bad luck), in that he was consequently not at Captain Miller's side when that fine officer was killed in an accidental explosion while the *Theseus* was engaged in the Navy's next major combined operation under Admiral Sir Sidney Smith, when it inspired the Turks to resist General Bonaparte's army at the seige of Acre successfully, to the final ruin of the whole French adventure in Egypt. But that was the stuff of world war history, not the immediate reality of one naval officer's first ship-command, which admitted him to the more select band of captains (even captains by courtesy, of so small a vessel), with his lion's share of prize-money from the value of anything he took while in command of 'a Sixth Rate *or less*'. As a master and commander his pay was still little more than £100 a year. But from now on his prize-agents would begin to remit far more than that to England, to the tender care of his father: no less than with 'Captain' Hoste's command of the *Mutine*, the Rector of Tittlesham's ship had come in at last, to repay him a hundred-fold for his original investment of little William with Captain Nelson.

This was, nevertheless, Hoste's chrysalis stage, compared with his achievements (and profits) as a frigate captain. Only the very luckiest of officers made the jump from lieutenancies straight to postcaptaincies, after great battles or signal victories (like Israel Pellew after his brother's capture of the *Cléopâtre* in '93) without first passing through command of a smaller ship, and to the single epaulette of a post-captain of less than three years' seniority. But Hoste's final apprenticeship in the *Mutine* was none the less invaluable not only in completing his education while Nelson was still alive, and would continue to exercise his 'interest' actively on his protégé's behalf, but also because it provided him with experience of those waters in which the whole of his war over the rest of its 15-year duration would be fought, in the Mediterranean Sea and, above all, in the Adriatic.

His relationship with Nelson was never tarnished, through that defeat at Tenerife (which left Weatherhead dead and Nelson maimed) and Nelson's most ignoble period off Naples after his victory of the Nile. As an admiring pupil, Hoste never saw Nelson at his worst, vain and facile, as the Duke of Wellington did when he met the nation's hero for the first time (Nelson did not know who he was talking to then; but on the second occasion he did, and General Sir Arthur Wellesley decided that the little admiral was actually 'a very superior man' this time; but both impressions were accurate). Meanwhile, Hoste himself was on the crest of his patron's wave, and uncritical of him. Lady Hamilton looked him over, and thought that he had the makings of a 'second Nelson'. And when the whole war ground to a halt in the Peace of Amiens he not only remained employed (among other duties, helping Lord Elgin to sort out those marbles of his from the ruins of the Parthenon at Athens, while the Turks were still friendly), but also received word of his latest and most crucial promotion to command the *Greyhound*, a 32-gun frigate which carried with it automatic post-captain's rank, when he was only 22 years of age.

Returning home, more-or-less invalided, in the *Greyhound* (but Admiral Nelson's protégé still), he did not have to wait long before receiving the *Eurydice* (28) in the scramble for commands, when other captains low on the List had to wait (like the famous but unpopular Cochrane, or the meritorious but uninfluential Broke). And although initially employed on boring (and largely unprofitable) patrol and convoy duties in the Atlantic and off West Africa, it can hardly be by accident that he eventually came back under Nelson's command in the summer of 1805. Still (as always) short of frigate 'eyes', Nelson would have wanted to get the sharpest of them around him now – and in then putting them into the best of those frigates which were within his gift. It was this, one may suppose, that his favourite protégé was in due course exchanged from the elderly little *Eurydice* into the much more desirable *Amphion*, which was actually transferred from the command of William Bolton, Nelson's nephew-by-marriage. It had been enough, one may also suppose, to get 'that goose' on the Captains' List: now Nelson needed men he could trust.

It was in the *Amphion*, a faster and more heavily-armed 32 (more often described as a 36), that Hoste was to make his name; and she had actually been noted as a good frigate by Nelson himself two years earlier, when he had flown his flag in her en route from England to take up his Mediterranean command. But to Hoste's eternal chagrin she was not present at Trafalgar, having been detached on a diplomatic embassy to Algiers, that long-time autonomous pirate state with which the British had to maintain friendly relations in order to keep their fleets victualled when at war with Spain. Nelson was even then once again complaining of lack of frigates to the Admiralty: 'The last [enemy] Fleet was lost to me for want of Frigates: God forbid that this should.' But the honour of being his 'eyes' before Trafalgar went nevertheless to ships like the *Phoebe* (36) and the (ex-French) *Amiable* (32), and above all to Captain Henry Blackwood in the *Euryalus* (36), not to the *Amphion*.

Nelson's detachment of such a useful ship, with his favourite captain in her on an unimportant mission remains one of Trafalgar's minor mysteries, unlike his gift of the 90-gun *Prince of Wales* to carry Sir John Calder back to England to face a court martial, which thereby weakened his fleet in the face of the enemy to help a man who had never been his friend. For that was a typically Nelsonian act. But it is as useless to conjecture why he did detach the *Amphion* as it is to wonder how Hoste's career might have been different if he had been in attendance on his hero, as to try to imagine a Hoste future dominated by a live Nelson. And as regards Nelson himself, it is just as useless, anyway, to lighten the darkness by philosophising that his work was done and his fame secured untarnished forever by that French sniper, when it might have been all downhill thereafter with no more fleets to defeat and Lady Hamilton getting fatter all the time.

It is the facts that matter. And one is that Nelson had also done his work for the grieving William Hoste by getting him on the Captains' List when he was young, so that he had epaulettes on both shoulders, as a captain of more than three years' seniority, although still only 25. As it was, the young captain's own merit and the aura of Nelson's approval accompanied him after Trafalgar, as the British fleet returned to claim the Mediterranean under the command of Nelson's other grieving friend, Cuthbert Collingwood. As we have already observed in the case of the equally meritorious but far more troublesome Lord Cochrane, Admiral Collingwood was not the man to stifle frigate-captain talent, for all that he himself was slow and sure, rather than brilliant: not the least of Nelson's legacies to the Navy was that he had taught Cuthbert Collingwood to recognise merit, and not to despise eccentricity in his subordinates. Under Collingwood's senior command it was even to be another memorable naval eccentric, Rear-Admiral Sir Sidney Smith (1764–1840), under whom Hoste was soon to serve.

Sidney Smith's place in the history books rests securely in his celebrated defence of Acre in 1799, when as a senior naval officer he was largely responsible for stopping the French in their tracks and cheating Napoleon of his destiny (although this reverse no less ensured – or at least encouraged – the great man's speedy return home to France thereafter, to an even greater destiny, it may be thought). Hardly less dramatic, however, was Smith's own escape a few years later, after he had been captured during a naval reconnaissance of the French coast and faced possible execution as a spy. This adventure invites comparison with that of Horatio Hornblower, who effected an even more sensational escape in 1810 while en route to prison in Paris on a trumped-up charge of piracy, when also not being treated as an officer and a gentleman. But we shall be considering the nature of PoW status and the problems of escape from Napoleon's New Europe in more detail later. Meanwhile, it is not with Hornblower that Smith invites comparison so much as that other unusual officer, Home Riggs Popham.

Both Popham and Smith, for a start, boasted curious foreign knighthoods, the latter's having been conferred by the King of Sweden for naval work in the Baltic while the former's was a Tsarist reward. More than that, though, both were unconventional in the breadth of their interests and skills compared with the majority of naval officers, whom they also surpassed in intelligence and imagination, if not in bravery and professional competence, and zeal and ambition. Yet, for all this and in spite of the fact that both lived not only to reach admiral's rank (by seniority on the List) but to fly their flags at sea during the war (by undoubted merit), neither won the real fame which each thought he deserved as a 'great admiral'. But, to be fair to both, although this was partly due to their own characters (Popham, as we have seen, was something of a 'chancer', and Smith, in the opinion of many, was 'tricky'), it was more largely due to the change in the whole nature of the war itself. After Trafalgar there were no great battles to win – no more Glorious Firsts of June, St Vincents, Camperdowns, Niles and Copenhagens. Yet, because of this, if all the post-Trafalgar generation of admirals somehow seem lesser men in the shadow of battle-winners like old John Jervis and young dead Nelson – from worthy Collingwood, depressing Preaching Jemmy Gambier to that great professional, Edward Pellew – theirs was the Navy which now had the job of ruling the sea for Britannia. Only, although the great ship-of-the-line fleets of that navy (commanded by admirals with senior captains under them) were the guarantee of that supremacy, it was the frigate force, mostly in the form of single ships commanded by younger men, that was its day-to-day front-line instrument.

If the existence of this navy ruled out any threat of an invasion of Britain herself for the foreseeable future, it could not by itself win the war *in* Europe. In the immediate post-Trafalgar period, before that chance in Spain opened up (and even then only so long as Napoleon did not concentrate his whole power there), the British had no big continental ally to do their fighting: Austria had been humbled, the Prussian army virtually destroyed, and the Tsar had been first checked, and then turned into a neutral ally by that 1807 version of the Nazi–Soviet Pact of 1939, the Treaty of Tilsit. While Napoleon, at the zenith of his power, was busy creating his New Order, the British government could only fumble around, while King George's navy battled to blockade the enemy while maintaining the country's European and world-wide trade on which her economy as well as her ability to continue the war depended.

In William Hoste's Mediterranean war, to that need to fight and maintain trade simultaneously was added the spectre of another Napoleonic expedition to the east, towards India. That Napoleon may in fact never have seriously contemplated another Egyptian expedition is beside the point. The British knew that he had headed eastwards once, and that now he aspired to be the new Alexander as well as the new Caesar. And, anyway, if more proof that their suspicions were well-grounded was required, it was supplied by his continuing determination to hold another of those French 'Gibraltars', the island of Corfu, which had been seized in 1797 as a prelude to the invasion of Egypt. For this strategically placed base was not only reoccupied in 1807, but strongly reinforced and resupplied at great risk in 1808 in a daring French naval operation which made it invincible.

The truth was that, in spite of the superiority of the British fleet in the Mediterranean – at least in quality, if not actual numbers after every ship in every port had been counted – the Mediterranean was still far from being a British lake. By 1807 the French, or their allies and subject-states, had extended their control of the coastline from Spain and Italy to much of modern Yugoslavia down to Corfu at the mouth of the Adriatic. The British Navy might be firmly based in Gibraltar and now Malta, and able with a few ships to protect their only ally, Sicily. But with so many well-equipped bases – and bases well-experienced also in warship construction – at his disposal (notably Genoa and Venice, in addition to his own Toulon), Napoleon was far from powerless at sea, and the sea was still busy with French and French-allied ships.

It was Captain William Hoste's good luck that this Mediterranean war, which was to be the setting for his wartime career henceforth, was a little-ship war, and primarily a frigate one. Big ships-of-the-line there were, and occasionally they had their moments. In 1808, the French admirals Cosmao and Ganteaume concentrated two squadrons for that Corfu convoy, in a successful operation as risky as any of the British Malta convoys of the 1939–45 war. In 1809, having missed the Corfu convoy, Collingwood caught another, destroying two ships-of-the-line with it. And, of course, there was Hornblower's battle of Rosas in 1810, which ended another French squadron break-out attempt. Yet the famous names of the Mediterranean now were those of frigate captains rather than ship-of-the-line captains and admirals: not only Hoste of the *Amphion* (and later 'the bold *Bacchante*'), but also Cochrane of the *Impérieuse*, Jahleel Brenton of the *Spartan*, and Patrick Campbell of the *Unité* ('the smartest ship in the sea', boasted her proud captain). These, and smaller craft, were the ships which increasingly did the work (and took the prize-money), expanding their operations from their traditional duties of reconnaissance, escort and patrol to increasingly aggressive descents on enemy coastlines, and eventually even to reconquest. Dear old Cuthbert Collingwood, slowly working himself to death aboard his giant flagship, the *Ville de Paris* (110), not only as fleet commander but also as his country's roving ambassador and Viceroy of the Mediterranean, summed it all up very typically in 1809: 'All our frigate captains are great generals, and some in brigs are good brigadiers . . . the activity and zeal of these gallant young men keep up my spirits.'

Hoste was fortunate, initially, to be commanded by such a man, with Smith as his immediate superior. For, if Collingwood was no Nelson, at least he recognised talent – even in its most uncomfortable Cochrane-form. Also, as Nelson's friend, he kept faith with Nelson's intentions, quickly giving Hoste 'the best cruise' in his gift, which might provide not only the 'pewter' (prize-money) every young captain needed, but also a chance of what every young frigate captain desired even more, a French frigate. Sadly, no French frigate immediately presented itself. But then, under the enterprising Sidney Smith, Hoste learnt his new trade of combined operations during descents on Naples and Calabria, including the landing which preceded the battle of Maida in 1806, where in miniature the steady, well-trained British redcoat line first proved its superiority over the hitherto irresistible gallantry of the French column. (In this battle, also, his younger and far less talented younger brother George – the future Colonel Sir George Hoste, Rugby School and the Royal Engineers – was blooded, while smaller brother Edward was being readied for service in his big brother's ship.)

In fact Hoste performed so well that when the worn-out *Amphion* returned to England for a major refit in the summer of 1807 Collingwood asked for both to be returned to him, the man specifically, because he was 'active, vigilant and knows the coast' and the ship because like every British admiral, he was short of frigates. So both were back in the Mediterranean within six months, escorting a big convoy and with the reinforcement of 13-year-old Edward Hoste as a 'First-Class Volunteer' thanks to his brother's 'interest'.

This coincided with the period of renewed French activity in the Mediterranean after Napoleon had finished off the latest coalition against him at the Treaty of Tilsit. Under that treaty's secret provisions, the Russians not only agreed to support the French in closing Europe to British trade and to use her navy against her late ally if necessary, but also abandoned her footholds in the Mediterranean to Napoleon. It was thus, after having already gained control of Venice and the province of Illyria at the head of the Adriatic Sea through his defeat of Austria, that Napoleon was able to add the naval bases of Ragusa and Cattaro in modern Yugoslavia and the greatest base of all, Corfu in the Ionian Islands, to the whole of the Italian Adriatic coastline. It was against this background of continental triumph that he hatched his plan for the capture of Sicily and reinforcement and resupply of Corfu. But this plan involved a naval operation which, although partially successful (as regards Corfu), was actually to be the French fleet's last major enterprise in the Mediterranean – and a classic example of the frigate's 'eyes of the fleet' role even if it did not end in a battle.

For that last, Admiral Collingwood is usually held to blame. But, to be fair to him, the defence of Sicily rather than a battle had to be his priority – and Sicily *was* defended. Also, he was almost as desperately short of frigates as Nelson had been back in 1798. And Nelson, after all, had then failed as completely to catch a much bigger French fleet at sea as he did later on, in the long 1804-5 run-up to Trafalgar, while chasing back-and-forward across the Atlantic. The sea – even a 'small' sea like the Mediterranean – was a very big place in those days of poor communications. Without enough frigates it was simply far *too* big once an enemy had evaded the blockaders round his naval bases, which he could always hope to do in the right conditions.

Even as it was, the French expedition eventually degenerated into a pursuit once they had first been headed off from Sicily and then finally spotted (by the frigate *Active*) off the Ionian Islands. Jahleel Brenton then took up the pursuit from the *Active* in his *Spartan*, hanging on all the way from Cape Bon to Sardinia, and Hoste himself, in the *Amphion*, finally reported them back in Toulon. Within a week there was a British fleet on station there: the French had briefly evaded their jailer, but were now back in prison, never to escape again in any really significant force until the very end of the war (and then only briefly, to be harried back by a fleet commanded by Admiral Sir Edward Pellew).

Chasing such fleets was in fact risky work for British frigate captains, not only near coasts and islands against which they might be pinned themselves if the wind changed, but because even in the open sea French ships-of-the-line were not to be pursued incautiously since some of them were in the right conditions actually faster than many British-built frigates. But the arrival of the British fleet now released Hoste from blockade duty for one of those independent or semi-independent (and much more profitable) missions which favoured young captains more often received – and which, of course, Colling-wood happily gave to the favourite of his own much-lamented friend Nelson. Indeed, the nearest happy hunting-ground to Toulon for prizes and action was the Franco-Spanish coastline down to the Costa Brava, which was the scene of Hoste's next fight, when he chased and drove ashore the fast military transport *Baleine* under the guns of Rosas fortress.

The *Baleine* incident in fact admirably further illustrates both the frigate-function and the effect of a tight blockade. In the first place, the *Baleine* herself was no ordinary merchant ship, but a converted frigate which still carried 30 guns and – as the French no doubt intended – could only have been chased and taken successfully by something as big as another frigate. That they had been reduced to running military supplies in such a fashion is not simply a testimony to the problems caused by the blockade, but also of their transport problems in general, which made such high-risk operations necessary. The trans-port of anything by road in those days was far slower and more laborious than by sea. Spanish roads, of course, were notoriously bad, and especially to be avoided if possible even while the Spaniards were friendly; when, very soon, they became hostile, and blood-thirsty guerrillas lay in wait behind every rock, the sea became even more attractive, to the subsequent enrichment of Cochrane, Hornblower and dozens of other British captains fortunate enough to be given Spanish patrol assignments, and who in the end put a virtual stop to French coastal supply. (By contrast, of course, Wellington *never* had any supply problems once he had organised his army's road transport, for the Navy ensured the arrival of everything he needed to the nearest convenient port: in the final analysis, the Peninsular War was as much a triumph of his organisational ability as of his generalship.) But perhaps the most eloquent memorial of all to the power of the British Navy and the efficiency of their blockade (as well as the inadequacy of early nineteenth-century roads – even Napoleonic ones) is to be found in France herself, between the two great seaports of Nantes and Brest. For there, and from one end of Brittany to the other although Nantes and Brest are a few days' sail apart, Napoleon caused *a canal* to be built, because Pellew, Hornblower and their successors had made the easy sea route uneconomic. (This great work can still be navigated – at least on each side of the Guerlédan Dam, which now divides it into two.)

That young Captain Hoste was trusted by his commander-in-chief as well as favoured was demonstrated after the *Baleine* action when he was given the diplomatic task of delivering a royal figurehead to Britain's new but leaderless Spanish allies. In fact, the Austrian Archduke Charles proved unsuitable in this role. But the failure of this (typical frigate) special assignment was of no consequence: Spanish hatred of foreign invaders was by itself more than sufficient to inspire an increasingly savage and unconquerable resistance which might actually have been less effective had it been centrally directed – or, more likely, *mis*directed – in the usual Spanish manner. And, in any case, although the Spanish and French Mediterranean coasts would henceforth become a marvellous Tom Tiddler's ground for enterprising captains like Cochrane and Hornblower, Hoste himself was now redirected to join another talented frigate captain, Patrick Campbell of the *Unité* (36), in an equally promising theatre of operations from which prize-money would soon be flowing back to England to support his father's expensive tastes, the Adriatic.

William Hoste was now in his prime. Still only in his twenty-ninth year, he was already a captain of seven years' seniority, with 16 years' service behind him, most of which had been spent at sea and at war – and with nearly all that sea-warfare experience in the Mediterranean, where he now practised his art.

It has already been suggested that, of all our frigate captains, Cochrane was the greatest (and Pigot, of course, was clearly the worst). But all such historical comparisons are invidious, and in daring, professional skill, bravery and ingenuity there is really little to chose among the five good ones. Pellew was professionally (and financially) the most successful during this war (and also the most senior from the beginning). Hornblower was the most 'judicious', ashore and afloat – and as 'worthy' as Broke, who was (as we shall see) the best gunner among them. But, with Hoste, one can see very easily why Nelson loved him, for his merit as a young officer was evidently equalled by a boyhood attractiveness which continued in manhood: he was a loving (even *too* loving) son and a delightful elder brother as well as a good captain whose crews would follow him anywhere. Near enough, he *was* (as Emma Hamilton said), 'a second Nelson' – and even in his least-attractive 'man-of-his-time' hunger for the honours and prizes he later on felt he had earned. Professionally, the only lesson he failed to learn (from Sidney Smith, not Nelson) concerned the proper use of the irregular guerrillas of the Adriatic in fighting the French, whom he affected to hate intensely (as required by Nelson). But then, as the Duke of Wellington and Captain Hornblower both discovered the hard way, guerrillas *were* unreliable when they came up against French regulars. And, when it came to the French, the testimony of Madame Vallié, his sometime prisoner, suggests that his treatment of his enemies was very different from the sentiments of his letters home.

In William Hoste, all in all, one can discern that quality of inspirational leadership (even with one eye always fixed on the main chance of personal advantage) which powered the British Navy at its best in the age of Nelson. Indeed, Nelson himself exemplified it: as aspiring second lieutenant in the *Lowestoffe* frigate, Nelson had seized his chance to board a prize in heavy seas, forestalling another officer with the shout '*It's my turn now. And if I don't come back* [fail/don't survive, that is] *it's yours!*' And then, as a captain, Pellew had emulated Nelson in delighting in outclimbing his midshipmen to the maintop. Even as an admiral, Pellew led the way in cutting wreckage free, axe-in-hand with the best of them in an East Indian storm. Cochrane, Hornblower and Broke all famously led their own boarding parties. By the same token, Hoste – and by the hero-worshipping testimony of 'litle Ned', his brother – was first up the mast off Malta in 1808 when lightning set fire to the top-gallant sail, extinguishing it in the dark with his own uniform coat: it was just such inspirational *leadership* which inspired the 13-year-old Ned to stow away in defiance of his brother's orders in the boats of the *Amphion* when they were sent to attack the beached *Baleine*, just as the leadership of the brutal Captain Hamilton filled his boats with volunteers when he cut out the *Hermione* back in '98. *Leadership*, when all the confidence of training and tradition, and the memory of past victories, is stripped away, was what gave the British Navy its sharpest cutting edge, enabling it to snatch so many of its successes against the odds. When led by men like Hoste, when men like Hoste were given the opportunity to lead, it was virtually unbeatable.

And now, the Adriatic was Hoste's great opportunity, given to him at last by Cuthbert Collingwood in memory of Nelson, but also by right of merit.

CHAPTER FOURTEEN

The war in the Adriatic; and, among other matters, how Midshipman O'Brien reported back to the Amphion

The naval war in the Adriatic, in which Hoste and his fellow captains were henceforth to play a major role, receives but little space in the general histories of the period. Yet for all that (and apart from demonstrating the economical use of naval forces, chiefly in the form of frigates), it cannot be regarded as one of those wasteful side-shows which Britain's military weakness and naval strength led her to mount after Trafalgar, like Admiral Duckworth's unsuccessful attack on the Dardanelles in 1806, which only served to increase the French influence with the Sultan in Constantinople.

Rather, the Navy's presence in the Adriatic, apart from being a necessary British precaution against another French drive to the East, was part of the great and continuing trade war at sea. There, as elsewhere, the determination of the merchants and manufacturers of a nation of shop-keepers to do business with Europe collided head-on with Napoleon's Continental System, which was designed to exclude them. And there, as elsewhere (and benefiting from the hard-pressed pound's devaluation), the shop-keepers finally defeated the System.

Through the recurrent crises of this unending economic war (the latest of 1807–8), the ports of North Germany and the Baltic were more important to the British than the Mediterranean, as their treatment of Denmark shows. But their manufactures also poured into South Germany and Austria through the great trading (and smuggling) centre of Trieste, at the head of the Adriatic, *via* Malta (on which prosperity suddenly descended now, unhealthy though it was). And, apart from commercial profits, the connection with Austria was vital to Britain throughout the war. Napoleon's defeat in Russia in 1812 and old Blucher's Prussian ride-to-the-rescue at Waterloo in 1815 have tended to overshadow the contribution of the almost-invariably defeated Austrian army to the struggle against France. But that army's powers of recuperation were heroic, and Austria was at the heart of every one of the great coalitions which did the fighting for the British in Central Europe, and which in the end won the war for them.

So the Adriatic was a busy sea for the British, where protection was required for her ships and those of whatever country might be smuggling her merchandise. But it was also a rich hunting-ground for those protectors, when the French controlled every mainland port and sea-base (and, where Italian roads were merely normally bad, those of Illyria and Dalmatia were impossible). Most of the traffic was small stuff, admittedly (compared with the fat Indiamen of distant oceans), and much of it had to be destroyed for lack of prize-crews to take the captures back to the busy prize-court in Malta. But during Hoste's first descent on this sea (down to the end of 1809) he took 218 vessels while in company with the *Unité*, the bulk of his estimated £60,000 total prize-money during the war (£6 million in modern money?) representing the accumulation of such small rewards.

Also, it was to his advantage that the Adriatic did not then merit the stationing of a substantial British squadron. At first there were only four French frigates at Venice and Ancona, together with several Venetian (French-allied) frigates, and the remains of the original Russian presence in the Adriatic, which comprised four ship-of-the-line and two frigates in Trieste, which were theoretically hostile under the secret provisions of Tilsit. But although this Russian force was definitely not friendly, and the Franco-Venetian frigate strength was undoubtedly hostile, this was not the sort of opposition which required the big battalions of the British fleet. So in his first years in the Adriatic, Captain Hoste – *Commodore* Hoste, even – was not to be much encumbered by senior officers with more post-rank years to their credit, who might have stolen his thunder (not to mention his prize-money).

Also, his duty was exciting as he bearded the enemy off Trieste in 1809, so that one British escaped prisoner-of-war was inspired to remember the sight of him there quite unforgettably: 'one small British Frigate proudly standing in, reconnoitering a large Russian Squadron moored in the Mole, and capturing vessels hourly, in their view, even under their guns – 'twas truly flattering that we belonged to a country and service that swayed so triumphantly – feared and admired by all Europe.'

This escaped prisoner was Midshipman (future Commander/Captain) Maurice Hewison, who was then with Warrant Officer

(Master's Mate/future Post-Captain) Donat Henchy O'Brien, one of the bravest and most resourceful Irishmen ever to honour the British flag, or any other flag, and Hoste's own future first lieutenant.

Hewison and O'Brien had two months earlier been part of an escape group which had broken out of the notorious French Colditz fortress prison-camp of Bitche, in Alsace, and as brilliantly as any of the famous escapers of the 1939–45 World War. And although neither officer features by rank or service with our other frigate captains in this narrative, they and their stories deserve a place in this narrative as of right none the less, not simply as an irresistible digression, or even as an example of the stakes and hazards our captains latterly faced in their duties, but as evidence of how their war was changing, as it pointed to future wars.

Among our captains, it will be recalled, two have already faced captivity, albeit in very different circumstances. Hornblower, taken prisoner by the Spaniards while still a midshipman (but an acting-lieutenant), had had his acting *commissioned* rank then confirmed while still a prisoner, and had then been not only treated with perfect propriety by the Spaniards as an officer, but had subsequently been released freely, without exchange for an officer of similar rank in the best eighteenth-century tradition, as a reward for saving the lives of certain shipwrecked Spaniards off Corunna. The eighteenth century is well supplied with such examples of civilised wartime behaviour, including that of Cochrane when he was captured in circumstances inspiring admiration among his enemies off Cadiz, and then paroled in record time, a matter of hours rather than days, and finally formally exchanged, to fight again, in return for a more senior Spanish officer a week later.

That was how eighteenth-century gentlemen, fighting their kings' private wars, behaved when war was still more about *winning* than *killing*. However, in the new era of peoples' wars, for 'liberty and freedom', Napoleon soon began to change these customs, only inhibited somewhat in the case of the British because they soon had ten times as many French naval and military prisoners as he had of theirs. At first, indeed, he appeared still to subscribe to the principle of the exchange of officer-prisoners of equal rank, who until their exchange could live a quite comfortable and reasonably free life on the basis of their word-of-honour not to escape home to fight again. But very soon, and greatly to the embarrassment of both the British government and their own word-of-honour prisoners, the French Emperor began to cheat on the well-established rules, failing to exchange like for like, restricting the customary privileges of officers whose paroles already bound them more securely than locks and bolts, and – worst of all in point of honour – insisting on the return to duty not only of paroled

French officers for whom he had not released a British equivalent, but of parole-*breakers*.

A case illustrating all this is provided by none other than Hoste's own fellow frigate captain, Jahleel Brenton. Not long after the outbreak of war in 1803, Brenton's *Minerve* (32) had been wrecked off Cherbourg while scouting its approaches, and he had been captured with his entire crew. As had already been noted, Brenton was one of the Navy's finest seamen, and it is pleasant to discover that his behaviour and powers of leadership were no less admirable in adversity than on his own quarterdeck: he looked after his men like a father on the long journey to prison-camp, marching every step of the way on foot himself while hiring a carriage for the sick and shoeless and encouraging his officers to do the same by his example. When in camp at last (British PoWs ended up in one or other of the great Vauban frontier fortresses which the expansion of France had left far behind her new frontiers) he discharged his duties as Senior British Officer with the same skill, courage and determination as had characterised his command afloat, to maintain the rights and secure the welfare of all prisoners. In any imagined film of the adventures of the PoW escapers of this war, whose exploits deserve celebration as much as those of their *Wooden Horse/Great Escape/Colditz* descendants, Jahleel Brenton's part would once have surely been taken by the late Jack Hawkins.

As Senior Officer, and having given his parole, Brenton could not escape himself. But then, back in 1803, this would not have occurred to him because he did not need to do so: he expected to be exchanged as soon as a French prisoner of equal rank (of which there were already not a few) was offered. And one was very soon produced: a certain redoubtable Captain Jurien, who a few years later was to distinguish himself when in command of the *Italienne* (44) and two other frigates for his brave fight against the 80-gun *Defiance* when caught off the sands of Les Sables d'Orlonne in the opening phase of the Basque Roads operation. But then, after Jurien had arrived back in France in 1803, Brenton failed to appear in England. Indeed, he did not even learn of Jurien's return for nearly a year, until he received news of his country's angry protest on his behalf. Worse still, not only did the French ignore this protest, but when Jurien himself heard of it, and very properly avoided re-employment, he was ordered back to sea by Napoleon. Effectively, this marked the end of the whole system of exchange, although its demise was never formalised and exchanges continued to take place, but much more rarely and only when they suited Napoleon. This indeed, was how Brenton finally got back home in the end, two years later than Jurien. Even then it was not for Jurien that he was swopped, but for a ship-of-the-line captain, Louis Infernet, who had been taken with his *Intrepide* (80) at Trafalgar. Infernet was not only one of the heroes of that battle, who had fought his ship to the last, when one-third of his crew were dead, but was also Marshal Massena's nephew, whose release (and immediate promotion to admiral's rank) was directly solicited from Napoleon by his uncle. So this hardly ranked as a genuine exchange.

The whole prisoner situation had in fact degenerated by then, and in some ways much more seriously than in the mere breakdown of gentlemanly usages in the treatment of officers in France. That the treatment of other rank prisoners in England left much to be desired, especially those in the infamous hulks (old worn-out warships moored off-shore) is undeniable. But such cruelties were more the result of abuse by individuals and of endemic eighteenth-century corruption – plus the problem of handling a steadily increasing number of prisoners (nearly 200,000 perhaps) acquired during so long a war. It was never, as one may suspect it was in France, the result of higher policy. In the end, it was probably only the disproportionate numbers held by France and Britain that best protected the British. Even so, there were circumstances in which British officer-prisoners were at some risk when first captured, notably when carrying out land-reconnaissances or involved in landing or encouraging French royalist *émigrés* and other 'traitors to the Revolution'. Sidney Smith, as has been noted, was imprisoned in Paris after having been caught at this sort of work, but managed to escape. Commander John Wesley Wright, who was captured in Quiberon Bay in 1804 when possibly involved in similar operations, was less fortunate: while imprisoned in Paris (*not* paroled in an official PoW fortress) he allegedly committed suicide, but in circumstances so unlikely and suspicious that murder seems more probable. After the undoubted murder – albeit publicly and by firing squad – of the Duc d'Enghien in 1804 the British always believed the worst of Napoleon, with some justification. Both Captain Horn-blower and Colonel Colquhoun Grant, Wellington's Chief of Intelli-gence in the Peninsula, had no illusions about their chances when being transported to Paris under close arrest. Grant had long been a thorn in the French Army's side, working behind their lines, and Hornblower's part in that alleged disinformation plot before Trafalgar laid him wide open to reprisal – arguably legitimate reprisal, too. Neither, accordingly, much fancied his chances once Joseph Fouché's feared secret police got their hands on him, and each brilliantly seized his chance to escape en route (always the best time to run) before it was too late. Not surprisingly, after Hornblower had gone to ground with the help of the royalist Comte de Garcay, he was referred to in the British press as 'Bonaparte's martyred victim'. To be 'shot while escaping', or otherwise officially to lose one's life 'accidentally' then, is not an invention of our familiar twentieth-century tyrannies. For every ten naval officer escapers during the Napoleonic

War there was an eleventh who died violently, while escaping (and not infrequently in outrageous circumstances), while others got away only to disappear suspiciously afterwards, without a trace. Of course, wartime escapers in any age, even in countries which in the future subscribed honourably (as opposed to nominally) to the Geneva Convention, cannot reasonably be expected to go unpenalised on recapture, and such was the case on both sides of the Channel in the last French war. But it is not fanciful to discern the beginnings of the twentieth century's bad habits in Napoleon's regime, when there was still some attempt to cling to eighteenth-century customs in Britain. It may be convenient for some to suggest that Napoleon's empire was but an early attempt to invent a European Common Market, after the revolutionary armies had carried new ideas of liberty and the rights of man across Europe in their knapsacks, together with that meritocratic chance of promotion from the ranks. Yet the truth is also that his imperial armies paved the way for arbitrary government, secret police, pillage and confiscation, so that the final battles against him were called 'Wars of Liberation' by contemporaries, for all that they also brought reactionary governments in their aftermath. Total wars like that in Spain were the result of his policies, and the shape of twentieth-century things to come: it is no accident that Spain added the word *guerrilla* to the English language, dating it exactly to the year 1809 in the Oxford English Dictionary.

As regards the breakdown of prisoner exchange, there was admittedly a certain logic in Napoleon's attitude all the same, for a complete exchange of officers, one-for-one of equal rank, would have emptied his prisons of British officers (particularly skilled naval ones) while still leaving many French prisoners in Britain. It was therefore very much to his advantage (if not to his honour) to get back as many officers as possible, and then to return them to duty *without* releasing a similar number of equal-rank prisoners, while still paying lip service to the system. And this he proceeded to do on a grand scale, for the British protest over Captain Brenton's release in specific return for Captain Jurien (to whom they had then quickly written directly: '. . . you are hereby required to return to this country according to the terms of your Parole Agreement') was but one item in a much bigger complaint over the release of no less than 500 French officers, in exchange for whom not one single British prisoner had yet arrived.

Worse was to follow. For when the British quite understandably baulked at being caught out again in this way, Napoleon not only turned a blind eye to the many French officers who broke their parole in England by escaping, but positively condoned such action when it was committed not merely by young men, but by generals like Lefevre-Desnouëttes, who should have been setting an example in honourable behaviour. Indeed, if a report in *The Times* of 1812 can be believed, he even executed one of his properly exchanged officers for protesting about his comrades' parole-breaking. Certainly, where Britain was a famously difficult – indeed, actually impossible – place from which to escape in the twentieth-century world wars, there were many such successful enemy escapes in this one – no less than 464 in the years 1809–12 alone. But few of these involved much ingenuity or daring, only money. For the escapers, being on parole, were already free, and getting them across the Channel was a big and profitable business for those of the large British smuggling fraternity willing to diversify their operations. This, actually, became a business so outrageous that the law relating to it was changed in 1812, increasing the offence of aiding escaped PoWs from a misdemeanour to a felony, for which the punishment was transportation to that 'fatal shore' of Australia for anything from seven years to life.

What made all this distasteful (however logical, honour aside) was that Napoleon not only condoned it while stigmatising Britain as *perfide Albion*, but his servants no less expected *their* British prisoners to keep their paroles while severely curtailing their rights. And in this the French were assisted by the British government itself: in supplying Parliament with that 464-escapes figure during the debate on the change in the law mentioned above, the Foreign Secretary, Castlereagh, proudly reported that during the same period not one single British officer had broken his word. But, then, no British officer dared to do so when proven parole-breaking spelt the certain end of his career, and possibly even his return to his captors. With the virtual breakdown of the exchange system British prisoners thus seemed condemned not only to increasingly uncomfortable and boring semi-imprisonment on half-pay in some provincial French fortress-town for the duration of an endless war, but also to the loss of all chances of promotion, fame and fortune which that war was giving to their uncaptured comrades. Ironically, it was the new and less-civilised practices of the prison-camp jailers and secret policemen which were to resolve this problem for the prisoners, though the solution rendered actual escape much more difficult and dangerous even before the escapers set out on their hazardous odysseys across Napoleon's European police state. For example, those three famous escapers, Sidney Smith, Horatio Hornblower and Colquhoun Grant, were not being treated like eighteenth-century prisoners when they escaped, but were either closely guarded or actually in prison. Thus they had no word-of-honour or parole to break, and did not have to behave like officers and gentlemen. By the same token, *any* prisoner who deliberately relinquished his relatively comfortable half-pay existence as a paroled officer and got himself closely confined (first usually by committing some minor misdemeanour, but thereafter – if he was recaptured the first time – because he was literally in prison) cleared all the eighteenth-century's technicalities from his path. What now faced him was, of course, bad enough: harsh jailers, locked doors and barred windows, precipitous prison walls patrolled by trigger-happy sentries – and then hundreds of miles through a Europe well-policed not so much to capture escaped PoWs as to catch much more numerous smugglers and conscription-avoiders or army deserters; and while he *might* find sympathisers or kind hearts along the way even in France, he might equally find hostile policemen in satellite countries far beyond her frontiers, all the way to the far-off sea, where he would be tantalised by the sails of patrolling British frigates which he somehow had to reach.

It required daring and resolution to attempt such escapes. But, of course, the escapers were chiefly drawn from that very class of British officer from whom our frigate captains are drawn: likely young men (midshipmen, masters' mates and lieutenants) whose stock-in-trade was daring, resolution and the tackling of practical problems in conditions of hardship. So, although *out* of their element, they were also in some sense in it. and it was thus that, in spite of all obstacles, nearly *one-quarter* of Napoleon's British junior naval officer/warrant officer prisoners (or perhaps more, allowing for the inadequacy of the records) schemed and dared, and climbed and risked, and talked and walked and fought their way back to sea during the war. And if that quarter is in reality but a small number, little more than 100 (say, the junior officer complements of ten rated ships), this digression is none the less justified here not even simply as an elongated footnote which began and will end with Hoste's *Amphion* cruising brazenly off Trieste, illustrating the hazards and the changing times which our surviving frigate captains and their crews faced over the years, and the way these were surmounted. For it also leads up to Hoste's acquisition of the man who became his trusted first lieutenant, Master's Mate (future Captain) Donat Henchy O'Brien.

In the all-time honours list of great escapers, Donat Henchy O'Brien certainly ranks with the men of Colditz. Equally certainly, he was one of those with the greatest incentive to escape, since captivity until the war's end (whenever that might be) would have then most likely left him in the no-man's land of technically uncommissioned rank forever. When he was captured in February 1804, after the wreck of the frigate *Hussar* (38) off Ushant, he had actually passed his lieutenant's examination (having earlier, by a most curious coincidence, served in the *Amphion* herself as an acting-lieutenant while she was with the Channel Fleet in 1803). But, being only 19 and quite without 'interest', he had not by then found promotion, and was still in the warrant rank of master's mate, which the French at first identified as keeping him in other rank status. He was, however, one of those indebted to Captain Jahleel Brenton – then himself still improperly detained, but always a determined fighter for prisoners' rights – for his eventual transfer from the Givet other ranks' fortress prison to the relatively more free Verdun depot, with all the other British officers.

Escape planning and preparation was much easier at Verdun, either aiming westwards, on the shorter but more dangerous route through France to the well-policed Channel coast, or eastwards, which was longer and presented the great obstacle of the Rhine, but which thereafter ran through countries where the authorities *might* be less dedicated and efficient and the people more friendly. In fact, accumulating failed-escape experience made both routes problematical. An added western hazard was that on the coast the escapers ran the risk of being shot as spies if caught (and O'Brien very nearly suffered this fate when his first attempt failed). But then, even though rewards were offered, there were poor French peasants who neither hated all Englishmen (especially in Brittany) nor loved their own government (increasingly, there were also the *réfractaires* – conscription evaders – also on the run, with whom lucky escapers might be confused). However, not all German policemen were anti-Napoleon, and his arm was long beyond his frontiers, even though the Austrian authorities were quite reliably pro-British. It was, indeed, by non-French police, beside Lake Lucerne, that O'Brien's second escape came to grief, after he had brazened his way across the Rhine, past eleven sentries, as a cowherd mixed up in a herd which was conveniently also making the crossing. And the escapers' favourite ploy of passing themselves off as Americans (which Colonel Colquhoun Grant used to good effect on a French general while still in British uniform) rarely seems to have deceived policemen, once their suspicions were aroused.

Still, O'Brien first ran in 1807, with three other young officers, after having de-paroled himself to his satisfaction, shinning down Verdun's 70-foot town wall. And then he escaped again (after his first recapture within sight of the sea) while being taken back to the maximum security 'Mansion of Tears' at Bitche. Escape while en route avoided the disadvantage of high walls and locked doors in the first place, which both Hornblower and Colquhoun Grant capitalised on; but any unplanned run for freedom thereafter left the escaper without any essential escape equipment, most importantly money and a compass, demanding extraordinary luck or at least special knowledge, as well as cheek, courage and endurance. In his escape, Hornblower was exceptionally fortunate in meeting up with the kindly Comte de Garcay, an aristocrat of the old school, although other lucky escapers were also on occasion given shelter by French peasants who equally despised the New Order. Colquhoun Grant, for his part was both an experienced intelligence officer with contacts and a fluent linguist. O'Brien, in his spur-of-the-moment second break, had only the rags he was wearing, and only got as far as he did by at first pretending to be one of the peasants who were hunting him.

Such cheek and extraordinary presence-of-mind saved him in his third escape attempt, during an ill-planned mass break-out from Bitche which failed when the alarm was raised before the escapers had cleared the walls. Determined to avoid further punishment, he turfed a dead-drunk non-escaper from bed and substituted himself therein: the drunk was not suspected, and O'Brien was able to return to his own prison quarters undetected afterwards. This experience caused him to plan more carefully for his fourth and final attempt. But by then, in any case, he was able to plan better because, in concentrating inveterate escapers in the high-security Bitche fortress, with its concentric ring of walls totalling 200 feet, the French had also concentrated British escape know-how. So this time he was not only equipped with sufficient home-made rope for each descent, together with a compass, money and a working knowledge of German as well as French, but was also one of a small group which included the equally experienced and resourceful Midshipman Maurice Hewison.

Hewison was another fledgling frigate officer who had actually passed his lieutenant's examination just before his capture, but had not yet been appointed to a lieutenancy. A meritorious member of an equally meritorious Anglo-Irish family (his elder brother George was a lieutenant in Collingwood's flagship, the *Royal Sovereign*, at Trafalgar) he can indeed be taken as an example of how *bad* luck worked: first he was born rather late (in 1786), so that he needed all the luck he could get, short of significant 'interest' as he was, if he was to make post during hostilities. In such a long war he might have done so, nevertheless, had he not been captured – while still a midshipman – in 1803, during a land raid near Brest. Now, six years later, he was still a midshipman, and would miss real promotion. But he was also a frigate-product, having graduated through the *Nemesis* (28), the *Mermaid* (32) to the *Diamond* (28), and an inveterate escaper of the sort that ended up (or *didn't* end up) in the 'Mansion of Tears' at Bitche. He had, indeed, been sent there after a truly heroic break-out in company with Midshipman Butterfield, of the *Impétueux* (32), when both had taken an unusual southwards route through the length of France, only to be captured within sight of the sea in Aigues-Mortes, at the mouth of the Rhone.

His experience, together with that of O'Brien and the third and fourth members of the group, an East Indian Company officer and a ship's doctor (who later practised successfully in Bloomsbury), decided the escapers to head east-south-east this time, towards Austrian territory. First, however, they had to beat the various walls of Bitche, which they conquered in three 70-foot stages with a single home-made rope knotted to bear the weight of one man at a time, so that three could pull it free and it could be reused for the next drop, leaving no evidence of escape behind it.

After this they headed east, towards the Rhine, which they crossed in a stolen boat even while the doctor and the East India Company soldier began to weaken from unaccustomed privation. Before they entered pro-French Bavaria, they were forced to leave the soldier behind with a friendly Black Forest German (though, happily to relate, he eventually made a successful home-run too). Keeping away from the bigger towns and villages the remaining three finally reached Austria, where the local police didn't believe their claim to be Americans for a moment, but readily pretended that they did, allowing them to reach their objective, Trieste. There the Russian squadron was still moored, but a British frigate – which they believed to be Campbell's *Unité* – was cruising just out of range, snapping up any vessel not provably neutral.

By then, in spite of innumerable hair's-breadth escapes, O'Brien and Hewison were both bright-eyed and bushy-tailed (which Hewison always seemed to be, taking comfort from his strong Protestant faith as well as his patriotism while escaping – 'every difficulty and disentanglement only give cause to joke on the occasion'). And now, by one of those anomalies which made a mockery of Napoleon's Continental System, there was still a British vice-consul in residence in Trieste, (just as, in his eventual foray into the Baltic, Hornblower was to find a self-styled British consular agent in Stralsund, who licensed trade, but who also served the neutral King of Sweden and the hostile King of Bavaria). Indeed, Napoleon's failure and the success of British capitalism were even more exactly demonstrated by this whole final episode in their escape story. For they had actually been passed on by the sympathetic Chief of Police in Salzburg, complete with a covering letter, to the Chief of Police in Trieste (one of his relatives), recommending them to the United States consul in Trieste – who, in the most civil manner, then passed them on to his (illegal, unofficial) British consular colleague, who in turn kindly obtained a boat for them, and pointed them in the right direction.

At last, Captain Hoste comes into the story again, for it was the *Amphion*, not the *Unité*, which was by then closer to Trieste. But even now the escapers' adventures were not over: they saw a ship's boat (which was big enough to undertake cutting-out operations) heading towards them as they reached the open sea. At first they feared it was a Russian patrol, but it turned out to be from the *Amphion*; and, more than that, by an amazing stroke of luck it was commanded by Lieutenant George Jones, who recognised O'Brien from his past service in the frigate. Lieutenant Jones, however, was on a raiding mission, so that after they had paid off their Triestino boatmen they joined him in an attack on two Venetian vessels which proved too strong for them. In the ensuing fight several British sailors were killed, and both Jones and O'Brien himself were wounded; after which, when the boat managed to get back to the *Amphion* in some disarray the escapers first encountered an irate Hoste, who was unaccustomed to defeat and casualties, and took them for foreigners. Thus their high adventure ended in a mixture of near-tragedy and semi-comedy before Hewison's explanation and further recognition of the former Acting-Lieutenant Donat Henchy O'Brien of the 1803 *Amphion* turned them at last into honoured guests, and the heroes they really were: 'When misfortunes cease', recalled Hewison, 'how soon does buoyancy possess the mind, and all sufferings become buried in oblivion.' And that buoyancy was such that within 24 hours the unwounded Hewison begged his way into another of Hoste's small-boat raids, this time on inland waterway shipping which the Venetians had hitherto regarded as safe.

So were the naval careers of two very tough young men restarted. They were soon on their way home, the story of their exploit travelling with them (and their returned luck too, for they narrowly missed recapture shortly afterwards, when on their way to report to Admiral Collingwood they nearly took passage on the frigate *Proserpine* (36), which was caught by the French off Toulon). However, although both then speedily received their lieutenancies, and appointments into ships-of-the-line, those lost PoW years were never quite to be made up during their subsequent wartime service. Both continued to fight with distinction, Hewison in the *Magnificent* (74) in the forthcoming assault on the Ionian Islands, then in the *Clarence* (74) in the Channel, and finally as first lieutenant in the *Prometheus* (16). As for O'Brien, within a year he was back in the *Amphion*, rising eventually to become first lieutenant of Hoste's next ship before his final wartime promotion to commander. That he did finally make post in 1821, but without a ship, was surely due to his Hoste connection. But, with Hewison (who had retired from the Navy with the honorary rank of commander), he remains one whose merit was cheated by bad luck: theirs was the *mis*fortune of war – any war.

By contrast, William Hoste had already benefited from an abundance of all three success-ingredients, for all that his relative youthfulness compared with all our frigate captains rendered it virtually impossible that he would ever fly his flag as an admiral in *this* war, unless it continued into the 1820s. It had, after all, taken the very well-placed Pellew 22 years to get to the top of the Captains' List to achieve that unmeritorious rank; and even the perfectly placed Nelson, a captain at 21 in 1776, had taken another 21 years to become an admiral. But Hoste, seizing his great opportunity now with both hands, was to do the next best thing very soon, under the local and temporary rank of commodore, which would entitle him at least to the honour of his own pennant, and an eleven-gun salute to go with it, as well as the temporary command of a 'frigate group'.

More immediately, however, he had to take the measure of the Adriatic in a war which seemed to be opening up at least with Austria's latest defiance of Napoleon, and elsewhere with the Spanish national rising and the British invasion of Walcheren in the Low Countries. The Walcheren operation – a good idea disastrously executed – was soon enough over, and Napoleon quickly smashed the Austrians again, at the battle of Wagram. But, in spite of the evacuation of the first British invasion army in the Spanish peninsula after its defensive victory at Corunna, the war there was only just beginning. For in April 1809 Sir Arthur Wellesley arrived in Lisbon with a British army which was five years later to carry that war victoriously across the Pyrenees, into France. And in the war in the Adriatic, Austria's latest defeat did not end British naval operations. The French did indeed hold every mainland naval base and port there, from Venice to Bari, and from freebooting Trieste by way of Spalato (modern Split), Ragusa (modern Dubrovnik), and Cattaro (Kotor), to their Corfu 'Gibraltar'. But all William Hoste really needed was a reasonably safe and convenient base, which he found in the island of Lissa (modern Vis), halfway up the present coast of Yugoslavia, well out to sea, and with an excellent deep-water harbour developed by the Venetians in their great days of empire. From strategically perfect Lissa, the British could turn the Adriatic from a French lake into a British one.

Initally, however, it was the French who were now on the offensive, for Hoste could not prevent them from collecting their easy mainland dividends after Wagram, the ports of Trieste and – sadly, because a number of his recent prizes were lost there – neighbouring Fiume. But he nevertheless had a highly profitable time, with dividends being regularly remitted by his agents to the tender care of his well-loved (and unwisely trusted) father, to be spent almost as fast as they were received. And, better for him even than prizes, he was then left in sole command with the withdrawal of Commodore William Hargood's squadron of three 74s, the *Northumberland, Excellent*, and *Montagu*, and then Campbell's *Unité* and Brenton's *Spartan* (to which little brother Ned was transferred for further experience – in as pretty a compliment as the admirable Brenton ever received from any brother-captain).

Brenton went to join the British counter-stroke against the French in the Ionian Islands, which was carried out by 1,800 soldiers commanded by Brigadier-General John Oswald, reinforced by marines and seamen from two other 74s, Hewison's *Magnificent* and O'Brien's *Warrior*. And this force in a series of neat little combined operations speedily dealt with all the enemy garrisons except that on

Corfu, with ten 18-pounders from the *Magnificent* playing a useful part in the reduction of Levkas under Lieutenant Hewison's command, while Ithaca, the one-time kingdom of Ulysses, fell to a marine sergeant and seven men. (Corfu, with its well-supplied 4,000 defenders, was too tough a nut to crack, and remained uncracked for the next five years under its determined French Governor-General, Donzelot, to whom was to fall the honour of being the last Frenchman to surrender his imperial outpost, long after the war had been lost in greater battles nearer home.)

But the Ionian Islands were outside Hoste's Adriatic stamping ground, in which his star could now shine all the brighter in the absence of senior officers in big ships and other frigate aces like Brenton and Campbell after he began to receive the frigate reinforcements which were now to come under his command. Even before the latter arrived, he ranged up the coasts of Italy and Dalmatia at will, with only a small sloop in support and confident that he could handle any enemy frigates. 'They are afraid of the weather, and are very badly manned,' he reported home. 'We are well-manned, and do not care a fig for the weather.' Fortunately for him, the four Russian ships-of-the-line (any one of which could theoretically blow him out of the water with a single broadside) were not only doubtfully seaworthy, but also even more doubtfully hostile in spite of the provisions of the Treaty of Tilsit: according to Collingwood's intelligence, the Russian commodore's dislike of the French was such that he had expressed himself ready only to join the British. And apart from them there were only a few French and Venetian frigates here and there – and Hoste had always wanted a French frigate.

That this judgement had some truth in it, as events turned out in the Adriatic, nevertheless conceals two other truths about the British and French navies respectively which were to deliver a number of unpleasant shocks to the former during the last years of the sea war. For the British, victory over the enemy (though never over the sea itself) had become so normal that it was taken for granted not only by those first-rate captains who won their fights because they *were* superior, but also by *all* captains, no matter that by now many of them had never faced a really tough opponent. Such, indeed, was the overall numerical (as well as professional) superiority of the British Navy by then that skill in the chase of weaker and more profitable game was more often at a greater premium than the superlative gunnery of earlier years: on her long voyage home from the Indian Ocean the worn-out (but still fast) French ex-frigate *Cannonière* (formerly 40, but by then converted into a blockade-runner), was sighted and pursued on no less than 14 occasions in 93 days before she and her £150,000 cargo were finally captured almost within sight of home by the 74-gun *Valiant*. It is hardly surprising that an emphasis on smart ship-handling and its aberration, excessive spit-and-polish, increasingly replaced regular gunnery practice, if not the more useful skills of combined operations which the Navy was also often called on to demonstrate. And, to be fair to the usually quite competent and always brave captains of the spit-and-polish class, they still usually won (or muddled through) in the end, at least to successes which admirals like Gambier considered good enough, where men like Nelson would have been disappointed (and Cochrane, as we have seen, was outraged enough to ruin himself). 'Hearts of Oak' summed up their recollection of the recent past and expectation of the future exactly:

> We'll still make them fear, and we'll still make them flee,
> We'll drub them on the shore as we've drubbed them at sea.
> If they run, why, we'll follow, and run them ashore,
> For if they won't fight us we cannot do more . . .

ending with the inevitable

> We'll fight and we'll conquer again and again!

What this jingoism concealed, of course, was that all these conquests had been over a navy first comprehensively ruined by the Revolution, which had destroyed Louis XVI's experienced naval officer corps, and then continuously debilitated by Napoleon, who starved it of resources and first-class equipment for its splendidly-designed ships. The Emperor's short-sighted naval policies, together with the endless naval defeats which were at least partly their result, drove many good seamen into privateering, which was encouraged and reached its high point in 1810, while other good men actually preferred to join his (ever-victorious) army, further weakening his navy. Compared with the British Navy, French naval discipline was easier – and slacker. But the French sailor's life afloat was, if anything, more unpleasant and frequently shorter: where attention to hygiene and general health on British ships kept their sick lists down in all except the most unhealthy climates, losses on French ones were often appalling even in harbour.

In spite of all this, however, it never paid to underrate the French. In all wars, whether by land or sea, the unconquerable spirit of the fighting men even after a succession of defeats is a phenomenon insufficiently explored by military historians. The Austrians, as has been noted, came back quite quickly after Austerlitz to be 'drubbed' again at Wagram – and were to come back *again* before very long, to do better in the 'War of Liberation', among all the other battle-scarred worms which have turned over the centuries. And, in *this* world war, there were now younger French naval officers who hardly remembered the humiliations of the Revolutionary period, and who certainly did not subscribe to the sentiments of 'Hearts of Oak' – men like Captains (future Admirals) Duperre, of the *Venus* (44) and Pierre Bouvet, variously of the *Atalante* (26), *Minerve* (48) and finally *Bellone* (44), and their Commodore (also future Admiral) Baron Ferdinand Hamelin – not to mention Commodore Bernard Dubordieu, whom Commodore William Hoste was soon to encounter. All these were France's new model frigate captains, and although they were too few and too late, the first three of them were now to teach half-a-dozen British frigate captains their lessons the hard way in and outside the ramshackle French naval base of Grand-Port, on Ile-de-France (Mauritius) in the far-off Indian Ocean.

CHAPTER FIFTEEN

The battles of Grand Port and Lissa

Just what constitutes 'a battle' is of course open to interpretation. Gunners, for example, are inclined to dismiss any land engagement fought in the absence of field artillery as no more than a vulgar brawl, while their comrades of horse (four-footed or tracked) and foot may consider numbers the deciding factor. At all events, however, *Bolton's Dictionary of Dates*, which is somewhat more exhaustive for the period than *Everyman's*, lists no less than 133 named battles for the years 1793 to 1815; and this total increases to 138 if the year 1792 is added, when the French were certainly fighting the First Coalition even if the British were not yet at war (except that is with 'the Tiger of Mysore' in India, whom Colonel Arthur Wellesley did not finish off until 1799). Yet even Mr Bolton's impressive list is far from comprehensive, for all that he offers it as 'invaluable to students, quiz solvers, writers and journalists'. In its inclusion of but one Anglo-American fight (and that chronologically misplaced) it virtually ignores the 'War of 1812' (1812–15, in terms of battles). And it hardly does justice to the war at sea in leaving out not only Algeciras (1801) and Rosas Bay (1809), both of which *Everyman's* includes, but also the undoubtedly major sea-battle of the Glorious First of June (1794 – and *also* missed by *Everyman's*). But, in particular for our purposes alas, both dictionaries of dates forfeit bonus points anyway for omitting the two most interesting purely frigate *battles* of the war, Grand Port (1810) and Lissa (1811).

That these two engagements were battles within any reasonable meaning of the word derives from their nature. In terms of their importance, they deserve a place in the history books not only because they were multi-ship set-piece occasions, not the single-ship duels or the rather untidy frigate chases which could involve half-a-dozen or more ships in chance encounters which otherwise characterised frigate warfare. For their outcome was of even greater importance than the actual battle itself: Grand Port was the disastrous opening to a successful Falklands-style long-range operation which ended with the reduction of France's 'Gibraltar' in the Indian Ocean; and Lissa marked the end of French naval power in the Adriatic. As such, both were significant examples – Grand Port eventually, Lissa at a stroke – of British sea-power in the later stages of the war. But also they have a special place as of right in this narrative both as interesting 'frigate occasions' illustrating the use of such ships and as evidence of the weaknesses and strengths of the British Navy after so many years of war as demonstrated by the personalities of Captain Nesbit Willoughby, of the *Nereide* (36), and Captain Robert Corbet, of the *Africaine* (40), representing the old navy of Captains Hamilton and Pigot, and of Captain (acting Commodore) William Hoste, of the *Amphion* (36), who, like Captains Hornblower and Broke, commanded in the Nelson tradition.

Nesbit Willoughby (born 1777, to survive – amazingly – until 1849) was another of the Navy's great eccentrics. C. Northcote Parkinson, in his *War in the Eastern Seas*, sums him up shortly and best as 'a man of courage and resource, able, cruel and . . . apparently immortal'. That last adjective is the most interesting, which he turned into a noun with his naval nickname: 'The Immortal'. To survive in Nelson's navy a man had to be tough as well as lucky. 'Little Hoste' survived accidents, but malaria got him in the end. The originally weak and always undersized Nelson had malaria too, but avoided yellow jack (which killed most of his men) in the Indies somehow, and then survived the loss of an eye (at Calvi), an arm (at Tenerife, thanks to Betsey Fremantle's nursing) and a head-wound (at the Nile), as well as all the grape-shot and flying splinters which cleared so many quarterdecks before a sniper on the *Redoubtable* finally got him, by which time he may have thought that he too was immortal. Willoughby certainly survived the most appalling injuries (and fought on while he was still recovering from some, while suffering from new ones which the Navy thought – incorrectly – afterwards precluded him from further active service). But, apart from being a victim of violence of the enemy (and accidental damage), Willoughby had the additional disadvantage of being one of those officers who compounded the cruelty of Captain Hamilton, of the *Surprise*, with the bloody-minded awkwardness of Captain Lord Cochrane. Entering the Navy in 1790, at the age of 14, he soon distinguished himself in the capture of the French frigate *Duguay-Trouin* by the British *Orpheus* (32) in 1794. Having subsequently shared in the huge prize pay-out for the capture of Amboyna and Banda in the Dutch East Indies, he was promoted lieutenant by Admiral Rainer (Pellew's predecessor in the East) in 1798. But then, very shortly after, he was court-martialled for insubordination – only to be reinstated as commander of a brig soon after having been dismissed from his ship.

After that, ill-health returned him to home waters, but he recovered to take part in the battle of Copenhagen in 1801, during which he boarded and took possession of the Danish ship-of-the-line *Proctesteen*. But he was soon in trouble with his captain again, this time actually being dismissed from the Navy. Thanks to Napoleon, however, he was back in service in 1803, first as a volunteer, but soon promoted to the rank of lieutenant again, in which rank he distinguished himself by talking the French *Clorinde* into surrender, as an alternative to the massacre of her crew by the insurgent negroes of Haiti. After that his career prospered, first in the *Acasta* frigate with Admiral Duckworth in the Dardanelles, and then in the east, as master and commander of the *Otter* sloop. Even in her he had not changed his ways, however, although he was acquitted of cruelty in another court martial (a member of which was, significantly, one Captain Robert Corbet, who is unlikely to have convicted even Hugh Pigot, had he lived, given his own customary brutality).

By 1810 Post-Captain Willoughby, by then in the rank through promotion to the frigate *Nereide* (36), was proof that there were still hard men in the Navy who, like Captain Corbet, of the ex-French *Africaine*, commanded in the style of Edward Hamilton, if not Hugh Pigot, with only their personal bravery mediating their cruelty, but without Hamilton's cool professional judgement of the odds. For, as it turned out, both captains then came unstuck in the attack on Mauritius.

For a variety of reasons, none of which does much credit to clear thinking on the part of either the Admiralty or the Honourable East India Company, the British had been disgracefully slow in mounting an invasion of this troublesome French base, from which a succession of enemy frigate captains – some of them highly enterprising, like Captain Bergeret – had preyed on trade in the Indian Ocean with considerable success. As a cheapskate alternative, a blockade of sorts had been mounted, which was only intermittently effective. Most recently, however, a series of daring raids on the islands had been carried out, most notably by Captain Willoughby himself, whose real talent seems to have been for commando-work rather than sea-fighting. And now, at last, a proper and well-equipped invasion force, headed by the *Illustrious* (74) and consisting of some dozen frigates and transports, with over 6,000 soldiers and marines, was on its way in 1810.

Meanwhile, however, an opportunity seemed to present itself to the blockading British frigate squadron to neutralise Grand Port, in which three French frigates and a sloop were anchored, before rumoured French reinforcements arrived there. Grand Port was an extremely tricky anchorage, but Willoughby himself had reconnoitred it, and although he was then still recovering from a firearms accident which had seriously injured him, he was angry at having failed to intercept the most recent arrivals there. Accordingly, he led the way in an attack, signalling that his *Nereide* (a 12-pounder 36) was 'Ready for Action' against an 'Enemy of Inferior Force'.

French reinforcements were indeed on the way. But the Grand Port squadron, under Commodore Duperré and Captain Boubet, was hardly inferior to the attacking force, anchored as it was under the protection of shore batteries and consisting of the big *Bellone* (44) and *Minerve* (36), both 18-pounder frigates, together with the smaller *Ceylon* (32) and the *Victor* corvette (18/20).

The British had in fact grossly underestimated both the strength of the defence and the difficulties of getting at it, so that matters went speedily from bad to worse. Only Willoughby's own *Nereide* reached her appointed station among the rocks and shoals, the (ex-French) *Magicienne* (36) and the *Sirius* (36) both running aground helplessly, and the more powerful *Iphigenia* (a 18-pounder 36) anchoring too far away to do much damage.

Catastrophe followed disaster. During the long hours that followed the *Nereide* was battered to a pulp, with Willoughby once again dreadfully wounded and his crew massacred, proving only that the British, like the French, could sustain appalling casualties before their inevitable surrender (only 51 men were left alive and unwounded out of 281, one in three of whom was killed). The *Magicienne* and the *Sirius* were meanwhile burnt by their retreating crews, and the *Iphigenia* herself was captured by the finally-arriving French reinforcements, Commodore Hamelin paroling the crews of all three British frigates since he had no room for them on his own frigate.

Debacle followed catastrophe when Hamelin despatched the (ex-British) *Iphigenia* (now the French *Iphigenie*) with the *Astrée* frigate to cruise nearby, with a corvette in attendance. These fell in with Captain Corbet in the *Africaine* who, instead of retreating, unwisely chased and fought them. For his pains he was mortally wounded, and his crew of 295 suffered over 160 casualties before the *Africaine* surrendered.

It is perhaps fair to distinguish Nesbit Willoughby from Robert Corbet. Where 'The Immortal' was probably simply hard to the point of cruelty as well as an awkward subordinate and a rash captain (in addition to being insanely brave, of course), Robert Corbet seems to have been a brutal captain of the Pigot type. As a subordinate, however, it was his bravery that caught the eye of his superiors, with his true character masked. A lieutenant in 1796, he was commended by Nelson himself for his capture of the *Hirondelle* privateer in 1802, while master and commander of the *Biter* brig, and he was subsequently made acting-captain of the *Amphitrite* frigate in the spring of 1805, his post-captaincy being confirmed a year later. Transferring to the *Nereide*, he took part in Home Popham's South American venture, and was from there sent to the East Indian station. It was in the East Indies that his Pigot-colours emerged, when he fell foul of Admiral Pellew on account of his cruelty, being involved in a near-mutiny which resulted in the hanging of one of his crew. Finally court-martialled, he pleaded that his crew had been a bad one, drunken, insubordinate and malingering, with bad warrant officers, requiring a firm hand. Men like Pellew, with their experience of 'bad' post-Spithead-mutiny crews, would have known what that meant: bad crews were made by bad captains who, like Corbet, over-used the cat-o'-nine-tails (and Corbet's 'cat' had special knots in it). But captains of the time were still usually beating cruelty charges, and Corbet survived these even though his excessive use of starters (rope-ends or sticks used to encourage laggards) was noted with disapproval by the court.

His behaviour in the *Africaine* does not seem to have changed: he was well-hated by her crew, although the rumour that he had been shot from behind during his last fight is incorrect – his foot was taken off by a cannon-ball. Nor, for that matter, can it be said that his crew did not fight hard, for they surrendered with a casualty list of well over 50 per cent. What is important, though, is that they fought *ineffectively*, firing inaccurately and inflicting little damage on the French before their ship was dismasted. The fact was that the *Africaine* was an unhappy ship *and* an inefficient one *because* she was commanded by a bad captain in whom cruelty was not offset by the sort of cool calculation and leadership Captain Hamilton of the *Surprise* had demonstrated in the Caribbean years before.

To the loss of these five frigates a final humiliation was quickly added, when ships of the returning French reinforcement squadron captured yet another British frigate, the East India Company's *Ceylon* (32 – but not to be confused with the French ship of the same name) – which could also have been serious, since she was carrying the commander of the invasion force, Major-General Sir John Abercrombie, and his staff. But then the real world of British naval superiority returned, with the arrival of the whole invasion fleet, led by Commodore Sir Josias Rowley, a skilled combined operations specialist, in the *Illustrious* and the equally able Captain Philip Beaver, in the *Nisus* (36). Not only were the battered *Africaine* and the *Ceylon* then quickly retaken, but also the frigate *Venus* (44) and all her prisoners. After that the invasion, brilliantly planned like the Egyptian landing of ten years before, went smoothly ahead, and everything fell

How to fight a frigate battle: the gunnery of Commodore Hoste's frigate squadron is too good, and his ships are too well-handled, for the gallant Commodore Dubordieu's two columns to break his line off Lissa in 1811. By now Dubordieu himself is dead, and his *Favourite* is heading for the rocks – and Hoste will out-manoeuvre the *Flore* (pictured here apparently raking him) and her Franco–Venetian consorts. As of this day, the Adriatic Sea will become a British lake. (An engraving by D. Havell, after a painting by T. Whitcombe, from a sketch by Midshipman J. Few.)

God is on the side of the bigger battalions: there was no better frigate in the world in 1815 than the USS *President* and no better frigate captain than Stephen Decatur. But the British *Endymion*, copied from the French *Pomone* of 1794 (the *Forte*'s predecessor) and accompanied by a later British-built *Pomone*, were also good ships, and well-handled in the final pursuit of the unlucky *President*. So here they all are at the kill, with the smaller *Tenedos* and the ex-ship-of-the-line *Majestic*, one of the 74s *razéed* into frigates to deal with those American Humphreys ships (but which, since they were not re-rigged by frigate-experts like Pellew of the *Indefatigable*, were too slow to catch their special quarry).

Captain Sir Philip Bowes Vere Broke (1776–1841), baronet and future rear-admiral, posed conventionally beside long-range 18-pounder cannon in his *Shannon*, in his best uniform. But his portraitist, Samuel Lane, would have been better advised to have added Captain Broke's own special aiming gadgets to the cannon, and his marks on the deck beneath it, which his beloved navy embraced, even though he never used them himself in his last and most famous fight.

Frigate versus frigate . . . and by 1812 the leader-writers of the British Press and every British frigate captain *confide* that any British frigate can take any foreign one in single-ship action. But this time the foreigner is the USS *Constitution* – a Humphreys "pocket-battleship" with a well-trained all-volunteer crew, and the dismasted wreck on the right is HMS *Guerriere*. And before the year is out two more British frigates will end up in the same condition, to the consternation of the Royal Navy (but the satisfaction of both the American public and the British army. . .). (From an engraving by C.Tiebout, after a painting by T.Birch.)

Frigate versus frigate . . . and for the fourth time in a year an
American frigate meeting a British one. Only this time the
odds are the other way, for the *Chesapeake* is not a
Humphreys frigate, but the worst-manned nominal
38-gunner in the US navy – and Captain Philip Bowes Vere
Broke's *Shannon* (another nominal 38-gunner) has the best-
trained gunners in King George's navy. Yet at pistol-duelling
distance within sight of the crowds watching from Boston in
1813, and when both captains themselves behaved more like
duellists than frigate commanders, a few minutes' good and
bad luck settled "the fortunes of our respective flags".

Success story: Captain Sir William Hoste, Baronet (but with "Cattaro", not "Lissa", on his coat-of-arms), still looks young in this "original picture in the possession of Lady Hoste". But there are other pictures of Nelson's favourite teenager which show him just as young, although already a post-captain frigate commander. Thanks to Nelson's "interest" and his own merit he reached the Captains' List at 22. But it was thanks to his merit (and a fair share of luck) that he commanded at Lissa in 1811 – and entirely to his merit that he later became the navy's top combined-operations commander at Cattaro and Ragusa.

There were still wooden frigates in the world's
navies in the mid-19th century, although by then
powered by steam as well as wind. But by the 1860s
the old "ratings" and classifications of 1815 had
become meaningless. HMS *Warrior* – pictured here
in a contemporary engraving by T. G. Dutton
exactly as she is now to be seen, beautifully restored,
at Portsmouth – was actually commissioned in 1861
as a "steam frigate". In fact, however, she was not
the final descendant of the 1757 *Pallas* but rather the
first ironclad ancestor of the *Dreadnought* battleships
of the next world war.

Success story: the first Viscount Exmouth, once Captain Philemon Pownoll's saucy midshipman later the Channel Fleet's top-scoring frigate captain, and finally an enriched wartime admiral remembering his most hazardous *Indefatigable* days with regret. "We all grow old," was his reflect as C-in-C, Mediterranean Fleet, thirty years after he had commanded his first frigate, and twenty after he had captured the *Cleopatre* in 1793. But Edward Pellew (1757–1833) had nonetheless had good "last French War" (1793–1815), after having risen through the penultimate one (which end in 1783) to get on to the Captains' List just in time to screw the *Nymphe* from Lord Falmouth and Admiralty – and to illustrate the working of "interest"+merit+luck as the keys to success.

to the British – all the French warships (some badly damaged in the recent unpleasantness) and all captured British ships, naval and merchant (except the *Magicienne* and the *Sirius*, of course, whose burnt wrecks still lie under the waters of Grand Port harbour), together with the islands themselves, which were never returned to France. More drama was to follow, early in 1811, when three more French frigates and troop reinforcements arrived from the motherland at last. But the game was over by then in the Eastern Seas, and the only French frigate to escape from its postscript did so at the cost of its captain's career. (Long afterwards Napoleon remembered this occasion with irritation when himself imprisoned – how that wretched man had somehow avoided execution for cowardice because of the decision of an understanding naval officers' court martial. But then, the Emperor never did make any allowance for the odds at sea which he had stacked up against his captains, after having twice escaped Nelson's navy himself in the Mediterranean.)

Equally, though, after the news of these temporary embarrassments mixed with success arrived back in England no one drew any conclusions from the battle of Grand Port. Mauritius had, after all, been captured, and the Indian Ocean made even safer for British trade (before that, Admiral Pellew's innovations there had reduced war-risk insurance to half the rate for 'natural causes'). Captain Willoughby's over-confidence, his fellow-captains' incompetence in failing to follow his course into the harbour, and – most significant of all, perhaps – the poor gunnery of Captain Corbet's crew went unremarked. And, of course, both Willoughby's and Corbet's epic defences against over-whelming odds and their appalling casualty lists were accepted as comforting evidence of British courage, reflecting credit on them, their crews, the Navy, the Prince Regent and the nation at large. That Willoughby was not employed afloat again was due to his dreadful injuries, which included the loss of one eye, damage to the other, a smashed jaw and a neck so torn as to expose the windpipe. (But then, being 'The Immortal' he duly recovered; and, as we shall discover later, went on to an even more unlikely survival.)

No one noted, additionally, that the French captains Duperré, Bouvet and Hamelin had performed well, far from home, usually against odds, and in well-worn if not quite worn-out ships. So it was perhaps as well for the British that the next of this new breed, Commodore Bernard Dubordieu, came up against William Hoste, who had learned his trade under Nelson and whose confidence was soundly based on his own skill and on the quality of ships' companies trained and motivated by an inspirational young captain who had modelled himself on his idol.

Dubordieu had learned his profession the hard way, first in the French merchant service, which he had joined at the age of 16, and then two years later as a conscript in the Revolutionary navy in 1792. In that professionally demoralised service his total lack of aristocratic 'interest' at least no longer mattered, and merit was at a premium, so that he was quickly promoted to 'aspirant' (the more literally accurate French midshipman equivalent). Our third ingredient in the pursuit of fame and fortune, luck, was a somewhat more elusive commodity for likely young French officers in such hard times, especially for those caught in the Toulon uprising of 1793. Dubordieu, a youthful republican 'new man', was taken prisoner in the frigate *Topaze* (38) there, and consigned to a prison hulk in Gibraltar. But during all his short life he was nothing if not a man of action, who made his own luck: he not only escaped in 1795, but led a party of fellow-escapers in the capture of an armed transport, which he then sailed through the blockade to Brittany. Promoted into the *Gaiété* corvette, he was captured again two years later, by the *Arethusa* (36 – another of those British frigates which must have seemed omnipresent to the French). But this, at least, was in the pre-Napoleonic days of exchange, and by 1799 he was back in action again, as a lieutenant in one of the few French frigates which escaped capture or destruction during the Egyptian campaign.

In spite of the French Navy's *égalité* (but perhaps rather because of a mixture of old-fashioned bad luck and the succession of defeats which overtook it after the renewal of war in 1803–4, and the consequent lack of opportunities for distinction), Dubordieu had to wait until 1806 for his next chance. But then he performed splendidly, winning *Legion d'Honneur* membership for gallant conduct during a West Indian raid. Yet although that also raised him to the French equivalent of post-rank (*capitaine de vaisseau*) he then had to wait for another three years before he achieved the rare distinction of catching a British frigate, the *Proserpine* (and nearly the recently escaped Lieutenant Donat Henchy O'Brien with her), off the French coast in 1809. For this he received the Cross of the *Legion* – a bar to his DSO? – and was at last given a command worthy of his ardour and courage: the depredations of the relatively small British naval forces in the Adriatic, led by Captain (acting Commodore) William Hoste, had become intolerable, and who better than Bernard Dubordieu to bring them to book after Grand Port?

Commodore Dubordieu accepted this challenge joyfully, in the knowledge that he had three advantages over a formidable enemy. First, he had secure bases up and down the Adriatic, from Venice and Chioggia in the north, then down the Illyrian and Dalmatian coast from Trieste and Fiume, past Spalato, Ragusa and Cattaro to Corfu on one side, and all the way down Italy on the other, with Ancona only 300 sea-miles from Hoste's only base, at Lissa. Secondly, he only had to threaten that base (which was as yet unfortified) to bring Hoste to battle, for it was from there that all British operations and the licensing of the semi-piratical privateers who aided them was organised. And, finally, he now had a force more than sufficient to deal with the enemy: against Hoste's *Amphion* (38), two 32s – the *Active* and the *Cerberus* – and the *Acorn* sloop (18), he now had three big 44s – his own *Favorite*, the *Flore* and the *Danae* – and the *Uranie* (40), plus a big Venetian 44, the *Corona*, and the smaller *Bellona* (32) and *Carolina* (28), as well as two 16-gun sloops and a number of gunboats and smaller craft. Altogether, this Franco-Venetian force then had more than twice the number of ships, and far more than three times the number of men and weight of broadside.

Thus began a nine-month battle of wits in the Adriatic. Dubordieu, having fought the British at sea for most of his life, was no beginner, and probably wanted both to work up his squadron and assess the value of its Venetian contribution (which in fact turned out to be far from negligible). In the course of this period he sighted and chased the *Amphion* once, while she was in company only with the *Active*, but seems to have otherwise preferred to manoeuvre, taking numerous prizes (at least, so he claimed), raiding Lissa in Hoste's absence, but not seeking to put everything to the test too quickly. But meanwhile he also fought a skilful propaganda war which embarrassed Hoste not a little, claiming that an allegedly bigger British squadron was unwilling to fight. And this war-of-words became all the more galling for Hoste (after his own earlier assertions of superiority) after his only reinforce-ment, the *Volage* (22) collided with the *Amphion* during one of those sudden and dangerous squalls for which the Mediterranean and the Adriatic were both notorious. The *Volage* was in fact another of those puny 'frigates-by-courtesy', like Hornblower's *Atropos*, little more than a sloop and better for taking merchantmen and unrated smaller craft than for fighting 18-pounder enemy frigates. But she rammed the *Amphion* amidships, and the *Amphion* was an old ship by now. So it was back to Malta for both of them.

This was the danger-point in Hoste's career, with his squadron reduced to virtual impotence and Dubordieu at large and unbeaten. And worst of all, there was a new commander-in-chief in the Mediterranean now: Cuthbert Collingwood's health had finally broken down in 1810, and that brave old man had died quietly on the first day of his voyage home to the England he loved so much and served so well. Under his successor, Admiral Sir Charles Cotton, whom Hoste did not know, it was all too likely that an exciting plum job like the Adriatic would not be his for much longer. It must have been a close-run thing, for Hoste had not even enough 'interest' now to secure Donat Henchy O'Brien's promotion to be his first lieutenant. But Cotton was an experienced admiral, and no one by then knew the Adriatic better than William Hoste. So, finally, that third ingredient of luck, which with his merit and 'interest' had so often helped him to shine, reasserted itself sufficiently to return him to Lissa just in time to transform disappointment into triumph. For there, now in the form of a direct order from Napoleon, luck brought Dubordieu to him.

The battle of Lissa, which resulted from that order less than a week after Hoste's return there in early March 1811, provides several ironies and one coincidental curiosity. To take that curiosity first, this was not the one and only battle of Lissa in which 'frigates' were involved. Fifty-five years later, during the Prussian blitzkrieg war of 1866 against Austria, the Austrian Admiral Tegethoff led a somewhat ramshackle fleet in a gallant assault on the much more modern (and more ironclad) navy of Italy, Prussia's ally, in the same waters. There were still 'frigates', so-called, in the mid-nineteenth century navies, but in that age of steam-and-sail, increasingly large guns (even in turrets now, too), and new armoured protection, these ships had meta-morphosed into the forerunners of the battleships and dreadnoughts of the future. No one quite knew how to fight battles in this new age, but Admiral Tegethoff, reckoning on the inferiority of his ships in any variety of battle, took his inspiration more from Salamis and the ancient galley-warfare of the Mediterranean (if not from the more recent battle of Hampton Roads during the American Civil War): he went pell-mell for the Italians, ramming his way to victory and directing naval designers and strategists for years afterwards down the blind alley of close-quarter fighting, in ships furnished with huge rams (which proved successful thereafter only in sinking their sister-ships by accident).

Commodore Dubordieu, ordered now not to raid Lissa but to take it and with 500 soldiers on board for that purpose, favoured the same direct pell-mell tactics once he discovered the *Amphion*, the *Active*, the *Cerberus* and the *Volage* reunited and awaiting him off his objective, Port St George, in line at right-angles to his approach. Given his orders, he had no choice but to fight. However, given his superiority in ships, men and guns – he had six of his frigates with him, including all four big 44s, together with a 16-gun brig and several smaller vessels – he also felt he had a good chance of victory. And given his courage and the training his crews had had over the previous nine months, he would no doubt have fought even if the odds had been more equal. So he came on without pause, in two three-frigate columns against Hoste's single line of four ships, aiming his own *Favorite* at the *Amphion*, which was at the head of the British line.

The first irony here was not so much that this was the classic French column-tactic on land – columns against lines – but that it was also exactly Nelson's own one at Trafalgar. And, more than that, Dubordieu himself took Nelson's own position, leading his captains and crews from the front, vulnerable in the most honourable and dangerous place on his own quarterdeck and ready to be the first man to board the enemy, rather than from further back in the column, from where he could have controlled the attack better. Finally (and most ironically of all in this reversal of Trafalgar roles), however much the French commander may or may not have had the dead British admiral's tactics in mind on this, 'the happiest day of my life' as he called it, there can be no doubt that the memory of the man to whom he owed everything was in the forefront of Hoste's mind. In the final flutter of signal-flags up the mast of the *Amphion* he did not bother to expect every man to do his duty, but more simply and directly reminded them to REMEMBER NELSON.

All these ironies aside, the fact was that, given the likely skills of an experienced British frigate squadron commanded by Nelson's favourite pupil, poor brave Dubordieu had chosen the very worst tactic. Indeed, equally by the tactics of the future he was at fault in allowing Hoste to 'cross the T' in classic fashion, raking the French with repeated double-shotted broadsides to which they could not reply.

The result of this devastatingly one-sided opening to the battle changed the odds to favour the British before the Franco-Venetian squadron had a chance to fight, with their leading ships being dreadfully knocked about. Dubordieu himself realised too late his rashness in planning to break Hoste's line, which was not only closed-up so tightly that the British frigates were almost touching each other, but was deliberately drawn up dangerously close to the rocky shore of Lissa. But by then it was too late, as the final British broadsides (including fire from their close-quarter smashing carronades) repelled his alternative attempt to board, mortally wounding him together with most of his officers. Out of control, his *Favorite* plunged onwards onto the rocks while the British frigates went about smartly onto the opposite tack (narrowly missing the shore themselves in doing so) to deliver further broadsides from their as-yet-unfired starboard batteries.

With this, as the rest of the Franco-Venetian ships also at last changed course to run more-or-less parallel with the British, the second phase of the battle began. But it was, to all intents and purposes, already over. The French *Flore* and the Venetian *Bellona*, the other ships of Dubordieu's column, attempted to catch the *Amphion* between them, but were outmanoeuvred by Hoste and so badly damaged that the former struck her colours then, and the latter did so later. There was a bad moment when the *Cerberus*'s rudder was damaged, and the little *Volage* found herself up against the *Danae*, whose broadside was three times heavier. But then the next most powerful of the British frigates, the *Active*, burst through to rescue first her and then the *Cerberus* from the combined attentions of the remaining Venetian ships, the *Corona* and the *Caroline*.

The final phase was one of pursuit, capture – and escape, with *Bellona* being taken by the *Amphion* (in the persons of Lieutenant Donat Henchy O'Brien, a midshipman and four seamen in a small leaky boat), and the *Corona* by the *Active* after a brave two-hour fight. Much to Hoste's chagrin and outrage, the *Flore's* captain raised his flag again (claiming afterwards that he had never lowered it), to join the damaged *Danae* and *Caroline* in their retreat, while the wrecked *Favorite*, set alight and abandoned by her crew, burnt until the flames ignited her powder magazine, blowing her up with the dead Dubordieu still aboard.

With these events the battle of Lissa was over (except for a final small flurry of action off Port St George in which the initiative of two midshipmen from the *Active* frustrated an attempt by a small Venetian warship to attack the shipping there while the British were otherwise engaged). But although only half the enemy squadron had been accounted for finally after the escape of the *Flore*, it was a decisive victory. More than 1000 of the attackers had been either killed, wounded or captured, excluding the unknown totals in the three frigates which got away in varying states of damage. None of the British ships was unseaworthy, although they had suffered some 200 casualties (out of about 900 men engaged), and both the captured enemy frigates were repairable, decisively reversing the balance of power. The Lissa base was secure in the immediate future, and in fact forever after: when Napoleon ordered another attack on it a few months later, insufficient naval forces were available, and with its subsequent fortification and the arrival of a British battle-squadron of ships-of-the-line in the Adriatic it was never threatened again.

For Hoste, however, the results of the greatest day in his career throw interesting light on the way times had changed over so long a war. Most immediately, he dashed off an angry letter to the unrepentant captain of the *Flore* ('. . . sir, I might have sunk you, had I not considered you as having surrendered.'), with predictable lack of result. But he eventually returned in triumph to Malta, to the accolade of his peers who were best able to appreciate the perfection of his handling of both his squadron and his own ship in an action against brave enemies who had outnumbered him six to four in ships and two to one in men and broadsides. Indeed, although he now had no great surviving patron among the new generation of admirals, he was professionally made by Lissa. On his subsequent return to England in the worn-out *Amphion* – with his two prizes and with O'Brien at last confirmed as first lieutenant – he was well-received by the Admiralty. The pick of the new frigates under construction was his for the asking, and he could choose his own officers and the theatre of war in which he led them. But this was June 1811, not June 1793, and all the years and naval successes in between had somewhat devalued the other rewards of victory. So, where there had been an instant knighthood for Edward Pellew after his reassuring capture of the *Cléopâtre* 18 years earlier, there was no knighthood for the victor of the battle of Lissa (let alone the baronetcy he felt his due), only the Naval War Medal which went also to his fellow-captains. But there it was: naval captains had to do more than just beat the French in this eighteenth year of the war, which itself was reaching its final climactic period, to get their knighthoods.

The year of Lissa had in fact been another one of extreme economic crisis for Britain, from which she was to emerge into one of extreme military crisis during 1812, in what must have seemed to many a make-or-break situation. In the economic war, she had in the end triumphed by 1809 over Napoleon's first attempt to ruin her. His second attempt, which reached its danger-point during 1811, almost brought her to her knees. After two disastrous British harvests in 1809 and 1810, there were food shortages, industrial riots and machinery-breaking, with a depreciating pound, many bankruptcies and a serious decline in gold reserves, all of which brought the French closer to achieving what their continental land victories had failed to do.

Of course, the British weathered this economic storm in the end, just as they had survived its predecessor, and fought on through the military crisis year of 1812 to emerge into the transformed situation of 1813. But, as always in this long war, it is all too easy to shrug off these crises in the knowledge of what was to come. The 1793–1802 volume of Sir Arthur Bryant's wonderfully readable history of the war (which was all the more exciting for having been written during the darkest days of the struggle against Hitler) was entitled *The Years of Endurance*, and that covering 1802–12 *The Years of Victory*. But notwithstanding the victories of that second period it was in reality no less one of endurance, and never more so than during its last two years. To take the Peninsular campaigns as an example, 1812 witnessed Wellington's most perfect victory, Salamanca, which, but for the egregious incompetence of his Spanish allies, would have annihilated Marshal Marmont's army as Nelson had done Admiral Brueys' fleet at the Nile. But it was an opportunist battle, when Wellington was actually retreating. And the year before the British government had itself contemplated the evacuation of the whole Spanish peninsula in spite of his earlier successes, on the grounds that the war there was unwinnable. We *know* that it turned out very differently, just as we *know* the fate of the army which Napoleon was then gathering for the war with Russia. And in 1812 Waterloo was an unknown village in Belgium, and St Helena was an island-speck on the map, of significance only to its inhabitants and a few sea-captains who needed fresh water.

The 1811–12 truth is that Britain had very nearly collapsed economically and that Napoleon was marshalling the largest army the world had seen since Xerxes had invaded Greece in 480 BC. A final settlement with Russia was his objective, and any sensible betting man, having studied past form, would have known where to put his money.

The additional fact that, before he had marched eastwards, Napoleon had – with some help from the British themselves – finally brought the United States into the war against his enemy was almost irrelevant to Britain's desperate situation. If (as seemed likely) she lost Canada, and even all her older North American possessions, these colonies were hardly the greatest jewels in her crown, and their loss would have been as nothing compared with her likely loss of the Napoleonic War itself. For once he had dealt finally with the last unconquered country on the mainland of Europe, Napoleon could have turned at his leisure to deal with Britain's little army in Spain, while tightening the economic screw on her decisively. With all the resources of Europe available to him, Napoleon might even at last have concentrated on building a great navy (as Rome had done against Carthage, as every classically educated person remembered). As it was, there were numerous ships-of-the-line then under construction in his well-equipped dockyards – three in Venice, in the Adriatic, alone. Indeed, he himself might turn again in that direction, southwards and eastwards, leaving a marshal (preferably one as yet not defeated by Wellington) to settle Spain with a huge new army. For, as his orders to Dubordieu testified, Napoleon had not forgotten his Egyptian expedition. He had left unfinished business in the decrepit Turkish empire. With the bases he already had in the Adriatic he could begin that business again, perhaps to follow Alexander's path to India if the British still refused to see reason.

The British transfer of ships-of-the-line to what had once been a frigate captains' happy hunting-ground (and William Hoste's in particular) was perhaps in part a recognition of this worrying possibility. What is certain is that Hoste himself returned to a new situation there which was at first less than either satisfactory or happy for him, until his merit raised him above it. This, however, he cannot have foreseen when he left England in his spanking-new 'bold *Bacchante*' a 38-gun (18-pounder) 1,000-tonner, crewed as only a famous frigate hero could hope for, whose success in both battle and prize-taking was well-known. Sadly, his reputation for the latter must have rankled, since apart from his failure to obtain a knighthood his homecoming had been marred by the discovery that his adored and admiring father, the Reverend Dixon Hoste, had squandered all the profits of his *Amphion* captures with the abandon of a drunken sailor trusted with pay and shore-leave in Portsmouth on a Saturday night. But, for the rest (and even because he now needed to recoup his fortunes), it would have been a happy departure. He had his trusted Donat Henchy O'Brien as his first lieutenant, to play a more dashing Hardy (or Bush) to his Nelson (or Hornblower). With O'Brien, he had the pick of the country's (or, more exactly and preferentially, Norfolk county's) likely lads as midshipmen and juvenile 'volunteers', including not only brother Ned again but also other offspring of influential blue-blooded fathers and deserving naval· families: the wheel had turned full-circle over his 19 years' service, and it was he who now disposed of that vital 'interest' which had once given him his chance. Sadly, although he looked after these youngsters with the same care as that which Nelson had given him, some of them were to die under his command in the years to come, with other 'old *Amphions*' who now accompanied him, as others before them like his friend Weatherhead had done at Tenerife so long ago now. But that was the fortunes of war and the price of admiralty, and it still lay in the future. What mattered then – *now* – was that he was taking the *Bacchante* to war. And he was taking her to serve under the overall Mediterranean command of that legendary ex-frigate captain, Sir Edward Pellew, who had come home enriched from the East Indies to take over from Sir Charles Cotton, and could be relied on to recognise a kindred spirit. (And when they finally met, Pellew did take instantly to Hoste – although at that moment he was actually cruising rather morosely off Toulon in his 120-gun four-deck *Caledonia*, complaining about his captains' incompetence ... and, one may suspect, mourning his days in the old *Indefatigable*, when only the sea and the rocks off Ushant were his routine worries).

And then, under the legendary Sir Edward, there was anyway the almost as legendary Admiral Sir Thomas Fremantle, now flying his flag in the Adriatic in the 74-gun *Milford*. Hoste did not know Admiral Fremantle personally any better than he had known Admiral Cotton, but short of returning to the Adriatic flying his independent commodore's pennant again the prospect of serving directly under Fremantle must have seemed the next best thing. Fremantle, in his time, had been a *very* dashing frigate captain: not only had he once supported Captain Nelson's *Agamemnon* in the harrying of the 80-gun *Ça Ira* in his delightfully named frigate *Inconstant* (not an incongruous frigate name, of course, because so obviously *feminine*!), but he had also sailed into Leghorn thereafter to save – and woo and win – the beautiful Betsey Wynne from the advancing French revolutionaries. That Betsey (with whose sister Nelson had danced during the Christmas festivities of '96) was, as an heiress, a richer prize than Captain Fremantle ever captured at sea, was the captain's good luck, no more. Her importance for the then-Lieutenant Hoste was that she had nursed Nelson back to life in her husband's ship after Tenerife, to superintend the lieutenant's future career and his advance to the

Mutine and a post-captaincy. And the importance of her husband to the now-Captain Hoste was that both had been Admiral Nelson's friends, and that Captain Hoste might therefore hope that one of his patron's senior 'band of brother' graduates would give him patronage and the 'good cruises' which Admiral Collingwood before him had done, with the 'Immortal Memory' of Nelson in mind.

In fact Fremantle proved quite the opposite; though whether that was because of the toll of years of war and the cares of senior command which frayed Pellew no less, or because of a certain prickliness on the part of the victor of Lissa, who had not quite got his full reward and was accustomed to independent command, it is hard to say. But with the whole war lurching to its tremendous two-year climax such petty squabbles are not even footnotes to history, only important in our specialised story. For now, as the events of 1812 and 1813 began to unfold, the bets which might have been laid earlier began to be swallowed up by extraordinary reality.

As the first of these two years progressed, and the greatest military genius of the age collected and launched his *Grande Armee* against Russia, and with the new problem of an American invasion of Canada, where there were few redcoats, it is really quite surprising that the British government kept its cool so well (and not least after the assassination of the Prime Minister, Spencer Percival, by a lunatic that spring), in the aftermath of the country's most recent economic crisis. But, behind the shield of a navy with 1,000 ships at sea, it persevered. Its worst shocks were, indeed, about to occur at sea. But they did not for one moment interrupt the steady flow of supplies and reinforcements which was now reaching Wellington's army in Spain – and far more speedily and safely than anything his French enemies there could expect, thanks to the efficiency of the British Navy and the inveterate hostility of the Spanish guerrillas. (Indeed, those two were also now co-operating with increasing success, notably on the Biscayan coast where none other than Sir Home Riggs Popham, having triumphed over his South American court martial, ably commanded an inshore squadron.)

This was, indeed, quite dramatically, one of those *tout le monde à la bataille* moments in history. Among the survivors of our 1793 intake, all those who could and would now be heading for the sound of the guns – all, that is, except that greatest of fighters, Captain Lord Cochrane MP, who was still condemned to inactivity by the naval system he had so unwisely and unforgivably offended. And, for the rest, even the battered Sir Nesbit Josiah Willoughby, complete with black eye-patch and innumerable scars, was rejoining the fray – this time (since his own country regarded him as unfit) as a soldier of the Russian army resisting Napoleon's invasion. Horatio Hornblower was heading in the same direction, flying his commodore's pennant as commander of a Baltic inshore squadron (and with the special secret duty of rescuing the Tsar from St Petersburg if the worst came to the worst – an assignment for which a 'judicious' officer with Wellesley 'interest' was well-fitted; except that a 44-gun frigate would have been a better command-ship than the lumbering 74-gun *Nonsuch*, perhaps?).

Meanwhile, on the other side of the continent, Pellew was off Toulon in the huge *Caledonia*, probably envying young Hoste, of whose adventures in the 'bold *Bacchante*' more anon. For now it is the turn of the last of our special frigate captains, Philip Broke, whose steady merit had been rewarded with the *Shannon* some years earlier but who had since then had little opportunity to shine. Chances of prize-money, let alone glory, had been more rare for donkey-work captains on patrol in the Western Approaches, the Irish Sea, and even off the French coast – and even more so across Britannia's Atlantic Ocean on the neutral North American coast, where he was in 1812. But President Madison was to change that.

CHAPTER SIXTEEN

Joshua Humphreys and the United States Navy

In the context of the Anglo-French World War of 1793–1815 the Anglo-American War of 1812–1814/5 was a mere sideshow, as irrelevant as it was unnecessary and embarrassing: it neither helped the French when they looked like winning nor hindered the British and their allies in the conduct of those victorious campaigns in Spain, Central Europe and eventually France herself which brought down Napoleon. Ending in a draw when the Americans lacked both the will and the means to continue and the war-weary British equally lacked the will, if not the means, this wretched affair rewarded both nations appropriately for their original stupidities with more unexpected and humiliating failures than moments of triumph – appropriately, that is, for their respective governments, not the brave men on both sides who died as a result of the miscalculations and incompetence of their elders.

All this is not to say, of course, that this fools' quarrel did not have results, the most important of which served decisively to re-direct the future expansion of the United States when that new nation's development was this period's other most significant world event. But for our purposes in this story its consequences were naval, and of special interest in the field of frigate development and warfare. For the War of 1812 was nothing if not a frigate war.

For the record, indeed, the United States of America were finally goaded into declaring war on Great Britain by the British Navy itself, and for four worthy maritime reasons: unfair restrictions on American seaborne trade, the illegal seizure of American shipping, an outrageous blockade of (and intrusions into) American territorial waters, and the scandalous impressment of American citizens into the very navy which was doing all this. For only *some* of these reasons the United States Navy (such as it was) had already fought two undeclared but hot little wars, one against their former ally France, between 1798 and 1800, and the second – more a police action than a war, and which was not finally concluded until 1815 – against the egregious Barbary Corsairs of North Africa who had been variously preying on or blackmailing all Christian nations for centuries. 'Freedom of the Seas' and '(Neutral) Sailors' Rights' were slogans which the Americans cherished now, and would maintain in the future all through the British Navy's campaign to suppress the slave trade, until Mr Lincoln's Union navy took the opposite point of view during the American Civil War when the boot was on the other foot.

But no matter, for in reality all this was flumdiddle, for American maritime interest in 1812 did *not* want war, however much they disliked the British Navy: they were making far too much money. But with the expansion of the United States (not least now into the limitless lands of the Louisiana Purchase) the new nation's destiny was becoming manifest. Unfortunately, nevertheless, a continued migration of Americans *northwards*, into British North America, tempted politicians in that direction just as much as *westwards*, if not more so: destiny was equally manifest in that direction. The expulsion of the French from Canada had paved the way for the American revolution by making the presence of Redcoats (and Redcoat-taxes) unnecessary. After 1763 – Britain's victorious 'Seven Years' War – all settled North America had briefly been British. The expulsion of the British from Canada would now make the whole sub-continent truly all-*American*.

That was the true driving force behind the War of 1812, hidden in a fifth reason for going to war, which quite unjustly accused the British of encouraging the Red Indian tribes in their resistance to American encroachment. The Indians were already hugely outnumbered, as well as militarily outclassed. But the settler-fear of the 'Red Savages', who had often had the edge over the front-line families in colonial and early post-colonial days, was real enough, and another strong emotive reason for dealing finally with the British. And now, when Napoleon seemed to be about to win the war in Europe and British resources were stretched to the limit, the time appeared to be ripe for such a settlement. There were, after all, only 5,000 British regulars in the whole of North America. And although President Madison had only 7,000 regular soldiers of his own, he could draw on tens of thousands of citizen-volunteers whose fathers could remember beating much bigger red-coated armies – and who, no doubt, would be welcomed by the Canadians (particularly the French-speakers among them), if not by those 'Loyalist' Americans who had emigrated northwards.

Such memories also conveniently overlooked the decisive presence of the troops of King Louis XVI in America during the Revolutionary War, and the even more decisive intervention of the French Royal Navy. Now, in fact, the armies of the Emperor Napoleon were incomparably more numerous and formidable. But there was not the slightest possibility that they could intervene in an American war – or effectively in any overseas adventure – with his Imperial Navy in a state of terminal decline. In American waters, even, the British Navy had become so dominant that the convoy laws had been relaxed there, and the Navy's presence had been reduced to one or two obsolete ships-of-the-line and a handful of patrolling frigates and sloops more concerned with regulating trade and recovering deserters than with war.

Still, the American 'War Party' expected to win quickly in Canada, while letting the sea (which was anyway the province of the New England 'Peace Party') more-or-less take care of itself, with no outside aid required.

Not the least of the ironies of the ensuing war was that the War Party's attempted conquest of Canada ended in a stalemate of failed invasions by both sides. On balance, indeed, while the Americans eventually came to rule the Great Lakes, the British (whose hearts were never really in the war, but who were loyally supported by all their colonists) had the defensive best of it, even though the American army redeemed early humiliations with a heroic little victory at Lundy's Lane. The historic importance of this drawn fighting lies in its influence on the future establishment of a permanent Canadian–American frontier (thereby also directing the United States *west-wards*), not to mention its prevention of a ghastly prolonged 'War of Canadian Reconquest, 1814–16' if the invaders had at first been successful. But our concern is not with the land warfare which at the beginning came as a salutary shock to the over-confident Americans, but with the sea warfare – the *frigate* warfare – which if anything came as an even greater shock to the British.

As already noted, President Madison started the war with only 7,000 soldiers. But such a diminutive army was actually quite adequate for his requirements, as well as appropriate to democratic parsimony, a permanent shortage of federal cash and the ingrained American dislike of soldiers and standing armies which the former colonies derived from their recent history and also inherited from their ex-Mother Country. Such an army, which could be cheaply aug-mented by volunteers as required, was more than good enough to deal with uprisings among the already outnumbered Red Indian tribes of the frontiers of that period (and not least because those fears of British machinations were groundless, of course). Even, as things turned out, it proved sufficient now at least to fight some sort of war against an admittedly half-hearted Britain, as those dreams of conquest dissolved.

When it came to a navy, however, the needs of a nation which was still substantially dependent for much of its prosperity and standard of living on seaborne trade might logically and properly have resulted in the creation of something more formidable. Indeed, the United States had already found herself forced to fight not only the French at sea (which she could do, of course, only because the French were being beaten there by the British), but also those Barbary States of North Africa. And the rules for her requirement had actually been laid down quite concisely by George Washington himself: 'Europe . . . must be engaged in frequent controversies, the causes of which are essentially foreign to our concerns . . . Our detached and distant situation invites us to pursue a different cause,' he had advised his countrymen in his farewell address. But having thus laid down the principles of isolationism he felt the need to warn them of the need '. . . to keep ourselves, by suitable establishment, on a respectable defensive posture'.

The most eminently 'suitable establishment' was a navy. Sailors, unlike soldiers, were unlikely ever to become the instruments of tyranny. And the new United States not only had a great many of them (when army enlistment was always unpopular), but had inexhaustible supplies of ship-building material and superb expertise in ship-building. There was, as always, the problem of raising federal funds, however. But, worse than that, there were *political* problems, with the pro-navy (and pro-British) Federalists at odds with the pro-French (and therefore anti-navy) Republicans, who could not even agree at least that a navy might be of use against one or other of these foreign ogres. Fortunately, nevertheless, there were the Barbary pirates, who became the Fathers of the United States Navy. Initially, indeed, the USS *Crescent* (36) was built as much as a safe (frigate) method of transporting blackmail money – and ransoms for captured American sailors – to Algiers and Tripoli as the beginnings of the mighty American fleets of the twentieth century. But the Federalists were able to go on from there to pass a law in 1794 authorising the construction of six more frigates, with an establishment of 2,000 regular officers and men.

It was thus (with the Republicans still voting against such folly) that the launching of some of the finest frigates ever built came about. Indeed, in the absence of any precise instructions regarding dimensions, armament and cost, old Joshua Humphreys, the Pennsylvanian Quaker who happened to be America's foremost ship-builder, came up with a truly deadly weapon in naval warfare: charitably, one must assume that it was his half-a-lifetime's accumulated experience and the logic of his country's new navy's likely predicament at sea, not

his non-violent principles, which went into the United States class of
frigate. But what he produced would, anyway, have gladdened the
heart of Britain's next naval genius in eventual succession to St
Vincent, Admiral 'Jacky' Fisher, from whom the future Dreadnought
of 1906 and the battle-cruisers of the 1914–18 war derived. Fisher's
intention, in the laying down of new classes of ships-of-the-line with
an all-big-gun armament and Parsons' oil-fired geared turbines, was
for ships which could catch and sink anything afloat, and escape from
any combination of enemies which might be too strong for them (even
though that last, given the size of Britannia's navy, would be an
unlikely occurrence).

With an eye to the realities of his country's needs, when 'our navy
for a considerable time will be inferior in numbers', Joshua
Humphreys would have designed a big frigate for preference, anyway,
rather than an improvement of the tried-and-tested 74-gunner, if that
had been the specification. Before the war ended the Americans would
be building ships-of-the-line – and even a monster among them to
retain their supremacy on the Great Lakes. But what came out of his
cogitations in the 1790s was as close to Admiral Fisher's requirement
as anything short of a ship-of-the-line could get: nominally a 44-gun
frigate, it was vastly bigger than any frigate afloat, at some 2,200-tons.
And its size not only enabled it to cram on more nicely-calculated sail
(to give the Constitution and her sisters a maximum logged speed of
over 13 knots – and the later President was a faster sailer than the
Constitution, all things being equal), but also a devastating armament.
Notional gun-reckonings – this one 36, that one 40 – are always
approximate, where frigates are concerned, as we have seen; and the
proportion of 'long guns' (long-range guns) to bigger (but short-range)
carronade smashers further complicates the equation. But, where the
cream of the British frigate fleet mostly mounted 'long' 18-pounders,
augmented by 32-pounder carronades and a couple of 12-pound
bow-chasers, the Constitution and others of her class were armed with
24-pounder long guns on her main deck (and 30 of them), as well as no
less than twenty-two 32-pound carronades and the usual bow-chasers
– 54 guns in all, delivering a prodigious weight of broadside for a
frigate both at long and short ranges.

In fact, such heavyweight armament was not uniquely American.
The 1,400-ton French Forte, which was taken by the British (ex-
French) Sybille in the Indian Ocean in 1799, carried a comparable one,
her 52 guns including thirty 24-pounders (actually firing 27-pound
shot) and ten 32-pound carronades. But, also with her crew of 500, she
was an exceptional ship – and exceptionally unlucky perhaps to
encounter an unusually powerful (ex-French) British antagonist, rated
a 38 but actually a 44, which had been taken five years before (by the
50-gun two-deck Romney).

Most important of all, though, in that *Forte–Sybille* duel was the disparity in the skill and training of the two crews. Although numerous, the French were sloppy and indisciplined, and their captain an elderly man, albeit brave, whereas the British Captain Edward Cooke (who was mortally wounded during the fight) was one of the best in the fleet, with a crew to match at a time when the British were coming up to the peak of their wartime efficiency. By 1812, however, as Grand Port had demonstrated, the confidence of British captains and their crews was by no means always matched by their gunnery and general combat-efficiency. But now, while they were still usually (though not invariably) good enough to beat anything Napoleon was able to send to sea, they were to come up against an enemy whose ships were not only bigger and more heavily-armed, but whose crews were also not simply more numerous but *qualitatively* as good or better, man for man, overall.

The reasons for this qualitative difference are not hard to find. In the first place, the United States Navy – at least in the opening phase of the war – was an all-volunteer service, in which pay and conditions were better than those in the British Navy (in which the proportion of pressed men and unwilling recruits had been high from the beginning and was even higher now, after nearly a generation at war). Nor, for that matter, can the US Navy be regarded as an inexperienced one. Many of its officers, including all its captains, had fought in their country's earlier wars against the French and the Barbary pirates. But, more than that even, not a few of its sailors had themselves served in and been trained by the British Navy in circumstances which provided one of the most publicised causes of the war.

Just how many Americans – *genuine* Americans – had been pressed into King George's fleet is difficult to establish. Indeed, what constituted a genuine American was itself a vexed question. Just as Colonel Colquhoun Grant (successfully) and Midshipman O'Brien (unsuccessfully) tried to pass themselves off as Americans in France, so thousands of British sailors all the time were trying to become Americans in order to avoid impressment: an estimated 12,000 bogus citizenship papers were then being issued every year in New York, at $2 each, many undoubtedly being bought by British naval deserters. The official British view during the war was that the King's subjects could *not* become foreigners, but desperate captains were in any case not choosy in distinguishing foreigners from Britons to make up their crews, no matter how obviously foreign they might be. Hornblower, presented with a handful of sullen and silent Spanish-Indian survivors from the sunked *Natividad*, read them in with the typical aside, 'Never mind, we'll make topmen of them yet.' Everything was grist for the British Navy's mill, not excluding Frenchmen or others from countries with which Britain was at war. Usually well over 10 per cent of any

'British' crew could be expected to be foreign. The *Victory* at Trafalgar was probably unusual in having only 8 per cent; it is probably significant that at the other extreme Pigot's *Hermione* had nearer 20 per cent, if men with foreign-sounding names are added to undoubted foreigners, especially as a further 10 per cent were Irishmen, some of whom might well have been classed at least as unreliable in view of the troubled state of Ireland in 1797. In the case of the *Danae* mutiny of 1800 the presence of so many foreigners, including both French and American, in an undermanned crew which also included many recently pressed men, was the undoubted real cause of that ship's loss.

Genuine Americans comprised the largest single foreign nationality, with (for example) 28 in the *Implacable* ship-of-the-line in 1808, as compared with a total of 40 from continental Europe and 12 from elsewhere (80 in all, out of a crew of 563). More eloquent, however, are the figures of undoubtedly illegally impressed Americans who were discharged from the British Navy as a result of successful United States protests: 2,410 for the first half of the war (1793–1802) and 6,057 from 1803 until the outbreak of the American War in 1812 – more than enough, even taking only that second total, to man the entire US Navy. And to these (or at least to those of them who volunteered) can be added both the British deserters who joined the American service *before* 1812 and those who, having been captured by the Americans, liked what they saw and then joined their erstwhile enemies. That there were at least some of the former was demonstrated in one of the most disgraceful and high-handed British actions in peacetime, which particularly rankled with every American. For in 1807, the British admiral commanding the North American station heard somehow that there were such deserters on the American frigate *Chesapeake* and actually ordered the captain of one of his smaller ships-of-the-line, the *Leopard*, to wait his chance to take them off the American warship as soon as she was outside American territorial waters – which the *Leopard* then did in a surprise attack, forcing Commodore James Barron to strike his flag. (That the British government subsequently apologised for this outrage, reprimanding all concerned and offering reparations, is beside the point: politic reprimands for offences against the Americans were part of the British Navy's custom-and-practice. We shall meet Commodore Barron again in a tragic sequel to the *Leopard–Chesapeake* affair, and the ill-fated *Chesapeake* herself will appear again in due course.)

British attitudes to the Americans were, to say the least, equivocal in 1812. At one chauvinistic extreme, the former colonials were heartily disliked, if not invariably despised, as 'Jonathans' and 'Yankees' – provincial (and republican) ex-Britons who had made a good thing out of the French war commercially, and who were now stabbing their mother country in the back in her war against the blackest of tyrannies. If Nelson had been alive, he would have fought them gladly, as Hoste, his pupil, was soon to volunteer to do, and all the more so after they had humiliated his beloved navy. But although blood had not yet become thicker than water (and that turned-around 'Special Relationship' was even further in the future), the beginnings of a half-rueful, half-admiring attitude was also a product of this war. Soon, in what can perhaps be regarded as the first recognition of American technology, the British would be hurriedly building their own versions of Humphreys' super-frigates. But also the commander of one PoW hulk in the Medway (the ex-Spanish *Bahama* ship-of-the-line, which had come down in the world since her capture at Trafalgar) reflected that 'these Americans are the sauciest of dogs I ever saw; but damn me if I can help liking them, *nor can I hate men who are so much like ourselves*'. And this affinity was even more significantly demonstrated by the recollection of a captured British sailor from the frigate *Macedonian*: '. . . that we had been trying to shoot each other's brains out so shortly before seemed forgotten. We ate together, joked together . . . a perfect union of ideas, feeling and purposes seemed to exist'. It is hardly surprising that this man quickly changed sides: he fitted all too easily into a navy which not only spoke the same language, but fought in the same way under officers who used the same tactics, manoeuvring for advantage to fire their well-aimed broadsides on the downward roll, at their adversaries' hulls, not on the upward roll to damage masts and rigging in the French style. Nor, indeed, was it surprising that Commodore Bainbridge USN easily bamboozled those long-time allies of Britain, the Portuguese, into believing that he was a British captain, and that his USS *Constitution* was HM Frigate *Acasta*, in order to leave an encoded message in the Cape Verde Islands for Captain Porter of the USS *Essex*.

The significance of all these factors completely eluded the British Navy at the outset of the war. To be fair to the Admiralty, however, there can have been no reports of any American naval preparations for this conflict, for in the years preceding it there had been none. The taut little 54-ship navy which had given the French a bloody nose and performed bravely in the Tripolitanian police action had not been maintained by the Republican Party's President Jefferson, whose discerning enthusiasm for French wines had not been matched by any appreciation of the need to lay down more naval ships for the future. Indeed, the navy had actually been progressively reduced by successive parsimonies in 1800, 1803 and – in spite of all British insults – as late as 1810. However, its formidable nucleus, which had been built during the last decade of the eighteenth century, still remained available, with no shortage of dockyard facilities and crews. And this consisted of a trio of Humphreys' frigates, the *United States*, the

Constitution and the *President* (nominally 44s but actually 'pierced' for well over 50 guns), and five smaller ones, the *Chesapeake*, the *Constellation*, the *Congress* and the *Essex* (nominally 36 to 38), and the *John Adams* (28), together with a few sloops and brigs.

To be fair again to the British Admiralty, this force did not really present a great threat to the Navy which then disposed of nearly 200 ships-of-the-line and 250 frigates, as well as upwards of 500 smaller vessels from sloops-of-war to inshore bomb-ketches. The outcome of a conflict between such ill-matched navies was inevitable, sooner or later, and although the British at first had only one Fourth-Rate ship-of-the-line and seven or eight cruising frigates on the North American station, no strong reinforcements were detached there on the out-break of war. The main problem was expected to be the possible depredations of licensed American privateers, especially in the West Indies, where the capture of France's last island possessions had resulted in the abandonment of the convoy system and the reduction of naval duties to mere police patrols. This was in fact a correct perception of what was to come, for while the ships of the regular United States Navy were not on the whole very successful commerce raiders, their private enterprise captains became a considerable irritant, if never a real danger as the French had been in the Channel in their heyday. What the otherwise confident British did *not* realise was the fighting quality of American navy captains and crews in general, and the strength of their heavy frigates in particular. In fact, they now faced a new naval challenge which was to be paralleled curiously in the first months of both the world wars of the twentieth century, on each occasion in the South Atlantic and against another enemy whose individual ships and crews were first class, though her navy was numerically inferior.

The first of these involved a squadron of modern German cruisers which, under the command of the chivalrous Admiral Count (Graf) Maximilian von Spee, were in the South Pacific when the war broke out in 1914. This squadron – composed, in 1800 terms, of the equivalent of half-a-dozen well-designed French 44s and 38s – made short work of two elderly British cruisers off the Chilean coast in the battle of Coronel, demonstrating that cold equation of war by which, given equal skill and bravery on each side, the weaker goes to the wall. (In theory the British might have run away, but it was Admiral Cradock's preference and duty to do as much damage to the enemy as possible, and his tragedy that by the custom of modern war he could not strike his flag honourably when beaten, but had to go down with his ships and his men.) But then, having broken out of the Pacific with the intention of destroying the British communications and fuel base at Port Stanley in the Falklands, von Spee was caught and destroyed in his turn by that same equation. For Admiral Fisher, aided by modern communications and technology, had reinforced the British South Atlantic squadron with two big battle-cruisers, faster and immeasurably more powerful than any of the German cruisers. Against such ships in 1914 cruisers had no more chance in a stand-up fight than frigates had had against ships-of-the-line in Nelson's day.

Twenty-five years later – or 127 years after the events soon to shock the British in 1812 – Commodore Henry Harwood faced much the same problem in those same South Atlantic waters as Admiral Cradock had done in the Pacific at Coronel. There, while in command of three cruisers – the small 8-inch gun *Exeter* and the smaller 6-inch *Ajax* and *Achilles* – he caught up with a true descendant of Joshua Humphreys' heavy frigates, the pocket battleship *Admiral Graf Spee*. It was, admittedly, three ships against one (and in the War of 1812 three smaller British frigates could have taken on Humphreys' frigate with some chance of success). But nineteenth – and twentieth –century advances in guns and gunnery more than cancelled out this numerical superiority: with her six 11-inch guns the *Graf Spee* could have blown all three British ships out of the water before they even got in range. Indeed, she nearly did just that, before taking refuge in the neutral port of Montevideo. Harwood had in fact fought a good tactical fight, determined at all costs to inflict as much damage as possible on a raider which was far from any proper repair facilities. Fortunately for him, the German captain (another honourable man in the von Spee tradition) fought hesitantly, failing to close with and finish off any of his enemies – probably because he did not wish to sustain any such damage. And for the British this outcome was sufficient: they delayed the departure of the *Graf Spee* as long as they could, and then deceived the Germans into believing that the battle-cruiser *Renown* (with her 15-inch guns) was waiting outside, with the aircraft-carrier *Ark Royal* and the big cruiser *Cumberland* in attendance. So, rather than have his ship interned, Hitler ordered the scuttling of the *Graf Spee* in the estuary of the River Plate.

One must be careful not take the pocket battleship/Humphreys' frigate analogy too far, of course. Their similarity lay in their awkward 'intermediate' nature, but in fact the American ships were in their day the more formidable, even though they did not actually embody any new technology themselves, other than advanced ship-building design. The *Graf Spee* was an ingenious ship, but by 1939 the day of the surface raider was over, and it was the submarine that had inherited the role of the frigate and the privateer, to be countered not by other submarines but by a mixture of radar-assisted escorts and aircraft.

No such new technological weaponry existed to counter ships like the *United States*, the *Constitution* and the *President*. Under the stimulus of so long a war, and at a time when the industrial revolution was accelerating, there were then men of an inquiring and inventive

turn of mind who were working on ideas which would make future
wars even more unpleasant. Cochrane was playing with poison gas;
Sir George Cayley had already published his remarkable researches
into heavier-than-air flight (only lacking the right engine); Robert
Fulton had been hawking his submarines and 'torpedoes' from one
unresponsive country to another, but Colonel Sir William Congreve's
rockets did see action in Europe and America (though they were most
destructively used by Lord Exmouth – Edward Pellew – in his battle of
Algiers in 1816, after the war). Above all, steam-power was by now so
well understood that the United States Navy was not only offered but
actually *built* a revolutionary 'steam frigate' during the war to a Fulton
design, the 20-gun *Demolgos*. But she (alas?) came too late to be tried
out against the British blockade, and was never developed further.
Steam-propulsion, like jet-propulsion in the 1939–45 world war,
came just too late to play a significant part in the proceedings of
1793–1815, and nearly all innovations of the period were hampered
either by primitive technology or by the conservatism of those in
power and their dislike of 'infernal devices'. So this war, at its most
advanced (and for all that Britain's industrial revolution played a
decisive part in her victory) was fought with no more than refinements
to the existing weapons of 1793, which had already proved themselves. And among these the heavier frigate, which the French had
already developed (and as distinct from the weaker and smaller old
ship-of-the-line, which was then obsolescent), was really no more than
a master ship-builder's intelligent perfection of the class, maximising
the speed and armament of a single main gun-deck warship *more than
ten years* before it was properly tested in battle. It is perhaps surprising
that the French themselves did not further develop the *Forte* class –
except, of course, that the British had taken the *Forte*, like the *Sybille*
before her. But as it was, anyway, the shock of the encounter of
Captain James Dacres' HMS *Guerrière* (nominally a 38, but actually
carrying 49 guns) with Captain Isaac Hull's Humphreys'-built USS
Constitution (nominally 44, but actually 54) was almost as profound
as if the American ship had been a secret weapon, even though she was
as familiar to the British as the *Guerrière* was to everyone along the
New England coasts which she had for so long patrolled.

Not that this was the first hostility of the war, which began at sea in
the best tradition of that age of long-delayed communications in the
same way as it was to end, with one of the combatants unaware of the
actual belligerent status of the other. Indeed, in 1812 the British
Orders in Council dictating the behaviour of British naval officers,
which constituted the official cause of the war, had been withdrawn by
the time the first shot was fired. But, like Master and Commander
Hornblower of the *Hotspur* when he saw the French frigate *Loire* (40)
heading towards him off Brest in 1803 with her guns run out, the

captain of the patrolling British *Belvidera* (32) did not wait to exchange the usual courtesies with the *President*, the *Congress* (38-plus) and two sloops when they headed towards him: he turned and ran, and only escaped by the skin of his teeth. If either of the American frigates had been alone he would no doubt have fought. But then, in any case, the British North American squadron concentrated, and it was Captain Hull's turn to run next, in the *Constitution*, when he was nearly ambushed by the *Shannon* (38), the *Aeolus* and the *Minerva* (both 32), and the *Belvidera*, with the big *Guerrière* and the even bigger (though obsolete) 64-gun *Africa* nearby. The *Constitution* escaped in almost windless conditions by luck and brilliant seamanship, to the rage and chagrin of Captain Broke of the *Shannon*. He too, at this stage of the war, would not have hesitated to engage any enemy frigate, of whatever country, in single combat, like all his fellow British frigate captains. As professionals, the majority of those captains would have been aware of the size of the *Constitution*. But as British captains, whose frigates had emerged victoriously from 100 single-ship actions, many of which had been won against far bigger French adversaries, they took success for granted. The true situation (which would soon be acknowledged by the Admiralty itself) was that *no* single British frigate could tackle a Humphreys frigate by itself, any more than any British cruiser could have fought the *Graf Spee* single-handed later on, and that in the future they must operate at least in pairs – and preferably pairs of bigger frigates of 36 guns or more, and those at least 18-pounders, since the Americans carried long 24s. But meanwhile Hull knew himself to be overmatched, and being a mature and experienced ship-captain from the Tripolitanian war and a fine sailor, eluded his enemies by the skin of *his* teeth (and with much gnashing of British teeth), to preserve the *Constitution* as his navy's top-scorer in the months to come.

However, with so many American merchant ships now heading for home (and representing a bonanza in prize-money, even though most of them beat the inadequate blockade), the British squadron concentration was neither maintained nor reinforced: John Paul Jones, from the previous American war, was forgotten, and Joshua Humphreys and his fellow 'Jonathans' were discounted, together with the lessons of the battle of Grand Port. And it was in that situation, when the *Guerrière* was cruising by herself, that she next met the *Constitution*, which had broken out from Boston after her earlier fright without difficulty in the absence of a close blockade of the European variety.

Captain Dacres of the *Guerrière* was a lamb to the slaughter now, but he did not know it. Although still a young man in his twenty-ninth year, he was far from inexperienced as a captain, with six years' seniority after having been made post when only 22. But this, it may be thought, was an 'interest' promotion very different from Hoste's and mainly due to his family's influence: his father had been an admiral and his uncle Admiral Sidney Smith's flag-captain. On the evidence both of his handling his ship in the ensuing fight and of her gunnery performance he was certainly an indifferent sea-officer and captain, but he may not have been much below the average, when until now even below-average had usually proved good enough. What is also likely, anyway, is that he confided in the weight of the *Guerrière*'s broadside, which at 550 pounds was a heavy one, and that he had an unusually large crew, which totalled 270 even after the ten Americans among them had exercised their right not to fight their countrymen and had been sent below. But apart from that – and even if he had known that the *Constitution*'s 24-pounder broadside was close to 700 pounds and that her crew totalled 460 (among whom no ex-Royal Navy Britons chose to go below) – he not only would have fought, but had no choice in the matter. At this early stage of the war he probably expected to win fairly easily, as British frigates had almost invariably done against bigger ships bulging with men for as long as he could remember. It was not only unthinkable to turn away from a single-ship challenge, but he would be branded and condemned as a coward for doing so: failure at least to damage such a dangerous raider, curtailing her patrol if not taking her, would have meant professional ruin.

In fact he did end the *Constitution's* cruise – but not by damaging her, merely by being spectacularly beaten by her, first because of inferior tactics and poor gunnery, then through lack of initiative when the two ships briefly tangled after he had lost a mast, before he lost his remaining masts and the fight itself. Two hours after the first shot he had lost 78 men to Hull's 14, but the *Guerrière* was incapable of further resistance and was actually sinking as she wallowed uncontrollably in the sea. (Very skilfully, the Americans saved all the wounded in difficult sea-conditions as night fell; and, indeed, the behaviour of both sides after battle during this wretched war was usually one of its few saving graces.)

The aftermath of the *Constitution–Guerrière* fight is interesting both for its American and British reactions, after Captain Hull had chosen to terminate his Atlantic cruise in order to take his prisoners and the good news of his victory to New York, having burned the hopelessly damaged and unmanageable British ship. For this action not only curtailed his raiding sortie into the Atlantic but also ended his own wartime career – and perhaps justifiably too. He had left Boston without orders, and although the capture of a British frigate was a great coup, which caused him to be fêted in New York and discouraged the anti-war, pro-British party in New England, taking British frigates was not really the primary duty of the United States Navy, then or later. Of British frigates there was no end, and although the taking of them would duly inspire a tradition of navy success and heroism it was far less immediately important than the taking of some dull transport carrying soldiers and supplies to the war in Canada, which was the *real* war in 1812. So, although Captain Hull survived to be Commodore Hull, commanding the American Pacific Squadron in the 1820s, he never again captained a frigate against the British.

On the British side, meanwhile, excuses preceded reality at first. Yankee frigates, it might be admitted, were powerful ships. But the British were accustomed to taking more powerful ships, so the whole wretched affair might be dismissed as one of those hitherto rare flukes, deriving most likely from the *Guerrière's* initial loss of a mast, before she lost all three, never mind the presence on board the American ship of all those British deserters about whom the war had been started in the first place – hadn't it? So, really, nothing had changed, and the *Naval Chronicle* could confide that any 'English frigate of 38 guns should be able to cope successfully with a 44-gun ship of any nation'.

The editor of the *Chronicle* was evidently not apprised of the real broadside of an American 44, never mind the probable mediocrity of the average British 38's captain. And, in any case, the little *Minerva* had recently fought off the American *Essex* (32 – but all her guns were carronades) while successfully protecting all but one of a troop convoy heading from the West Indies to Canada. And the loss of the brig *Alert* (18) to the *Essex* really did not count: no mere brig could be expected to fight a frigate successfully (at least, except a brig commanded by that appalling bounder Cochrane), any more than a frigate (except perhaps a British one, and then only in unusual circumstances) could take on a ship-of-the-line. Admittedly, the British brig *Frolic* (18) had also recently fallen to an American brig of similar armament, the *Wasp*. But the *Frolic* had a slightly smaller crew and was hampered by recent storm-damage. And, anyway, she had soon been re-taken easily by the *Poitiers* (74), together with the somewhat damaged *Wasp* herself, in just such another unequal encounter.

But then, in quick succession before the year's end, two more single-ship duels were fought which could not be easily editorialised away by the *Naval Chronicle*. For in October, with the American coast still inadequately blockaded, a powerful squadron escaped from Boston on a commerce-raiding mission. This – apart from the little brig *Argus* – consisted of the *Congress* (38) and two of the Humphreys frigates, Commodore John Rodgers commanding the incomparable *President* and Captain Stephen Decatur the proudly-named *United States*. In a fit of caution many years later Adolf Hitler renamed his *Deutschland*, one of the *Graf Spee's* sisters, *Lützow*, just in case she came to an untimely end. But it was Decatur's *United States* which was to administer her country's and her navy's next great shock to Great Britain.

Stephen Decatur's claim to enduring fame (although a claim not perhaps so respectable now, when patriotism is no longer held in such esteem) is enshrined in *The Oxford Dictionary of Quotations* from his reply to the toast at a dinner given in his honour on his return from Algiers in 1815, after he had finally ended a generation of piratical assaults there on American shipping: 'Our country! In her intercourse with foreign nations, may she always be in the right; but our country, right or wrong!' This was a toast which Nelson, certainly, would have echoed. And, indeed, Decatur himself lived by it, and may even be said to have died for it. For, having served on the court martial which dismissed Commodore James Barron from the US Navy for surrendering the *Chesapeake* to the deserter-hunting HMS *Leopard* in that humiliating pre-war 'incident' in 1808, he opposed James Barron's reinstatement in 1820, and was subsequently killed by the angry and embittered Barron in a duel shortly afterwards. But that was in the future when the *United States* parted company with her consorts in late October 1812. For he then won his place in this narrative as of right: had any foreigner been included among our great frigate captains, Stephen Decatur would have been the most likely candidate, with a chapter of his own as a captain in the Pellew–Hoste class, and with more than a dash of Cochrane too.

A Marylander by birth, Decatur was in fact no Anglo-American by descent, but of French extraction (as his name indeed suggests). Not that any origin – or any 'interest' of the British variety – had any part to play in the navy of the new republic. Pure merit rather (plus luck, of course, as always), was the primary requirement, and Decatur's outstanding qualities seem to have been recognised quickly by his seniors. In so diminutive a service, with its tiny officers' corps, that is perhaps hardly surprising; but then, compared with his nearest contemporary in age, William Hoste, Decatur could not rely on that succession of opportunities which a big fighting navy in a long war provided, both to shine and to step into dead men's shoes. When his combat opportunity came on the Barbary coast in 1804, nevertheless, he took it with both hands. His ability had already secured him early promotion, and he was by then already well-placed as a first lieutenant in one of Commodore Preble's frigates. So, having distinguished himself in close combat with pirate gunboats off Tripoli, he was soon given command of a captured schooner. It was in this vessel (the aptly-named *Intrepid*) that he won that coveted promotion to full captaincy in a daring night raid on Tripoli harbour in which he avenged his country's humiliation by cutting out the American frigate *Philadelphia*, which had fallen into the hands of the Tripolitanians after going hard aground, and then burning her when he could not bring her out of harbour. Thus 'made' in rank, as well as in reputation, he had eventually been rewarded in 1808 by being given command of the *United States*, the somewhat more powerful if slightly less fast sister of the *Constitution* and the *President*. And he had worked her up to a high state of efficiency when luck presented him with the British *Macedonian* on 25 October 1812.

The 38-gun *Macedonian* was a newer version of the big *Guerrière*, commanded by a much more senior captain, John Surman Carden. Indeed, Carden's experience of frigates and frigate warfare was far more extensive than Decatur's: he had been rewarded with post-rank in the most enviable way, as a compliment to his captain when, as first lieutenant of the *Fisgard* (38), his ship had captured the French *Immortalité* (36) in single-combat during the Directory's 1798 attempt to invade Ireland (the *Immortalité* being one of no less than six French frigates which were lost on that occasion). Now he had 13 years' seniority, and some knowledge of the United States Navy with it; indeed, there is a story that he had earlier actually met Decatur, with whom he allegedly discussed the relative merits of British and American frigates. If that story is true, however, he can hardly have studied any of the Humphreys monsters very carefully, since he now at first mistook the *United States* for the much less dangerous *Essex* as the two ships converged. But whichever Yankee she might be, his situation and his reaction were the same as Dacres' (of whose fate he was unaware, but which would not have made any difference): he had to fight and expected to win. The main difference between the two men was that where Dacres seems to have been merely not very bright, Carden was another captain of the Corbet type, whose defects as a sea-officer were accompanied by cruelty. Admittedly, the evidence for this comes from one of those of his crew who subsequently went over to the enemy, and whose testimony may therefore be questionable. But Carden himself confirmed it indirectly at his subsequent court martial (at which, predictably, he was exonerated) by showing that same cloven hoof that Corbet had displayed in his cruelty court martial: he blamed his crew for his defeat, characterising the *Macedonian* as 'the worst Man'd Ship in the fleet'.

Qui s'excuse s'accuse. The truth was that when the fight took place (the *Macedonian* then being en route to reinforce the West Indies squadron) he had already commanded this crew for 18 months. Even a harsh captain like Edward Hamilton, when his severity was balanced by competence, could create an efficient fighting force. But a harsh *and* incompetent one was already halfway to disaster – and all the way, when up against Decatur and the *United States*. Carden's crew, indeed, took 40 per cent casualties (out of 256) before he – not they – surrendered that day: no one can say that they did not fight. What was significant so far as they were concerned was that they fought *inefficiently*, like a bunch of ill-trained Frenchmen, firing more slowly and far more inaccurately than the Americans – a sure sign of lack of practice and poor discipline, the blame for which belonged, *via* their officers, to their captain. But what was additionally significant in Carden's case was that he himself was out-thought and out-manoeuvred on all points by Decatur during the course of the fight, the *United States* sustaining only *twelve* casualties throughout. This disparity ironically recalled those early Anglo-French frigate meetings, in which the effect of faster and more accurate broadsides were cumulative. And indeed, this fight ended as all of them had done – except that this time the British ship was the one finally incapable either of returning the enemy's raking fire or of closing with him to try that 'last resort' of boarding; while, worst and most humiliating of all, that enemy emerged from the engagement virtually undamaged.

The only benefit the British derived from this defeat (though it had not really been Carden's aim in taking on a more powerful ship so confidently, and was also not apparent to the Admiralty) was that it did curtail Decatur's raiding cruise, just as the *Guerrière* defeat had done Hull's when his ship had also been virtually unmarked. But Decatur's decision was more soundly based. After a summer of military defeats and surrenders on the Canadian frontier his country needed news of a victory much as Britain had done when Sir John Jervis had decided to fight a bigger Spanish fleet back in 1797. And this time the British prize, though temporarily incapacitated, was still seaworthy and reparable, so that if she could be escorted back through the blockade she could be paraded as tangible proof of success. But time was of the essence, for the blockade was already building up: already the British had despatched three ships-of-the-line westwards, together with no less than 21 frigates and 44 smaller craft; and whether Decatur knew this in detail or not, he can have been in no doubt of the effect on them of the *Macedonian*'s loss, coming after that of the *Guerrière*.

Fortunately for him, the new commanding British admiral on the North American station, Sir John Borlase Warren, although by now concerned about the depredations of American privateers, was lamentably slow to tighten the blockade. So the *Macedonian* was sailed triumphantly into New York, to be enrolled in the United States Navy to the acclamation of the American public and the bitter shame and astonishment of the British – navy and public alike. And each was to receive more of such good-and-bad news very soon, with the news of a third frigate encounter, between the *Constitution* (now commanded by Captain William Bainbridge), and the British *Java* (38), commanded by Captain Henry Lambert.

Bainbridge and Lambert had each survived earlier disasters in their careers. The American, indeed, had been captured twice by his country's enemies, once by the French in 1798, and then by the Bashaw of Tripoli in 1803 when his *Philadelphia* had grounded on an uncharted reef off the North African coast. Even now he owed his command of the *Constitution* to another captain's bad luck, more than his own good luck (and undoubted merit), having been appointed to her after the surprisingly mean dismissal of Isaac Hull, the captor of the *Guerrière*.

Lambert, for his part, had distinguished himself in the *San Fiorenzo* (36), which had captured the weaker *Psyche* (32), commanded by Pellew's old friend Bergeret, after a hard fight in the Indian Ocean in which more than half the French crew had become casualties, in 1804. But six years later he had been caught up in the Grand Port defeat, when his *Iphigenia* (36) had been caught by Commodore Hamelin's reinforcements after the battle. Like Bainbridge, however, he had subsequently been exonerated for a loss which was judged not to be his fault, so that he had been speedily reappointed, this time to the *Java*, in which he was ferrying the new Governor of Bombay and a draft of naval reinforcements back to the East Indies. But now his bad luck finally swallowed up the good.

In most respects the *Constitution–Java* fight off the coast of Brazil was a rerun of the two previous Anglo-American duels. Lambert may have been a marginally more competent and less unpleasant officer than Dacres or Carden, but he certainly knew of the loss of the *Guerrière* and could have escaped if he had chosen to do so, for the *Java* was a fast ship. As the French *Renommée* (40) she had been captured with another French frigate by the *Nereide* and three other British 36s off Madagascar the year before, in a fight from which the French *Clorinde* (40) had disgracefully fled. Rerated by the British as a 38, she was still a typically fast and well-armed ship, and the presence of those naval reinforcements may well have further emboldened Lambert to try his luck. The 400 men he then had on board were certainly far in excess of the normal complement of even the largest British frigates of those days, which were more usually under-manned. Appropriate 'official' totals for any given ship are often misleading, anyway, since the actual number of guns carried rarely coincided with the nominal one. But big 44s theoretically carried 320 men, with numbers thereafter decreasing through the 230 of a 'standard' 36 of the Fifth Rate to a mere 160 in the smallest of the Sixth Rates, with their 20 or 22 nine-pounders. Carden, as a bad captain whose men would have deserted at the first opportunity, was unusually lucky to have 276 in his 38-gun *Macedonian* (which rated a crew of 250, but which actually carried more guns, of course). Some idea of the power of the Humphreys frigates can be gauged by the size of the crew of the *Constitution*, however, whose total of 476 was actually 56 *more* than the complement of the smallest of the old British Fourth Rate ships-of-the-line.

Most likely, though, Lambert was just another average over-confident British frigate captain, who would have dismissed the

Guerrière defeat as an accident. But as he was killed in the coming fight (so that it was his first lieutenant who was subsequently court-martialled – and exonerated and promoted) we shall never know his reasoning. And the course and outcome of the engagement were, in any case, no different from those of the previous two. The *Java* was perhaps slightly better handled, since she inflicted 34 casualties on the enemy. But in short order she was out-manoeuvred and out-fought, to lie helpless and dismasted with nearly one-third of her men out of action, at the mercy of Captain Bainbridge.

The effect of this third consecutive frigate defeat in Britain was predictable, though somewhat different in the way various interested parties reacted to it. The editorial writers of the *Naval Gazette* and *The Times*, whose earlier excuses and confidence in future victories were no longer tenable, were shocked and horrified, but were still able to fall back on the size of the Humphreys frigates. Some observers, like Larpent Wells, the Judge Advocate, combined common sense with a certain glee, even: 'People here are all very sore about the Americans, and our taken frigates. I think we deserve it a little. Our contempt for our descendants and half-brothers has always rather disgusted me . . . The Americans have faults enough; we should allow them their merits. Our sailors all thought Americans would not dare look them in the face. I think the Army rejoice and laugh aside . . . as they [*sic* – the Navy, of course] bullied so much before' (which was perhaps understandable in 1812, with the Peninsular War still in the balance, in spite of Salamanca, and the victorious advance into France still in the future, and Waterloo unimaginable).

So far as the rank-and-file of the Navy itself was concerned (and, as we shall see, not least its frigate captains) these three American swallows still did not make an American summer at sea. But the Admiralty was more realistic and more concerned – only more by the possibility of a re-animation of French naval spirit than because of the minor and quite easily containable problem of a few damnably good Yankee ships. Super-frigates could be matched by overwhelming force. And, anyway, if the Americans had super-frigates, so could the British. So, while that was put in hand, new orders went to British frigate captains and many more ships – ships-of-the-line as well as frigate-groups (with those new orders) – were despatched to the North American and West Indian stations. The Americans had no ships-of-the-line, of course – thanks to Thomas Jefferson and his party – although they were building them now. But nothing could have changed the outcome: the war – the *real* war – had changed even before the *Constitution* had set sail to meet the *Java*, and King George had ships to spare while Napoleon himself would soon be stripping his own navy of men to reinforce his depleted army.

What had happened, of course, had been his Russian catastrophe, out of which the last of all the great anti-French European coalitions had risen, phoenix-like. And, with it, an old phoenix-friend too: for among the handful of exhausted and frost-bitten survivors of the last of the *Grandes Armées* there survived also none other than Sir Nesbit Josiah Willoughby, who had got himself captured during the French advance and who – being 'The Immortal' – marched all the way back from Moscow as his captors died around him in their thousands. And even then his adventures were not over: after Napoleon had rejected the Tsar's polite request for his release he escaped from prison and got clean away, unencumbered by any word-of-honour, which the French had unwisely omitted to extract from him.)

With the vengeful armies of Russia, Austria and Prussia massing in Central Europe, and the victorious British Peninsular army advancing towards the Pyrenees, war with the United States was a minor matter of unfinished business for the British government and the Admiralty in the spring of 1813. Only for those at the sharp end across the Atlantic was it more than that – in particular for Captain Philip Bowes Vere Broke who, like every British frigate captain from the coast of New England to the shores of the Adriatic, was burning to avenge his navy's shame, and determined to do this with his incomparable *Shannon*.

CHAPTER SEVENTEEN

In which Captain Broke challenges Captain Lawrence to a duel

If the battles of Trafalgar and Austerlitz back in the autumn of 1805 had marked the end of the beginning of the Napoleonic half of this world war, the destruction of France's *Grande Armée* in Russia in the winter of 1812 emerges clearly as the beginning of its end. But although that end was only twelve months away in the spring of 1813, when the armies of the new Fourth (or Seventh?) coalition went to war, one may surmise that the main talking point among British naval officers (and British frigate captains in particular) was 'these d—d American frigates'.

Being for the most part practical men they had fewer illusions now, after that third defeat (an event the *Naval Chronicle* found 'too painful for us to dwell upon'). Yet among their young captains their confidence was none the less undiminished, if William Hoste is taken as typical: 'The Yankees may take a frigate or two, with ships twice as big and double the number of men . . . When fairly considered, our frigates are by no means a match for them; and yet with fifty more men I should be happy to try *Bacchante*', he wrote home. But his less ardent elders thought somewhat differently and pragmatically as they drafted their new orders to frigate captains.

The first duties of the heavily reinforced transatlantic squadrons were, of course, to protect maritime trade and troop convoys, pursue privateers and tighten the blockade, but it was inevitable that naval supremacy would also encourage those combined operations which had increasingly become the British Navy's business after they had disposed of all enemy battle-fleets. That they were then slow to take advantage of their superiority may have been due as much to Admiral Warren's liking for Americans as to this incapacity. But although his successor – Captain Lord Cochrane's Uncle Alexander – laboured under no such disadvantages, British subsequent raids and mini-invasions suffered mixed fortunes. Most humiliating of all was to be the eventual repulse of an army which included regiments of Wellington's veterans at New Orleans, when they were foolishly propelled against the future President Jackson's sharpshooters by the Iron Duke's bone-headed brother-in-law, General Pakenham, in an attack actually mounted after peace had been signed; while most humiliating for the Americans had earlier been the taking and burning of Washington City (which long afterwards embarrassed a young British diplomat, who remembered that the English had burned Joan of Arc, but stoutly maintained that the British had not even captured *George* Washington, never mind burned him thereafter).

But the land operations of this mutually unsatisfactory war lie outside the scope of this narrative, which is concerned only with its variously heroic frigate operations. And as regards these, whatever Captain Hoste might have reckoned, a meeting between his crack *Bacchante* and any Humphreys ship must have ended in carnage and probable defeat. Fortunately, the British Admiralty saw more clearly that their frigates were over-matched, for whatever reason, and planned and ordered accordingly. For there was, they concluded, no British frigate afloat which could single-handedly take on the *United States* and her sister-ships except something like Pellew's old and long-since worn-out *Indefatigable*, which was no real frigate at all, but a *razé*. This thought, indeed, had already occurred to Admiral Warren, who had asked for such cut-down ships-of-the-line to be included in his reinforcements. So now, as a stop-gap, the Admiralty quickly ordered three 74s – the *Majestic* and *Goliath* (veterans of the battle of the Nile in '98) and the *Saturn* – to be razéed, while at the same time laying down a new class of monster frigates of 60 guns (thirty-two 24-pound long guns and twenty-six 42-pound carron-ades), of almost exactly the same dimensions as the USS *President* (with a 174 × 45-foot gundeck, compared with Humphreys' 173 × 44). And even the use of despised (American) fir, as opposed to traditional (British, or wherever) oak was now acceptable, for the *Leander*, the *Newcastle* and the new *Java*.

None of these, and only the lumbering *Majestic* among the *razés* saw wartime combat. But then neither did any of the new American ships which were now building. For after the *Guerrière* victory the United States Congress had at last (but far too late) seen the light. Years before, during the undeclared war against France, it had contemplated building ships-of-the-line in spite of the opposition of Thomas Jefferson and his Republican Party, but had never authorised the money to construct any. Now, in addition to another six heavy frigates, four 'super-74s' – nominally 76s, but actually much more like three-deckers – were generously funded. Jefferson himself, whose many-sided brilliance (and incomparable taste in claret and Sauternes) was never matched by any naval enthusiasm, remained unconvinced: 'Frigates and 74s are a sacrifice we must make, heavy as it is, to the prejudice of a part of our citizens.' And perhaps in retrospect he was right to say so. If the *Independence* and the *Franklin*, the first of the new American ships-of-the-line, had been available in 1812, or had been commissioned in time to take part in the fighting, they would surely have caused the British more trouble and further humiliation. But they would still have suffered the same fate as the rest of the United States Navy was eventually to do, being cornered by superior forces at sea, or burnt to prevent capture at anchor (the fate of the *John Adams*), or driven into some backwater to end the war crewless and dismantled, as did both the once-victorious *United States* and her prize, the *Macedonian*.

By the early summer of 1813, however, the British blockade of the New England coast was still by no means as effective as it was later to become (allowing also for the fact that under sail such blockades were always at the mercy of the weather, of course, and that skilful and determined blockade-runners could beat it in the right conditions). In the case of Boston harbour, for example, although it was by then covered by the *Shannon* (38-plus) and the *Tenedos* (36) close in, with the *Hogue* (74) and sometimes another ship-of-the-line, the *San Domingo* (74) in support, the American *Chesapeake* (38-plus) was able to return safely from a not very successful raiding cruise in April, and the big *President* (56) and the smaller *Congress* (38-plus) got clean away in the same month. After she had completed a re-fit, the *Chesapeake* was bound to follow her sisters (and was indeed ordered to do so). It was the plain duty of her captain to avoid the blockading British frigates, whose captains' equally plain duty was to take no risks in preventing her from doing so by penning her in harbour – and, not least, to avoid another of those humiliating frigate defeats too. Not the least surprising thing about the extraordinary *Shannon–Chesapeake* duel which was soon to take place was that *both* captains ignored those plain duties, the American deliberately choosing to fight and the Briton deliberately creating a situation in which his enemy could either fight at an advantage or get clean away.

Altogether, this fourth Anglo-American frigate fight has a quaintly old-fashioned eighteenth-century air about it in those early nineteenth-century days of improved frigates and refined frigate fighting – at least before the exceptionally bloody fighting actually began, anyway. As in that first Anglo-French meeting between the *Nymphe* and the *Cléopâtre* back in 1793, patriotic cheers and counter-cheers preceded the first broadsides: but then there was of course plenty of time for such conventions in the slow-motion encounters of the age of sail, during which the ships were cleared for battle, flags raised defiantly (one in the *Chesapeake* bearing the legend 'Free Trade and Sailors' Rights'), and crews fed and rigged out in clean clothes. To the extent that the combatants usually had so long to wait in cold blood as the distance between them shortened and the echoes of those cheers died away, such engagements did indeed have the quality of a duel, and that description has already been frequently applied to them. But in this instance 'duel' more exactly and accurately describes what happened. Indeed, it does so quite *literally* in the case of Captain Philip Bowes Vere Broke, after his despatch of a formal challenge to the captain of the *Chesapeake* under flag of truce that very day, 1 June 1812, in one of the most remarkable letters to pass between belligerents.

'As the *Chesapeake* appears now ready for sea,' he began 'I request that you will do the favour to meet the *Shannon* with her, ship to ship, to try the fortune of our respective flags . . .' But then he went much further, in what can hardly be other than a calculated attempt to sting his enemy into fighting, for in precise detail he explained that the 74-gun *Hogue* had gone to Halifax to replenish her stores, and that he had sent away the *Tenedos* 'and all other ships' which might have interfered with the meeting. Then, for good measure, he listed the armament and crew of the *Shannon* (18-pounders and 32-pounder carronades), carefully denying the rumour of a reinforcement of 150 men from the *Hogue* which 'really never was the case'. After which he reminded his enemy that, as the greater might of the Royal Navy was gathering, it was now or never for such a duel, not for any personal ambitions but for 'nobler motives':

> You will feel it as a compliment if I say that the result of our meeting may be the most grateful service I can render to my country; and, I doubt not, that you, equally confident of success, will feel convinced that it is only by repeated triumphs in even combats that your little navy can hope to console your country for the loss of that trade which it cannot protect.

And, finally, 'We are short of provisions and water, and cannot stay here long . . .'

The fact that the new captain of the *Chesapeake*, James Lawrence, never actually received this remarkable missive, with all its calculated jibes and incentives, turned out to be beside the point, for in the event he behaved exactly as though he had – while Captain Broke himself no less behaved as though he had not the slightest doubt that his challenge had been received and accepted in the most gentlemanly manner. For he then waited alone in full sight of Boston with the *Shannon* hove-to and stationary, without the slightest attempt to manoeuvre either for advantage or even to avoid one of those raking broadsides delivered at right-angles which so often virtually settled such fights. He waited, indeed, exactly like a duellist at home who only needed 20 paces of level ground on Hounslow Heath to obtain his satisfaction.

Duelling by individuals in this murderously cold-blooded way was then in high fashion on both sides of the Atlantic, and in the very highest circles. Captain Decatur, as already regretted, was to lose his life in just such an affair of honour at the hands of the vengeful Commodore Barron in 1820, after he had prevented Barron's reinstatement in the navy, the meeting taking place on a favourite duelling ground at Bladensburg in Maryland, just outside Washington. But earlier – and much more infamously – Aaron Burr, a rascally politician who aspired to the presidency, had shot down one of America's foremost statesmen, Alexander Hamilton, in a duel at Weehawken in New Jersey in 1804; and two years later the future President Andrew Jackson had nearly lost his own life in killing his antagonist at a similar meeting. In Britain (where duelling was equally popular although a crime carrying possible indictment for murder for the seconds as well as the principals), William Pitt, the Prime Minister at the time of Trafalgar, was among the list of famous duellists, which included Castlereagh and Canning, who actually fought each other in 1809. Nor did the conclusion of the war, which ended such a long period of world-wide violence, put a stop to these bad habits in either country. In Britain the Duke of Wellington was to fight Lord Winchelsea, and in America Henry Clay fought John Randolph. These and many other duels mercifully ended without fatalities. But in the numerous meetings of hotter-blooded (and presumably more skilful) military and naval officers (who often fought out of sheer boredom, if not when drunk) there were many deaths. Cochrane was lucky to escape alive from a duel with a wrathful French royalist officer in Malta in 1801, after a ridiculous fracas at a fancy dress party which he had attended too well disguised as an ordinary British sailor, and then had been mistaken for the real thing and thrown out as a gate-crasher. But perhaps the nearest thing to the Broke–Lawrence ship-duel of 1813 was Midshipman Hornblower's challenge to the bullying over-age Midshipman Simpson in 1794, in which he – like our two captains – was a desperate man seeking to resolve his problem one way or the other.

In fact, neither Hornblower nor Broke was a hot-tempered duelling type, the major element in both their challenges rather being cold calculation. In his duel, Hornblower managed to reduce the odds against him (since Simpson was a far better shot) to exact evens by fighting the duel at point-blank range with only one pistol loaded. Broke could not go so far, but although he had supreme confidence in his own ship's excellence he certainly did everything he could to even the odds which, on previous American 'form', an outsider might have felt were against him. Actually, those odds were more in his favour, since the *Chesapeake* was not one of those Humphreys frigates which he had somewhat disingenuously described as the winners of 'repeated triumphs in even combats': his *Shannon* was in every way equal to the American *as a ship*, and more than equal as a fighting-machine in reality. But he can hardly have known the real condition of the *Chesapeake*, let alone the state-of-mind of her captain, who had *not* received his challenge, yet for whom the very sight of the enemy cruising alone off Boston did his challenge's work for him. Indeed, if he had known those crucial pieces of intelligence, he might well not have issued the challenge, but would have simply cruised alone temptingly, waiting for the bait of his ship to be taken in order to fight an entirely different sort of duel, for which his ship – of all the British Navy's 250 frigates – was ideally suited. But now, with that presumption, this frigate action – which was not to be the war's last, never mind the most typical, but was certainly among the most famous, shortest and bloodiest – ceases to be an interesting *ship*-fight, to become what in some sense *all* frigate fights were to a greater or lesser degree: the meeting of two captains, with luck and merit mediating the outcome, rather than 'interest'.

In age Broke (1776–1841) fits quite neatly among our special captains, younger than Pellew (born 1757) and Pigot (1769, and long-dead), but older than Hoste (1780) – a contemporary of Cochrane and Hornblower, in fact. Among them, however, and all naval officers in general, he represents the system almost at its best – at least in so far as steady and undeniable merit, without 'interest', had promoted him into the *Shannon*, in which he made his own luck in his last fight, for the good of his navy rather than for his own.

In origin he sprang from that class of minor gentry and squirearchy which contributed so many of its offspring to the Army and Navy – and to Parliament too, but not necessarily with any special 'interest' in the absence of some greater patron, to advance its 'young gentlemen' usefully. At least, the Brokes of Broke Hall, in the village of Nacton near Ipswich in Suffolk, evidently lacked significant influence, for all that one of their ancestors had been killed while commanding a ship against the Dutch in the battle of Sole Bay (or Southwold) in 1672. For, in spite of a vocation for the Navy, the young Philip Broke did not sail straight in as a 'volunteer' or 'captain's servant' under the patronage of some friend, or friend-of-a-friend, of the family, but was sent to one of the naval colleges at Portsmouth at the age of twelve, in 1788. In the small peacetime navy of those days it would in any case have been more difficult to find a berth afloat. But it was also the fact that these college products and 'academites' were not very popular with captains, who valued their privilege of taking in their own juvenile cannon-fodder to please their friends and patrons. As a probable result, Broke did not actually get to sea until 1792, and then only in a sloop, the *Bulldog* (18), not into a more desirable frigate.

Once at sea, however, his merit had a chance to show itself as he developed into the very best type of young naval officer, not only brave (of course) and professionally competent, but also equable in temperament, insatiably curious and (more rare, but by no means unique) cultured. Following his first captain from the *Bulldog* to the *Ecalair* sloop in 1793, he then moved on to the *Romulus* (74) in 1794, and into the flagship *Britannia* (100) off Toulon briefly, before appointment as third lieutenant in the *Southampton* frigate, a 12-pounder 32. In her he came under Commodore Nelson's overall command during the St Vincent campaign of 1797, again following his captain into the *Amelia* (28), in which he served in the squadron which captured all those enemy frigates during the French attempt to invade Ireland in 1798. That success resulted in his first independent command, first of the *Falcon* brig and then the somewhat larger *Shark* sloop, on convoy duty in the North Sea and the Baltic. This was not the sort of work which enriched impoverished young masters and commanders or gave them much scope for distinguishing themselves, as Cochrane was then doing in hostile Spanish waters. But it was none the less important and difficult work at a time when Russia had become an enemy and Danish and Swedish neutrality was collapsing, yet Britain's vital trade (particularly in naval material and stores) had somehow to be maintained. It was Broke's luck that his merit was observed and rewarded with promotion to post-rank in February 1801, at the relatively young age of 25.

That, however, was as far as luck and merit could take him, for he was not made post *into* a frigate (the most desirable form of such a promotion), and was then caught by the Peace of Amiens without a command. At the bottom of the Captains' List and without 'interest' he had no chance of a ship during the months of peace, and had to wait his turn when war recommenced. This, indeed, was the time when 'interest' was at a premium. Even Captain Lord Cochrane, who was famous for his *El Gamo* exploit and heroic handling of the *Speedy*, had had to exert all his 'interest' before receiving the wretched *Arab*. Broke, who was actually six months his senior on the List, now languished patiently on the beach for *four years* before finally getting the elderly *Druid* (32), in which he no less patiently patrolled the Irish Sea and the Channel for the following 16 months until at last his luck turned again, with his appointment to the brand-new Chatham-built 18-pounder *Shannon* in the late summer of 1806.

Not that the *Shannon*'s first 1806–7 cruise, or any of her subsequent ones, indicated anything like the favour which had made Cochrane's fortunes in the *Pallas*. Her first voyage, to protect the British whaling fleet off Spitzbergen in the Arctic Sea, was unrewarding if not unimportant. High-grade whale oil was an extremely valuable commodity, and the French had decimated the whaling fleet the previous year in a well-timed raid. But the French did not try the same trick again in 1807, and the *Shannon* returned to routine Atlantic–Biscay patrol thereafter for the next three years, when the chances of both action and prizes were steadily decreasing as Britannia's supremacy in the open sea became increasingly apparent. However, while even attendance on the Navy's easy capture of the Madeira Islands in 1807 must have made a welcome change, it is an incident during the winter of 1808 which points best to the climax of both the *Shannon*'s service and to the character of her captain and his influence on her crew.

On the night of 11/12 November 1808 the sound of gunfire was reported to him in the Bay of Biscay, and the *Shannon* was properly steered towards it, so that she arrived just in time to attend the capture of the French frigate *Thetis* by the *Amethyst* (36), in company with the *Triumph* (74). All that, given the nature of the British blockade, was nothing out of the ordinary – any more than was the small print of the prize-rules, which decreed that *all* ships in sight of such a capture were entitled to share equally in the profits of such an event. Which was fair enough, since *all* ships often contributed to the final cornering of the prize, in the days of sail. But in this instance Captain Broke judged that he had had no part in the fight, and accordingly put it to his officers and men that they ought to forego what they did not deserve, in favour of Captain Michael Seymour and his *Amethyst* crew. In fact the captain of the *Triumph* did not take the same view, so that in the end the *Thetis* prize-money (and head-money) was eventually divided up among all three ships. But although such windfall profits had by then become increasingly rare, with not only the French Navy and the merchant marine almost driven from the sea, but fewer French privateers now, and consequently less chance of recaptures, Broke thus proved that he was not avid for prize-money even before he was to demonstrate his priorities much more spectacularly off the American coast.

Initially, in fact, the *Shannon*'s posting to North America in the late summer of 1811 further reduced Broke's chances of either distinguishing himself or making money. From a frigate captain's point of view, as the experience of Nelson and Pigot had shown long before, detaining American ships (as well as stopping them to take off allegedly British subjects) was a legally risky business at the best of times. Now, almost as never before, American trade was important to the British. Indeed, it was to continue to be so even after war had broken out, with licences readily granted to Yankee traders prepared to continue business: just as Napoleon's *Grande Armée* marched into Russia wearing British-made boots and greatcoats exported under licence or smuggled into North German and Baltic ports, so Britain's Portuguese and Spanish allies – and, by extension, Wellington's army – ate American corn. (But then, of course, the United States was not at war with any country except Britain, any more than ever formally in alliance with France: the War of 1812 was a strictly private Anglo-American quarrel.)

What this meant before Mr Madison declared war was that the North American station was neither exciting nor profitable. When the war began even in spite of that ready issue of licences to continue trading, there were at last plenty of legitimate American prizes to be taken – although the Americans proved themselves better at this game, in which they had even better opportunities: the first year of this war was their privateers' 'happy time', as 1942 was to be off the American coast for German U-boat commanders. But prizes did not really interest Captain Broke now. Those that he took he burned – and for one very good reason: a prize retained meant a prize-crew detached, which would weaken his fighting strength for that occasion which he most desired, a meeting with an enemy warship. From the very outset of the war (in which, of course, he had taken part in that early pursuit of the *Constitution*) he regarded the frigates of the United States Navy as his proper prey – the prey, indeed, for which his *Shannon* was undoubtedly the best-prepared ship in quality, if not in weight of broadside, in the whole British Navy.

Even before the American war had broken out, Philip Broke had been a man with an obsession: he was a gunnery fanatic. But his fanaticism was not simply that of the good old well-drilled, quick-firing school to which all the best British captains had belonged. In addition to drill and speed, he was determined to achieve the most scientifically accurate shooting at long range as the irregularities of his cannon and cannon-balls would allow. The general standard of British gunnery had by then declined, as a number of fights between smaller British and American warships testified, as well as those recent frigate defeats. But accurate shooting had always been something of a rough-and-ready business, often consisting of little more than firing at the right moment on the roll of the ship. In the vast majority of all Anglo-French duels the faster broadsides delivered by better-trained and disciplined crews at close quarters had anyway been sufficient to secure victory. In his quest for perfection, however, Broke went much further: he personally superintended the mounting of every gun, had grooves cut into the deck behind each mounting marking the points of the compass, and supplied wooden quadrants for degrees of elevation and sights (of his own design and at his own cost) enabling gun-captains to aim parallel to the bore of weapon. Added to rigorous and regular gunnery drill, both for broadside and individual fire (and of the sort which the best of the Navy's captains from Pellew to Hornblower had always practised), these innovations resulted in one direct hit in four at ranges of up to 400 yards on a four-foot square of canvas fastened to a floating barrel.

Nothing quite like this had been seen before – even in the old days when well-trained gunnery had been more prized than smartness. As far as the latter went, the *Shannon* was nothing special: she was, as Broke himself was content to describe her, 'an unassuming ship'. But her reputation for exceptional gunnery spread, nevertheless, to the extent that Broke was ordered to exchange men from his gun-crews into other ships to spread the gospel, with the captain of the 74-gun *San Domingo* later recommending that *Shannon* practices should be standardised throughout the fleet. And, indeed, when setting out for Algiers in 1816, Pellew had Broke 'dispart sights' fitted on the guns of all his fleet – which, with the regular drills he ordered, resulted in some extremely accurate shooting against the stone forts there.

The great irony of the *Shannon–Chesapeake* meeting which was now to take place in 1813, however, is that this excellence in *long-range* gunnery not only played no part at all in the fight, but was by Broke's own deliberate choice not given a chance to do so: he waited like a duellist for the enemy to engage him at a distance hardly greater than he would have done if both had been fighting with Manton pistols at Hounslow Heath or Bladensburg. At such a range – at least, against an American ship of a navy which had battered three British frigates into submission – however good his own ship might be, the only certainty was that there must be heavy casualties (and especially on the quarterdeck, where the worst casualties usually occurred). In effect, he thereby threw away the one real advantage he had, seeming rather to ask the God of Battles to throw the dice for him.

On the face of it, that such a thoughtful and scientifically minded captain acted in such a fashion appears mysterious. But if the possibility that he knew of the actual state of the *Chesapeake*'s crew and battle-readiness (never mind the state of mind of her captain, whose identity he did not know) is discounted, it would seem that Broke's actions were more likely the product of a strange mixture of well-founded confidence in the innate perfection of his crew's training, ill-founded confidence in the superiority of his beloved navy, determination to avenge its recent humiliations, cool calculation and – not least – sheer desperation.

The first of these ingredients was obvious: the *Shannon* was, and was well-known to be, a crack ship. As such, however, she had inspired her captain with the same boundless confidence which animated Hoste in the far-off Adriatic when he reckoned that, with a few more men, he could deal with a Humphreys frigate. In a letter to his wife, Broke himself told her that he wanted 'one of these big American ships' – and what he particularly wanted (he also wrote) was the *Constitution* herself. What he had so far got over nearly a year of almost ceaseless patrol (and while scorning his prize-money) was precisely nothing. He had failed to catch the *Constitution* the previous year. More recently, the *Chesapeake* had reached Boston safely, and most recently of all the *President* and the *Congress* had escaped from that port. It was odds-on that the *Chesapeake* would get away again soon. And, in any case, his own stores were getting low, so that he would have to abandon this patrol soon if the American captain delayed sailing. His only chance of redeeming his failures and avenging his navy's defeats lay in offering himself as a sitting duck to an enemy who must himself be confident of victory, but who would also be – although a Yankee – a gentleman. His letter-of-challenge *might* have been merely good psychology. But it was also the literal truth, every word of it.

In fact, to his merit Broke now added luck – indeed, double or even treble luck. First, it was not a Humphreys ship he faced. But, much more importantly, of all the American captains he might have faced, he had unwittingly chosen not only the unluckiest, but the one who believed himself to be the unluckiest, whose belief now so flawed his judgement that he unwisely accepted the challenge he had never received.

James Lawrence, in addition to being as brave as he was unlucky, was among the most experienced officers in the United States Navy, and skilful with it. But the setbacks (as he conceived them to be) which had punctuated his life and career had embittered him, leading him to despise his seniors. Born in 1781, he had tried to get to sea when only twelve, but had been frustrated by his father, whose pro-British sympathies clashed with his own fierce patriotism. Only after the old man died was he able to fulfil his ambition, but although this got him to sea during the undeclared war against France in an early American frigate, the *Ganges*, he had no opportunity to distinguish himself. His first big chance came – as it did for most of the 1812 officers – in the Tripolitanian war, when he was chosen by Decatur to take part in the famous cutting-out and destruction of the *Philadelphia*, which Nelson himself considered a great feat of arms. But after that he did not receive the recognition he felt he deserved, eventually being given command of one of the useless little coast-defence gunboats which were the Republican Party's idea of a United States Navy. In this command he was casually humiliated by no less than Admiral Sir Cuthbert Collingwood, who removed several allegedly British seamen into his flagship, the enormous *Dreadnought* (98), without allowing a mere American lieutenant to make a big issue of the matter.

Another – and far worse – humiliation befell him as one of Captain

Barron's lieutenants in the *Chesapeake* in 1807, in the infamous incident when the British *Leopard* forced that ship to strike her flag temporarily to take off more British deserters. But only Captain Barron suffered for that surrender, of course, while Lawrence went on to be promoted first lieutenant of the *Constitution*, of which he was actually in temporary command for several months. Then, however, instead of the frigate he hoped for, he was relegated to the command of a succession of smaller brigs and sloops, ending up with the quite powerful little *Hornet* (18/20) in the autumn of 1811, all of which he considered beneath his merit and seniority.

War was what Lawrence needed (and for choice against the arrogant British), and his chance of glory (as opposed to mere prize-taking) came at last at the mouth of the Demerara River off British Guiana (modern Guyana) early in 1813. The *Hornet* had most recently been in company with the *Constitution* after the latter's capture and destruction of the *Java*, cruising off the Brazilian coast. There they had found the British sloop *Bonne Citoyenne* (18, ex-French) in neutral Bahia harbour, and – *à la* Broke – Bainbridge had actually sent in a challenge to the British captain to come out and fight the *Hornet*, with his big *Constitution* honourably standing clear. This old-fashioned offer the British captain had refused, not so much wisely (as he would almost certainly have been beaten) as properly, since he was carrying a fortune in gold and silver destined for Britain which he could not put at risk. Equally properly, having been warned by the locals that there was a British ship-of-the-line cruising in the same area (the *Montagu*, 74), Bainbridge then left for home (with the news of his *Java* victory), leaving the fast little *Hornet* to watch the *Bonne Citoyenne* for as long as prudent, and then to continue the raid, returning to Boston not later than April.

The *Montagu* duly arrived, chasing the *Hornet* into neutral waters. But Lawrence soon outwitted his lumbering pursuer, to head northwards and eastwards along the Brazilian coast, towards British and Dutch Guiana (the latter now being in British hands, together with much of the Dutch overseas empire). And it was off Guiana that he at last met an antagonist nominally worthy of him: the 18-gun sloop *Peacock*, commanded by Lieutenant William Peake. With her 24-pound carronades, the *Peacock* was slightly inferior to the *Hornet* with her 32s, but she could still have inflicted serious damage on the American had she been well-handled. Unfortunately, however, she only lived up to her name, being one of those shining spick-and-span British warships whose gunnery and fighting quality did not match her appearance, while the *Hornet* fully lived up to hers. For in 15 minutes she had stung both the *Peacock* and her captain to death, the British sloop sinking so quickly after surrender that several of Lawrence's men on board her went down with the wounded they were trying to rescue.

Lawrence was thus able to return home in triumph, having inflicted another humiliation on the arrogant enemy; an 18-gun sloop might not amount to much among the hundreds the British disposed by then, but coming so soon after the frigate defeats it represented a cumulative loss which a navy unused to losing *any* single-ship fights found intolerable. But then, once again (and all the more unendurable for coming in his hour of public acclaim), Lawrence received another fancied slight from above. For, after having been promptly promoted to captain, he wanted – and thought he deserved – the *Constitution*, but was given the relatively second-class *Chesapeake*. What made this even worse was that when the bigger ship's captain, Charles Stewart, agreed to exchange with him, the Navy Department rejected the idea. It was the *Chesapeake* or nothing, the stage-directions for this drama requiring someone more headstrong than the prudent Stewart to command the weaker ship.

The *Chesapeake* was, then, Lawrence's next piece of 'bad luck', and – given his state of mind – the final one. It was not that she was a bad ship, although she had the reputation of being an unlucky one. But, after her recent refit, she had nothing like the superb crews which had won those previous frigate engagements. Indeed, in spite of those victories, the American navy was no longer finding it so easy to recruit volunteers happy to take on the odds stacked against them at sea – or, indeed, to get the money with which to pay them (and when, anyway, there was quicker and easier money to be made in privateers). As a result, although the *Chesapeake* had a full crew with no pressed men, they were much more like a British warship crew in the earlier year of the war: to a nucleus of experienced men had been added inferior seamen, some foreigners and a number of raw hands, all of whom were in a mutinous state due to lack of pay. Worse still, these men were commanded by a scratch lot of officers, the two senior lieutenants being absent because of illness and most of the others young and newly-promoted. None of them – officers and men – had ever sailed as a crew, unlike Broke's 300, the majority of whom, although many had originally been pressed, had been together for six years now under a good and enthusiastic captain whom they trusted, and who trusted them.

All of this (apart from his actual orders, which were to get out as quickly as possible to raid the British supply route to the St Lawrence River) provided James Lawrence with good reasons to avoid the *Shannon*, but rather to delay until he had pulled his unhandy crew together. And that he could have done just that cannot be doubted, for he had always been a good commander of men, if not a good subordinate. But what he actually did was, of course, quite the opposite in every respect: with his crew *not* pulled together he sailed straight out to fight Broke, aiming (one may imagine) to solve all his problems by presenting his supposedly unappreciative masters and his country with something they could not shrug off: another British frigate. Like Broke, he expected to win (and all the hundreds of confident watchers on the Boston waterfront expected him to). So, like Broke, he was content to fight at close quarters and without finesse, no less ready to 'try the fortune' of their respective flags to the death.

The battle which followed more nearly resembled one of those old Hollywood sea-fights starring Errol Flynn not only in incident but also in duration than almost all of the duels of 1793–1815. It opened with face-to-face broadsides, developed from some loss of manoeuvrability on one side into an actual collision and the grappling of the two ships, and then was consummated by boarding and hand-to-hand fighting. And it was all over in 15 – or, in some accounts, only 12 – minutes.

Only this time the blood was real. Broke, leading his boarders, lay badly wounded, and 81 of his men were casualties, including most of his senior officers. But in the captured *Chesapeake* nearly half the crew – 146 out of 300 – had been killed or wounded, including Lawrence himself, who had been sniped by a British marine lieutenant in the grappling phase.

The British had ended their run of frigate defeats. But, really, nothing had been proved beyond what was already known from a hundred fights – namely, that when ships of equal strength met, the best-trained, best-led and fastest-firing crew would win, barring exceptional bad luck. Even as it was and with all her advantages, the *Shannon* had had all the luck: the *Chesapeake*, hard hit in the opening exchanges, had lost her head sails, and had then been half-raked; and after that, in the grappling-and-boarding phase when both Captain Lawrence and his first lieutenant were down (and his third lieutenant had questionably found more pressing business below), only an inexperienced midshipman was left to organise resistance to the swarming British boarders after the ship's chaplain had fired at (but missed) Captain Broke as he led them, before he was cut down. Time and again, whenever a ship was actually boarded, the capture of her upper deck – or her foredeck and quarterdeck – decided the fight. Years before, that had been how Captain Hamilton had retaken the *Hermione* and Cochrane had stormed the *El Gamo* (never mind Nelson's capture of those two huge Spanish ships-of-the-line off Cape St Vincent). In the smoke-filled confusion of the *Chesapeake* there was little that Lawrence's surviving second lieutenant could do from his command-post on the main gun-deck. His captain had been carried below famously crying, 'Don't give up the ship!' which earned him his place in American history. But by then the ship was as good as lost.

Now it was the Americans' turn to make the excuses – and they did their best, just as the British had done before them. The simple truth was that a better captain commanding a better crew with better luck had won, in a fight between ships of equal strength. But meanwhile Captain Lawrence must be honoured, even if he would have been broken and disgraced (if not shot) had he survived – and quite rightly. (In death, at least, he was lucky?) And, actually, although his inexperienced officers and motley crew had hardly written a new and glorious chapter in the history of the United States Navy, they had certainly died and been wounded in numbers equal to or greater than those of any of the defeated ships of the main belligerent navies of the 1793–1815 world war, French and British. As regards its cannon-fodder, if not the intelligence of one of its captains, the United States had rather less to be ashamed of when up against the *Shannon*'s specialists than the crews of their Humphreys ships had to celebrate for their victories over easier meat.

Still, victory in war is what counts – and in a country with an inconveniently free press it counts for even more. Even though the *real* war was now going the British way in Europe, a frigate victory after her invincible navy's three frigate defeats counted for even more, over these damned Yankees and Jonathans: it reassured the public and the London mob and the editor of the *Naval Gazette*, anyway, if not the more cautious Admiralty itself, just as Captain Pellew's victory over the French republican *Cléopâtre* had done 20 years before. So, where Commodore Hoste had received only a pat on the back and a new frigate after defeating a French squadron at Lissa and reconquering the Adriatic, Captain Philip Bowes Vere Broke received not a mere knighthood, but an instant hereditary baronetcy after the duel which ended his naval career in 1813. *Captain* Hoste (with his acting-rank now outranked by his commanding admiral, and therefore lost) would have to work much harder – and, even almost work himself to death, for *his* baronetcy. But, being Nelson's best pupil and the Navy's foremost exponent of frigate warfare after the promotion of Admiral Pellew, the elevation (and ill-health) of acting-Commodore Hornblower and the degradation of Captain Lord Cochrane, he would nevertheless win that now in the last years of his frigate war, by pure merit.

CHAPTER EIGHTEEN

The final years of frigate warfare

The *Shannon–Chesapeake* duel was neither the last fight between British
and American frigates nor the end of frigate warfare (as Captain Hoste's
further operations will show). But although those subsequent frigate
operations must now be explored, it is essential to place them in greater
context of the Armageddon of 1813–14, to which Waterloo in 1815
would be the postscript, and to which all naval incidents are really little
better than footnotes in the history of the war.

By then Napoleon's catastrophic defeat in Russia in the winter of
1812 was part of that history. And although he had performed
miracles of improvisation to conjure up new armies against the Fourth
Coalition (or whatever number it was; but the *last*, anyway), to give
the armies of Russia, Prussia and Austria a series of bloody noses, the
coalition had held firm and now scented victory. The *Naval Chronicle*
might carry columns about the *Shannon*'s victory and the guns in the
Tower of London would be fired, but it was for Wellington's triumph
at Vittoria three weeks later that the church bells would ring louder.
Before the year was out his Peninsular army would have crossed the
Pyrenees, to fight on French soil, and the French army in central
Europe would have been crushed by sheer weight of numbers at
Leipzig – the 'Battle of the Nations' – in which more than half a million
men took part in a struggle which had become the 'War of Liberation'.
Before the winter of 1813–14 was out the Allies were across the Rhine
and heading for Paris: the first world war had come a long way from
the days of its revolutionary beginnings, but it was ending now where
it had begun, on French soil.

Nevertheless, many men were still to die in this last apocalyptic chapter, not only on the banks of the Seine (in which the Tsar's Cossacks were soon watering their horses), or among the vineyards of Toulouse in the south, but also on the shores of the Adriatic, where Hoste was still campaigning. And the fighting in the dismal Anglo-American 'mini-war' was to drag on past Napoleon's first abdication in April 1814, and even after its own official conclusion, with its last shots fired at sea during the Emperor's final 'Hundred Days' which ended at Waterloo in June 1815.

In the Anglo-American frigate war the British *Phoebe*, with the sloop *Cherub* in attendance, finally caught up with the *Essex* off Valparaiso on the Chilean coast, in the same waters in which Admiral von Spee beat Admiral Cradock a century later. Captain Porter of the *Essex* was not unhappy with the meeting, hoping for another close-quarter duel like that between the *Chesapeake* and the *Shannon*. And, indeed, if the *Cherub* had kept her 20 carronades (a mixture of 24- and 32-pounders) out of such a fight he might have stood a chance, since the *Essex* (nominally a 32) was actually carrying 40 guns, all of which were short-range 32-pound carronade 'smashers'. But Captain Hillyar of the *Phoebe* had his Admiralty orders, which precluded fair fight. And, more than the *Cherub*, he also had 26 long-range 18-pounders among his 44 guns (although the *Phoebe* was only rated a 36). So, after both sides had first confidently opened the duel in old-fashioned 1793-style, with cheers and counter-cheers – only this time not 'Vive la Nation!' against 'God save the King', but 'King George' against 'Free Trade and Sailors' Rights!' – Hillyar fought a coldly calculated long-distance fight in which he smashed the *Essex* to pieces, with the *Cherub* hardly required. Out of the American ship's 255 men (the *Essex* was no Humphreys ship), the obligatory 50 per cent were killed or wounded before another 31 drowned while trying to swim ashore, in exchange for eleven men in the *Phoebe* and four in the *Cherub*. The British had learned their lesson and Hillyar knew his job, so that the fight resembled nothing so much as those future Anglo-German battles of Coronel and the Falklands, in which the stronger efficiently massacred the weaker.

Meanwhile, in the whole spread of the Anglo-American war at sea, the convoy system worked, even though American privateers continued to be an irritant and smaller United States Navy ships continued to win most of their ship fights, with the victory of HMS *Pelican* (18) over the badly-fought USS *Argus* off Liverpool three weeks after the *Shannon* duel being a well-publicised tonic, rather than a cure, and the capture of three British sloops in succession by the *Constitution* during a world-wide cruise (the last long after the war had ended) worth no more than a shrug. Frigates – especially

Humphreys 56-gun ones – always took smaller ships (with Captain Lord Cochrane by then a disgraced and forgotten man).

Much more interesting tactically, although actually almost as one-sided, was the final Anglo-American frigate action of the war, which ended with the defeat and capture of the finest of all the Humphreys frigates, the USS *President*, in the last days. Having been hemmed in for months by superior blockading forces, Captain Decatur was none the less determined to escape from New York, where the *President* had been penned for nearly a year. Peace had actually been signed in Europe, at neutral Ghent, some three weeks earlier when his chance came, after a gale had blown the blockaders off station on the evening of 14 January 1815. But this time his luck was out, as he ran aground on a sandbar (due to pilot error), only extricating himself after a crucial two hours' delay and with damage to hull and masts. Then he ran almost into the arms of the enemy, in the form of the *Majestic*, one of those ships-of-the-line *razéed* in 1812–13. Even in her damaged state the *President* could out-run a *razé*, but there were also three British frigates in the offing: the powerful *Pomone* (40), the smaller *Tenedos* (32) and – above all – the *Endymion*.

It is somehow appropriate that this, the last real frigate fight of the war (however unsatisfactory from the purist's point of view as a duel, because of the odds against the loser), should have involved the *Endymion* in which resides so much of the story of wartime frigate evolution at its best. For this is that ship which the British Admiralty ordered so many years before after the original French *Pomone* had caused such a stir in 1794, when her advanced design, performance and armament had been studied. From that captured *Pomone* (which had herself evolved from the powerful *Sybille* class) was derived the big new British *Endymion*, built in a private yard, of 1,240 tons, with 24-pounders on her main deck, and by all accounts 'an incomparable sailer'. So, if the *Shannon* had been the best *fighting* frigate in the British Navy, one of the best and most powerful *sailing* frigates in that navy was now in pursuit of the finest frigate afloat.

In a straight fight under broadly equal conditions the odds still might have been on the American ship, which was upwards of a thousand tons heavier and was pierced for up to 60 guns, although rated a 44. But then the *Endymion*, rated a 44, was nearer a 50; and, of course, she did not have to defeat the *President*, but merely to bring her to bay. By the same token, it was Decatur's plain duty not to fight at all, but to escape. To do this as the chase stretched out the pursuers (with the *Endymion* well in the lead), he endeavoured to immobilise the British ship with the various special-purpose dismantling shot designed to cut up sails and rigging, and with boarding parties readied for her quick elimination if the chance presented itself. For his part, the

British Captain Hope also aimed to slow down the American, while keeping well away on her starboard quarter.

For most of that winter's day and into the darkening evening this battle of wits was fought skilfully by both sides, but in heavy seas which made accurate gunnery difficult. Eventually, the *Endymion* was so cut about that she had to drop back, even though she had by then inflicted 85 casualties on the enemy for the loss of only 25. But the *President*'s sails and rigging had also been damaged and she was making water from her earlier grounding. So when the *Pomone* and the *Tenedos* then closed up on him, Decatur (who by then had himself been wounded) had no choice but to strike his flag.

Professionally speaking, never mind the civilised convention which allowed a captain to surrender without loss of honour when further resistance was out of the question, Decatur came out of this fight without damage to his reputation or career. In taking the *President* to sea when he did he had bravely run a legitimate risk in the line of duty: with peace negotiations (as he thought) still in progress, another American heavy frigate on the loose in the Atlantic might help further to concentrate the minds of the British negotiators. As it was he had had bad luck, and was quickly back in action against the Barbary corsairs, returning to a hero's welcome (and his famous 'Our country, right or wrong' speech), and to keep his final duelling appointment with Commodore Barron.

The British Navy had also, however, performed impeccably in eliminating a very dangerous raider with little loss. Only now such an event was no cause for any special celebration: the USS *President* simply became HMS *President*, an unrequired addition to a fleet already being run down, the frigate *Undaunted* having long since deposited the ex-Emperor Napoleon on his island principality of Elba. And in any case the British had by now recovered their cool, thanks to Captain Sir Philip Broke. After the *Shannon*'s victory the taking of the little *Argus* had necessarily been 'another event in every way honourable to British arms' (where it would previously have been hardly noticed, if the *Argus* had been French). But by the time the *Essex* was captured British confidence was serene again, reducing that ruthlessly well-handled affair in the considered opinion of the *Naval Chronicle* to 'an event of comparative insignificance'. So the *President*, the prize of another superior force, was no special trophy, going to the breakers in the same year that her last American captain died. (As a prize, anyway, she was presumably worth nothing to her actual captors, having been taken after peace had been signed, after which Crown Rights reverted to the Admiralty; but even if a different legal view had prevailed, the division of her value between the captains and crews of three frigates and a *razée* would not much have enriched any of them.)

Meanwhile, of course, the Anglo-French sea war had dragged to its close. On paper Napoleon had had a powerful fleet right to the end. In Antwerp alone there were 15 of the line, and other line ships were scattered throughout all the ports of Europe, where ship-construction continued unabated. But the Antwerp fleet was good only for harbour defence, and at Brest many crews had been transferred to the Army. Everywhere, above all, they were blockaded by strong and superior (although not always numerically superior) British squadrons ready to snap up would-be escapers (as the *Victorious* (74) did the brand-new *Rivoli* (80) off Venice). Even when French frigates did break out – usually in pairs – they rarely lasted long. Two were caught by the *Venerable* (80) off the Azores during this last year of war, and three more in the Atlantic after surviving an earlier brush with blockading frigates. Finally, as the Empire itself began to contract before the advancing Allied and British armies, the very boltholes into which they had been hunted began to fall. Venice was lost to the Austrians, with three of the line, a frigate and half-a-dozen or more ships in varying states of disarray. In Bordeaux another 74 was burned, to stop Wellington getting his hands on her, and yet another was taken by the Austrians in Genoa. That last was not lost without a gallant attempt by the Toulon squadron to escort her to safety, but they were headed off by a British fleet, only escaping themselves by brave seamanship and the skin of their teeth. This last episode is interesting in our story for that moment when the massive three-decker *Boyne* (98) could have sunk an attendant French frigate, but chose not to do so. 'It would have been a great shame, and could have done no good', her captain explained afterwards. And his commander-in-chief, one Admiral Sir Edward Pellew, though chagrined at the escape of the enemy ships-of-the-line, had no criticism of this adherence to the old custom. And who shall say that either of them was wrong?

It is time, now, however, to begin to close all the accounts, first of those officers with whom we have been specially interested, and then of that frigate class of warship in which they made their reputations.

Broke, whom we left ennobled but desperately wounded, never returned to sea again. But he did make a remarkable recovery from the cutlass-stroke that almost scalped him and left part of his brain exposed, which at the time many thought to be mortal. His 'hard hat' seems to have saved him, by somehow deflecting the blow. But then the fighting men of those times were tough men, who quite often recovered from the most appalling wounds if gangrene did not set in. Nelson, little and allegedly weak, was among the most famous of such survivors, after Tenerife, and a sergeant of the King's German Legion cavalry is on record as having ridden 15 miles to present himself at a Brussels hospital after Waterloo, a cannon-ball having taken his left arm off at the shoulder joint. Among frigate captains Sir Nesbit

Willoughby surely takes the palm, but Philip Broke, who later survived a serious riding accident after he had recovered from his wound, rates high. And, although he never went to sea again he none the less moved steadily up the Captains' List to become an admiral in 1830 and to hold that rank until his death in 1841. Also, if he never flew his flag, his was to be an honoured name in naval history, beyond the KCB (a newly instituted honour) which he received in 1815. It was in the flotilla leader destroyer *Broke*, on Dover Patrol picket duty, that Commander E.R.G.R. Evans repelled a German naval raid on the night of 20/21 April 1917, sinking two enemy destroyers. Indeed, after torpedoing the first of these he also rammed it at 27 knots, issuing cutlasses and pistols to his men (who also allegedly threw cups of hot cocoa at the enemy) to repel boarders. Broke would have liked and understood such an action: in his naval Valhalla, he would have been as reassured by it much as his contemporaries had been by his own *Shannon* fight.

What the mathematically inclined may have noticed, however, is that it took him 29 years to get from the bottom of the Captains' List to the top, longer than either Pellew or Hornblower, never mind Nelson. But, of course, peace slowed down the natural wastage of all those above him, with far fewer captains exposed to the wear-and-tear of duty and the perils of the sea, let along the fury of the enemy. For those below Broke on the List it was even worse, and for many of those not yet on that list at all chances of promotion now vanished altogether. Even before the end of the war the Navy's manpower had been slightly (but significantly) declining from its highest total of over 140,000 in 1809–11. After 1814 it fell at first drastically, and then progressively, to not much over 20,000 by the mid-1830s, only climbing again significantly in the 1850s as new naval threats emerged.

To look so far ahead is justified by the fact that there were then still naval officers afloat – the very lucky ones – who had served in Broke's time, and indeed in Nelson's. To take one such, there was Henry Dulcie Chads, whose misfortune it was to be forced to surrender the *Java*, in which he was first lieutenant, to Bainbridge of the *Constitution* after Captain Lambert had been mortally wounded by an American sharp-shooter. Lieutenant Chads had earlier had the bad luck to be with Lambert when he surrendered the *Iphigenia* to that French squadron after the Grand Port defeat, and now he compounded his misfortune by failing to destroy the *Java's* code book. But he was none the less a lucky man, for it was more than ever then not in the British Navy's interest to penalise those frigate captains – even such a temporary one as Lieutenant Chads – for losing against 'overwhelming odds'. Long before the *Java* fight, Thompson of the *Leander* had been knighted after surrendering to a more powerful French ship; Carden of the *Macedonian* was 'most honourably acquitted' by a searching court martial after having fought rather incompetently against the *United States*, and he also lived to become an admiral. Chads, therefore, after having been put ashore with the *Java* prisoners, speedily exchanged and duly exonerated (as senior surviving officer) in the *Java* court-martial inquiry, was promoted to command the *Columbia* sloop (18). At the height of the war he might have expected to make post within a year or two, but peace now caught him, and after his sloop paid off in 1815 he was unemployed for eight years. Then his luck turned, first with the *Ariadne* sloop (18) in 1823, and two years later the frigate *Alligator* (28) – with automatic post-rank, of course – in which he served as Senior British Officer in one of Britain's earliest colonial 'little wars', in Burma in 1827.

Chads was by then in his late thirties, but was evidently an intelligent officer who kept up with change in changing times. For although he only received two sea-going commands (both in frigates) during the next 18 years, he served on two committees, one investigating screw-propulsion and the other coast defence (against the French, naturally), before his appointment to command HMS *Excellent*, the gunnery school at last established by the Navy and named after a ship once commanded by an earlier gunnery enthusiast, Cuthbert Collingwood. This was in 1845, and Chads was now in his fifties, but once on the List the years were a captain's greatest ally, and he lived to fly his flag at sea, and gain his knighthood, as fourth-in-command of the Baltic fleet during the Crimean War when in his sixties, 32 years after he had struck the *Java*'s flag. 'Interest' was by then a thing of the past in its classical eighteenth-century form, but his merit had in the end been well-assisted by luck and longevity. Yet, as regards both of those last two, the top prize goes not to him, but to an officer junior to him in 1812, Broke's second lieutenant in the *Shannon*, Provo Wallis.

The naval career of Provo Wallis provides in its early phase an example of the bending of the Navy's rules at its most extreme and in its final one strict adherence to them at its most embarrassing. Initially, also, he illustrates another variety of 'interest' which must have enabled not a few humbler 'gentlemen's' sons to aspire to the quarter-deck. Born in Halifax, Nova Scotia, in 1791, he was the son of the chief clerk to the commissioner for the important naval dockyard there, a man whom any captain would have been well-advised to cultivate. As a result the infant Provo was entered on a ship's books as 'Able Seaman' at the age of four. Whether or not he then actually went to sea at the age of nine (as he claimed), his promotion to lieutenant at the age of 17 was as exceptional as illegal: of all our special captains, none reached this rank until at least 20. Even Nelson, who managed it at 19, was meticulous in not supporting Hoste's promotion until the rules had been observed. Thus advantaged, however, Provo Wallis was second lieutenant of the crack *Shannon* at 22; one may assume that he was meritorious, but by then he was certainly experienced – and then he was lucky also. For, with his captain badly-wounded and the first lieutenant dead, it was he who brought both the *Shannon* and the *Chesapeake* into Halifax as acting-captain.

After such a famous action all the surviving officers could hope to be marked men in the Navy. One of Broke's midshipmen went on to become an admiral, but more immediately Provo Wallis was at once given command of a sloop as master and commander. With the outbreak of peace and swingeing naval cuts he, like Chads, joined the ranks of the unemployed. However, the *Shannon* was much more happily remembered in the corridors of the Admiralty than the *Java*, so he was honoured with post-rank in 1819, a full four years ahead of the otherwise more senior Chads. After that, naturally, the List itself did his work for him with the passing of the years, as he moved up it. Inevitably, he became an admiral before Chads, reaching the rank three years before that otherwise much more able and successful captain, for all that he did not fly his flag at sea as Chads did. Both then moved up by seniority also within the ranks of the admirals, though Chads finally dropped out of the race in 1868, in his eightieth year. But by then, in any case, the Admiralty was at last nerving itself to change a system which had obviously long outlived its usefulness (in so far as it had ever been useful): in 1870 new rules for the retirement of admirals were introduced, which gratefully settled all of them in their final moorings, but which none the less excepted *all those who had commanded a ship during the 'French Wars'* – a graceful acknow-ledgement of the great, but long-past, Age of Nelson to which the Navy looked back with such pride. Presumably the Admiralty thought that time would soon render that small print irrelevant, anyway. But in Admiral Provo Wallis's case it did not; he lived on, and on, and on – and on, even, long past when he had reached the very top, as Admiral of the Fleet, in 1877. It was not until 1892, when wood and sail (and frigates) were history and the armoured steel battleships of the *Majestic* class, with their 12-inch guns and their triple-expansion engines, were on the drawing board that the last of the old '*Shannons*' died, in his hundred-and-first year and the ninety-seventh since he had been entered on the books as 'Able Seaman'.

By then, of course, all our other frigate *dramatis personae* had also long since departed the scene. Of them, ironically, it was Cochrane who remained on active service longest, even though he played no further part in the last of the French Wars after the Basque Roads battle in 1809. For, as earlier sketched, he nevertheless survived all his enemies (longevity again aiding merit!), to have all his ranks and honours restored to him by new admirers, not only to be returned to his original place on the Captains' List, but to become Admiral of the

Fleet in 1854. Yet, for all that, he probably found this triumph hollow, since the government refused to employ him in his country's first European war since 1815, and would have none of those chemical 'secret weapons' still exercising his mind after over 40 years, which he now proposed to use against the Russian naval bases in the Baltic and the Black Sea. Whether these would have been any more successful than Britain's first fumbling attempts to copy German poison gas at Loos in 1915, is another Cochrane might-have-been. However, he was then not only a Grand Old Man and the Navy's greatest sailor since Nelson but still a fighting captain at heart in his eighties, no doubt mourning his happy frigate days in the *Pallas* and the *Impérieuse*. But Admiral of the Fleet the Earl of Dundonald, *alias* 'Cochrane the Dauntless', *versus* the Tsar of All the Russias was a confrontation never put to the test.

There was no such irony in the subsequent careers of the remaining three of our heroes, all of whose operational careers continued beyond the war's end successfully.

Pellew, for his part, saw the fighting cease off Toulon in his huge *Caledonia* flagship, being created Lord Exmouth in May 1814, and hauling down his commander-in-chief's flag in the Mediterranean in August, only to be reappointed to the same command in March 1815 as a prelude to his operations against the Barbary pirates of Algiers in August 1816. He, more than anyone, encompasses the whole 22-year war from a commanding position on the quarterdeck. But those years had taken their toll of his spirit, if not his splendid body. 'We all grow old', he wrote bitterly. Certainly, he had often been unhappy as an admiral both in the Far East and in the Mediterranean. And when ordered to deal with Algiers he was unhappy with that prospect too, carefully choosing no one he valued to serve with him for fear that he might get them uselessly killed. (In the event, he discharged his orders successfully enough, with his usual efficiency and great attention to accurate gunnery; but the corsairs' final comeuppance was still 14 years in the future, when the exasperated French finally invaded North Africa, setting in train a century of romantic and grisly events which would produce Beau Geste of the French Foreign Legion and the return to power of General de Gaulle in the 1950s.)

Pellew, like Cochrane, is perhaps another who remembered his frigate days most happily, in the *Indefatigable* (and with Mr Midshipman Hornblower straining at the leash under him). Having never been one of Nelson's 'band of brothers' he came ashore finally in October 1816. He lived to become Vice-Admiral of England in 1832, a year before his death, but is one of the most-forgotten of all the great sailors of that age.

His one-time midshipman, Horatio Hornblower, 'outlived' him by many years. Indeed, Hornblower – a special case, admittedly – was actually ennobled a month or so before him, and flew his flag as an admiral in the West Indies in 1821 only 16 years after reaching post-rank (a truly amazing progression up the list; but who are we to quarrel with his biographer, Mr Forester?).

Hornblower can be taken as representing that class of naval officer who were above all 'judicious'. When it came to tact and diplomacy in the handling of others, friend, foe or neutral (but particularly superior officers), where on a scale of one to ten Cochrane usually scored *zero*, Hornblower always scored *ten*. And this, in a long and complicated war, was a quality of increasing importance in naval officers, who so often found themselves representing their country far from home, with no sage advice (never mind actual orders) to assist them. Young frigate commanders needed it. Admirals like Pellew, who had to deal with other admirals like poor Troubridge as well as the Honourable East India Company and its servants, needed it. Honest fighting men and gunnery enthusiasts like Cuthbert Collingwood, when he found himself British Viceroy of the Mediterranean as well as commander-in-chief, had to develop it. That Hornblower's masters discerned it in him accounts for his assignment to independent command in the Baltic in 1812, where he mightily encouraged the Tsar to resist Napoleon, helped to save besieged Riga and schemed to detach the Prussians from their French alliance as the retreat from Moscow turned into a rout.

Having recovered from a dose of typhus (caught from the Russian army), Hornblower was raised to a peerage, after he had *judiciously* detached the great port of Le Havre from Napoleon's cause, in favour of King Louis XVIII, while suppressing a mutiny in a blockading sloop off that port in March 1814. A popular and enlightened captain, he privately sympathised with mutineers, not only remembering Pigot of the *Hermione* but also his own experiences in the *Justinian* and the *Renown*, one may suppose. But as a *judicious* British naval officer he shot the elderly chief mutineer in cold blood without a second thought, in the interests of his service, his country, and the peace of Europe, and after the war scotched an attempt to rescue Napoleon from St Helena just as cold-bloodedly by deliberately breaking his word-of-honour. 'England was worth fighting for, was worth dying for,' he then reflected. 'England was worth a man's honour.' Put to the test perhaps Philip Broke would have come to the same conclusion. Theodore Roosevelt certainly thought Captain Hillyar of the *Phoebe* had not behaved honourably in the run-up to his duel with the *Essex*, though the facts hardly justified such an assertion. But Hornblower's action was in the end only the ultimate expression of Decatur's 'Our Country – right or wrong' and the final requirement of de Vigny's 'servitude et grandeurs militaires', anyway (although, of course, he was then saved by that fortune which more often favours such heroes in fiction than real life).

William Hoste never had to face such a decision in his 'good war'. But even his luck seemed to falter after Lissa, as we have seen, not only when he failed to receive the honour due to him (and also discovered his father's profligacy), but also when he returned to the Adriatic in the *Bacchante* in 1812. For there he found that having been Nelson's favourite protégé cut no ice with Nelson's devoted friend and loyal captain, Admiral Sir Thomas Fremantle. Rather, the Admiral seems to have taken an almost instant dislike to his most distinguished subordinate. Where the blame for this lies is hard to determine. If it was not mere ignoble jealousy on Fremantle's part, then perhaps the burdens of command warped his judgement, for the Adriatic was a notoriously worrying station, with the problems of neutral shipping and the enemy's possession of the whole coastline at a time when Napoleon's star was still in the ascendant. But also the young Hoste – still in his early twenties although well up the Captains' List – may well have been prickly after his setbacks in England, and may also have expected too much as of right. Also his health was beginning to break down. He had contracted malaria long before, and had this time returned via the infamously unhealthy base at Malta. Ill-health rarely makes for good temper.

Fortunately, Hoste still had one trump card: recurrently sick or not, he was an able and energetic officer who knew the Adriatic like the back of his hand. And Fremantle – himself a good officer and a Nelson graduate – could not but recognise that, whatever his personal opinion might be. Where Hoste patrolled, things happened: not only prizes (small, but numerous), to gladden any admiral's heart, but real injury to the enemy – 'Sir . . . For those last forty-eight hours we have been doing nothing but burning, sinking and destroying the enemy's vessels,' wrote Hoste to him.

Napoleon's defeat in Russia and the formation of the Fourth Coalition transformed the game, even though it also complicated it in doing so. Henceforth Austrian land forces were on the offensive against the French Adriatic garrisons, aiming to recover their lost Illyrian provinces, while local independence movements tried to set up their own little republics there and in the territories of the ancient but now finally defunct Venetian Republic. But even with Russia and Turkey both also interested parties in Eastern Europe, the opportunities for the defeat of the French on land by British combined operations were irresistible, no matter who the final beneficiary might be (provided of course, that it was not Russia). Particularly, after Trieste and Fiume had been safely delivered into Austrian hands, two smaller but important targets beckoned south of Lissa: the hitherto invincible fortress ports of Cattaro (modern Kotor) and Ragusa (Dubrovnik), where the locals were in revolt. In sending Hoste to investigate the former, a land-locked base surrounded by mountains,

Admiral Fremantle may not have expected his least-favourite captain to perform the miracle which the young man had long been pestering his superior to be allowed to attempt, for he then failed to supply him with the men and guns which the task seemed to require. But if Fremantle expected Hoste to burn his fingers he must have been mightily disappointed. For, with the assistance of one blockading sloop, the *Saracen* (18, commanded by an able master and commander, John Harper), Hoste proceeded to do the impossible. Triumphing over unreliable Montenegrin allies, appalling weather and the mountains themselves (up which his crew hauled long 18-pounders from the *Bacchante* to look down on the defenders), he forced Cattaro's surrender. And then, while still enmeshed in the political problems caused by his conquest, he surpassed even this achievement by going on to capture Ragusa, which gave in to him on 28 January 1814. (Almost on the very eve of the fortress's surrender another British frigate arrived, commanded by a captain senior to Hoste. But, once again, if Fremantle intended to do him a disservice thereby he failed, for the newcomer refused to take the credit from the *Bacchante*'s captain.)

These two great feats of arms, which equalled – or perhaps even surpassed – Cochrane's frigate land warfare in the *Impérieuse*, were overshadowed by the Allied invasion of France from the east and the south, which brought over 20 years of warfare full-circle. But Captain Hoste's achievements, supported by the loud cries of gratitude from Austria, which had been quick to seize their fruits, could not now be denied: the baronetcy which his grateful country now conferred on him, which should have featured *Lissa* as its coat-of-arms battle-honour, came to him bearing the name *Cattaro*.

Nevertheless, Ragusa (which no less ought to have been included on those arms) fell not a moment too soon. Hoste's recurrent bouts of malaria had recently been accompanied not only by the fatigue and wear-and-tear of operations frequently carried out in appalling weather conditions, but also by all the routine dangers of war in which Nelson's pupil had always fought from the front, like his master. Indeed, his health was already breaking down completely when he faced his last captain's crisis, after he had sailed on southwards towards the toughest nut of all, Corfu. Historians look at wars broadly, knowing their endings, and by then the French had lost this war, as the Germans had by the late summer of 1918 and the final Armageddon of 1944–5. But those who died in the final winning of those wars still risked as much as all those before them, and no less lost the fruits of all those earlier years of hardship. So, perhaps, Hoste's finest hour was when the *Bacchante* grounded off his enemy's main base, in which there were gunboats and a frigate. Because then, having had to jettison most of his main-battery guns to lighten ship and escape, he made plans to blow her up if the enemy attacked her, while leading his crew in small boats to attack *them*; but then his – and his crew's – luck held at the last, so that they lived to cheer him from the ship when he was invalided home, and the *Bacchante* left for safe American patrol.

Perhaps that 'luckiest', which was earlier fastened on William Hoste, should be qualified now: he had a 'good war', more accurately, and a very lucky one too, because of Nelson, but also because of his merit and in spite of Admiral Fremantle and malaria. But of all our special frigate captains (as always, apart from Pigot), Hoste was the *un*luckiest also, in not seeing old bones: accident-prone before he became the sickliest of them, he died young, in his forty-eighth year, as much a casualty of war eventually as Pellew's Captain Pownoll and his long-dead friend, Lieutenant Weatherhead – or even the egregious Pigot. However, he still had another 14 years ahead of him before 1828, during which he smelt the sea again, even if only in command of the Royal Yacht for a year or two, after nominal 'active service' in command of the permanently-moored Portsmouth guardship *Albion* (74) – the only ship bigger than a frigate that he ever commanded. But by then (since happy endings are always the best ones), he had also contracted a marriage which was not only pleasant and successful, but also rich – which was just as well, because of the burden of his ever-troublesome but long-lived father, who had reduced his hard-earned prize-money to a mere million (or thereabouts). And, anyway, even if he never lived to reach the top of the List and become an admiral, he also won an honour which few admirals achieved.

The Royal Navy has a share of the monuments in St Paul's Cathedral. But some of these, it has to be admitted, are more the result of heroic death than pre-eminent merit: not simply all those who died in the revolutionary (and badly-designed) nineteenth-century battle-ship *Captain*, as a result of bad weather (and bad design), but some captains of the Age of Nelson: Nelson's own Captain Westcott, of the *Majestic* (74), who died at the battle of the Nile, Admiral Duncan's admirable Captain Richard Burges(s), of the Fourth Rate *Ardent* (64), whose crew did not mutiny at the Nore in 1797, but who was then killed at Camperdown, and Pellew's 'thick-headed' Captain Faulknor, whose gallant capture of the much more powerful French frigate *La Pique* in his *Blanche* and death 'in the moment of Victory' on 5 January 1795, is engraved in exciting detail. (It was one of those rare victories-by-boarding, like the *Shannon–Chesapeake* fight, after his disabled ship had collided with the enemy, and the two had been lashed together by Faulknor himself, during which 'bold and daring manoeuvre He was shot through the Heart'.)

No such *Naval Chronicle* journalese distinguishes Captain Sir William Hoste's memorial in St Paul's, for he never had the chance of blowing up the *Bacchante* immortally off Corfu in 1814. But his memorial is none the less a more eloquent one for all those who have studied his career, which was more spectacular than most of all those frigate captains who kept the seas for Britannia between 1793 and 1815.

'Erected by his brother officers and the Admirers of his Services', the inscription below his effigy reads. What would have pleased him even more than words, however, is the actual siting of his memorial: it is to be found just round the corner from that of Nelson himself, on the right hand of his mentor and friend.

And so our tally of frigate captains is complete.

CHAPTER NINETEEN

The Eyes of the Fleet

The main activity of the British Navy in the years after 1815 – apart from the bombardment of Algiers in 1816 and the massacre of the Turkish Navy in 1827 – was its long campaign to suppress the slave trade. But the frigate was quite unsuitable for this type of work: too big even in its smallest form, unnecessarily well-armed, and above all far too slow to catch slavers designed for speed (and often by those superlative Yankee ship-builders, too).

In operations requiring some sort of real presence, however, the frigate was still a useful and cost-effective warship. Captain Chads' *Alligator* led the way into the Irrawaddy in 1827, and the *Imogene* and the *Andromache* fought the 'battle of the Bogue' at Whampoa in 1834 at the beginning of the wretched Opium Wars. 'Send a gunboat' really meant 're-route the nearest frigate'. So frigates were still built, some of them monsters, like the French *Belle Poule*, whose 60 guns included 32 long 30-pounders. But then everything had got bigger and bigger: the United States Navy's *General Pike* corvette, which was laid down in 1813, was not only bigger than most 1793 frigates, but more powerful than any of them, with her 24-pounders.

During the first half of the nineteenth century, nevertheless, the *appearance* of the world's navies did not change much, any more than the apparent perception of the admirals of those times: billowing clouds of canvas and the more modern black-and-white checkerboard of gunports was the rule at sea, behind which Britannia's 80 ships-of-the-line and her 65 much more hard-working frigates were the ultimate deterrent – even though most of all of those were more usually at anchor, if not 'laid-up in-ordinary' for activation only in emergency, apart from the hulks in which those convicts not sent to New South Wales were kept. But appearances all the while became increasingly deceptive. The industrial and technological revolutions had begun to accelerate even during the war, in which the American *Demologos* was the real Shape-of-Things-to-Come. Once warships had been liberated from paddle-wheels, which were both inefficient and vulnerable to gunfire, in favour of almost-invulnerable screw propulsion, steam would cease to be an auxiliary to sails in warships, and bigger (and more accurate) guns would start a new battle with defensive armour.

Britain, although industrially pre-eminent and capable of building the most advanced navy, nevertheless had a vested interest in not leading the way: always having the largest old-fashioned fleet (and tradition of victory-in-spite-of-incompetence), she copied when she had to counter. So her first screw-propelled frigates were built to answer France's new 40-gun *Pomones* in the 1840s. And – much more enjoyably for those who go to Portsmouth now – her *Warrior* of 1861 was therefore a smashing answer to France's *Gloire* of 1860: where the *Gloire* was no more than an ingenious conversion from an obsolescent 92-gun wooden (but steam-driven) ship-of-the-line, still with masts but now with cast-iron armour-plate, pioneered during the Crimean War), the *Warrior* was something else. With her single deck of main guns – albeit 68-pounders now – she might still be classified as a 'steam-frigate' in the days when there were still lumbering three-deckers afloat (and when her first captain was one of Cochrane's younger sons, 42 years after the Basque Roads). But, at 9,200 tons and 100 feet longer than the hybrid *Gloire*, she was not so much the last of the frigates as the first of the new *battleships* – the 'line' ships of the twentieth century. To all intents and purposes, the frigate-succession from the *Pallas* of 1757 was now lost in nineteenth-century confusion. Only two ships survive from their age, as museum pieces, if the British *Warrior* is dismissed as a new species temporarily wrongly named. And, appropriately perhaps, because theirs was a frigate navy, both are American. In Baltimore the smaller *Constellation* is still to be found, but – better still – there is an actual Humphreys survivor in Boston: 'Old Ironsides' herself, the USS *Constitution*, the veteran not only of the War of 1812 (and the conqueror of the *Guerrière* and the *Java* therein), but of the previous undeclared French and Tripolitanian Wars. She was due to be scrapped in 1830, but Oliver Wendell Holmes wrote a poem then which saved her to become the oldest United States Navy ship still in commission – and a not-unworthy representative of all our stars, from the *Pallas*, through the *Nymphe* and the *Inde-fatigable*, and all those French beauties, to Cochrane's *Impérieuse*, Hoste's *Amphion* and 'bold *Bacchante*' and Broke's deadly *Shannon*.

The new age, anyway, became apparent in 1862, in the battle of Hampton Roads in Chesapeake Bay, during the American Civil War. There the former United States wooden steam-frigate *Virginia*, transmogrified into the armoured Confederate States Ship *Merrimack*, quickly disposed of the old-fashioned *Congress* (44) and the *Cumberland* (24) – the first with her armoured ram – before being stopped in her tracks by the much smaller (but technologically far more advanced) Union turret-ship *Monitor*. Because of her first success and the (second) battle of Lissa in 1866, rams would be in fashion for a few years to come, in battleships. But *frigates* would shortly disappear, their all-purpose role being taken over by a succession of different classes of warship, from big, formidable battle-cruisers and other varieties of 'cruiser', through fast new torpedo-boat destroyers and eventually new 'frigates', which were the answers to all those innovations which Cochrane would have loved: torpedoes, submarines and aircraft (even if he would have hated the radio, which would have kept giving him orders).

But, anyway, if there was at least eventually a 1914 HMS *Cochrane*, as well as a 1917 *Broke*, and belatedly a 1950s *Pellew*, the twentieth century has never been the age of *our* frigate-warfare, and *our* frigate captains, who made their own decisions (and their reputations, and sometimes their fortunes), for better or worse. Evans of the *Broke* might issue cutlasses to his men, Mountbatten of the *Kelly* might make his reputation and Vian of the *Cossack* might storm the *Altmark* in a neutral Norwegian fiord, and Commodore Harwood might stop the *Graf Spee*; and there was never any lack of frigate-style gallantry, daring and professionalism in either the British Navy or in those of her sometime enemies, sometime allies, of the nineteenth century during the twentieth-century sea-wars. But never again would any of the captains of those wars have such complete responsibilities – and opportunities – as those which Horatio Hornblower looked forward to when he thought of *promotion, distinction and prize-money* as inseparable from service in a frigate at the beginning of the last of the French Wars. Certainly, no young captain would sit down at his desk and pen a challenge to an enemy captain, as Broke did in 1813 in the *Shannon* – or despatch a letter to the Admiralty, as Hoste did from the *Bacchante* in 1813, beginning 'Sir – I have acted without any precise orders from my admiral . . . [but] . . . upon motives which at the time I considered as best calculated to avoid giving umbrage either to Russia or Austria, and most for the interest of Great Britain', when his admiral was perhaps a fortnight away, and London a month, at best. Theirs was not only another time, another system and another navy, but also another world.

It is surely no accident that in our world their sea-war has produced such a notable (and best-selling) crop of hero-captains in fiction:

Alexander Kent's *Bolitho*, Dudley Pope's *Ramage*, Richard Woodman's *Drinkwater*, C. Northcote Parkinson's *Delancy* and Patrick O'Brian's *Jack Aubrey*, as well as Mr Forester's (and our own) *Horatio Hornblower*. And it is no good arguing that all these are 'too good to be true' – that, for example, Hornblower was too noble in spurning prize-money in preference for duty, or too ingenious in planning his sea-fights and his commando operations, and too daring (and lucky) in their performance. For Hornblower (who was only chosen from among the others for the completeness of his career) in no way out-performs all the real-life Hornblowers and Aubreys and Ramages among whom he has been set – men like Pellew, Hoste, Broke and, above all, Cochrane. And if they were perhaps exceptional, there were others not far behind them in merit, if not opportunity (among whom the American Stephen Decatur undoubtedly deserves to be counted). Even the worst of the frigate captains – madmen like Pigot, sadists like Corbet, and brave brutes like Hamilton and Willoughby – have their function in the story, not only by throwing the good ones into sharper relief but by generally out-performing the fictional villains in their villainies. We shall not see their like again in any conceivable conflict, not for the lack of their virtues and vices in modern men, but for lack of opportunities which frigates in their age provided. It was their good fortune, by whatever additional conjunction of merit and 'interest', that they found themselves in command of such maids-of-all-work which are best-remembered as Nelson's 'eyes' – 'the Eyes of the Fleet'. But whatever sentimental sailors may think, ships are inanimate things, and it was men like Pellew and Hoste who were the British fleet's eyes in its longest and most victorious war. Even glimpsed fleetingly, in these pages, their war and their adventures have surely been worth the telling.

Author's note

This book owes everything to other books, and to their authors, who have given this author such pleasure over half a century. In the first place, and at intervals thereafter down to the present day, there have been the novelists (and novelist-historians), from Henty and Marryat long ago to Forester in the 1940s and 50s, and his more modern successors, Patrick O'Brian, Dudley Pope, Alexander Kent, C. Northcote Parkinson and Richard Woodman. But, no less, there have been the historians (among whom two of those novelists also figure largely). Earliest among those was Arthur Bryant, whose *The Years of Endurance* and *The Years of Victory* still read as excitingly as they did when the last World War – 'Second' or 'Third' according to taste? – had not yet become history. Most of all, however, I am indebted to the late (and great) Michael Lewis, sometime Professor of History at the Royal Naval College, Greenwich.

By a happy chance I had the privilege of reviewing Professor Lewis's *A Social History of the Navy 1793–1815* when it was first published by Allen and Unwin in 1954. This was like first reading Chapman's Homer: after all the battles and biographies (and novels) of previous years it revealed the British Navy in a new and much more complete perspective – how it was put together, how it worked. Here, it seemed to me, was the blue-print for the real-life Hornblowers. I said as much in my review (and was given enough space to do so by a kindly literary editor), and this started a correspondence with Professor Lewis, who generously admitted that the Hornblower comparison had not occurred to him. The germ of this book, with the feeling that frigates and frigate captains (particularly those on their way up) had never quite been properly separated from other aspects of naval history, dates from that time. But for nearly 40 years other things got in the way.

If most is owed to Professor Lewis (and not only for his *Social History*) much is also owed to the authors of many other splendid naval histories covering this period. The story of Edward Pellew's life and career has been most fully told by C. Northcote Parkinson in his *Edward Pellew, Viscount Exmouth* (1934), while that of the egregious Pigot, together with a blow-by-blow account of the *Hermione* mutiny, is to be found in Dudley Pope's *The Black Ship* (1936). Mr Pope's *The Devil Himself* (1987) traces the course of the *Danae* mutiny of 1800, and an account of the 'Great Mutinies' at Spithead and the Nore is to be found in *The Floating Republic* (1935), by G. Mainwaring and D. Dobree. Not surprisingly, there is a considerable literature on the amazing career of Thomas Cochrane, but Christopher Lloyd's *Lord Cochrane* (1947) and more recently Donald Thomas's *Cochrane: Britannia's Last Sea-King* (1978) are as good as anything and better than most. William Hoste – if not a 'Sea-King' then certainly a Sea-Prince' – was less well-served until Tom Pocock's excellent *Remember Nelson* (1977) (although the widowed Lady Hoste published Hoste's *Memoirs and Letters* in 1833, apparently at the suggestion of Captain (ex-First Lieutenant) Donat Henchy O'Brien). A detailed account of the *Shannon–Chesapeake* fight is to be found in Kenneth Poolman's *Guns off Cape Ann* (1961), and its background in C.S. Forester's *The Naval War of 1812* (1957) and Reginald Horsman's *The War of 1812* (1969).

There are, of course, many other social, technical and general histories of the British Navy covering in greater detail many of the areas so lightly touched in this book. Christopher Lloyd's *The British Seaman* (1968) and Henry Baynham's *From the Lower Deck: The Navy 1700–1840* (1969) provide fascinating worm's-eye views, and the sequel to Professor Lewis's 1793–1815 social history, *The Navy in Transition 1814–1864* (1965) gives another absorbing overall portrait. Most recently, Brian Lavery's handsome *Nelson's Navy: The Ships, Men and Organisation 1793–1815* (1989) is both well-constructed and well-illustrated.

Among the more general histories, A.T. Mahan's *The Influence of Sea Power on History 1660–1783* (1890) is of course a starting point. After that, Professor Lewis's *The Navy of Britain* (1948) and G.J. Marcus's *The Age of Nelson* (1971) not only approach the subject usefully from different directions, but also contain excellent bibliographies. The relevant chapters in E.H. Jenkins's *A History of the French Navy* (1973) provide another perspective, and Douglas G. Browne's *The Floating Bulwark* (1963) is informative on ship development. C. Northcote Parkinson's *Britannia Rules: The Classic Age of Naval History 1793–1815* (1977) is, in its 1987 paperback version of less than 200 pages, ideal for holiday reading both for its lightness and its light-but-sure touch.

Although too big to take on holiday, Mr Parkinson's *War in the Eastern Seas 1793–1815* (1954) contains much on the frigate warfare in that far-off theatre of naval warfare, including a full account of the battle of Grand Port and much information of Pellew's years on command in the East. As for books on any of the other aspects of the war, from those great battles which have been here been 'off stage' to an analysis of the *guerre de course* and economic warfare, the bibliographies of Mr Marcus and Professor Lewis will point the way. Of books on Nelson, there is of course no end. But Tom Pocock's *The Young Nelson in the Americas* (1980) casts a bright light on the hero's rise to frigate command and – indirectly – on Hugh Pigot's career in those same pestilential waters.

Readers seduced by the tale of Donat Henchy O'Brien must hunt for his *My Adventures during the Late War* (1902), failing which *Escape from the French: Captain Hewison's Narrative 1803–1809*, edited by Antony Brett-James (1981), may do as well. What happened to French (and American) prisoners in Britain is traced in Francis Abell's *Prisoners of War in Britain, 1756–1815* (1913). What happened to the British ones in France is much more fascinatingly chronicled by (who else?) Professor Lewis in his *Napoleon and his British Captives* (1962).

To all these authors, and others unnamed, my admiration and thanks.

Anthony Price

Index